The Ayahuasca Visions of *Pablo Amaringo*

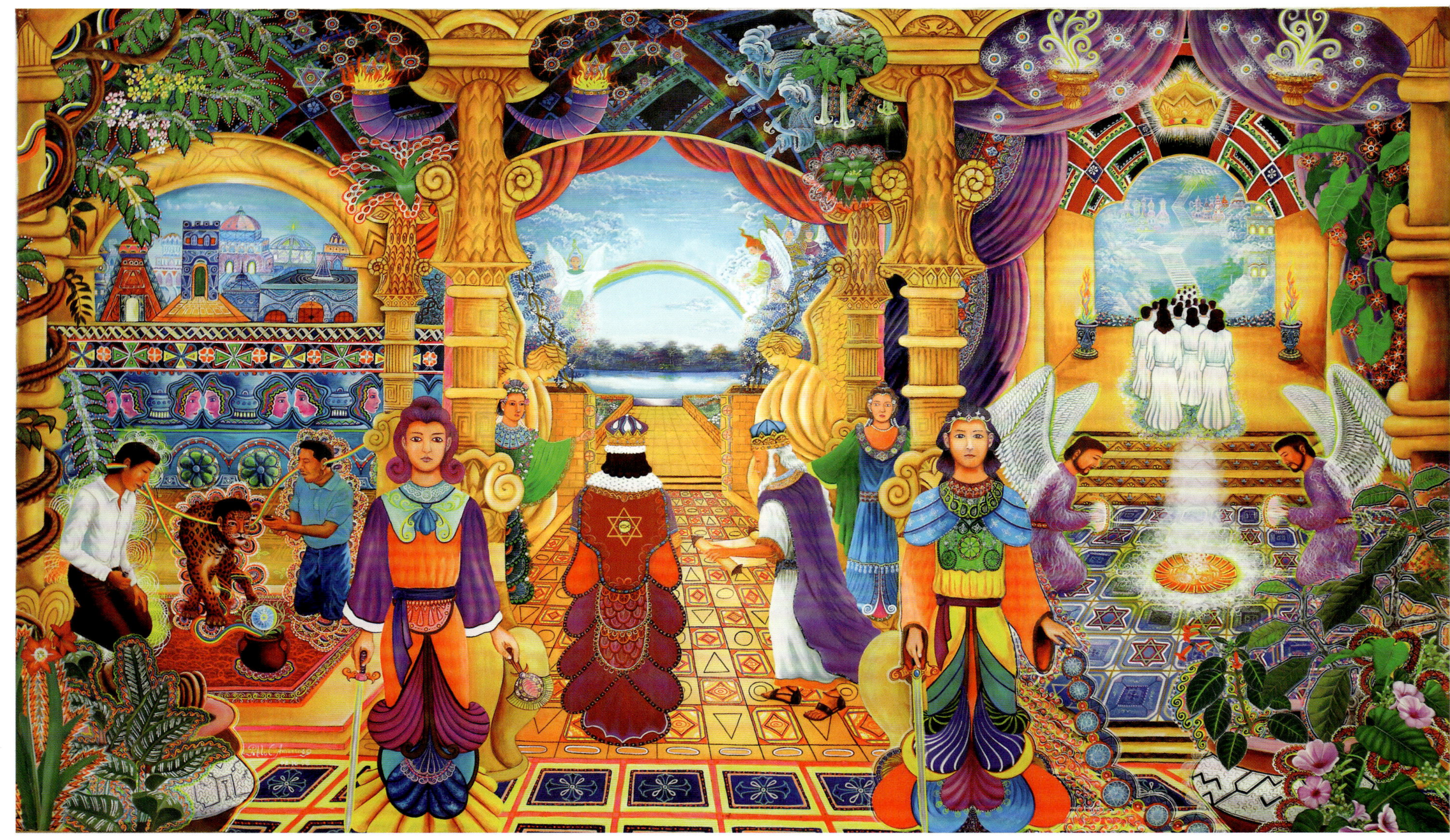

TEMPLO SACROSANTO
2001, Acrylic on Canvas
250 x 150 cm.

This is the sacrosanct temple of the Pleiades. If I had enough money I would like to build a temple like this by a lake. I would make a port to arrive at and a ramp to enter at the center. How people would love to visit a place like that! I have seen it already in my vision, and it is just like this.

The Ayahuasca Visions of *Pablo Amaringo*

Howard G. Charing, Peter Cloudsley,
and Pablo Amaringo

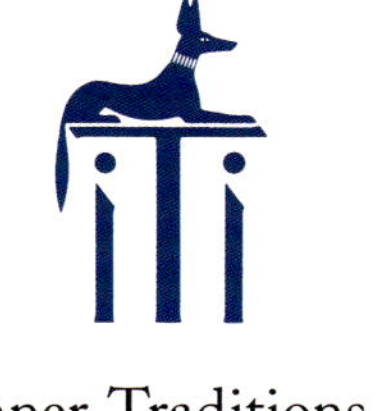

Inner Traditions
Rochester, Vermont • Toronto, Canada

Inner Traditions
One Park Street
Rochester, Vermont 05767
www.InnerTraditions.com

Note to the Reader: The information provided in this book is for educational, historical, and cultural interest only and should not be construed as a guide to or advocacy of the use or ingestion of ayahuasca. Neither the author nor the publisher assumes any responsibility for physical, psychological, or social consequences resulting from the ingestion of this substance or its derivatives.

Library of Congress Cataloging-in-Publication Data

Charing, Howard G.
The Ayahuasca Visions of Pablo Amaringo / Howard G. Charing, Peter Cloudsley, and Pablo Amaringo.
pages cm
Includes index.
ISBN 978-1-59477-345-7 (Hardcover)
1. Amaringo, Pablo, 1938-2009—Themes, motives. 2. Visions in art. 3. Ayahuasca ceremony—Peru. I. Cloudsley, Peter. II. Amaringo, Pablo, 1938-2009. III. Title.
ND419.A44C49 2011
759.985—dc22

2010047749

Printed and bound in China by Reliance Printing Co., Ltd.

10 9 8 7 6 5 4

Text design and layout by Priscilla Baker
This book was typeset in Caslon with Copperplate and Cezanne used as display typefaces

To send correspondence to the authors of this book, mail a first-class letter to the authors c/o Inner Traditions • Bear & Company, One Park Street, Rochester, VT 05767, and we will forward the communication, or contact the authors directly at **www.ayahuascavisions.com**.

This book is dedicated to the wisdom and beauty of Pablo Cesar Amaringo. We were privileged to have known him as a dear friend and to have worked with him on this book, which he would have been so thrilled to see for himself.

HOWARD G. CHARING AND PETER CLOUDSLEY

I also dedicate this book to honor the memory of my father, Victor A. Charing, and to my mother, Anita, and my daughters, Katie and Elizabeth.

HOWARD G. CHARING

I dedicate this book to my mother and father—an artist and a zoologist—who taught me to enjoy the rapture of nature and love all plants and animals, however poisonous, dangerous, or sinister they may be.

PETER CLOUDSLEY

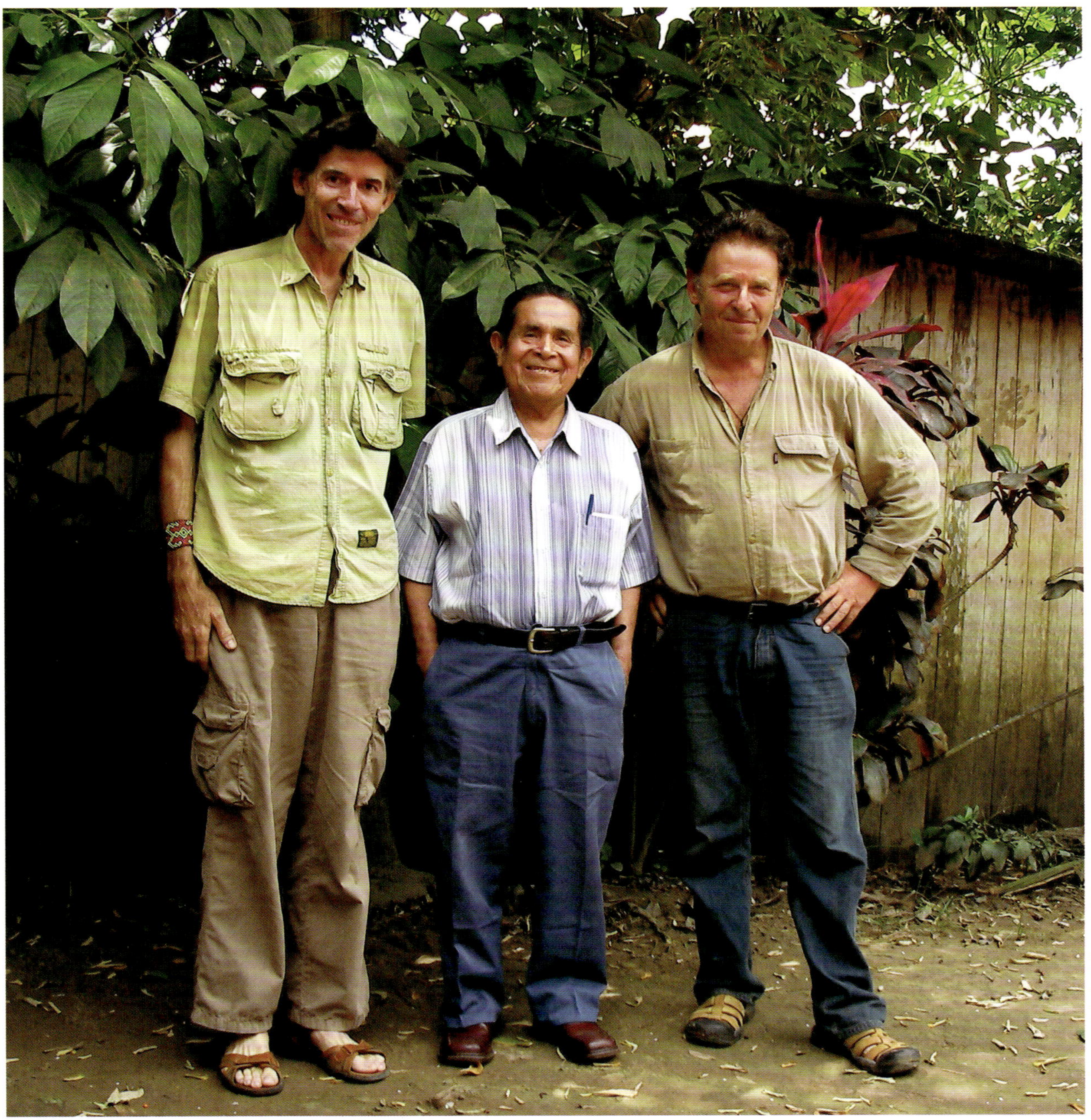

Peter Cloudsley, Pablo Amaringo, and Howard G. Charing

ACKNOWLEDGMENTS

Warm thanks are due to Dennis McKenna, Jeremy Narby, Graham Hancock, Jan Kounen, Robert Venosa, and Stephan V. Beyer for their contributions to this book. We also thank David "Slocum" Hewson for permission to use his portrait of Pablo that graces the introduction (see page 2). We are also most grateful to the president of the Department of Ucayali in Peru, Jorge Velásquez Portocarrero, for his contribution and his commitment to honoring Pablo's legacy. At Pablo's funeral, Sr. Portocarrero announced that the new cultural center and library in Pucallpa will be named in honor of Pablo.

We are also grateful for the assistance of a number of other people in the making of this book. First among these is Jon Graham, acquisitions editor at Inner Traditions, for his enthusiasm for this project and his firm commitment to publishing a high-quality book. We also thank Linbert Gonzales, one of Pablo's students, for his assistance in identifying plants; Judith Diaz for her outstanding work in transcribing hundreds of hours of voice recordings; Jose Carlos Mendoza for his photography; and Alan Matthew for photographing the mural paintings. In addition, we would like to acknowledge the assistance of Patrick Hamouy for the translation of Jan Kounen's contribution from French into English, and Sofía Doig and Ioana-Maria Iliut for their support with the transcriptions.

We wish to thank Pablo's son, Juan Vasquez Amaringo, for his friendship and support throughout the process, and, finally, the people of Peru for their generosity and openness while we have worked on this book.

CONTENTS

Foreword by Jorge Velásquez Portocarrero ix

Preface by Howard G. Charing x

Preface by Peter Cloudsley xii

Introduction by Pablo Amaringo 1

Part One

PABLO AMARINGO, THE MAN

Memories and Legacy 3

With contributions by Dennis McKenna, Ph.D.
Jeremy Narby, Ph.D.
Graham Hancock
Roberto Venosa
Jan Kounen
Stephan V. Beyer, Ph.D.

Autobiography of the Artist 18

Part Two

PABLO AMARINGO, THE WORK

THE COLOR PLATES 25

Glossary 170

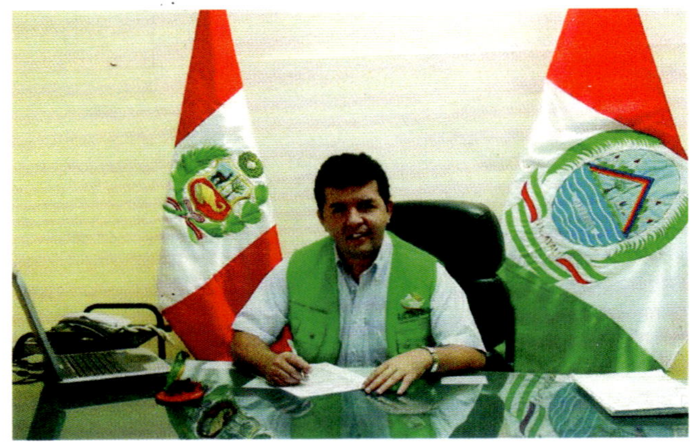

Hacer el prologo de la vida y obra de **Pablo César Amaringo Shuña**, no resulta empresa fácil, dada la sencillez de sus orígenes y la grandeza ecuménica de su obra. Su procedencia, de una familia numerosa y pobre, asentada en un pueblo perdido en el verde profundo de la Amazonía Peruana: Tamanco-Perú, crisol donde se forja un espíritu inquieto teniendo como escenario la flora y la fauna; vitales, ubérrimas, dinámicas, majestuosas y misteriosas.

Su corto paso por la escuela formal, no borró su formación amigable con la naturaleza; los azahares de su inicial vida citadina, su salud quebrantada y los desencuentros con la formalidad llevaron a Pablo César, a buscar nuevamente el abrigo de la naturaleza y allí; en la profundidad de la selva se produce el reencuentro con el mariri, con los genios de las plantas y los ángeles etéreos del bosque: Nace un shaman, un médico, un maestro curandero.

Pronto, hace una parada en el camino y sentencia **:** *"la ayahuasca no es algo para jugar. Incluso puede matar, no porque sea tóxica en sí misma, sino porque el cuerpo puede no ser capaz de soportar el reino espiritual, las vibraciones del mundo espiritual";* deja el shamanismo, siente que su misión es comunicar la sabiduría de la naturaleza, el reino espiritual, las vibraciones de ese mundo, enseña más allá de las palabras y de la dinámica no lineal del conocimiento, enseña con sus trazos las lecciones aprendidas en sus visiones.

El manantial de su escuela **Príncipe Espiritual** (Usko Ayar) es la vía para enseñar a amar y comprender la cultura y el medio ambiente, nadie puede amar algo que no conoce; sus líneas sin retoques; sus colores extraídos de la floresta, del cosmos sempiterno, de la librea de las aves y el canto de los genios, se materializan una y otra vez en armoniosas visiones de un mundo que no "vemos", pero que es nuestro hogar, nuestro hábitat, nuestro planeta.

Cruza el océano el ave de su pincel visionario, Pablo César alcanza el pedestal de los elegidos, en 1992 se le otorga el Premio Global 500, desde el programa ambiental de las Naciones Unidas, junto a Jacques Cousteau, Chico Méndez y Jimmy Carter y otros, su obra de amor a la naturaleza, de espíritu y vibraciones cósmicas nos señala hoy el camino.

Ahora en la morada celeste, multicolor, iridiscente y llena de espiritualidad, que con genialidad iluminó en sus cuadros, nos ha legado la semilla de su obra que trasuntando espacios, llenó un vacío de la ciencia, el compromiso del la humanidad con el espíritu de la naturaleza y el medio ambiente.

....

Jorge Velásquez Portocarrero
Presidente del Gobierno Regional de Ucayali
Ucayali Región Ecológica
Pucallpa-Perú

FOREWORD

To write something about the life and work of Pablo Cesar Amaringo Shuña is challenging, given the deep spiritual nature of his work. He came from a large and humble family in the remote village of Tamanco, deep in the verdant Peruvian Amazon. It was here, surrounded by majestic and mysterious flora and fauna, that Pablo's inquisitive spirit was forged.

He had a brief formal education, which did not detract from hard lessons learned from life; he had problems with his health and experienced difficulty conforming to the conventions of a small jungle village. But Pablo was always able to retreat into nature and commune with the spirits of plants and beings of the forest, and this led him to become a shaman, a doctor, and a *maestro.*

When he stopped practicing as a shaman, Pablo declared: "Ayahuasca is not something to be taken lightly. It can kill not because it is in itself toxic, but because the body may not be strong enough to receive so much knowledge and wisdom." After this he discovered a mission that would last the rest of his life: to communicate the teachings of the spiritual world beyond language, by painting his visions.

Pablo's painting school, Usko Ayar, became his instrument for teaching love and understanding of culture and the environment, and no one can love something he does not know. His lines were faultless and his colors were lifted from the forest and the plumage of birds. His visions materialized out of an invisible world, yet one that is our home, our habitat, our planet.

He crossed the ocean like a bird with a visionary brush, and in 1992 Pablo was chosen for the Global 500 award of the United Nations environmental program, together with Jacques Cousteau, Chico Mendez, Jimmy Carter, and others. His dedication and love for nature and the spirit world continue to show us the way forward.

Now, from his iridescent celestial resting place that illuminated his pictures with genius, he has left this legacy as a seed for us to plant. His wisdom fills a gap in science and is a model of humanity's commitment to the spirit of nature and the environment.

Jorge Velásquez Portocarrero
President of the Department of Ucayali, Peru,
2006–2010

PREFACE

HOWARD G. CHARING

The genesis of this book was in January 2007 during a beautiful *ayahuasca* session at Mishana in the Peruvian Amazon. My visions that night were of the vivid creations and forms of Pablo's paintings. The session culminated in what I can only describe as a lightning flash of inspiration to work with Pablo on a new book of his paintings.

The following day I was still filled with excitement from this vision, and knew then with absolute certainty that this book would be done. I discussed the idea with Peter—he and I had worked together, since the 1990s, organizing ayahuasca and plant diet retreats in the Amazon. We decided to visit Pablo in Pucallpa at the earliest opportunity, which was in February 2007, to discuss the idea of doing a book with him. When the three of us spoke, Pablo's face immediately lit up with enthusiasm and there and then, without further ado, we agreed to collaborate on this book.

All in all, this was a complex project. We formed a detailed plan, the first step of which was to catalog and have all of Pablo's available paintings and sketches professionally photographed, and later digitally scanned. Pablo gave us hundreds of pages of his notes and journals, which he had kept in his house. We had many meetings with Pablo to discuss and explore the multifaceted qualities of his paintings. Each session generated new questions, which necessitated further trips to Pucallpa before we were in a position to complete the narratives that accompany the paintings themselves.

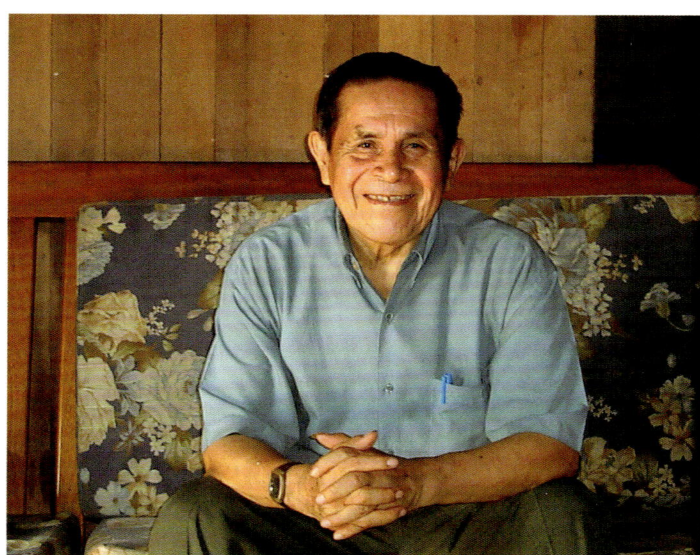

Pablo Amaringo at home

In our meetings with Pablo we were continually amazed at his vast eclectic knowledge. We also enjoyed his personal anecdotes, spiritual wisdom, and gentle humility. Pablo was a master in the authentic meaning of the term and being with him was an enriching and transformative experience. Pablo would often describe the outer aspects of a motif or theme and then subtly hint at a deeper meaning or metaphor. Each time I returned to Lima, I needed to meditate on, as well as forensically study, each painting for hours to comprehend its subtle and transcendent nature.

Much of Pablo's work is allegorical. For example, although he said that the supernatural serpents such as the sachamama, the yacumama, and the huiramama actually existed, they were, in his own words, "semi-mythological," as well as descriptions of the forces of nature embodying the natural cycles of rain that fertilize and sustain the forest. I also came to understand that the heirarchy of shamans was a metaphor for the evolving destiny of human consciousness.

It was very touching that Pablo trusted us to communicate his visions and teachings and deeply gratifying to be documenting oral traditions and knowledge that might otherwise have been lost to the world.

We recorded all our meetings with Pablo in both audio and video; all this material has been archived. Some of his communications were made outside of our meetings. For example, when he showed me a commissioned work in progress—a painting of Jesus ascending into the clouds, witnessed by his disciples—I asked Pablo if he regarded Jesus as a shaman. He whispered, "Yes, he was a sumiruna."

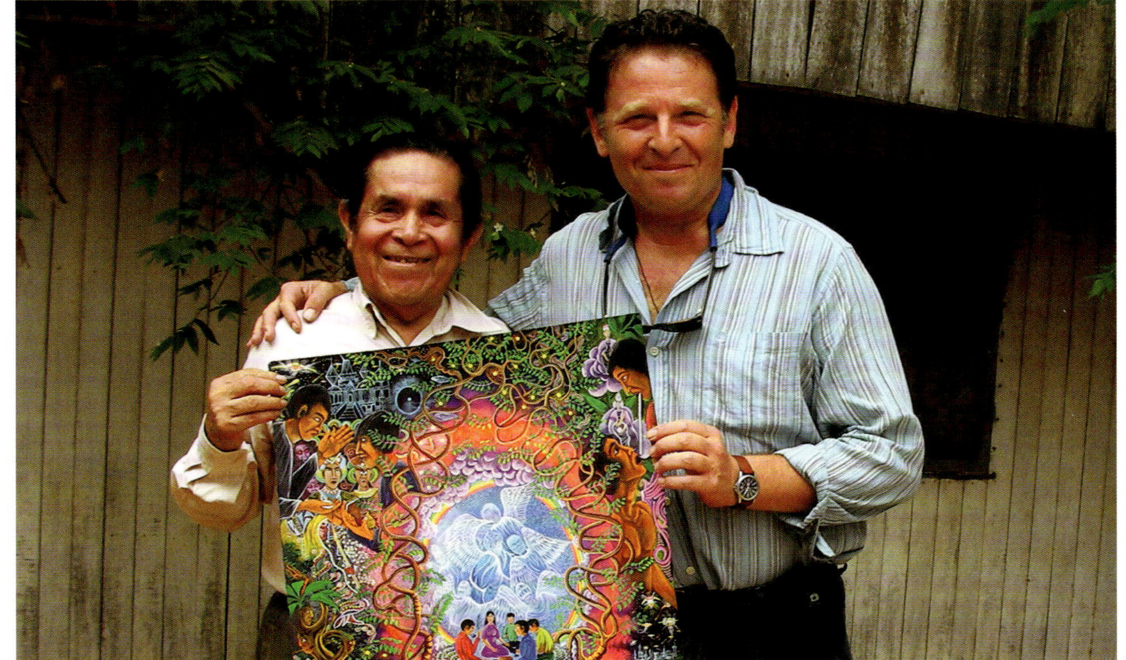

Pablo and Howard with one of Pablo's paintings

Pablo's paintings are imbued with power and are far more than two-dimensional images. While he was painting them he would also chant his *ícaros* (magical incantations). He said, "If you concentrate and meditate on the paintings, you will receive this spiritual energy." Although he had stopped drinking ayahuasca many years prior, he had the ability to perfectly recall each of his visions. On one occasion he said to me, "I do not need to drink again; ayahuasca has connected me to the spirit world."

Peter and I had many discussions regarding writing conventions for this book. For example, we standardized variable Quechua spellings, and for expediency we have frequently used the term "shaman" (*chamán* in Peru), even though it is a relatively recent import in the Amazon (see the glossary). We have also retained all the original Quechua language titles and Spanish subtitles of the paintings.

I have been truly privileged to know Pablo as a friend and maestro. He always made me welcome: "Mi casa es tu casa" (my house is your house).

On two occasions in 2008 Pablo suffered acute dengue fever, which severely debilitated him. After this, he never fully regained his strength and vigor. In 2009 he became visibly frail and I knew deep down that he might not make it through to the book's publication. I have to think that he knew this too, because he said to me in March of that year, "I fear that I will go before I paint all that I have seen. But this is no problem . . . I will finish painting them the next time when I come back." I knew that this book would be his testament as a visionary, sage, and artist.

Howard G. Charing has worked with some of the most respected and extraordinary shamans and healers in the Amazon rain forest and in the Andes. Since the 1990s he has organized specialized retreats to the Amazon rain forest with Peter Cloudsley, at the dedicated retreat center in the Mishana Nature Reserve. He coauthored *Plant Spirit Shamanism: Traditional Techniques for Healing the Soul,* published by Destiny Books.

PREFACE

PETER CLOUDSLEY

In February 1980 I arrived in Peru for the first time, equipped with a Uher reel-to-reel tape recorder, to research Andean fiesta music for the British Library. Previously I had been a harpsichord maker with my own workshop in Clerkenwell, London, where I enjoyed listening to music while I worked. In addition to early music, which I have always loved, I was fascinated by field recordings of ethnic music, especially from Peru.

I will never forget my first experience of a fiesta in Tinta, in the Department of Cusco. I connected my microphones and pitched myself into the streets of this normally tranquil village where, on this day of the year, the *campesinos* abandoned their agricultural work to make music and dance wildly, while unmarried women improvised hilarious lyrics, some of which made fun of me.

I was overcome by a surreal intoxication. *Aguardiente* (see glossary) was generously and obligatorily offered to me, and I could not refuse. Flour was thrown everywhere, then water, and I was "danced" willy nilly several times around the square before I could break free from the viselike grip of very strong women. That day I participated in my first "Indian experience" and felt I had broken through a veil into another world.

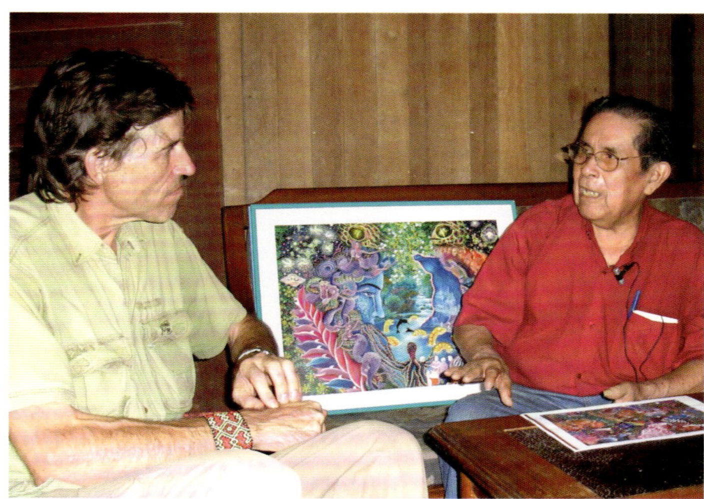

Pablo discusses one of his paintings with Peter.

In subsequent years I attended many more Andean fiestas, observing their finer details and appreciating that a fiesta is more than just a music festival. It is a dramatic enactment of a primordial ritual, a collective shamanistic experience wherein the dark side of a community can be expressed and healed. Fiestas are always held on particular days of the year and often in special places.

A foreigner had to work harder in those days to be accepted, trusted, and not stereotyped as a "gringo." Since then Peruvian society has opened up and modernized, and the boundary between the two worlds has allowed interpenetration, although many of the obstacles to crossing the cultural veil into the magical dimension are as challenging today as ever—whether you participate in a fiesta or an ayahuasca ceremony.

My exploration of Andean cosmovision broadened in the late '80s to include Amazonian shamanism, and I soon found myself in Pucallpa, being welcomed at the house of Pablo Amaringo. He was the ambassador for ayahuasca, a guide for seekers in the ancestral Amazonian world, and his willingness inspired and supported me in my research. I went on to interview maestros in the Peruvian Sierra and along the coast who work with their clients in other traditions with San Pedro,* tobacco, coca leaves, and guinea pigs, for example. I recorded their ceremonies and chants, and made pilgrimages to sacred places, such as Las Huaringas in northern Peru.

Each time I went back to Pucallpa, I visited Pablo to see his latest paintings. The spirits inspire and teach us, he explained, but we must be willing to evolve and change. To have a good vision we must develop the imagination, and this, I realized, was exemplified in his artwork. Pablo's imagination was so highly developed that he could remember past visions whenever he wanted to by chanting or whistling his ícaros, without

*San Pedro (*Trichocereus pachanoi*), is an entheogenic cactus used in the Peruvian Andes and coastal region.

drinking ayahuasca. He always said he never painted anything he had not himself seen.

I realized that Pablo's narratives were full of clues for working with ayahuasca—experiencing the most profound mysteries of life and wondering at their meaning and purpose. If one could access these experiences in every ceremony, there should never be any reason for despondency. The apprentices in Pablo's paintings confront anxiety and trials—dangerous animals, poisonous plants, and wicked *brujos* that originate in the conditions of the rain forest and may appear unrelated to modern life. If the apprentices prevail, they will serve their community as healers and find a meaning to life.

But of course, things are not always as simple as that. Even when the mother plant rewards us richly, most of us are so captivated by modern life that when we return to the mundane world, we easily forget what we have learned.

Riverine communities in the Amazon have little exposure to advertising and television, and this could be an advantage. Their spontaneity and joie de vivre suggest that they find meaning in the details of daily life: fishing, hunting, and tending their modest plantations. A house in the Amazon is simple and natural; people there do not need walls to protect their property. There is abundant fruit on the trees and fish in the river, and people eat to their hearts' content and give freely to their neighbors because ripe fruit and fresh fish soon rot, and there are no refrigerators. In contrast, our culture sees life as being separate from nature, promoting the illusion that fulfillment can be found in accumulating prestige or wealth.

Working with Pablo was occasionally challenging. His mind worked like the mind of a shaman and mystic. Sometimes the secrets he so much wanted to share seemed impenetrable, but this was part of my journey of discovery.

Sometimes his explanations played intriguingly with ambiguities and hinted at the ineffable. At times we struggled with Pablo's interviews, and they challenged Howard and me not to arbitrate too much on what might be meaningful or otherwise. In *Unicornio Dorado,* for example, he contrasts the Western rational path to the wisdom of the indigenous way, which, he said, is faster. He had tried both routes and believed that ultimately both were needed if our spirituality was to evolve sufficiently to lift humanity out of the crisis in which we find ourselves.

The first painting to captivate my imagination was *El Barco Fantasma.* Here we can imagine the indigenous peoples' first sighting of the robber barons in the nineteenth century. Peering through the undergrowth at the edge of a river they see a huge steamer hissing at them and seemingly returning the incredulous looks of the Indians through the eyes on its prow. The clattering engines shatter the primordial tranquillity of the river at night, and the steamer's electric lights cause the natives to perceive the steamer as an Amazonian spirit accompanied by welcoming mermaids and sylphs.

Pablo reflects the way in which the indigenous people made sense of their initial perceptions of Europeans, and how Amazonian mythology forged a vibrant hybrid of the two cultures. The smoke and steam rising from the boat's chimney emerge from a cauldron for brewing ayahuasca. The multiple decks of the steamer with strange Europeans dressed in sumptuous evening dress was Pablo's metaphor for order, not only among humans but also in nature. If this is destroyed, he said, our world will descend into chaos.

It is difficult to work with ayahuasca. Its preparation and use are beset by exigencies that anthropologists have referred to as "taboos": rules that do not appear to have any reason to exist. These rules govern such things as diet, attitude, the phase of the moon,

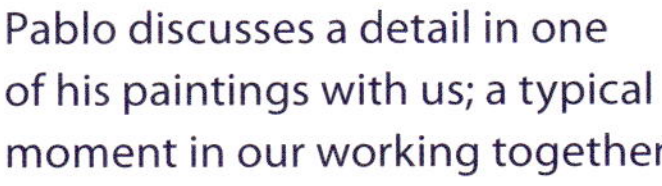
Pablo discusses a detail in one of his paintings with us; a typical moment in our working together.

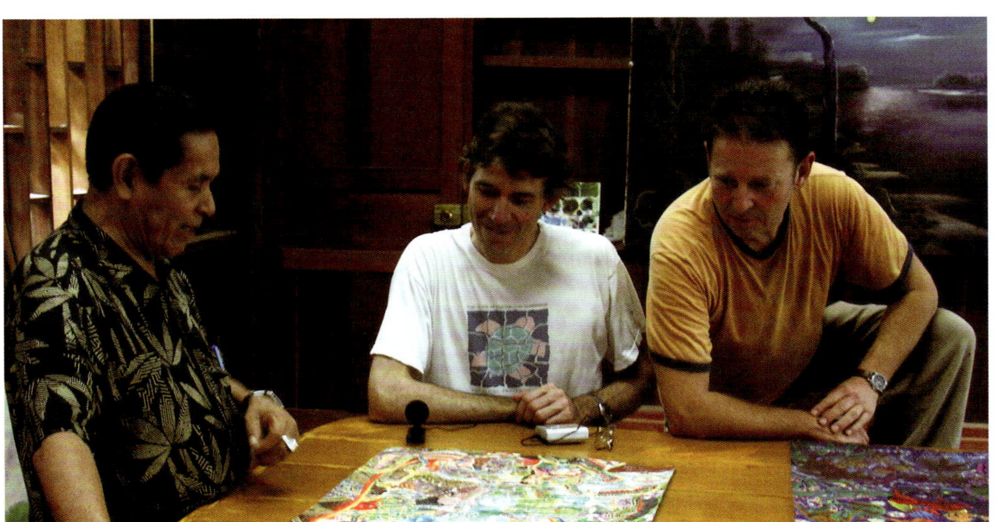

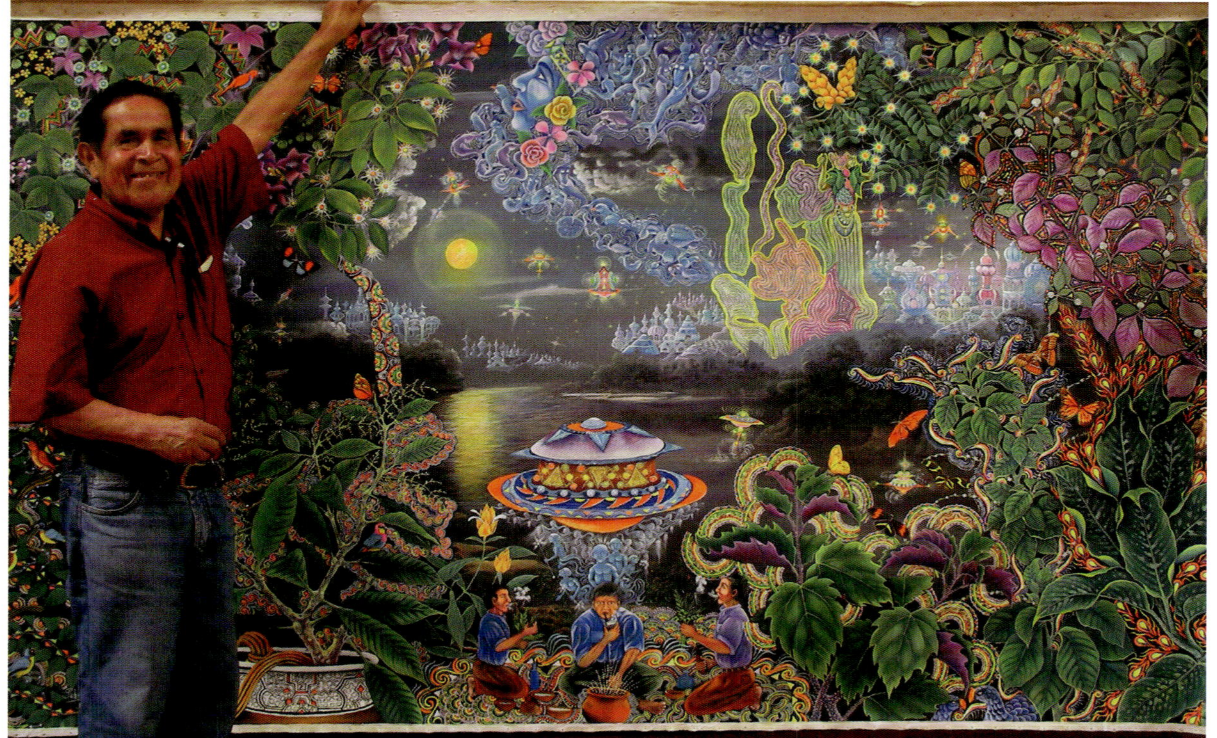

Pablo with his mural painting *Misterio Profundo*

menstruation, and so on, and have a crucial influence on the effectiveness of the ayahuasca brew. Pablo explained that from a shamanistic perspective all the rules have rationales, which we ignore at our own peril. Shamans tell us that the mother of ayahuasca is jealous and will not open herself to those who do not respect her. The only known way in is through the tradition of the Amazonian Indians, which the *mestizos* later learned and gradually adapted to their own needs. (Mestizos still respect native shamans and generally agree that indigenous ícaros are the more powerful ones.)

When I asked Pablo if he had any advice for Westerners wanting to learn from ayahuasca, he said that the quality of the shaman was paramount and it was preferable to work with an indigenous one.

Pablo believed that the aim of this book was to develop the imagination and prepare the reader for learning. Pablo saw the imagination as the seed for a new government of every person's consciousness.

Peter Cloudsley is a musicologist and writer who, since 1980, has created an archive of traditional music and interviews in Peru and collected for the British Museum. He published *A Survey of Music in Peru* in 1993, and two CDs: *Fiesta Music from Peru* (2000) and *Shamans of Peru* (2002). He established the Amazon Retreat Centre in Mishana in 2004.

INTRODUCTION

Pablo Amaringo

This book is very different from my first book, *Ayahuasca Visions: The Religious Iconography of a Peruvian Shaman,* because I have felt much freer to express myself in it. For the former book everything was written down from the beginning and we gave it an academic appearance so that it would be taken more seriously, or at least recognized as a piece of anthropology.

Eighteen years ago, one did not expect to get much credence for subjective experiences, and my fears of being misinterpreted or criticized for not being Catholic were greater. Now I can afford to be quite open about personal matters, and I hope this new book will enchant and fascinate readers. I have told my personal stories behind the visions and my experiences with Amazonian people and folklore. All of this should provide guidance to people following the way of plant knowledge and ayahuasca—to live life more creatively and take more care of the earth.

The pictures themselves have messages and teachings that train the mind to see what could have happened in the past and what can happen in the future. They open up other ways of seeing, which you could call sacred or Divine. I would like my pictures to inspire a different idea of religion, one that is not given in exchange for something, but is free.

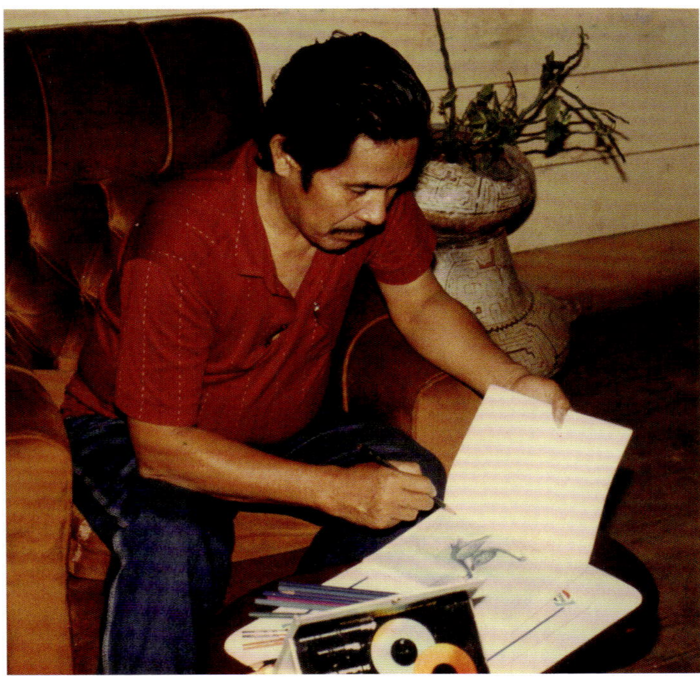

Pablo as a young man, working on a sketch of a goose

Each of us has a function in the working of life, starting when we are born, continuing while we grow to our zenith, and after that when we decline and die. So I say to people: Prepare yourself well from an early age, so that when you are older you have something of the shaman in you. You should take into account that when you are old, there may be nobody to help you and you can no longer work. Or your mind might work a little, but still it is difficult to adapt to such a fundamental change in your condition. As you age, a Pandora's box opens and out come demons of every kind. To survive in the high seas you need to be very balanced; otherwise you go over and die from any trivial thing.

The way to do this is by doing good and leaving seeds for others, and this is what this book attempts to do. The best thing you can leave is a seed for others to work with. I am not just a person; I am a *spiritual* person. I always communicate with the great universal force, which is the rock of perfection—Dios—that I have seen in my ayahuasca visions, and which has always spoken to me. If we doubt, we do not please Dios, who is watching and observing the wisdom of everything we do. Without his strength and the strength of the spirits, we would not even be able to speak. Life is a gift given by spirit.

We do not know what this spirit is or what it wants to do with us. We want to change the system to correct all the bad things that are happening in the world, but no one seems to be able to do much good. We need a government of every person's consciousness, yet this is the very thing people fear is coming. I say it will come not suddenly, from one year to the next, but a change is getting near, in which this book will play a part.

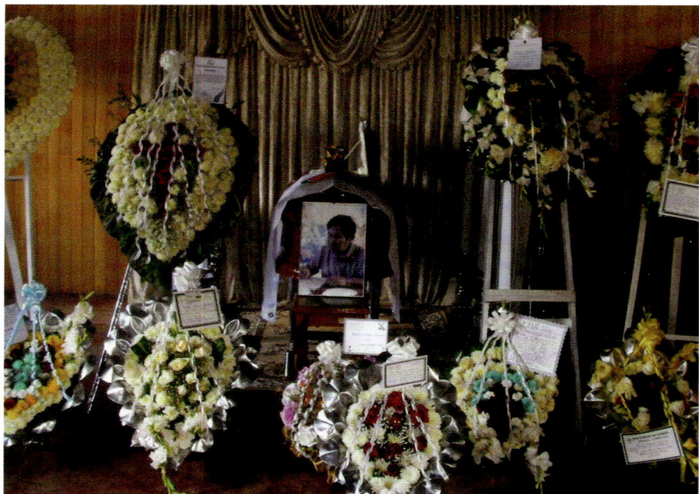

Pablo's funeral wake, November 17, 2009

Everything should be right about this book, not in the sense of its authority, but being complete—giving, thinking, and acting completely.

If we are handing on information, we should try to give the whole picture. Mysteries as well as vicissitudes are also information from which we can discover how to learn. We can learn from dreadful things too, but how? Recognize your mistakes, but do not think of making them when you live. Live with faith; do not give in to doubt and fear!

Once I was arriving in Norway by plane and the plane's undercarriage would not unfold, so we circled for forty minutes to burn up fuel before attempting a crash landing. Everyone onboard looked pale and nervous, including my nephews and two students who were with me. I was ready to die and told them not to fear, you must not die like an iniquitous person, condemned for doing wicked things. This is why I think well about what I do.

Reading this book requires the reader to be curious, because its meaning will not be understood from a superficial reading. It requires readers to ask why and what the book is trying to teach them. It is my hope that this book will be published in order that people might benefit from what I have learned, and I have faith in its success.

Editor's note: On November 16, 2009, after a brief illness, Pablo Amaringo died at his home in Pucallpa, surrounded by family and friends.

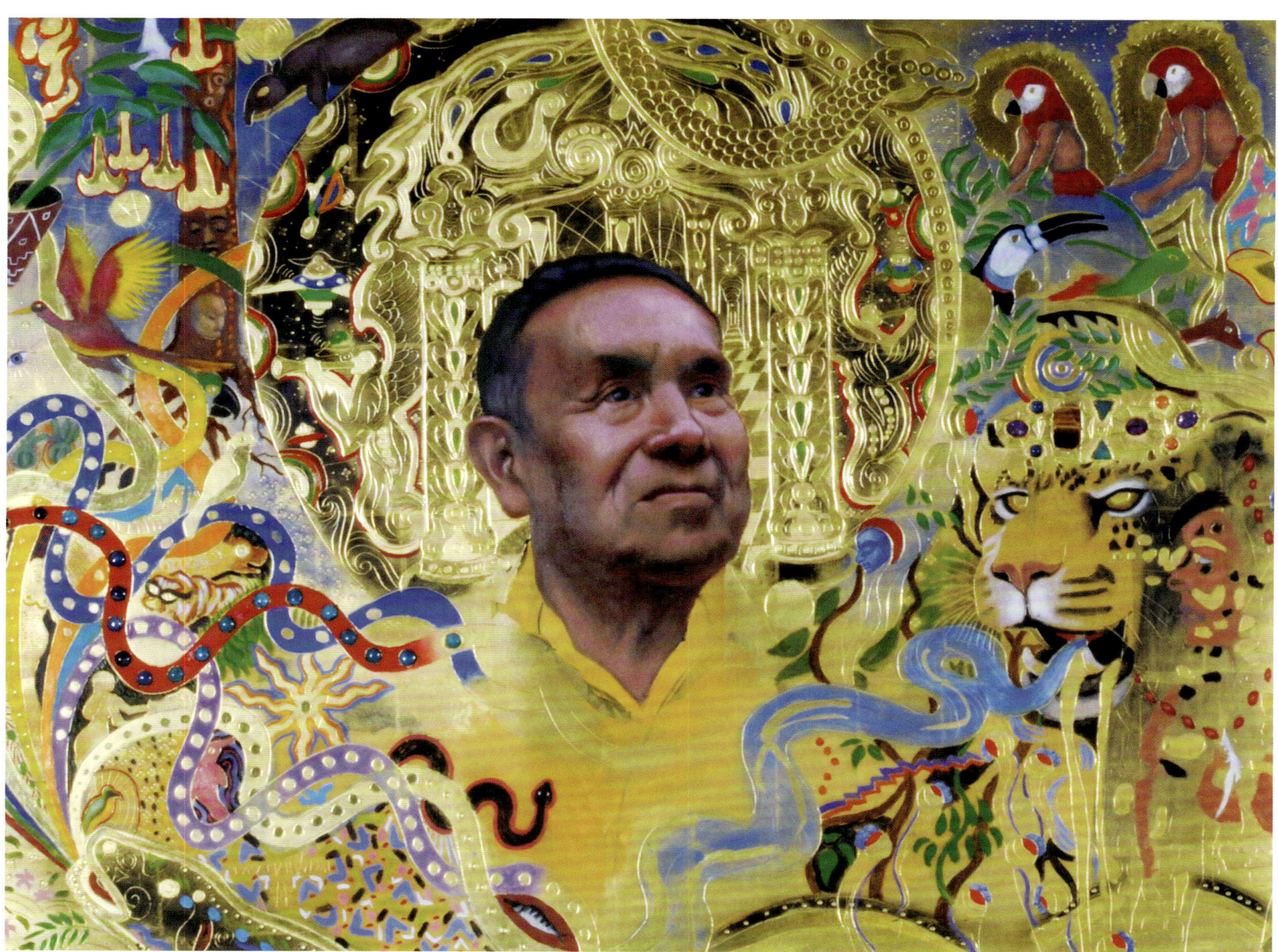

Icon Don Pablo Amaringo by David "Slocum" Hewson. 24-karat gold water gilt with embedded precious stones/oil on wood. For more information please go to www.davidhewsonart.com and/or www.amaruspirit.org.

Part One

Pablo Amaringo, the Man

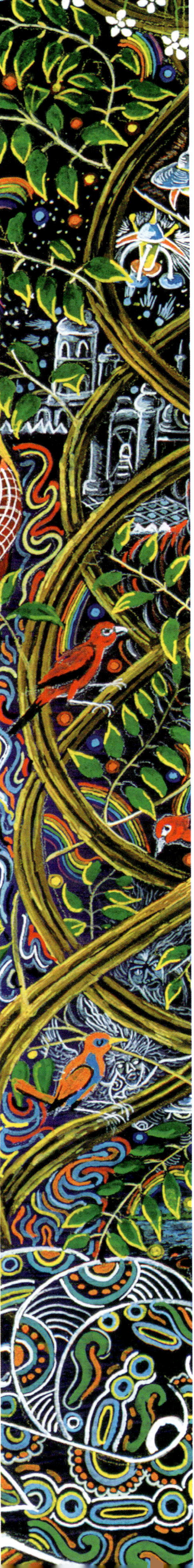

MEMORIES AND LEGACY

EARLY ENCOUNTERS WITH PABLO AMARINGO—PAINTER OF VISIONS

DENNIS MCKENNA, PH.D.

I first met Pablo Amaringo in May 1981, when I was finishing up some ethnobotanical fieldwork in the Peruvian Amazon. It was at the end of a grueling but rewarding six months of collecting specimens and material for phytochemical investigations on a project that was eventually to evolve into my doctoral thesis on the botany, chemistry, and pharmacology of ayahuasca. Ayahuasca is the now-famous but at that time little-known visionary brew that is the portal to the shamanic universe of the Amazon.

It had been a long trip. I had returned to Pucallpa for a few days to collect a few more specimens and to visit my chief informant there, the ayahuasquero Don Fidel Mosambite, who had been my major informant when I first arrived in Peru. It seemed appropriate, somehow, to stop and pay my respects to this wonderful man before catching my flight back to Lima, and then Vancouver.

So it was that on a sunny Sunday afternoon I found myself in Pueblo Joven José Olay, a tiny settlement on the outskirts of Pucallpa, near Don Fidel's home. I had stopped in at a local cantina to slake my thirst on the hot day, and was trying to order a beer and a little food in my broken Spanish (it has since improved) when a diminutive man with a kind face and a soft voice introduced himself in equally broken English and asked if I needed some assistance with my order. I was grateful for his help and offered to buy him a beer. In the conversation that ensued I learned that he was a maestro, a teacher, and, specifically, that he taught English in the local one-room school in his village. It was one of those chance encounters about which one thinks little at the time; a pleasant conversation in a local watering hole, a casual encounter that began what became, over the years, a warm friendship that would change both of our lives.

We passed the time in the dusty shade of the drowsy afternoon, learning what we could of each other through the limitations of our linguistic filters. It transpired that Pablo was not only a teacher, but a musician and an enthusiastic amateur painter. He invited me to his modest home on the main drag of this village (or what would have been the main drag if there had been any automobiles, which there were not).

While I waited in his living room, nursing a glass of lemonade, he went into a back room and rummaged around for a bit, returning with a stack of paintings on cardboard or particle board. They were mostly representations of animals and plants, things he had seen during his extensive ramblings in the jungle. Though I murmured politely as he showed me painting after painting, they were workmanlike but unremarkable, the sort of effort that might be the product of a first-year art student.

Eventually, as the afternoon dissolved into evening, I took my leave, telling Pablo that I was tired and had to return to my hotel to pack my gear in order to catch a plane to Lima the next day. I thanked him for his kindness and hospitality, made another insincere comment or two on the paintings, and prepared to depart. Pablo asked if I would like to return the next day for a *fiesta de la musica*. He wanted to gather together some friends and give me a little concert, a proper send-off for my long journey back to North America.

I started to demur, but he would not be put off; he insisted that I come to his house the next afternoon. As my plane did not depart until early evening, I had no real excuse, so finally I assented and told him I would stop by around lunchtime the following day. It was perhaps one of the best spur-of-the-moment decisions I have ever made.

When I arrived, bringing *cervezas* (beer) and a

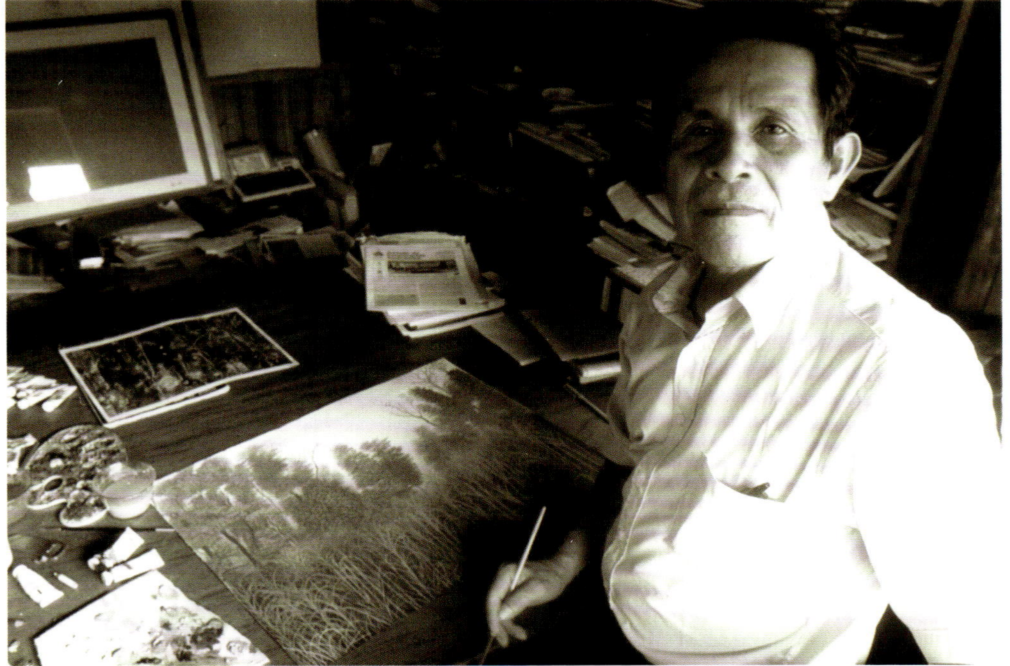

Pablo and one of his early landscapes

bit of *comidas* (food), Pablo had gathered several of his friends together and they were unpacking musical instruments of all kinds: a battered guitar, drums, flutes, ukeleles, tambourines, and bells—the typical ensemble of Peruvian folk music. This little band of "jammers" then proceeded to regale me, for about the next four hours, with a truly amazing repertoire of traditional folk tunes.

The beer and laughter flowed freely, food was consumed, stories were told, and all of it transpired in an atmosphere of warmth and friendship, just a bunch of *amigos* hanging out, jamming, and having a good time.

I was truly moved.

Suddenly, I was no longer an *extranjero,* an alien foreigner dropped in from a parallel universe; I was just one of the guys and the guys were eager to share their music, their laughter, and their life with me. It was a moment I will never forget. As it happens, I had a few cassettes left, and my cheap tape recorder, which had served me well over the past months, still had some life left in its failing batteries. So I was able to capture a little of the performance, and that tape—tinny, scratchy, and about as bad a recording as it's possible to make—remains one of my most treasured possessions to this day. My head was full of the music, but my heart was sad as I bid Pablo and his band of merry men good-bye, not knowing if I would ever see any of them again. I returned to Vancouver and threw myself into my work, spending long days and sometimes nights unraveling the chemical secrets of the hard-won samples I had collected.

Years passed and although Pablo and I had exchanged addresses and I had heard from him once, there was no further communication from him. I had responded to his one brief letter with an equally short missive, the best I could do as a busy graduate student (or so I justified to myself).

In the fall of 1981, shortly after the conclusion of my fieldwork, I met Luis Eduardo Luna for the first time. He was in town to attend an anthropology conference being held at the University of British Columbia; though we had not met, we knew of each other, as he had been a friend of my brother Terence since 1972. When he sent word that he was coming to Vancouver, I invited him to stay in my tiny apartment, even though I had just moved in a few days earlier with my new girlfriend, Sheila (who is now my wife). Eduardo was a model houseguest. We spent many hours talking late into the night, after he had returned from the conference and I from my long days in the lab. Another birth took place there and then, of another friendship that I still cherish.

Suddenly, it was 1985. I had completed my thesis the year before, published the findings (such as they were), and moved to San Diego to begin the first of an endless chain of postdocs. In the mail I received an unexpected invitation from my new (and now old) friend, Eduardo. It seemed that he was organizing a satellite symposium on ayahuasca that was to be held in conjunction with the 45th International Congress of the Americanists, scheduled for that summer at the University of the Andes in Bogota, Colombia. Could I be persuaded to attend and present some of my findings? It took no persuasion; I told him I was honored, and I was ready to go.

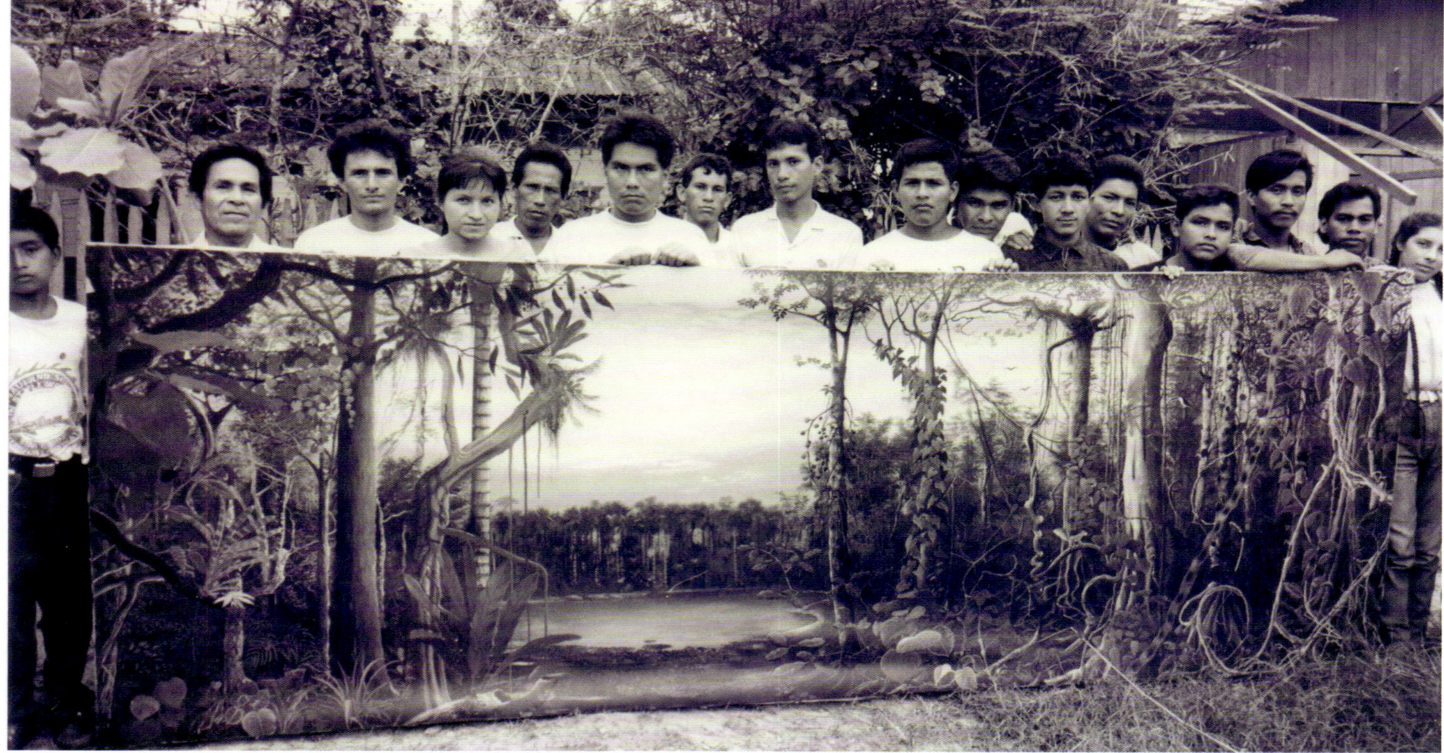

Pablo (second from left), circa 1985, stands with his art students, displaying a mural they worked on together.

That July I met up with Eduardo at his home in Florencia, in the province of Caqueta, Colombia. I had passed through Florencia once before, in 1971 while I was on the way to La Chorerra in the company of my brother and our unlikely hippie entourage. It felt strange to be returning to this forsaken spot on the map, the place where, nearly a decade and a half before, I had had my first encounter with the *Psilocybe cubensis* mushrooms, an encounter that changed my life forever. (The chronicle of our journey to La Chorrera and the hyperspatial portal lurking there has been related extensively in my brother's book, *True Hallucinations,* so there is no need to belabor it here.)

We stayed at Eduardo's home for a few days and journeyed together to Bogotá for the conference. Afterward, we parted company. I had an obligation to travel on to Iquitos to conduct some business, and we agreed to meet again in Pucallpa to embark on six weeks of travel and collecting in various parts of Peru. Eduardo showed up right on time, encountering me waiting impatiently in the cantina of El Pescador—the tiny, squalid hotel in the town of Yarina Cocha, a few kilometers from Pucallpa.

No sooner had he dropped his bags than we left for an ayahuasca session with Don Fidel; I was eager to introduce him to my informant, still going strong since I had last seen him in '81. The next morning, after a light breakfast, we determined to go to Jose Olaya to see if we could find Pablo. We found him at home and introductions were made. Eduardo's presence, with his perfect Spanish, enabled a much less superficial conversation with Pablo to take place this time.

In short order, the subject of ayahuasca came up (I had not discussed this at all with Pablo in our previous encounter, four years prior) and we learned that not only did he know about it, but that he had been a practicing ayahuasquero for many years. Suddenly my perception of this odd, funny little man changed dramatically. He was not just an ayahuasquero, but a very powerful one. He related to us the circumstances that had led him to follow the path of the medicine; how in his late thirties he had been diagnosed with a serious heart problem, a congenital defect that doctors told him was likely to shorten his life by decades. There was nothing they could do, they said. In despair, not knowing what else to do, Pablo sought out the local shaman and submitted himself to the medicine, not knowing whether this or any other measure could help him.

He related an amazing story; how, in his first or second encounter, he had been visited by "spirit doctors" (he described them as "German doctors"). He found himself in a curved space, an operating room, surrounded by high-tech machines and doctors in white coats. He related how the doctors opened his chest and removed his heart, still beating, all while Pablo watched in terror, convinced he was going to die; how the doctors did things to his heart, fixing it before his eyes, and replaced it in his chest and closed him up; how, after this experience, he never had any further heart problems (his doctors in Pucallpa were baffled—they couldn't explain it); how, following this miraculous healing, he had responded to the message from ayahuasca, that in order to maintain his health and vitality he had to become a student of ayahuasca; how he learned to use it to maintain his health and to cure others. Which he did, over many years, until it came about that he got into a shamanic conflict with other ayahuasqueros—evil *brujos* (sorcerers) who were bent on killing or harming him.

He went on to tell us how, at that point, he determined to give up his practice. He saw himself at a crossroads, he said, where his only choice was to kill his enemies or to be killed by them. Not wanting either of these grim options, he stepped back from the world of ayahuasca and never ingested the brew again. Eduardo and I were struck by this story and while we were ruminating over his tale, Pablo proceeded to bring out some of his paintings to show us. As we were examining these (his work had improved somewhat since he had first shown it to me years before, but his paintings were still fairly conventional) Eduardo asked him if he had ever tried painting his ayahuasca visions. Pablo seemed puzzled by the question; the idea had really never occurred to him! Eduardo made some compliment about his technique and gently suggested that he ought to give it a try. Pablo was noncommittal, and the moment passed. We spent another hour or so in conversation about inconsequential matters and then took our leave.

The next morning, we decided to drop by Pablo's house again, with no particular agenda except to say hello. Pablo was excited and showed us three canvases, the first three visionary paintings he had ever produced. Intrigued by Eduardo's suggestion, he had been up all night producing these paintings. They were still somewhat crude by the standards of his later work, but it was clear to both of us that these works were of a wholly different order from anything he had shown us before. They seemed to come from a place of vision and inspiration—a direct download from the magical ayahuasca universe, its details remembered and rendered perfectly from memory, though it had been many years since he had taken the brew.

Both Eduardo and I noted with slight amusement that the paintings were unsigned. So egoless was this man, so naively unaware of such conventions, that it did not occur to him to spoil the effect with the imprimatur of his creative ownership. Eduardo, much more qualified than I to judge the quality of Pablo's artistic efforts and quick to discern their commercial potential, lost no time in suggesting that he should include his name on any further works he might produce; but those first two remained unsigned and are hanging, still unsigned, one in my den in Minnesota, the other in Eduardo's study in Helsinki.

We returned to visit Pablo the next day, to find that he had turned out three more paintings in the preceding twenty-four hours. They were signed this time, as he proudly pointed out. They were, if anything, even more intricate, colorful, and inspired than the works of the previous day. And thus began Pablo's remarkable career as one of the world's foremost visionary artists.

It was as though Eduardo's simple suggestion had triggered something in Pablo; once he took to the idea, it turned on a floodgate of creative expression, with ideas and images pouring out of him almost faster than he could put brush to canvas. That original inspiration and its prolific result continued and his technique improved while his fame grew. His later works are more sophisticated and detailed, reflecting his years of

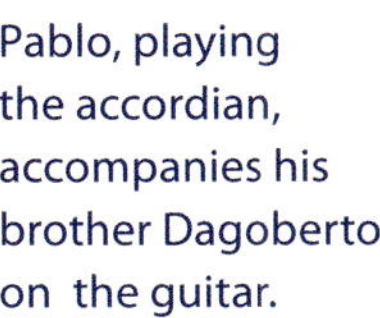

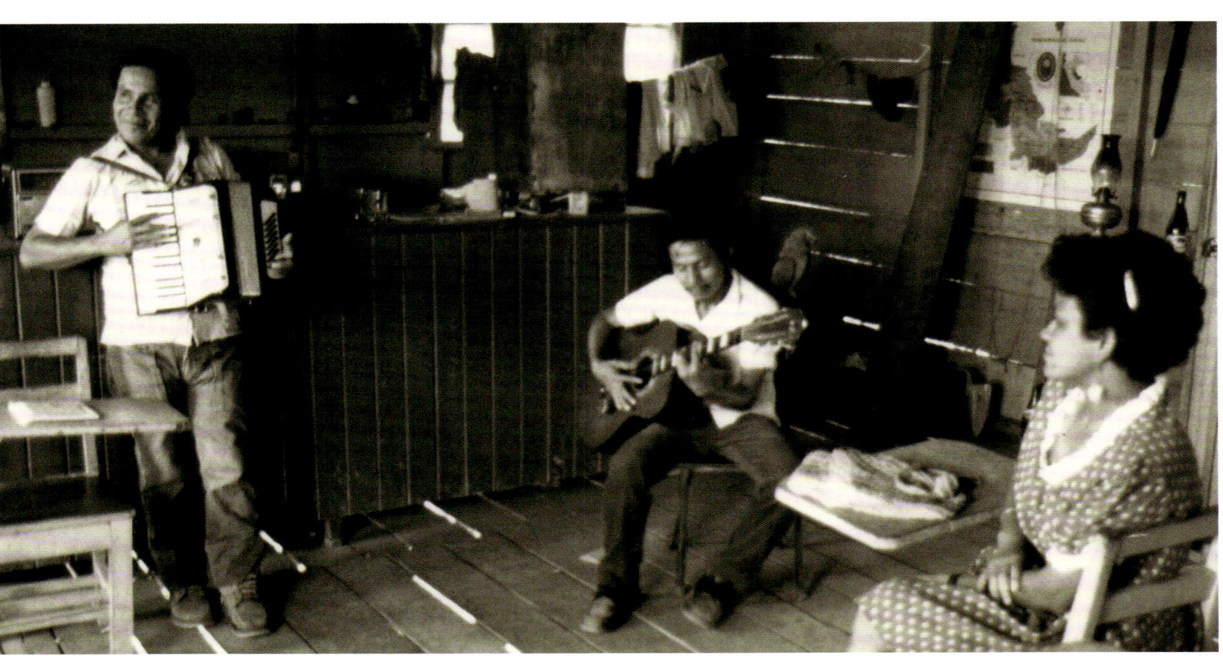

Pablo, playing the accordian, accompanies his brother Dagoberto on the guitar.

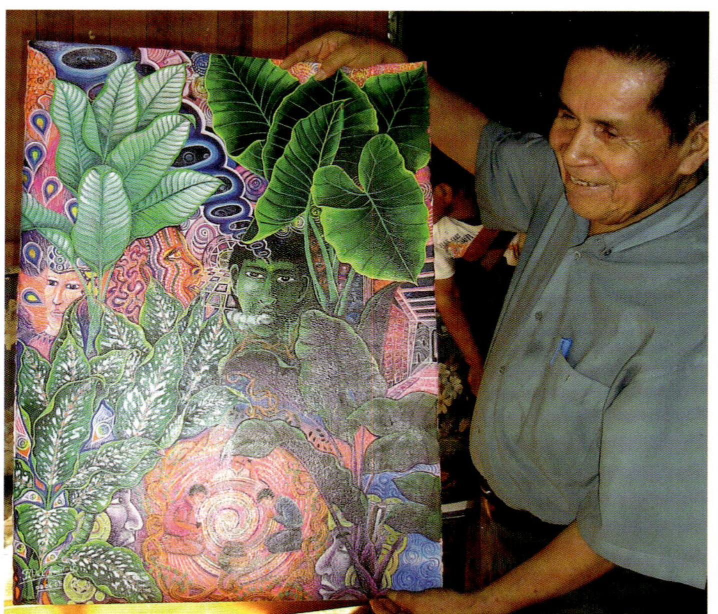

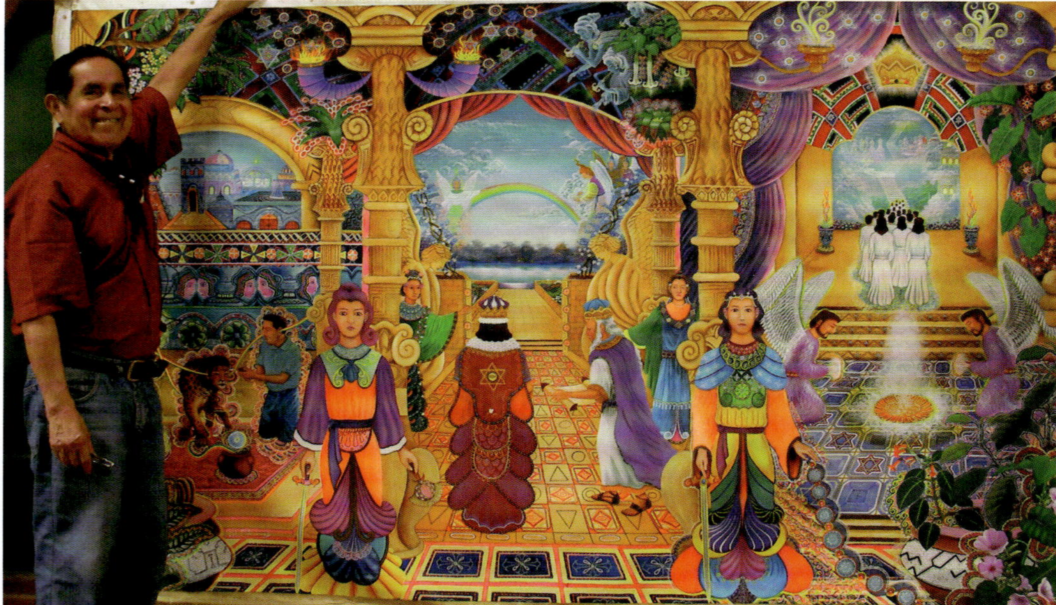

Pablo proudly displays his visionary art.

experience, and yet they clearly spring from the original creative impulse that moved him to put brush to canvas and generate the first of his visionary works.

In the years that passed subsequent to this fateful encounter, initially with Eduardo's help in arranging sales and international exhibitions and later independently, Pablo became famous and revered worldwide, not only for his paintings but for the Usko Ayar school of Amazonian painting, which he founded with Eduardo's help in the late 1980s. Through the school he taught many young people in his community how to paint and gave them a means of livelihood, a way to help support their families by producing and selling wonderful paintings depicting the marvelous plants and animals of the Amazon.

There are now many derivatives; one cannot wander into to a gallery or tourist shop in Pucallpa or Iquitos that does not have a few paintings from Usko Ayar, or, more frequently, crude knockoffs of the genuine articles. But few of Pablo's students have ventured into visionary painting and while their works are wonderful, masterfully done, highly detailed, and taxonomically accurate, they are largely representational. Only Pablo can claim the title of curator and official artist in residence of a museum of marvels, committing to canvas, for the world to see, the bizarre, beautiful, magical, and terrifying reality that is the ayahuasca dimension.

The results of Pablo and Eduardo's collaboration in the late '80s culminated in the publication of his first collection of visionary paintings. *Ayahuasca Visions: The Religious Iconography of a Peruvian Shaman,* published in 1991, brought Pablo's work to the world. Pablo's paintings, reproduced in high-quality full color, together with Eduardo's detailed translations of Pablo's interpretation of each painting, have given students of folk art, anthropology, Amazonian mythology, and ayahuasca a window into this shamanic realm that few will ever experience firsthand.

Pablo's creative output did not end with the publication of his first book, and although he was subsequently invited to hundreds of conferences and workshops, no additional collection of his paintings was published. Recently some new collaborators, Howard Charing and Peter Cloudsley, teamed with Pablo to create the second collection of his work, which includes numerous examples of his more contemporary paintings, many of which have never been widely shown before.

The collection builds on Pablo's previous work and illustrates its evolution over the last two decades. Any collector of Pablo's work or student of Amazonian art or mythology will want to have and cherish this new work. The collaboration has done justice to Pablo's legacy. Always and forever, Pablo will remain the maestro, the explorer, and chronicler of the visionary worlds of ayahuasca.

Dennis McKenna received his doctorate in botanical sciences in 1984 from the University of British Columbia. His research has included the pharmacology, botany, and chemistry of ayahuasca. He has also conducted extensive fieldwork in the Peruvian, Colombian, and Brazilian Amazon. He coauthored *The Invisibe Landscape* with his brother Terence and is an assistant professor at the Center for Spirituality and Healing at the University of Minnesota, Twin Cities.

Making the Invisible Visible

Jeremy Narby, Ph.D.

Before Pablo Amaringo began painting his ayahuasca visions, a number of erudite observers had provided vivid written accounts of their own ayahuasca experiences, but it was difficult for those who had not partaken of the brew to get a clear picture just from words. Pablo changed all that; he seemed to have found a way to take snapshots of his hallucinating mind. And by looking at one of his hyperrealist paintings, one could take a look for oneself, from the safety of "ordinary consciousness," *sans* ayahuasca.

Like the works of Hieronymus Bosch or M. C. Escher, Amaringo's powerful images show worlds within worlds and multiple dimensions, all in intricate detail and in defiance of reasonable categories. His paintings have philosophical implications because they suggest the existence of an autonomous realm of visions (agreeing with Plato), and a way of grasping it (through experience, mnemonics, and pictorial art).

Pablo Amaringo dared to step off the conventional path and follow his heart. Over many years of self-teaching, he accumulated deep knowledge about life. As a friend of humanity he went on to found an art school, where he shared what he knew. In his view, art and knowledge can change the world.

The first time I met Pablo, he said his explorations had led him to conclude that reality is so complex that he "would have to live ten thousand years just to understand *something*." As he said this, he held his index finger and thumb close together to indicate a small quantity. Ten thousand years just to understand a little bit! This view, which speaks to the limits of human understanding, may not comfort those who believe in rapid progress, nor is it taught much in universities, but it provides a precious antidote to anthropocentrism and self-importance.

Pablo Amaringo spent decades acting as a pathfinder and a go-between. With dazzling style, his work honors plants, animals, Amazonian cultures, and other beings and worlds. By finding a way to make the invisible visible, Pablo Amaringo has raised the stakes.

Jeremy Narby is an anthropologist and writer who grew up in Canada and Switzerland, studied history at the University of Canterbury, and received a doctorate in anthropology from Stanford University. Narby spent several years living with the Ashaninca in the Peruvian Amazon, cataloging indigenous uses of rain forest resources. He works as the Amazonian projects director for the Swiss NGO, Nouvelle Planète.

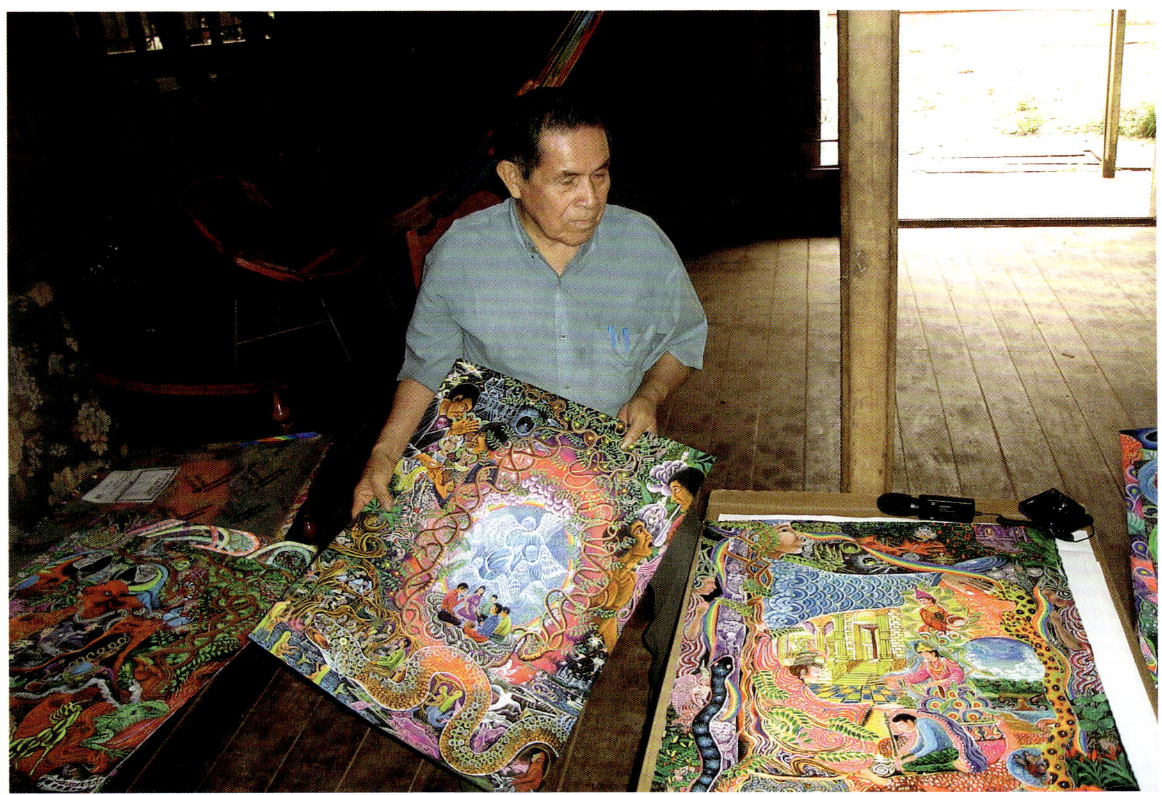

Pablo arranging his art at home

Pablo Amaringo: A Special State of Consciousness

Graham Hancock

Pablo Amaringo was an artistic genius, but he was also so much more than that—a phenomenon, a force of spirit and of nature, a seeker after mystery, and an inspiration to others.

While I was researching my book, *Supernatural: Meetings with the Ancient Teachers of Mankind,* I came across a copy of Pablo's book, *Ayahuasca Visions,* and was immediately—and forcefully—struck by the correspondences between his stunningly beautiful and enigmatic paintings and the prehistoric rock and cave art of Europe, North America, and South Africa that was then the focus of my research. How could it be, I asked myself, that this Peruvian shaman living and working in the Amazon in the early twenty-first century could be portraying—admittedly in his own absolutely unique and special way—the same themes, patterns, supernatural entities, and symbols that are so evident in, for example, the art of Chauvet Cave in France, dated to thirty-two thousand years ago, or the art of the San in the Drakensberg mountains of South Africa, dated to eight thousand years ago?

None of these artists, Pablo included, could possibly have known each other or been comparing notes. Far from it—they were separated by thousands of years of time and thousands of miles of geography. And yet they all seemed to have tapped into the same mysterious source of inspiration and been transported by it into the same strange and exciting "otherworlds."

I found the answer when I read the text of *Ayahuasca Visions,* written by the anthropologist Luis Eduardo Luna. The source of Pablo's inspiration lay in experiences unleashed by drinking the powerful visionary

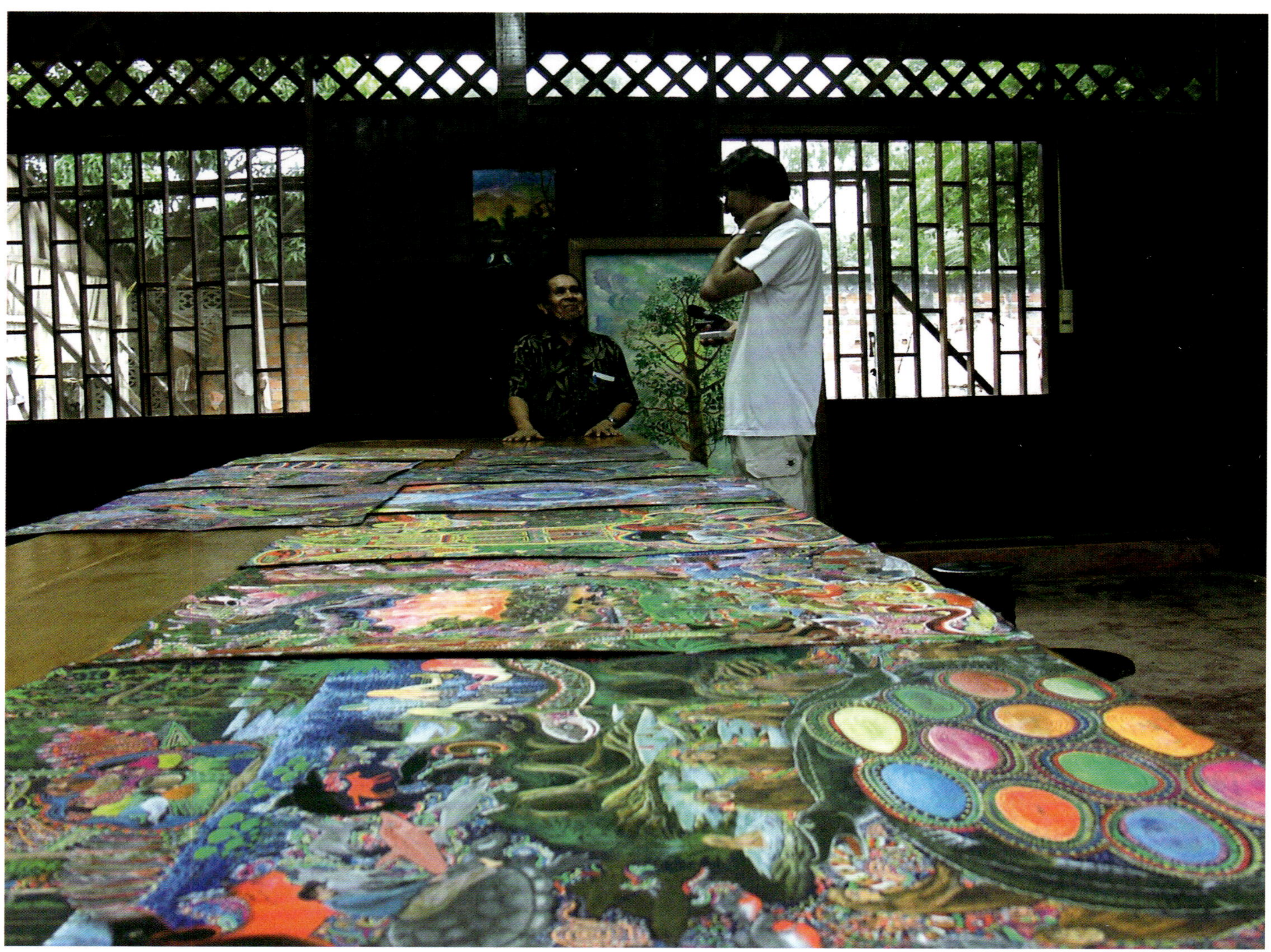

Pablo in his art school with his paintings and Peter Cloudsley

brew known in the Amazon as *ayahuasca*—the "vine of souls" or the "vine of the dead." Like all shamans everywhere, past and present, Pablo's access to the spirit worlds depicted in his art was not attained in the "normal," alert, problem-solving state of consciousness that we use to deal with day-to-day life in the physical realm, but in a deeply altered state of consciousness, a pellucid, trancelike, visionary state.

In Pablo's case that special state of consciousness was induced by the consumption of ayahuasca, and I soon discovered that the best archaeological work on prehistoric cave and rock art all around the world, from all periods of history and prehistory, had concluded that those ancient artists had been shamans also, and that their art also was an art of altered states of consciousness.

Here, then, were the common factors underlying all the great visionary art of the world: altered states of consciousness, shamanism, and direct experience of non-ordinary realms. From the moment this became clear to me, the direction of my own research also became clear. I determined that I must travel to the Amazon and experience ayahuasca myself. It was the beginning of a long journey, far longer, richer, and more creatively fulfilling than I could ever have imagined—a journey that still continues for me today. Without Pablo's extraordinary, transformative art to guide me, I would have been lost and bewildered at first, but with it I was more quickly able to find my feet and sense of direction, and more confidently able to negotiate with and, above all, learn from the entities I encountered—entities from non-ordinary realities, whom I truly believe are the ancient teachers of mankind.

For those who have not yet had the experience of ayahuasca and the benefit of her love and guidance—for ayahuasca *is* a spirit, she is love, she is a teacher, and she is female—Pablo's art can play a vital introductory role. He stands at the leading edge of a lineage stretching back thousands of years to those shamans who took the first daring steps in the night of prehistory and who launched themselves on the great adventure that would make us truly human.

Look on his art in wonder, remember its venerable heritage, and learn the lessons it has to teach. It is truly a window on the unseen realities just beyond the reach of our everyday senses, which surround us all the time and are deeply and intimately connected to us and to everything we think and do.

GRAHAM HANCOCK is the author of the bestsellers *The Sign and the Seal, Fingerprints of the Gods, Keeper of Genesis, Heaven's Mirror,* and *Supernatural.* His books have sold more than five million copies worldwide and have been translated into twenty-seven languages. His public lectures and broadcasts have further established his reputation as an unconventional thinker who raises controversial questions about humanity's past. His first work of fiction, *Entangled: The Eater of Souls,* is a fantasy-adventure novel that tells the story of a battle of good aganst evil played out against the frame of time. It was inspired by and features ayahuasca.

A Holy Message of Absolute Brilliance

Roberto Venosa

As is so often the case, we attract to ourselves that which we open up to with our consciousness: higher levels of thought, conundrums, and attendant enigmas are always waiting at the edge of our abilities to recognize and, hopefully, understand them. Such was the case with my introduction to the art of Pablo Amaringo.

In 1992, shortly after experiencing my first ayahuasca journey, I was glancing through a friend's library and, either through intuition or serendipity, I pulled out a book that would add significantly to my recently altered consciousness, as well as my artistic expression. That book was Pablo's *Ayahuasca Visions* and it featured paintings that amazingly captured, in form and color, an authentic representation of the hallucinatory, holy cosmic *yagé* opera that any other artist would consider difficult, if not impossible to execute. Those images, however, were profoundly inspirational, and provided the initial stimulus for me to attempt my own interpretations of the inexplicable, divinely mysterious, sometimes terrifying but gloriously beautiful visual world of ayahuasca.

After that, fortuitously, I had the pleasure of meeting Pablo on a number of occasions, both in the United States and in the Amazon, and I can report that I never met a sweeter, more humble individual . . . but with a brilliant intellect, an equally powerful spirit, the wisest of souls, and vast knowledge of the transcendent realms he once traversed as the shaman—*vegetalista*—that he was. And although Pablo refrained from ingesting the sacrament in his later years, he continued to paint the wonderful visions that overflowed in his repository of yagé experience. As an artist, I know it would take numerous lifetimes to be able to paint the visions from just one aya journey.

There is just too much, a delicious abundance, of heretofore unknown forms and colors that inundate the inner eye during the journey. I discussed this with Pablo and he agreed that there was not a canvas or palette large enough to capture the smallest iota of the overall ayahuascan visual storm. But Pablo's creative output was nevertheless Herculean as well as generous. After his retirement from active shamanism in 1977, Pablo started planning for more earthbound activities, and opened his Pucallpa home to teach painting to orphaned and abandoned children. In 1984, he turned it into the Usko Ayar Amazonian School of Painting, which flourished and expanded exponentially, producing an abundance of Amazonian master painters, such as Juan Carlos Taminchi and Anderson Debarnardi, among many others. It was so typical of Pablo to compassionately share the gifts that Mother Huasca had presented to him.

Although Pablo's technique and color scale can be considered somewhat primitive or naive by fine-art standards, his depictions of the yagé realms in their manifested power of emotion and otherworldly magic transcend all academic critique. Pablo was also a deeply versed master translator of the ayahuasca mythologies, in which snakes, leopards, celestial palaces, and aliens and their spacecraft all converge on his canvas, presenting an indigenous encyclopedia of the inner, outer, and transcendent worlds of yagé. Celestial architecture, as well as and in contrast to his underworld iconography, never fails to captivate the viewers and take them on a vicarious journey that offers a view into the dynamic consciousness-altering experience magically exteriorized through Pablo's brush and palette.

The high mission of art, through its illusions, is to foreshadow higher states of reality, and no one did this better in the depiction of the ayahuascan worlds than Pablo. Art should inspire, it should reach into the emotional center and ring the bell that awakens us to our higher self. This is what all great artists have attempted to do throughout the ages through their own inspired art—an art that comes not *from* them, but *through* them from some Higher Power that lures us onto the path of light leading to the ever-elusive but divinely attainable source and center of all Beingness. This is what ayahuasca alludes to in its holy message, and in its absolute brilliance, it has chosen Pablo Amaringo as one of its divine messengers.

Fantastic Realism painter, sculptor, and film artist Roberto Venosa has exhibited worldwide and is represented in many major collections. In addition to painting, sculpting, and film design (pre-sketches and conceptual design for the movie *Dune,* and *Fire in the Sky* for Paramount Pictures, as well as the upcoming *Race for Atlantis* for IMAX), he has recently added computer art to his creative menu. There have been four books featuring his work, including *Illuminatus,* a retrospective collaboration with Terence McKenna.

The Power of the Man and His Painting

Jan Kounen

At last, it's arrived—a new book on the work of Pablo Amaringo with his new paintings and his commentary about them. When he was alive I had the pleasure of going to see him in Pucallpa, where he would tell me about his paintings. I enjoyed the pleasure of hearing his melodious voice, seeing the sparkle in his eyes, and feeling his joyful embrace. Of course, and most especially, I delighted in seeing his original visionary work.

Pablo has a special place in the world of ayahuasca. He is considered the founder, the central pillar of painted visions of ayahuasca. He is among those few who have a deep knowledge of both painting and the "medicine."

I must tell you that I was "changed" when I took ayahuasca some ten years ago with Guillermo Arevalo (Kestenbetsa) Shipibo, who is a traditional healer. It threw me into another world. To be more precise, it started with the visions and then I was guided to the other side, to a universe that I perceived as real and consistent. This experience challenged many of my beliefs, which were mainly materialistic, and I underwent a paradigm shift in just a few nights. All this does not happen without pain, and initially I was immersed in great confusion. However, the process makes sense. I had to relearn, to step back and rebuild my universe.

The important thing for me was to share, to bring back information. I could not live peacefully at home alone with the weight of this new reality. The sharing was possible; it was both the path of healing for me and the responsibility that I gave myself in return for the medicine.

Pablo helped me, talked to me, showed me, and explained. If I tell all this it is to show the power of the man and his painting. Healers are rather reserved, reluctant to describe the nature of their vision to strangers. Pablo, however, indulged me without measure; he was inexhaustible. In this way, he helped me to solidify my desire to communicate: Yes, we can communicate. Let's do it.

If you have not had the ayahuasca experience, you will enjoy this pictorial journey, just like the beautiful world of a different dream. On the other hand, if you have shared the experience, or if you are an ayahuasquero, you will acquire a wealth of information on the practice itself, on the worlds of the spirits of plants, and on the healers' techniques.

We all seek a better understanding of the world. This is the natural movement of the human creature. Physicians and historians will provide information, both from their areas of expertise. The poet will be more efficient in getting some information across about love.

Pablo dedicated his energy to sharing vital information from additional levels of reality, from other realities that govern our ordinary reality. During these experiences, one opens to these fields of realities. Pablo did not satisfy himself by merely describing this other world; he also extracted the working mechanisms of it—he unfolded them in space. In his paintings time does not exist. The temporality of the ceremony is shown in a space adjacent to the past or the present. The ayahuasca proposes a language that unifies time and space—it is practiced in a space beyond the senses. Time breaks out at the same time as thought. Knowledge comes from a state beyond thought, where the healer has learned to remain in a state of spiritual apnea. In the practice of traditional indigenous medicine, this is normal: plants teach.

Man eats different plants, and in doing so purifies himself physically and mentally. The spirits of plants, or "plant intelligence," heal him first and then teach him to cure another human being. Step-by-step, they show him what plant or what song to use to do this. It's a long process of several years, which will never end. The "medicine" tells him and shows him the cosmos; it proposes a new reading of life and death. The spirits of the plants expose to him the mechanisms of the psyche, proposing a meeting with the world of the soul. In a way, it is like nature's university, and the natives call it "cosmovision." It must be the root culture of humanity. The plants were on our planet before we were. The Western world, having long ago turned to exploring other areas, has unfortunately forgotten that science. In this university Pablo has a special and unique professorship. In fact, we can say that he has created a new department—the department of communication and the plastic arts.

I can tell you a short story illustrating the influence that Pablo's art has on other artistic domains. I went to see him in preparation for my movie *Blueberry*. The day before my visit, I had participated in an ayahuasca ceremony with Olivia Arevalo (Panshin Beka), a great healer who was present in Pucallpa. I knew her. For me she was a lovely elderly lady with the soul and joy of a little girl and I had gladly accepted her invitation. But I quickly realized that this ceremony would not be an easy ride. Early in the morning, Panshin Beka changed completely. Her child's look disappeared, leaving a pair of snake eyes. She glued her pipe to her lips and smoked *mapacho* (locally grown tobacco) all day. In the evening, there were four of us: Maria (Panshin Biri) who was Guillermo's mother, Kestenbetsa, and Panshin Beka.

Unusually, Kestenbetsa was wearing the traditional ritual costume and only Olivia (Panshin Beka) sang. The nice old lady turned into a relentless warrior of love. In my mind I begged her all night to stop sending me so much love—it was too much. Her songs carried me to the most sensitive part of myself, scrubbing it raw. Water flowed continuously from my eyes, which had opened to the visionary world. I died several times but I survived. This is one of the rules of the medicine: symbolic deaths are the doors.

The next afternoon, still intoxicated, I was with Pablo. In a painting I saw a very specific snake that had been at the heart of the ceremony with Olivia, and I questioned Pablo on this detail of the painting. He replied by telling me that this snake was the main life force nestled deep in the cells of the human body. (I photographed the details of this painting, which gave me specific references that helped graphic designers build the final vision of my film *Blueberry*.) Pablo's painting captured the snake-dragon rising from the body of the healer to get the hero's soul and bring it back to his body (similar to a sequence of the experience that I had lived). Pablo had unwittingly helped to create a new vision of medicine.

In 2008, at the Chimera Festival on visionary arts organized by Romuald Leterrier, I discovered that I am in another painting of ayahuasca. The painting by Juan Carlos Taminchi describes how I was inspired by the spirits to make *Blueberry*. I do not know the painter/healer Juan Carlos, but he saw the film and reintegrated this "vision" into the world of the Amazon, which was a nice loop in the game. I talk a lot about myself here, but in so doing I describe the influence of Pablo and also his importance to the arts, because all ayahuasquero artists—whether painters, filmmakers, or musicians—have a great appreciation for his work. Pablo Amaringo is to ayahuasca paintings what Kandinsky is to abstraction: a mark in history, the beginning of a movement. Let's hope that his story takes its rightful place in our world. Other artists from the Amazon have the same approach as Pablo: learn ayahuasca and paint it. Among the most talented are Jhefferson Saldaña Valera, Paolo Del Aguila, and Juan Carlos Taminchi. The seed is germinating; the movement can only grow.

In the summer of 2009 I briefly met with Pablo in Iquitos. He was surrounded by a group of people who listened to him talk about his painting. He had not changed; he still had the same joy, the same energy, and observing him, I saw how his stories fed him as much as his listeners.

I wish you a beautiful journey into the world of Pablo and ayahuasca. His paintings emerge from his heart like singing *guérriseurs.*

Rama kano abanon (Now I'm going to open your vision)
Ayahuasca abanon kano (the vision of the ayahuasca)
Mato quenpen youshonban (I'll open it)
Jakon akindra shaman (I will do it nicely)
Quepen quepen vainquin (I open, I open it)
Nete Yabi quepenquin. (I open his world)

Dutch director, screenwriter, and actor Jan Kounen was born May 2, 1964, in Utrecht, the Netherlands. He studied at the Arts Decoratif of Nice (E.P.I.A.R.), concentrating on cinema, animation, and pixillation, and graduated in 1988 with a superior national diploma in plastic expression. Kounen has directed numerous fims, including *Blueberry,* which he also coauthored, and which uses shamanic rituals and native entheogens to resolve major plot elements. He is known for his interest in Peruvian culture and shamanism. The text for "The Power of the Man and His Painting" was translated from the original French by Patrick Hamouy.

The Shamanic Art of Pablo Amaringo

Stephan V. Beyer, Ph.D.

On November 16, 2009, after a brief illness, famed visionary artist Pablo César Amaringo died at his home, surrounded by friends and family, and leaving behind a mass of uncataloged paintings and hastily jotted notes. We are more than fortunate that Howard Charing and Peter Cloudsley had already been working with Amaringo for months to get his collection in order, annotate his more recent work, create a digital archive of his art, and protect his paintings from deterioration in their humid tropical environment. One result of these dedicated labors is the remarkable book you now hold in your hands.

Pablo Amaringo first became known outside his native Pucallpa with the 1991 publication of the beautifully produced book *Ayahuasca Visions,* a collection of his paintings depicting visions he had received during his years of practice as an ayahuasquero. *Ayahuasca Visions* is accompanied by his own explanation of each painting and the annotations of anthropologist Luis Eduardo Luna. Entirely self-taught, Pablo had begun his painting career with portraits and meticulously detailed Amazonian landscapes; from the mid-1980s on, with Luna's encouragement, he dedicated himself to painting his recollections of his ayahuasca journeys.

In contrast to the abstract patterns of indigenous ayahuasca-inspired art, Pablo's work is characterized by detailed and naturalistic depictions of the substantive content of his visions—the spirits, trees, animals, intergalactic travelers, underwater cities, crystal palaces, spaceships, wise shamans from other planets, sorcerers, and spirit boats revealed to him by ayahuasca—as well as naturalistic depictions of the shamans, patients, audiences, healings, and jungle settings of the ayahuasca ceremony itself.

His art almost paradigmatically falls within what has now come to be called outsider art, sometimes naive art, and sometimes visionary art. It is direct, intense, dense with content, and bright with color; the perspective is nonscientific and two-dimensional. Where there is a narrative, the events are presented simultaneously, within the same frame. His painting is enormously detailed, personal, idiosyncratic, and visionary.

One such vision directed Pablo to use his artwork to speak of the spirit world and the difficult times faced by humanity. As a result, in 1988 he founded the Usko Ayar Amazonian School of Painting in Pucallpa, dedicated to documenting the ways of life in the Amazon. The school's mission was the education of local youth in the care and preservation of the Amazonian ecosystem. They were taught to visualize internally what they were going to paint—to evoke visions, like those of ayahuasca, that could be shared with others.

The work of the Usko Ayar school has been extremely influential, creating a distinctive and recognizable style—particularly landscapes characterized by extremely detailed and naturalistic renderings of jungle plants and animals—and an international market for Amazonian art. What we can now call New Amazonian art—not only of Pablo Amaringo and his students at Usko Ayar, but also of such independent practitioners as Elvis Luna, Yando Ríos, and Francisco Montes Shuña—is finding its way to a global audience and into the commercial art market, through exhibits, both academic and commercial, and through the Internet.

This accessibility has in turn created a strong interest in ayahuasca visions generally, stimulated ayahuasca tourism, and created local markets in Iquitos and Pucallpa for paintings in the Amaringo visionary style. I think it is fair to say that the surge of foreigners seeking out ayahuasqueros in the Amazon, beginning in the mid-1990s, was driven in large part by Pablo's extraordinary paintings. Indeed, as depictions of ayahuasca experiences have grown normative, it may be that in addition to the experience prescribing the art, the art is prescribing the experience.

Of equal importance with his art, Pablo introduced us to an immensely rich, complex, and voraciously absorptive mestizo shamanism in what was then the remote jungle of the Upper Amazon. His striking visionary paintings were filled with battleships protected by pyramid-shaped lasers; electromagnetic boa constrictors; spaceships from the edge of the universe; poisonous space snakes from Mars; spaceships from Venus, Mars, Jupiter, and Ganymede; beings from distant galaxies with skin as white as paper; singing spaceships from the constellation Kima; magnetizing mirrors; and, of course, doctors and nurses performing spiritual medical procedures.

Similarly remarkable was the way in which Pablo's own thinking absorbed and then transformed outside philosophical influences. The spirits depicted in his visionary paintings include Krishna, Vishnu, Shiva, and "the great gurus of India." The Indic word *samadhi* turns up in the name of Queen Samhadi the Illuminated; and we may see the Indic word *kundalini* in the name of the spirit King Kundal. Buddha appears as a spirit who is a "celebrated king of the Sakias," or as a "great Chinese guru . . . from the great family of the Sakias."

This is not a remote and insular shamanism of the sort constructed by anthropologists. Rather, Pablo inherited and expressed a shamanism that had been enmeshed—probably for generations—in all the currents of the modern world, borrowing and reshaping them according to its own vision.

And the paintings are irreducibly shamanic. Indeed, Pablo says that what he produces are more than paintings; they are crystallized ícaros, the magical songs of the mestizo shaman. The paintings have ícaros sung into them as though they were medicine. He explains: "I chant ícaros when I paint, so if ever a person wishes to receive teaching or healing, they should cover the painting with a cloth for two or three months. On the day they remove the cover, they should prepare themselves by bathing and meditating. When it is uncovered they will receive the power and knowledge of the ícaros that were sung into it."

We are now, thanks to Charing and Cloudsley, in a position to trace Pablo's trajectory during the intensely productive decades following *Ayahuasca Visions.*

The art itself has remained essentially the same—colorful, packed with detail, showing events unfolding simultaneously—although perhaps experimenting more with three-dimensional modeling, particularly of the human face. The content remains eclectic. He still speaks about electromagnetic nets, stellar fields, UFOs from another galaxy, flying saucers, and Queen Samhadi; he still depicts the now more familiar creatures of Upper Amazonian mestizo folklore—dolphins, mermaids, magic stones, and wandering spirits of the dead.

And he maintains as well the tremendous richness of his imagery. He has continued to extend his mythological reach; he now depicts angels, Christ, and Confucius ascending the stairway to heaven, as well as unicorns and gnomes. He draws from everything he has seen or read or heard about in conversation with the foreigners who flock to him, as well as from the seemingly inexhaustible mythic resources of the Upper Amazon and his own endless imagination.

What has changed most is the quality of his annotations. His descriptions are now less academic, less anthropological, more personal. He is now more willing to talk philosophically; he no longer fears being

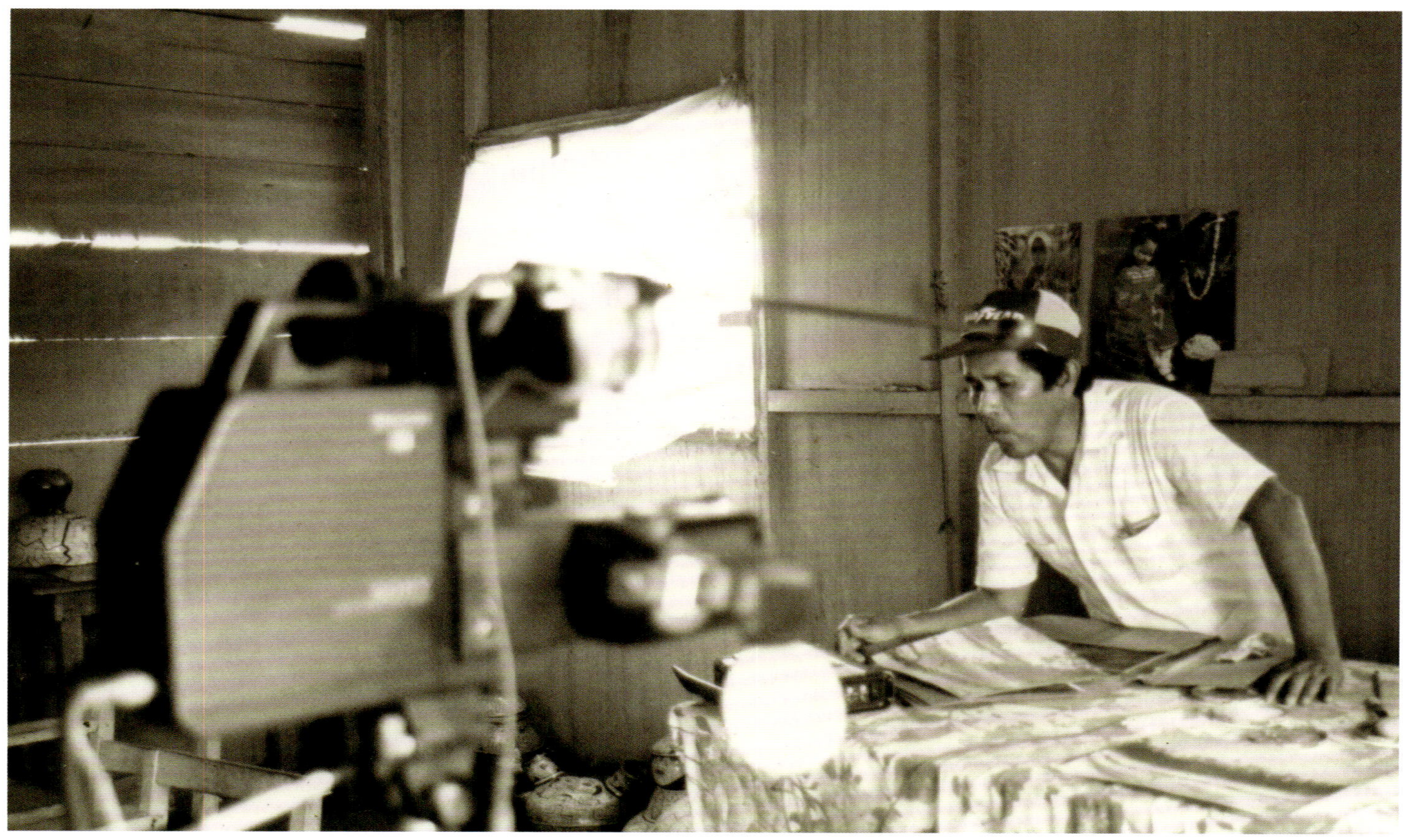

Pablo, in his studio, being filmed for a 1984 documentary for Helsinki TV.

misinterpreted or criticized as being insufficiently Catholic. This is perhaps due to the growing strength of his own voice over the intervening decades. His fame has given him opportunities to interact outside the relatively narrow social and religious constraints of Pucallpa, which remains, in many ways, a small town. And I think it is due, too, to his deep personal relationship with Howard Charing and Peter Cloudsley, within which he felt free to express himself more than ever before.

It is here that the personality of the artist shines through. Pablo had always been a kindly, humorous, and self-effacing man; these qualities are particularly evident here. Throughout his notes he articulates the ideal of *confianza:* human relationships of mutuality, trust, and generosity. He says, for example: "People will often claim to carry out justice, but usually it is little more than an agreed boundary, one side of which belongs to you, the other to your neighbor. Goodness, on the other hand, is having just enough food for yourself, but still you share it with your neighbor. Goodness is greater than justice. You give of yourself. It makes demands on your heart, but you feel happy."

Howard Charing and Peter Cloudsley are uniquely qualified to put together all of this new material. They have long experience working with shamans in the Upper Amazon and have published dozens of interviews with them. Howard coauthored a book on Amazonian plant spirit medicine, for which Pablo Amaringo wrote the foreword. We owe them our gratitude for guiding us deeper into the art, the thought, and the spiritual world of this wise and gentle artist.

Stephan V. Beyer is the author of *Singing to the Plants: A Guide to Mestizo Shamanism in the Upper Amazon* (Albuquerque, New Mexico: University of New Mexico Press, 2009). He has a law degree and doctorates in both religious studies and psychology, and has been a university professor, a trial lawyer, a wilderness guide, and a peacemaker and community builder. He studied sacred plant medicine with traditional herbalists in North America and with shamans and ayahuasqueros in the Upper Amazon, where he studied the healing plants with doña María Tuesta Flores and received coronación by banco ayahuasquero don Roberto Acho Jurama. He has worked with ayahuasca and other sacred plants in the Upper Amazon, peyote in ceremonies of the Native American Church, and huachuma, the San Pedro cactus, in Peruvian mesa rituals.

AUTOBIOGRAPHY OF THE ARTIST

Editor's note: The substance of this autobiography was recorded in interviews between Peter Cloudsley and Pablo Amaringo from March 2008 to August 2009 and was constructed by Peter on behalf of Pablo.

I am the seventh of thirteen brothers and sisters. Six of my siblings—four brothers and two sisters—are still alive and live in Pucallpa. I was born in Tamanco, in the province of Requena, the department of Loreto, Peru, in 1938. When I was just two years old my great-grandfather died at a very old age. At that time, I already understood what was going on around me and thought like a rational person. Thus, although I could barely walk, I appreciated the social mores and subtleties of his wake and funeral, which was typical for those days, with much singing of religious music. It took place on my father's land, which adjoined my grandfather's land and the land of my *padrino* (godfather), Cesar Augusto Machado, farther inland.

At this time our settlement, Puerto Libertad on the River Guanache, consisted of just three families: my padrino's family, originally Portuguese; my family; and my grandparents, who were initially from Pasto, Colombia. Before finally arriving in Tamanco, they had attempted to settle in places such as Chachapoyas and Cajamarca.

In those days, big riverboats unloaded at our house because my father had a *bodega* and *trapiche* (sugar mill) for extracting cane sugar, while my mother had cattle, pigs, and hens. The River Guanache runs into the River Ucayali upstream of Iquitos in the province of Requena. My father was governor and founded the Guardia Civil (military police force) in Tamanco, which still exists today. He and my grandfather also had the church built, where the faithful would gather. I was very religious when I was small and would pray to the saints, as was the custom there. Thus, I grew up in wisdom and abstained from playing with my siblings or friends. I was a different sort of boy and never played rough games. Neither was I involved in fighting. I was intelligent and respected my parents, padrinos, grandparents, and their *compadres.** Everybody loved me and held me in high esteem.

As a youth, I could not stand seeing people suffering and could not understand why bad things happened to people. I wondered what the purpose of my life was and where I would go after I died. I would cry when I saw people dying, and I worried about them. People told me they would go to heaven, and I would think, "Where is that and what is that?" It did not make any sense to me. I thought, "If I am only going to die, why have I been born? It would be better if I had not existed in the first place."

Later I used to think that if spirits exist in an invisible place called heaven, and if I can see the moon for myself, surely there ought to be people up there, too. I would look at the rivers and absorb their musical sounds. Looking into their depths, I reckoned there had to be people like us down there, too. I wondered and asked about everything, in search of answers. My father used to tell me not to go on asking stupid questions because they did not have an answer, but I persisted.

I used to love looking after the cattle and rounding up the cows. My heart was very open to people around me, and regardless of whether or not they were members of my family, I would run and pick fruit for them, or offer them cane juice, chich, or masato to drink, or try to help them in some way. I was much appreciated by everybody, whereas my brothers were withdrawn and barely talked to anybody.

I understood many things at an early age, and by the time I was three I could read. Calligraphy fasci-

*A compadre is a bond that is made through Catholic ceremonies such as baptism or confirmation. The padrino or madrina of the child become compadres of its parents.

nated me, especially Gothic. Later I became interested in fiestas and weddings, which in those days were sacred affairs. There was much decoration and people wore crowns to go into church. A Spanish priest named Agustin Lopez Pardo used to visit. He was a short, fat man who founded the city of Requena and the local school. In those days, Requena drew many children from surrounding areas who came to study.

When I was ten I went to Pucallpa to finish my primary school education, because in those days, education in a little town like Tamanco was basic. I arrived with my oldest brother, Fortunato, to the house of Juana, my mother's sister. Although I was only a boy, I was keen to work, so my uncle took me to where he was working in a soft drink factory. Here I worked for two or three years, washing bottles and sticking labels on them, giving some of my earnings to my aunt for food and keeping the rest because I needed to pay for my studies. My aunt and her family were pleased with me because I also helped to fetch water and firewood.

I already knew how to build a house and do many jobs that a grown man should know, and I helped my uncle make wooden boats. Later I worked in a shop, was assistant to an accountant who began training me as an accountant, and later still, I made metal components in a shipyard called Raymond y Rosas.

I sketched a little at that time but had no notion of wanting to be an artist. My main concerns were to understand the world, struggle against misfortune and death, and be human. It still worried me that we all get old and then die. I asked my father and grandparents how they could live knowing this. I asked what part of us persisted and where it went after death. They said if we were good, we would go to heaven; if bad, to hell; and if half good and half bad we would go to purgatory. I did not like the sound of this and wondered what to do. Then I decided I should become a priest to free my family from suffering and burning in the afterlife.

I inquired with the religious authorities and they said my father would have to deposit 100,000 *soles* in the priests' chest for my studies.* They were effectively saying that God was for the rich people, not for the poor, and I thought something was wrong. I explained that the economy of the *chacra* (cultivated land) had taken a downturn, and my father was no longer so well-off. Then they suggested I go to Lima to study and work at the same time, and pay them in monthly installments. I had nowhere to go in Lima and concluded that the church was just a business and I no longer wanted anything more to do with it.

By the time I was fifteen years old, I had decided there was no God and no angels or spirits. The religious authorities appeared to be deceiving the people, and it was better to leave well enough alone. I could live without thinking about spirits and tranquillity, but my mother was very Catholic. Once I saw her praying and I said, "Mama, what are you doing? It is stupid. How do you know there is a God when he never appears? I have not seen him and neither have you." I actually said that, but she was such a noble woman, she did not reply or scold me. She remained quiet.

I went to look for work in the river port of Pucallpa and luckily found a job. I said to myself, "Before, when I believed in God, I could not find any work or help. Now that I have stopped believing, I seem to have everything." The captain of the port respected me as though I were his son. He made me his secretary and I was happy. He offered me five soles for the first month, but afterward gave me ten. After six months he increased my wage to fifty soles.

One day he told me to paint two armchairs and, as I had never painted anything before, I carelessly slapped on the paint. There were lumps everywhere and it looked awful, but my boss did not reprimand me. He asked, "How is it possible you are good at everything except painting?" I was a little hurt because he had always seemed so impressed by everything I did. This made me think that if I were to paint, then I would learn to do it well.

After two years working at the port, the captain gave me more responsibilities. One day I was carrying a heavy weight and I felt a terrible pain in my chest. In a few days I realized I was seriously ill with a heart problem and sensed that I was going to die. In a dream, I saw angels coming down to take me up to heaven. When I woke up I said, "God, if you really exist, let me live, and I will never deny you again." After that, I slept for a day and began to recover. It took more than a year to recover and I had to stay at home, so I began drawing portraits in pencil, beginning with my own portrait. I also painted animals and plants on pieces of discarded paper.

I was just twenty years old and this is when my problems started with the authorities. We lived in poverty, and as I was unable to return to work, I started to think about what they used to pay me at the port.

*The sol was the Peruvian currency between 1863 and 1985 and is not the same as the *nuevo sol*, which circulates today. It was withdrawn due to hyperinflation, and replaced by the *inti*.

I looked at a fifty-sol note and thought, "How did they make this note? If I can paint, I can surely do the same." I made a good copy with my paintbrush. I was very innocent and naive; I did not think of it as being a crime; I did it for fun. My mama changed the first ten-sol note in the market, then a one-hundred-sol note, and then a five-hundred-sol note.

She did not know anything; she assumed the money came out of my wages from working at the port. The problem started when a man saw me through a window that opened onto an alleyway by our house, painting a thousand-sol note. He came in and asked if I would work for him in *his* house. I agreed, as I was still recovering from my illness. I painted forty-two one-thousand-sol notes. He then gave them to someone else to change in the Sierra. Just one bill remained, which he tried to change in a shop opposite the police station. The *señora* said it was a new note, so why was there no line running down the middle inside the paper? Two policemen, a *teniente* (lieutenant) and a *capitan,* were drinking there. They overheard and arrested the man but told him that if he informed on the person responsible, they would let him go. So he informed on me.

The chief of police knew me and came around at two in the morning but found no evidence, only drawings and portraits but no bank notes. I was in jail for two or three months because of this accusation.

They let me go that time, but later they caught me again. The person who bought the Chinese ink for me in Lima asked me to give him a note, and his neighbor's son happened to be a corrupt policeman who soon appeared at our house to take away the "evidence" of an offense. Once again, I reaped no benefit, but at least the evidence could not be used to convict me.

Nevertheless, I was still in trouble and there were tremendous complications, so I asked to do military service, as it was a way out of my difficulties. Military life was harsh and I deserted. The authorities came to my house and my mother said she did not know where I was. I slipped out of the back of the house with a small suitcase; my girlfriend had a canoe and basket of food ready for me to escape downriver.

I paddled all the way to Iquitos—the journey took twenty-five days. I had a blanket but no mattress so I slept in creeks on *gramalotes* (see glossary) with the canoe tied to me in case anyone tried to rob me. I arrived with a black face like a burned bread loaf. From Iquitos, I took a boat to the Brazilian border, which I crossed with a *salvo conducto* (a note conferring safe passage) signed by my *madrino.* From there I continued to Belem do Para, which was at the farthest extreme of the Amazon.

I knew no one there but met a man who needed someone to cut sugar cane to make *aguardiente* (see glossary), and I worked for him for eight months. One day I asked his daughter for a pencil, some charcoal, and paper, and I made a sketch of her. The man liked it and did not want me to cut cane anymore but wanted me to make portraits of his family instead. I then started saving money and was able to return to Peru with a false passport, *libreta militar* and *libreta electoral* (documents of identification), all in the name of Arturo Armentero. I had not heard from any of my family and I missed them greatly.

On the border I changed my savings into soles (old currency) and went to Tacshitea. After three months someone recognized me and went to the police. "Amaringo is here," they said. Again I was in trouble, this time for false documents. I was doing very well selling things I had brought from Brazil, which included clothes, soap, and mirrors. Immediately they confiscated all my merchandise.

It was not until 1970 that I finally got legitimate documents. For much of the time until then my girlfriend, who was from Huancayo, helped me by going

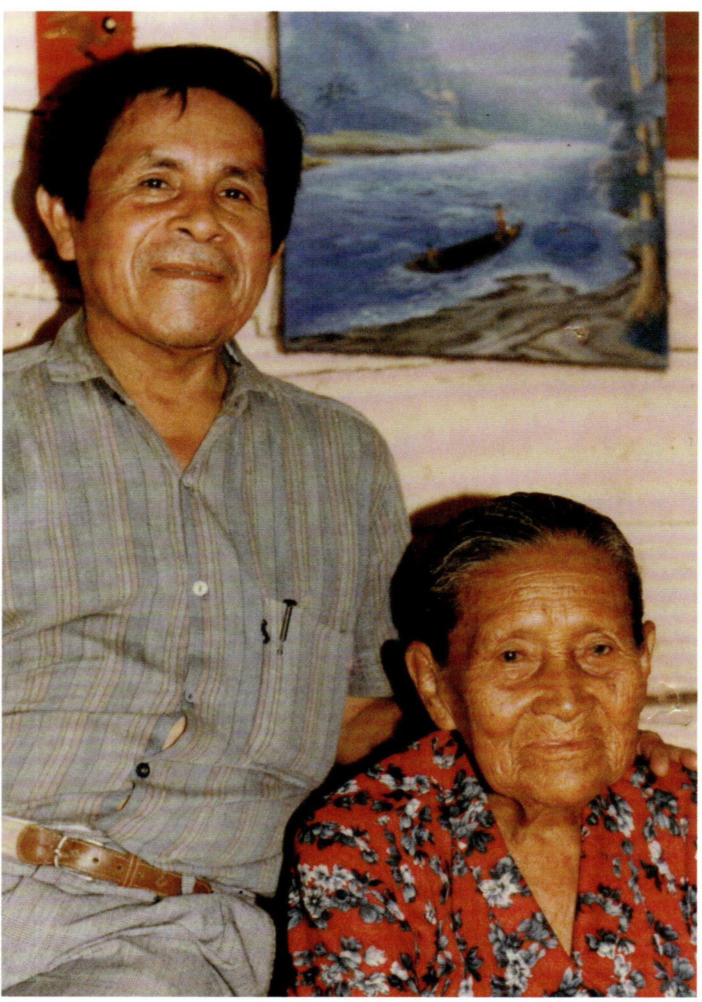

Pablo with his mother, Manuela, in 1992

out and doing the shopping and running the household errands. I had two children with her, a boy and a girl, but they lost their lives in a road accident coming from Huancayo. The girl was only thirteen years old when she died.

During this time I fell sick again and I went back to Tamanco to see my father. He healed me with ayahuasca. I thought ayahuasca must be a good medicine because it worked for me—I saw visions, and even today remember everything that I saw. But I said to myself, "It is the ayahuasca that has healed me, not a spirit."

And yet, after this illness I started to read the Bible. I discovered that life had no meaning unless one looked for the spiritual, whether through taking plants or by following a religion. However, conventional religion did not work for me, whereas I found the natural path of plants helped me to understand how the world came into existence and who created it. I saw that everything in nature is held in place by laws and I wondered who had arranged it all. This is what led me to believe in God again.

Scientific understanding helps us to have more respect for the universe because it brings us closer to what is, but it is not spiritual. Spiritual knowledge focuses on the primordial creativity of the spirit—on peace, love, goodness, and justice. Talking about these things is too abstract and will never give one a greater understanding of what they are. I cannot take out my consciousness and show it to you.

The spiritual domain is based on things you cannot see, but they still exist, because life is made of spirit. Your leg may have gangrene that you cannot see, but it affects you and you have to cut off the leg. Even microbes have other beings to keep them alive, and we call them spirits because we cannot see them. Life is made of the spiritual.

In 1967, when my sister was dying, I saw a woman shaman heal her just by chanting. Without taking any plants or medicines, my sister was well the next morning. That was when I decided that a shaman has access to a real but invisible world.

It caused me to reflect on many things that had happened in my early childhood in Tamanco. I used to go out in the dark at night without any fear and see people wearing coats and carrying boxes. When I told my parents, they scolded me and said I was being fanciful. They did not want to hear about it, so I would go out onto the terrace of the house, late in the night after they were asleep.

I began divining when I was only five, during the early years of the Second World War. I looked into the clouds and saw people from England and their allies—fighting, running around desperately, and weeping. I saw things that were happening to people, how they hid underground. When I told my father, he again said I was talking nonsense and that I must be mad.

I once saw the *huairamama*—the serpent mother-spirit of air—and my father threatened to whip me if a boa did not make an appearance that day. Later, when he went down to the river, he saw its tail.

I could see *malignos* and *tunchis* (evil spirits and ghosts) but when I told the adults, they would get annoyed, so I would hide and watch what these things did. I would go into the long grass or look deep into the water, or into the earth. I have never painted these things, only ayahuasca visions, so I still have much left to paint.

Once when I was returning from a nearby village, it was raining hard and there was thunder; I was soaked. In the rain, I saw an army of people going up to heaven: men, women, children, old people, and *señoritas*. I was amazed to think that those people were alive and I thought that perhaps one day I would understand what I was seeing and why. I am grateful to ayahuasca for giving me so much knowledge; without it I would never have learned so much.

I drank ayahuasca for the first time with my grandfather when I was ten. I was curious because people said that enemies attack when you drink the medicine. Before that, I had lain awake in bed and heard arrows firing without ever having taken ayahuasca. I had wondered why I was hearing these things, so I wanted to see the fighting for myself.

When I drank the first time, I felt a little afraid because I could not feel my body. I saw mermaids in the water under a renaco tree. They looked at themselves in the mirror, played, and watched television. In those days, I had already seen a television but not in Tamanco, where there was not even a radio.

The main entertainments in Tamanco were the guitar, accordion, concertina, drum, and *quena* (the traditional flute of the Andes). My grandparents played all these, as there was no radio or gramophone. They danced the tango, one-step, *tanguiño, marinera,* and *chimaychi.*

People lived in greater harmony then; television is a Pandora's box. I say that because my grandfather told me that devils come out when the box opens, and this is exactly what happens when people watch TV.

Tamanco had perhaps five hundred inhabitants.

After I left with my mother, my brother stayed on for another six years, finally leaving the house to a *señor*. Now even he has gone, and they say someone is looking after a piece of land for us. I do not have any photos of me as a child—there were no photographers around then.

My father looked after the bodega, selling things like clothes and supplies for rubber tappers and loggers—tools, rope, and lamps. He also held the position of governor, so authorities used to come to the house. He was very intelligent but spoke roughly. He spoke Portuguese and Tirol. I remember he used to buy products imported from England: biscuits, sweets, and specialties that arrived in Iquitos on steamers. People paid in sterling coins in those days, and as there were no banks, they often buried their savings.

Men dressed in Panama hats, ties, Swiss watches, and respectable clothes. Women, including my mother and sisters, wore gold pendants, pearl necklaces, and clothes made of Irish linen. They occasionally drank champagne. Many people had sewing machines. After the mid-1950s that prosperity was lost as Europe recovered from the Second World War.

Even after we moved to Pucallpa, the city was little more than a village; there were valve radios,* but no telephones, cars, or motorcycles. I had never been to Lima. The dirt road to the capital, which was finished in 1945, cut right through virgin forest and it was an impressive sight to see—such immense trees growing by the roadside. Nevertheless, it would still take up to a month to reach Lima. After this, novel things like newspapers started arriving, and Pucallpa began to grow into a city.

There was no poverty in those days. The only illness was beriberi, caused by poor nutrition, but that would only be likely after spending a year deep in the *selva* (rain forest). There was very little malaria, and dengue and measles were unknown. The people were healthy; they ate well and danced well. I would say they really knew what they wanted and appreciated what they had: farm products, plenty of fish and meat, and the forest remained relatively intact. *Otorongos* (jaguars) frequently came to rob pigs and drag them away from the house.

Only the children of Tamanco went to school; elsewhere there were no schools. The indigenous people had difficulty in school, as they did not speak much Spanish. I used to help teach them.

I was very agile, like an indigenous Indian in my canoe. I fished with a bow and arrow as well as with a hook, but my brothers did not. My mother was very religious and hardworking; she could hunt with a shotgun. She did business like a man and helped my father on the farm. She was whiter than he was. We all rowed downstream on a raft to Iquitos to sell our products and returned on the boat. The main products were chiclayo beans, rice, and livestock.

We had approximately sixty workers on our fifteen-hectare farm; it was happy and abundant. We often ate lizards. One day an immense Caiman crocodile killed my aunt; it chomped on her bottom when she was bathing in the river.

Our house was constructed of wood by my Spanish uncle, who married my mother's sister. (Some of my cousins and nephews are white like gringos, while some of my uncles have married indigenous Indians.) The house was on one floor but constructed high up on poles or *shungos* (see glossary); it was big and had many rooms and hammocks for visitors. (We held fiestas in the house when there were visitors.)

On the terrace, we used to play checkers in the evenings, and because we were up so high, the mosquitos didn't bother us. It was cool and we often fell asleep there on mats. It had a commanding view over the river and the white beach looked very beautiful under the moonlight.

Pablo Amaringo
January 21, 1938–November 16, 2009

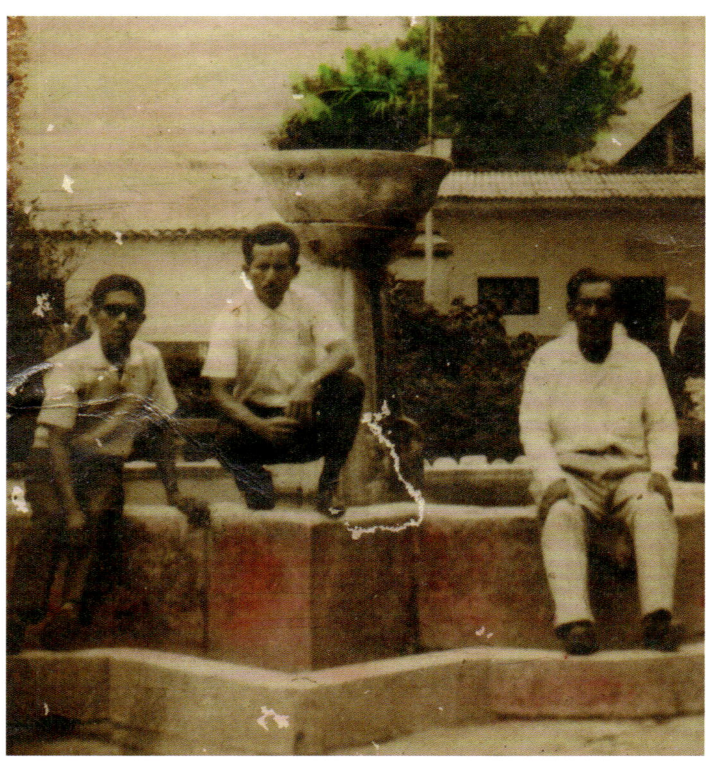

Pablo (far right) with friends at the Plaza de Armas in Huanuco, Peru, circa 1968

*A valve radio was an early type of radio receiver set, utilizing valves instead of operating by transistors (which hadn't been invented yet).

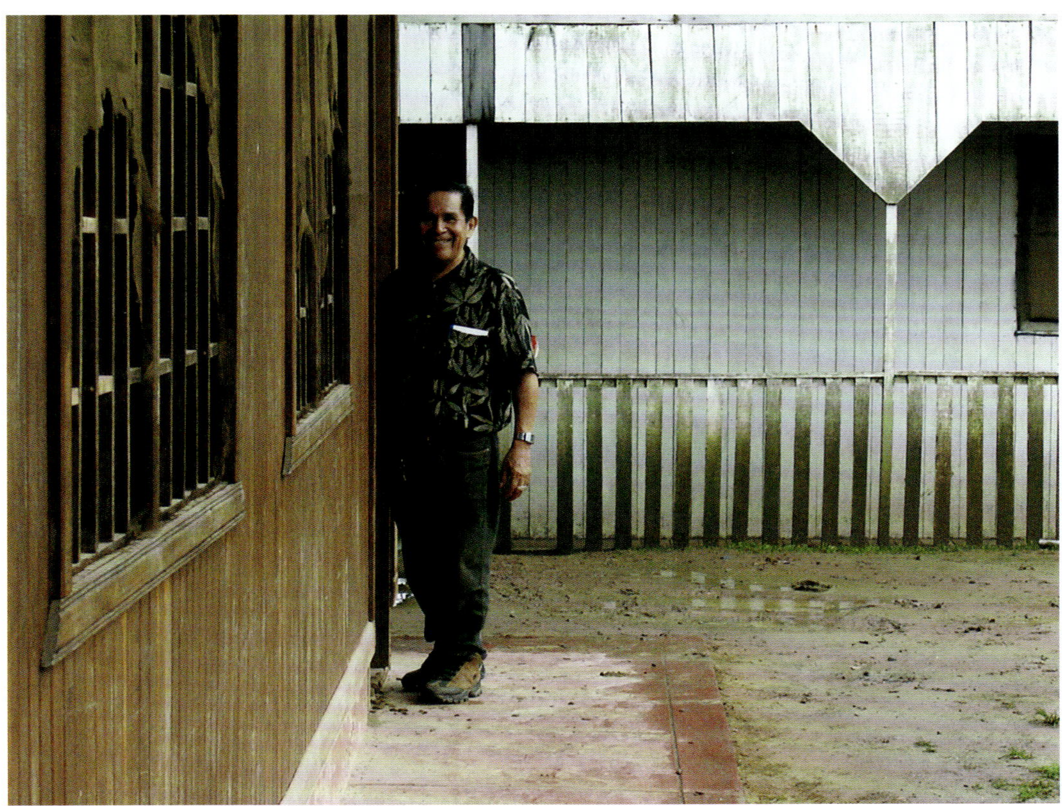

Pablo outside of his art school, Usko Ayar

With the publication of *Ayahuasca Visions* by Pablo Amaringo and Luis Eduardo Luna in 1991, Pablo's work was introduced to a worldwide audience. Pablo's paintings opened a unique window into the complex and magical world of ayahuasca.

During the 1992 Earth Summit in Brazil, Pablo was elected to the United Nations Environment Programme (UNEP) Global 500 Roll of Honor in recognition of outstanding practical achievements in the protection and improvement of the environment through the Usko Ayar School in Pucallpa, which he founded in 1988 and where he taught until his final illness in 2009.

Pablo also appeared in Jan Kounen's documentary *Other Worlds,* and as Jan states in this book, Pablo's art was the inspiration for some of the breathtaking graphics in his movie *Blueberry*—also known as *Renegade*.

Pablo's paintings have been exhibited in many countries, including the United States, France, Britain, Finland, Japan, Korea, Indonesia, China, and Peru. One of his paintings was exhibited in the United Nations Secretariat building in the exhibition *Myths and Legends of Peru* (2008).

Pablo was much loved and admired by many thousands of people worldwide.

For more information about this book, opportunities to purchase fine art reproductions of Pablo's work, and events and exhibitions of his work, please visit **www.ayahuascavisions.com**.

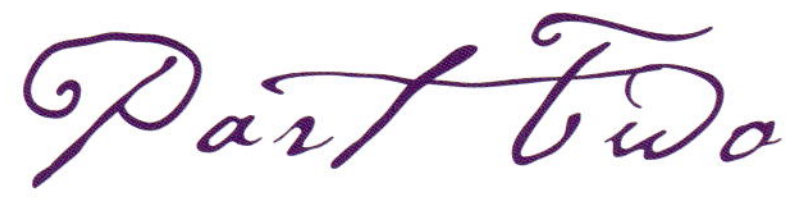

Pablo Amaringo, the Work

The Color Plates

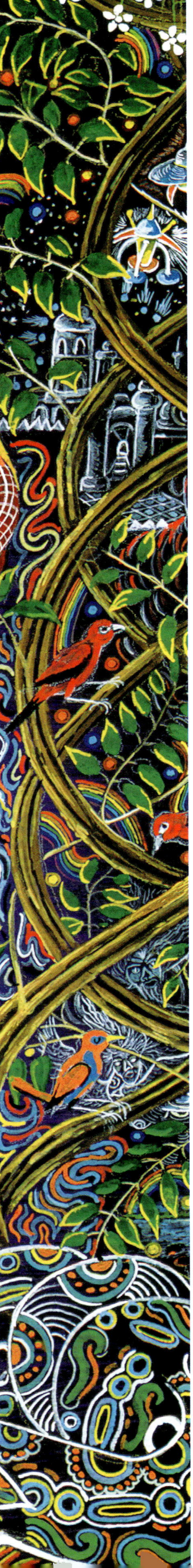

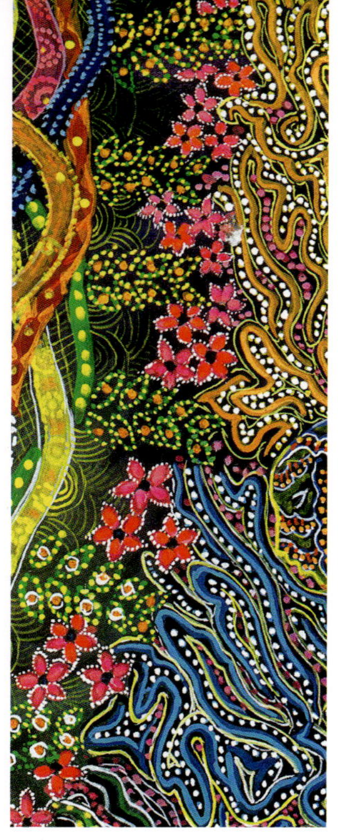

EL PRINCIPIO DE LA VIDA

This painting explores the mystical beginning of life, which can be accessed through drinking ayahuasca. The upper portion of the painting signifies that life exists throughout the cosmos. Universes inside universes, stars, celestial bodies, and an incalculable number of smaller worlds like our own can be found in the cosmic plan. For all this to come into being, spirits and the celestial hierarchy had to exist. The spirits are the creation of the Supreme Being, the totality of the dynamic energy that has always existed. Life has always existed; therefore it must continue. It is eternal.

The Supreme Being was first created in its consciousness and then manifested with an infinite explosive force, which was the Big Bang. Then spirits began to work in different dimensions according to their assigned tasks. All spirits originate from a transcendent level and are gradually transformed into denser mass that is the basis of all forms of life—plants, animals, and humans. We possess intelligence similar to that of spirits; indeed, we are not all that different from them.

They are intelligent and wise as we are, but our intelligence is subjective, not objective as theirs is. The intelligence of celestial beings is objective because these beings possess a broader and deeper perspective, so their knowledge far exceeds ours. The colored ribbons and strings of flowers flow like beads; they represent dynamic energy. No one can know or understand the nature of this energy.

There are three *huacras* (horns) in the picture; each one symbolizes a cosmological realm. The middle huacra represents the human realm; the upper one the realm of sublime spirits, wise ancient masters, the virtues, and the thrones. The huacra at the bottom connects to the subterranean realm; you see the *gnomos* (earth gnomes), guardians of mineral treasures, silver, gold, and diamonds. Their colors are symbolic of these metals and gemstones. The Shipibo woman is a sumiruna entering the subterranean world. A gnomo is helping her to understand the aboriginal peoples.

Humans and angels share a close bond, which is why angels watch over and care for us. Each of us has a guardian angel. If our actions are iniquitous or in conflict with their perfection, the angels withdraw. If our endeavors are benign, they come closer and help us to evolve spiritually. They themselves also evolve according to the work they carry out, such as protecting the natural cycles on the planet, the flow of rivers and oceans, and helping forests to thrive.

The first cell that divided for the first time was helped by extraterrestrial beings—spirits and angels. Cells have taken millions of years to evolve, and after making further cells they created marine animals, such as fish and large snakes, to live among the plants. Finally, they created terrestrial four-legged animals, large flying animals, and domestic animals.

Wild plants were created for changing the environment, while domestic plants, especially flowers, are for altering the mind, heart, and spirit of humans. In a garden it is best to grow domestic plants to put on your table and bring love and happiness. We do not understand plants and may look down at them, but they are our fuel and medicine, and they give us life. All this has taken many millions of years of work by spirits.

The human fetus while still in the womb recapitulates evolution; it passes through a snakelike

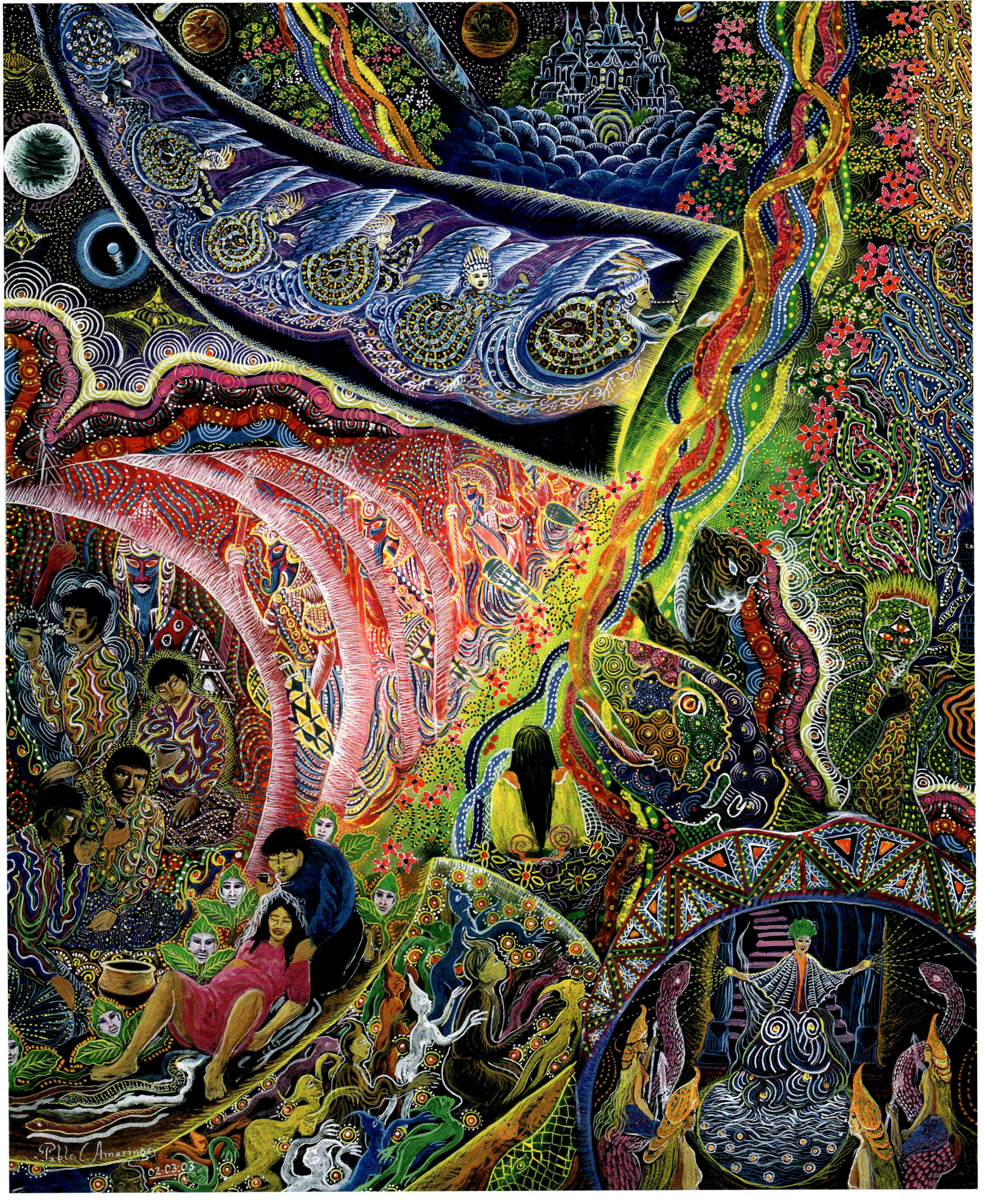

EL PRINCIPIO DE LA VIDA
2003, Gouache on Arches Paper
57 x 77 cm.

phase and later has horns. At this stage we are like a book in which you can read everything that will happen in your life, how many years you will live, and so on. I was very astonished when I saw these things; it is quite emotional. There are things you cannot see but that nevertheless exist. If we could see everything we would go mad, so we must train ourselves to survive the shock by following the *dieta* (see glossary).

The indigenous Amazonians have a different comprehension of the world; they think in a very different way from us and have different beliefs. This is why they appear primitive and uneducated, but they need to learn from us, just as we need to learn from them to understand each other. If you took a naked Indian to the city, it would be torture for him; similarly, if they took us naked into the forest we would suffer, because we are not used to their environment.

They are the way they are and have maintained a traditional way of life. We have learned to live in society and developed a different way of life. We light a fire with matches while they use the fiber of the *huimba* (*Ceiba pentandra,* cottonwood); the fiber of this seed pod is like fine cotton wool and is highly flammable. They also wrap it around the darts in their *pucunas* (blowguns), making them airtight and thus increasing the velocity and accuracy of the dart.

To the left a group of Shipibo *curanderos* (healers) are healing a woman of *boa chichuchishca,* which means "becoming pregnant by a boa." This condition is not caused by sexual intercourse. It occurs when a woman is careless with her underwear or the clothes she wears when menstruating. The snake can smell blood on her clothes and deposits its sperm on them. She cannot give birth like a human and it causes severe abdominal pain and blood hemorrhage. The curanderos prepare a medicine made from *huito* (*Genipa americana,* a medicinal fruit) for her to sip, while they chant ícaros and blow tobacco smoke over her. This releases the boa, discharging phlegm and blood. A woman is more vulnerable and sensitive when menstruating because she is purifying her body. A man in her company must follow the dieta during this time.

Around the woman are the spirits of the huito plant looking on like elves. The dye of the huito is used for elaborate body painting by Shipibo women at fiesta time, and additionally painted on their bellies to prevent them from becoming pregnant by an animal. This could happen when a woman swims in a river while menstruating. The Shipibo vegetalistas are helped by the warriors with spears and shields who are with them; these are the *achiapu* who defend the vegetalistas from harm. In the far right you can see people of malevolent character; these are *hechiceros* (sorcerers).

To the right are angels in the form of serpents entwined in a spiral representing DNA. The spiral connects to the spiritual realms where angelic beings nurture the genetic makeup that creates life.

The Oriental palace is the dwelling of the sublime ascended masters; it is the second celestial realm, not the celestial heaven of the Supreme Being. This is the realm where Confucius ascended the stairway to heaven while his disciples watched him. Christ was also triumphant as he ascended to this realm, climbing up to a cloud and then disappearing. It was his spirit that ascended, not his body, but as part of his spiritual transformation he materialized his body.

At the bottom right the spark of life and the origins of blood are entering the pregnant mother like waves as she sleeps. They penetrate the uterus, giving the child emotions and characteristics, just as electromagnetic waves produce a picture on a TV screen. It is what you are given to deal with all the problems of life. The first particles of matter were formed by *tingunas* (electromagnetic patterns). That is why this is called *El Principio de la Vida.*

ONDAS DE LA AYAHUASCA

At the top of the picture the sun radiates brilliant waves. As the source of all life on earth, the sun represents the blessings of the divine celestial pattern, the ultimate source of all life in the universe, which we call God.

We see that everything is energy and all matter is formed of pulsating waves and vibrating particles of electromagnetic energy. For us on earth the sun is the source of this energy, and we perceive it as light. Our eyes can see only a limited spectrum of chromatic light, as in the rainbow. Other frequencies, such as infrared and ultraviolet, are invisible. The sumiruna and his assistants in the ayahuasca ceremony here can perceive the iridescent rainbow of *arkanas* (see glossary) emanating from the alternate dimension that is normally invisible to the eye.

Ayahuasca is one of the most remarkable gifts from the plant realm, as it contains chemicals identical to the neurotransmitters found in the human brain. When you drink ayahuasca the sensory neurons that transmit messages inside the brain are enhanced so that a person can discover extrasensory perception and receive wisdom and knowledge.

If humanity can awaken to the spiritual laws of life and thereby stop damaging the ecological balance of the world, it will appreciate the limitless benefits of natural medicine provided by the plants and trees of the Amazonian rain forest.

The shamans in the ceremony are curing a man suffering from mental illness caused by an imbalance in his pituitary gland and hypothalamus. The shaman kneeling by him is performing *soplos* (blowing smoke) on his head and using his *shacapa* (leaf fan) to extract the troubling energies that are surfacing. The sumiruna is levitating and from his feet luminous electromagnetic vibrations appear that neutralize the dissonant energies in the patient's brain and restore his mental well-being.

The diminishing shapes of the arkanas moving upward symbolize the hierarchical structure of neurons in the brain. The stairway linking the rainbow arkanas represents the spiritual evolution of consciousness that leads to the universal "eye of understanding." A person who looks with the eye of understanding also sees with eyes of the heart, as love is a gift of the Supreme Being.

Coiling around the arkanas are serpentine forms with the spiral patterns that make up biological cells. All cells have a nucleus containing the double-helical DNA molecule. Similarly growing in spiral form is the ayahuasca vine, which emanates from the eternal spirit for our spiritual awakening.

Below the sun are winged celestial beings known as the "holy virtues." They maintain the physical order of the universe so that the movements of the planets, stars, and galaxies are governed by divinely ordained laws of motion. I have learned that these laws of orbicular motion control the movement of giant galaxies down to atoms and electrons.

Below, the *sachamama* (mother of the forest) projects from her mouth the seven rays of the rainbow, which provoke the *mareación* (vision). They arrive strongly, and just as they seem to be passing, another wave comes, rather like the waves of the ocean. The ayahuasca waves are entwined in a helical spiral of ultrasonic vibrations. These are ícaros and they contain the DNA code of all life.

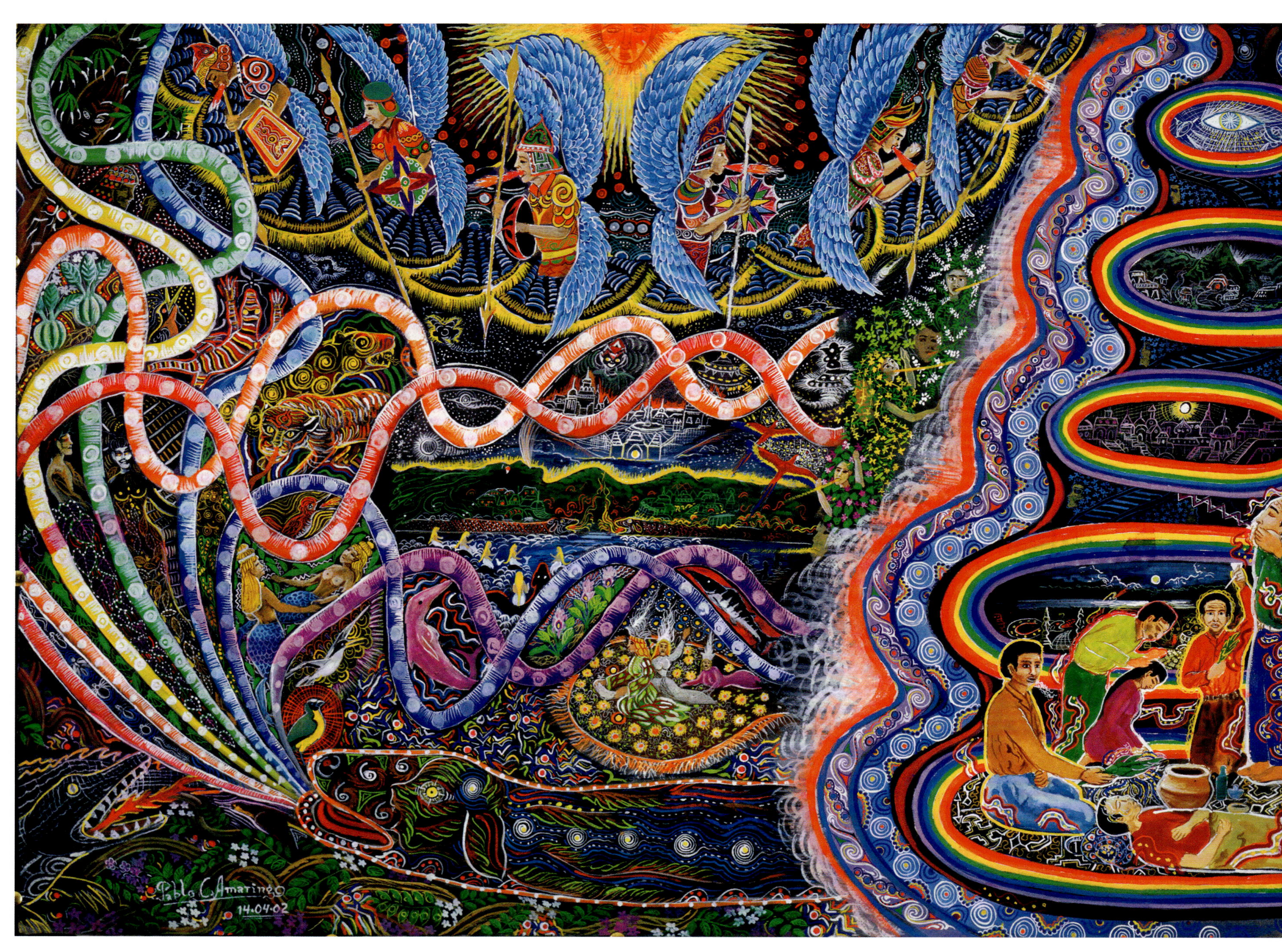

ONDAS DE LA AYAHUASCA
2002, Gouache on Arches Paper
57 x 76 cm.

Everything in the universe has a vibration composed of pure spiritual energy; it is the music of creation. When the ayahuasca wave reaches you, it teaches you different kinds of ícaros, which you can then sing to receive wisdom from the spirits directly. Some waves bring knowledge; others bring healing abilities or the power to repulse sorcery.

The sachamama is not merely a mythological being; it has been widely reported throughout the Amazon as a huge serpent that lives on land and moves so slowly that plants grow on it. You can be chopping a path with your machete and strike it unknowingly, until blood appears. If it sees you, it draws you into its mouth with its electromagnetic power and you cannot escape.

In front of the sachamama is the *chicua* bird (*Piaya cayana*), which is the guardian of ayahuasca and forewarns shamans of imminent danger. Just above is the *suisui* bird (*Thraupis episcopus,* blue-grey tanager) or *bodosque* (*Thraupis bonariensis,* blue-and-yellow tanager). The suisui has extraordinary hearing ability and can sense the heartbeat of the land and of people. It can distinguish people who mean well from those who harbor malevolent intentions; it is a good guardian for the shaman. Next to it is the *yuratibe* (*Pandion haliaetus,* osprey), an aquatic bird that can see into the depths of rivers and *cochas* (mountain lakes); it is also a good guardian for a shaman.

To the lower left is a *yanacocodrilo* (black crocodile), a powerful beast able to cause frightening turbulence in cochas when it moves. It is called upon by the shaman to demonstrate strength to his enemies.

Between the spirals of the ayahuasca waves you see the *sirena coyas,* or princesses, who teach shamans the medicine of the aquatic realm. To their right is the pucabufeo, whose ícaro is used for placing charges of attraction (usually on people). Further right is the *putu putu* (*Eichornia crassipes,* water hyacinth), whose leaves are eaten by the bufeos.

Next you see three golden-haired sylphs sitting among the flowers; their crowns of white fire are symbols of purity, intelligence, and wisdom. They are holding papyrus scrolls that contain the sublime teachings of aromatic flowers. The shamans learn the ícaros of the flowers, and how to make aromatic medicines and balsamic ointments from nectar.

Near the left edge of the picture is the *papastrueno* (*Dioscorea* sp., native yam), which is a difficult plant to find. Following the diet of this plant is very demanding and must be followed in secret. A maestro shaman with good resolve will learn the ícaro of the thunderstorm while asleep. Amazonian shamans use this to cause storms and bring rain to their chacras, so they will be abundant and luxuriant. If, on the other hand, he is a sorcerer, he can use lightning to kill a person or animal in an instant, wherever it may be.

To the right can be seen a striped lizard and two tigers. When the shaman learns the ícaros of these animals, they become his guardians and defend him from sorcery.

Sirenas (mermaids) are there in the cocha, riding on the coils of giant electric eels, or *anguilamamas,* who are the mothers of the cocha. Behind them are two giant *yacumamas* (mothers of the water) discharging electromagnetic radiation that will bring rain. At the edge of the cocha you see the *yana yakurunas* (see glossary). When a shaman is unable to heal an illness, he sings the ícaro of the yana yakurunas, who approaches the shaman with advice on how to proceed.

The mountainous landscape behind the cocha is formed by the body of a mythological being known as the *allpa gigante* (giant of the earth), whose slightest movement can cause tremors or serious earthquakes. A shaman that learns his ícaro can put enemies to sleep so they cannot attack him.

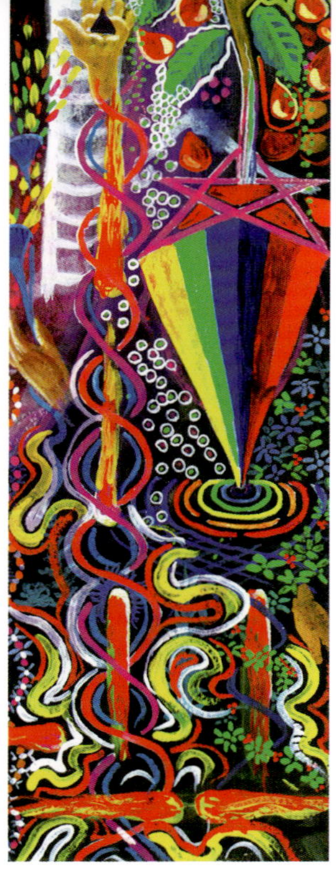

JEHUA SUPAI

ESPIRITUS SUBLIMES

Here you see a sumiruna, a great *maestro shaman* and man of esoteric knowledge who can transform his physical body into pure spirit. He is surrounded by a magnificent *aguajal*—a wet area where *aguaje* palms grow. An aguajal is a temple of nature, a beautiful sacred grove where the spirits like to gather. For a sumiruna it is also a ship that can take him anywhere in space and time.

He is wearing a *manto de fuego* (cloak of fire). To win this honor he must rigorously follow a dieta to learn from sublime teachers and gain spirit allies: anacondas, parrots, *guacamayos* (*Ara arauna*, macaw), black dolphins, red dolphins, and the *anguilamama* (mother of the *cocha brava*, which is a wild and mystical lake where few people dare to venture).

He chants *manta payariri,* an ícaro reserved for the aguajal. It goes, *"Manti payariri, ninangunacaya,"* meaning "Mantle of fire, strong as my medicine."

He calls the *yana puyurunas* (black beings of the clouds), whose faces appear in the sky above him. They teach how to heal using the wind, mist, and dew. They can heal illnesses arising from problems of love or separation, and also legal problems. The magnificent *sylphides* (sublime air spirits) form a celestial vault around the sumiruna, whose electromagnetic auras sustain life; they have dominion over the air, the storm, and wind.

Beneath the earth you see the gnomos who guard the precious emeralds, rubies, and diamonds buried there. When the sumiruna embarks on his voyage, these gnomos rise from the earth with gemstones. He takes an *ila* (tree that can fly into space) and transforms it into a ship; the roots become the prow and the tree's canopy becomes the stern. The sumiruna rides at the prow and the ship glides on the river like the morning mist, while he receives the ícaros of the tree spirits.

On the right, elemental forces from deep beneath the earth emerge. These forces are symbolized by the formation of a pentagonal rainbow prism. The rainbow and pentagram preserve and protect life. Just to the left the elemental spirits appear as a radiant caduceus (two serpents in the form of a double helix). The spirits show that animals, plants, and humans have a blueprint for constructing their own physical forms: DNA molecules embedded in the nucleus of every cell.

The aguaje palm (*Mauritia flexuosa*), or Moriche palm, grows only in special places where spirit beings can feel at home. It is good to have them grow near your house, as the leaves warn of approaching enemies by vibrating in the wind. The sound is recognizable. If it is *taraa,* it is an enemy; if it is *huaraaa,* it is a visitor.

Some palms have spikes on their trunks, which work like arkanas to protect vegetalistas from hechiceros. The *pijuayo* palm (*Bactris gasipaes*) is one of the most formidable arkanas, having clusters of long, sharp spines on its trunk like *virotes* (magical darts or arrows from the spirit world). It shoots these spikes out explosively and destroys the hechicero, just as he casts his malevolent spell.

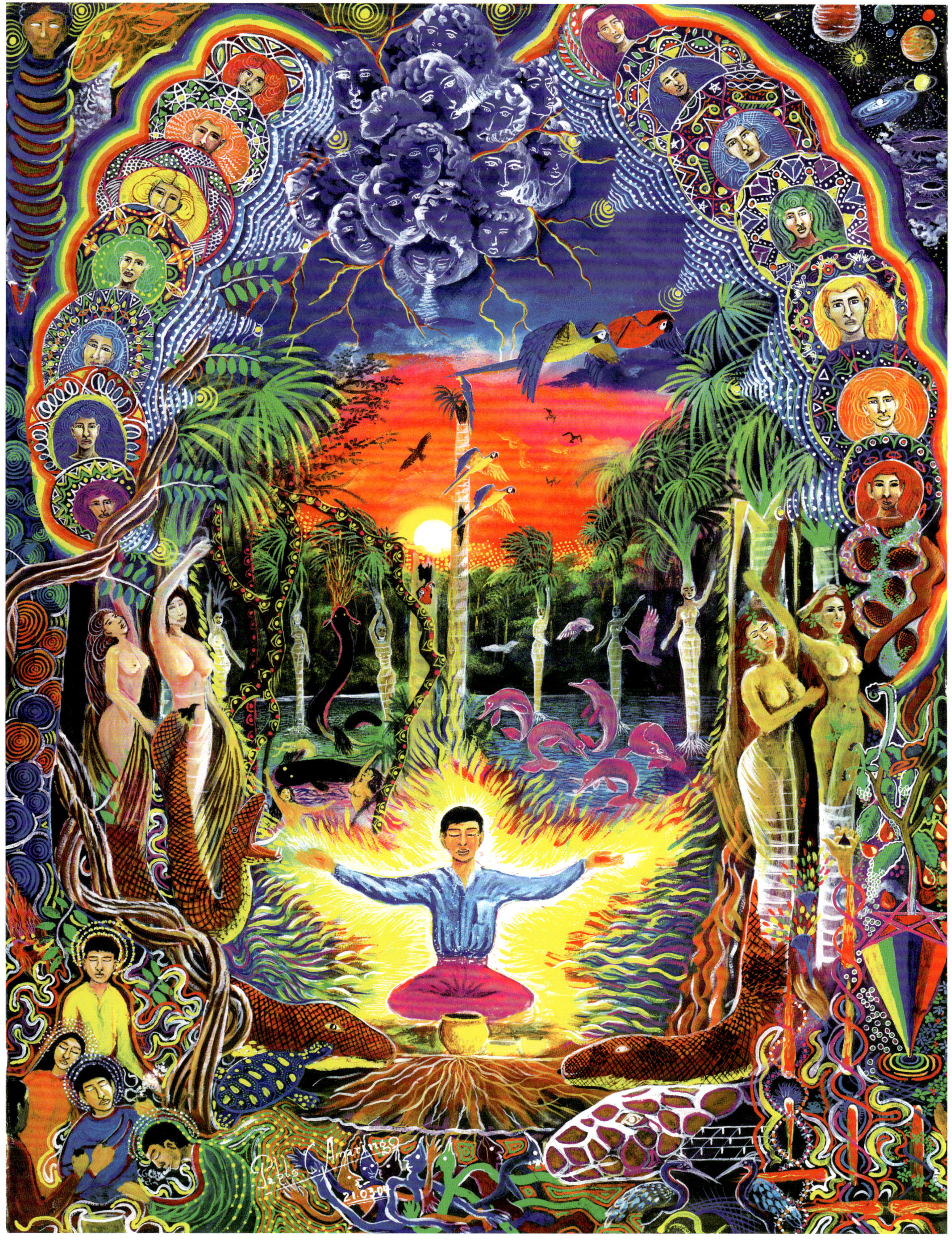

JEHUA SUPAI
Espiritus Sublimes
2004, Gouache on Arches Paper
57 x 77 cm.

Tree spirits—like nymphs—surround the sumiruna in the picture; they teach the ícaros of trees and contribute to his ability to heal.

Another protector is the *coto* (*Alouatta seniculus*, red howler monkey) in the center of the picture. When an enemy fires a virote, the agile coto intervenes and seizes it. The *tahuicuro* (*Monasa nigrifrons,* black-fronted nunbird) a dark-gray bird with a red beak, can also intercept virotes by shielding them with its wing. Another guardian is the wild *paloma torcaza* (*Columba fasciata,* band-tailed pigeon), which captures the virote with its beak while in flight. The roseate spoonbills (*Platalea ajaja*), seen here in flight, also defend the shaman, while the two herons below use their acute senses to warn of any dangers.

Here you learn everything necessary to defend yourself from attack from underground, because some sorcerers attack in this way. Cotos are useful for this and also the mother of the *curuinsi* ant, which makes its huge nest high up in trees. They are red, the color of the earth. When the curuinsi ants take leaves back to their nests, they are followed by a very large, thick snake, which is their mother. It follows the ants into their hole and makes its home there.*

Next to the ayahuasca vine are beings with luminous halos, the *achiparunas* that guard the sumiruna from dangers beneath the earth. By sitting upright with his feet crossed, the sumiruna receives the protection of underground animals, as well as power emanating from above. In this way the spirits come to him to defend him against his enemies. The yellow spotted turtle (*Podocnemis unifilis*) near him is also a protector ally.

There are more than forty kinds of palms in the region, but the aguaje in particular holds the most positive energy. When mature, guacamayos make their nests in it.

When old, the aguajes fall and rot, and after a time people look for *suris:* fat white worms considered a great delicacy in the selva. They are grilled on a fire and the fat that drips out is good for asthma and bronchitis. If you eat them for three months, you will be well again.

Aguaje is an important palm in the Peruvian Amazon. Its fruit is very popular, particularly with women, as it contains high levels of phytoestrogens. The tree can grow to heights of more than thirty-five meters (114 feet).

Another palm tree vital to healing is the *shacapa* (*Pariana* sp.), used to make leaf bundles that are tied together at the stem with fibers from the chambira (Astrocaryum chambira, *fiber palm*). When shaken, they make a rhythmic sound that is an important element in healing.

On the right, you see the *achiote* (*Bixa orellana*) tree, an effective cure against *mal aire* (see glossary).

*The authors have been unable to verify the existence of commensalism between snakes and ants.

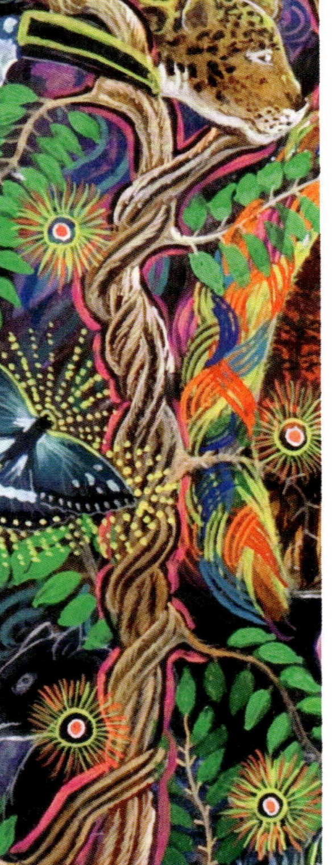

SUPAI PUCABUFEO

This is the legendary pucabufeo, which transforms itself into an attractive young man and seduces pretty young women with his charms. There are many versions of the legend but usually he appears as a fisherman or helper when a woman is alone, and uses his attractive personality to learn all about her and her business. Unknown to her, however, he is a magical being. The pucabufeo is more commonly known as the *bufeo colorado* (pink dolphin) in Spanish.

In the River Ucayali region, these beings often make their appearance in the port, offering fish, which is what the girls like. After a brief courtship, one of them will agree to live with the pucabufeo, but he is never there when other people are around, so he avoids being found out.

Often these pucabufeos will drink *masato* or *chicha* (yucca or maize beer) and get merry, or they come to fiestas where there is singing and dancing around a bonfire. Although they look like men, the women may know they are really beings from out of the water, but they are so infatuated they would rather deceive themselves.

In the morning when people ask what the stranger is doing in their village, he turns back into a dolphin and jumps into the water, leaving the girl pregnant. In the days of the rubber boom, rubber tappers would frequently be away for long periods. That was the ideal time to take advantage of innocent girls, and infants would be born half-pink. Early in the morning, the pucabufeo would leave fish and bananas in a canoe for the girl to bring home for her baby. By then she would know it was half-dolphin and half-human.

There was a man here who used to say he did not know who his father was and that he was the son of a dolphin. People have said to me that my father was a dolphin. There was also a woman who had a child with a bufeo on the condition that when the child was older, it would be taken back to the water. Another woman who lived near her was looked after by a bufeo, but he went away with their child when it was fifteen.

The pucabufeo appears as a gentleman who can speak normally. You always see a pucabufeo in this form wearing a hat to conceal his blowhole. In the old days, such occurrences would often happen because there were few firearms around. Nowadays the dolphins are frequently shot, so you have to go to very remote villages to hear of such things.

Many dolphins are killed for their body parts, which are sold to shamans who use them for making *pusanga* (love medicine). Several parts of the bufeo are used for this purpose, including the fat and a powder made from the penis. The teeth are used for making charms; it is well known that they are good for making businesses flourish. If the bufeo is a female, her vulva is extracted and secretly worn around the upper arm of the man under his shirt. Women are then compulsively attracted to him. Additionally, the shaman takes the fat of the bufeo and treats it with *sopladas* (blows tobacco smoke on it). The client then rubs it on his hands and arms before going out to a dance. There a woman will be overcome by a powerful attraction to him. Equally, it happens the other way around and women use it on men. This is the notorious use of pusanga.

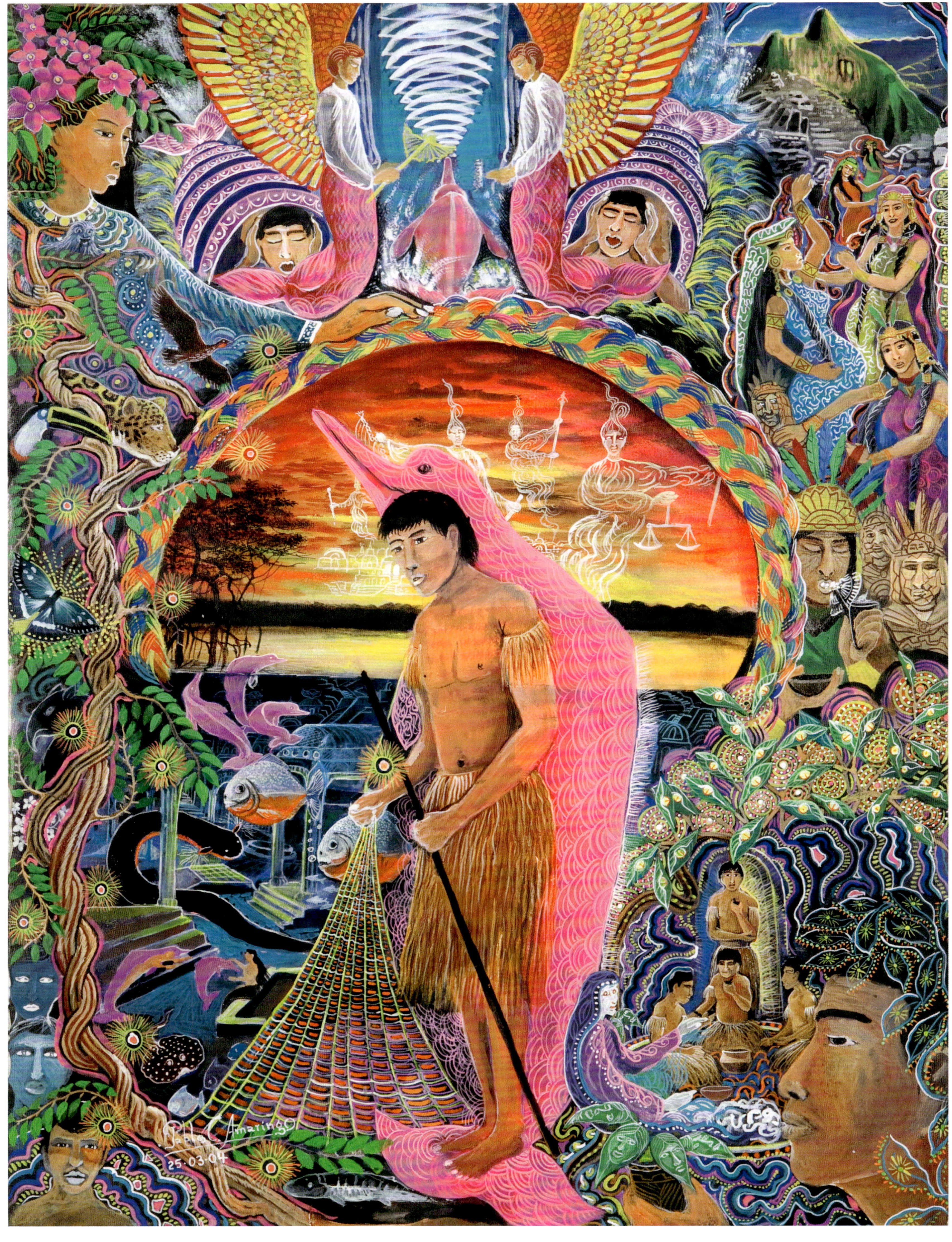

SUPAI PUCABUFEO
2004, Gouache on Arches Paper
57 x 77 cm.

My sister was severely affected once just from smelling one of these charms, although it did not affect me, as I am not a woman. A young shaman had left a little bottle in the house with tobacco, ash, and a bufeo's tooth, and closed with an unused stub of mapacho (tobacco) as a cork. It smelled aromatic and not knowing what it was, she smelled it. When we examined its contents we threw it away. When my father heard, he told me to get it back and he kept in a drawer. My sister was an eighteen-year-old señorita and we were living in Tamanco at the time. A year later she was married to a Spanish man and went to live in his house nearby.

A fortnight later my father threw the bottle into the river. That night he was near their house, looking after our cattle. He heard screams as though my sister were going mad. She left the house, breaking the door down, and rushed to the port, saying that her mother was calling her. Her husband came after her, trying to stop her. In the port some bufeos had gathered and she tried to jump in with them. Her husband called for help and we all went to stop her from throwing herself into the water because she could not swim. We got her home and had to tie her up.

She is seventy-eight and still alive today. Whenever we heard her say that her mother was calling her, she would throw things about and we would have to tie her up again. Sometimes it would take seven men to restrain her.

Once I was sleeping in a house near a riverbank and something touched my shoulder under the mosquito net. I turned to look and it was a mermaid with very long hair and tremendous breasts. I had never seen anything like it. I jumped and she slithered out of the house and splashed into the water. When I was working as a logger, sleeping by the water's edge or paddling in a canoe, I had many contacts with bufeos. I do not know why they always pursued me.

The multicolored arch is woven of mythological birds called *tibemama,* here depicted as osprey. The indigenous shamans sing the ícaro of this bird when they heal people, in order to acquire its ability to see into the river and foresee danger.

The angelic cherubim under the arch maintain balance and harmony between animals and humans. Animals have no hatred for humanity; they wish to be close to us but are timid and nervous because they are hunted.

The woman at the top left with the pink floral headdress is a sylph and represents the love of bufeos for humanity. She demonstrates that bufeos help people as brothers, and many times on the River Ucayali and in Yarinacocha, bufeos have rescued people from drowning and brought them to the surface.

Below the sylph appear several animals: *sachavaca* (tapir), toucan, butterfly, jaguar, and *pelejo* (sloth). Shamans use their qualities to heal people by singing their ícaros and performing sopladas. For strength, the shaman calls the sachavaca*;* for fighting and hunting skills, the jaguar is invoked.

Chukcabufeos, seen at the top, are bufeos with feathers or hair; they are like angels but come from the subaquatic world, not from the celestial. Chukcabufeos are guardians of bufeos and help them relate to humans, teaching them ícaros for attracting.

The spiral coming from the snout of the bufeo is the energy transmitted when their ícaro is chanted for attracting a mate. It is not for making your business thrive; the bufeo's tooth is for that purpose.

On the right is Machu Picchu with the face of a woman. Machu Picchu was the religious sanctuary of the *virgines del sol* (virgins of the sun), or *ñustas* (Inca princesses, in Quechua). Below, the ñustas are performing sacred fertility rites to bring sanctity and fertility to the land. They were married only to the Inca or to royal princes.

Farther down, the Incas in stone recall the respect they had for stone, which was alive for them. They constructed temples, palaces, and walls from massive stones shaped with such precision that even with modern machinery we are unable to replicate them.

The Inca priest with the feathered headdress is smoking his pipe, but it's not filled with tobacco. They used other plants such as *toé* (*Brugmansia*), *shillinto* (*Mascagnia psilophylla*), and the rhytidome of trees, such as the *capirona* (*Calycophyllum* sp.).

Below are *chacruna* (*Psychotria viridis*) leaves with gold nuggets surrounded by gold spirals. The Incas valued gold not for money or barter, but for crafting work devoted to their deities.

In the subaquatic world the anguilamama can transform into a *supay lancha* (phantom ship) and carry you through the water. Bufeos sometimes transform themselves into *yakucaballos* (water horses) so that bufeosirenas can ride them. When they get to the edge of the river the bufeosirenas remove their tails, as though they were trousers. Then they become sylphs and fly off into space to visit other worlds and star systems.

You can see the fishing net of the bufeo, and how he has transformed into a youthful and handsome fisherman.

At the bottom right is a curandero who can heal *daño* (harm) caused by the bufeo colorado. He blows the smoke of the leaves of the putu putu, which you see in his pipe. These leaves are also eaten by bufeos. Shamans who want to tame bufeos take advantage of this by covering themselves with these leaves. Putu putu is like an aquatic *maca* (a nutritive plant from the Andes) and is eaten by *vacamarina* (manatee) and *charapas*.

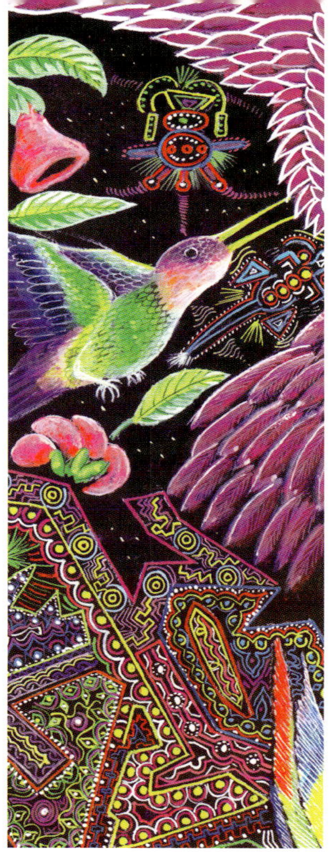

TRANSFORMACIÓN DEL SHAMÁN EN AGUILA

The shaman transforms himself into an eagle and flies away to bring back esoteric knowledge to his people. For a brujo or hechicero, it enables him to kill his enemy from a distance.

When a shaman transforms himself into kinetic energy and merges with the universe, he can see the past, present, and future as if it were all one eternal moment. These powers are granted to only the two highest grades of the shamans, the sumiruna and *banco sumi*. The highest level that a human can achieve is sumiruna. The banco sumi, a grade higher, is more of an angel or celestial being in human form.

Above are two celestial guardians bearing swords. These guardians are known as *tronos* (thrones). They bestow the powers of transformation on the shaman, who must master his courage. The soaring of the eagle represents the potential that we humans must ascend to—personal mastery and wisdom.

The dimensional aureoles are depicted as spiral forms, and when the shaman is about to transform himself, they begin to vibrate and gradually merge with the shaman below in the blue tunic, who is tending the preparation of ayahuasca. These aureoles symbolize the power and virtues that a person can have—intelligence, creativity, and insight.

The bird guarding over the ayahuasca is a *condor supai* that begins to sing, "Ewe, ewe, ewe." The shaman wearing the orange tunic is enveloped by a blue light, and later a white aura. The luminous auras that surround the shaman in his flight are a sign that the shaman has attained the virtuous powers of sanctity, justice, illumination, and love.

He opens his arms, producing wings and feathers. The shaman feels that his arms are no longer normal arms but powerful wings with the power to lift him, and up he goes. His whole body is taken over, but not yet his face. He feels half-man, half-eagle, and then even his face changes.

The eagle at the top has a crest behind its head, which is its compass and intelligence for seeing and hearing distant things. It is a fearful moment when the transformation takes place because his body is still on the ground while his spirit is flying high above, seeing everything. His sensory awareness expands and new neural paths are formed in his brain. He is filled with unlimited extrasensory power, which allows him to see and hear what is happening all over the earth.

The aureoles around the transforming eagle are like shields that allow him to hear the rhythmic movement of celestial bodies in the universe. All movement creates a vibration or sound; even the movement of nonphysical matter has a vibration, an ultrasound that underlies the harmonic structure of physical matter. You can sometimes visually perceive this when in the ayahuasca mareación; color and sound are the same (*synaesthesia*) and you realize that both are the vibration of matter. For this reason, when an angelic being manifests itself in the physical world, its body is perceived as a luminous display of resonating rhythmic vibration and color.

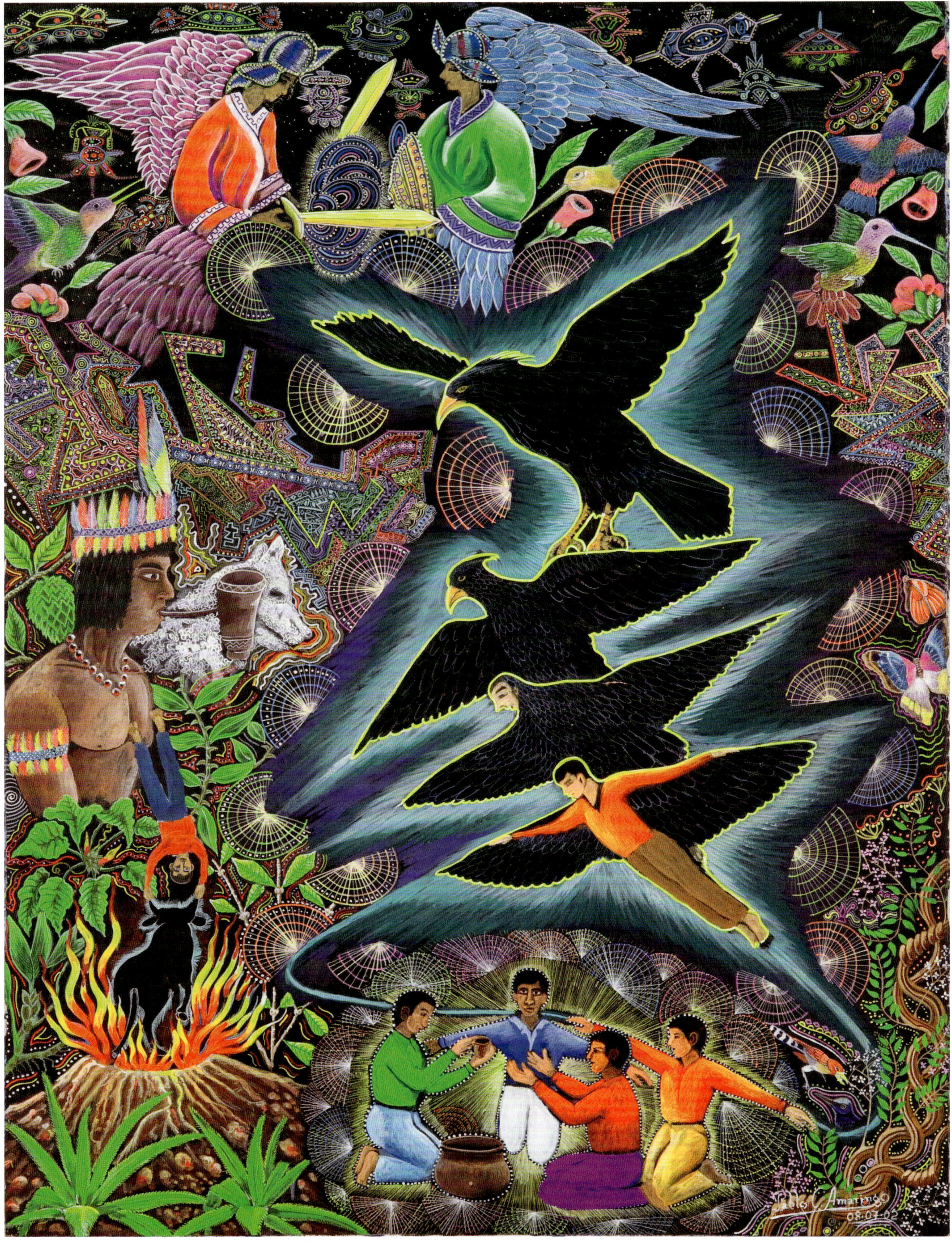

TRANSFORMACIÓN DEL SHAMÁN EN AGUILA
2002, Gouache on Arches Paper
57 x 76 cm.

On the left, the angular-looking complex matrices of galaxies are the structures of the neutrinos, which are the quantum particles that manifest matter. Here they symbolize the sounds of the universe functioning, and you learn that everything is part of a sublime celestial design; there is no disorder.

On the right are hummingbirds with the delicacy of angels and immense curative powers. When the shaman becomes one of these, he can extract poison from a patient.

On the top right corner are the spaceships of extraterrestrial beings attracted by the transformation. Sometimes they invite the flying shamans to a ride to other worlds and to share their understanding and knowledge. You learn to see as the spirits when the extraterrestrials take you to a place where you look at each other and your eyes interpenetrate and communication is total. Humans will evolve a great deal and one day will know the language of animals, but some languages will never be understood.

The indigenous man on the left with the *cashimbo* (tobacco pipe) is a Mashcopiro or Amahuaca banco sumi who can freely transform himself into an eagle, jaguar, *yacu toro* (water bull), or *sacha toro* (wild bull). These shamans can live to great ages by using plant balms and medicinal plants.

Behind his cashimbo you can see an *ailco sacha* or *perro del monte* (wild dog), which purifies your body when it licks you. White dogs will never do you any harm when they lick your face or arms; in fact, they are cleansing you.

At the bottom left is the *penca* plant (*Agave* sp.), very similar to the penca that is common in the Sierra. The *genio* (guardian spirit) of this plant is a snake that no one can see coiled up inside. It has its own ícaro and prayer, and should be treated with great respect, as though it were a being. When planted on the wall around a farm or house, it gives protection from thieves. If a door is left open and a thief gets in, he will fall and not be able to leave; the owner can then arrest him.

Once a priest was traveling in Huanuco and as he was passing an orchard said to the man with him, "I'm going to pick some oranges." "No, padre," replied the man. "The people grow penca on their wall." "That won't do anything to stop me," said the priest. "I'm going in." But the man would not accompany him. The priest was grabbed by the penca and soon the owner found him lying on the ground. "Why do you come secretly?" he asked. "Everything is protected here. You will be whipped fifty times and then you can leave."

The leaves just above the bull are from the *tomapende* (*Brugmansia suaveolens, toé*). Some sorcerers use this plant to cause *huaycos* (landslides and mudslides) by making it rain heavily and causing the river to flood. The *toro vilca* emerging from the hilltop symbolizes the huayco, and when people in the Sierra think one is coming they say, "Here comes the toro vilca." In the painting you can see the water streaming down the hill.

Before the huayco comes, some people get on a raft and go downriver with a smoky fire, or they start running for the mountains because they know their houses will be washed away two hours later, along with their animals and possessions.

The sumiruna foresees this disaster from afar while in flight, and grabs the bull by the horns, as you can see here. He spins it around so it cannot do any harm, thus preventing the sorcerer from causing any huayco.

Just to the left of the banco sumi is the fruit of the *guanábana* (*Annona muricata*). The guanábana helps to keep the shaman strong and is also used to heal cancerous tumors.

Above on the left you see the pink flowers of the *yacu toé* (*Brugmansia* sp.), a variety that grows near water. Its flower is crushed and used as a poultice on ulcers and tumors. The ícaro of this plant can be used to prevent people from wandering about and getting lost.

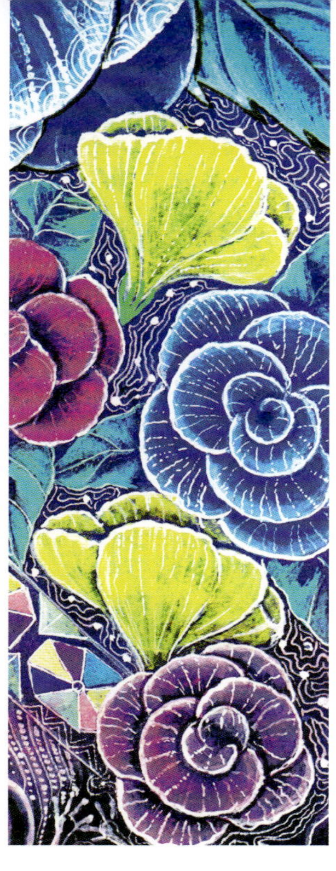

AYARI WARMI

VESTIDO DE MUJER ELEGANTE

The rose color in the center of the picture represents the realm of the earth, while the blue color represents the sky and the celestial realms. The picture reveals the eternal mystery of the feminine.

When a woman works with the spirit of ayahuasca and other plants, her radiant spiritual purity appears in the mareación embellished and garlanded with beautiful flowers. Just as lakes and rivers have luxuriant foliage and blossom adorning their banks, so a woman expresses the splendor of the entire natural world. She is the embodiment of heavenly beauty, tenderness, and grace. Her spiritual raiment and inner warmth are appealing, peaceful, and welcoming; as you can see in the painting, she is very beautiful.

Women symbolize and hold the quintessence of beauty, while men should develop wisdom to be of service to beauty. When a woman learns to sing ícaros, they are delicate and melodious. Her ícaros resemble tuneful bird songs, flowing water, or the sound of wind blowing through the trees. Her ícaros evoke the joy you feel when you visit a park brimming with brilliant flowers and majestic trees. Therefore, when a woman develops her innate esoteric knowledge she is much wiser and more capable than a man is.

As she smokes her pipe, she transmits her spiritual purity and impeccability. Coming out with the smoke from her pipe are *yura cukchas mallcas*—sublime healers who perform wondrous cures, or in Quechua, "the old white-haired wise ones."

The path of a man wishing to study esoteric knowledge is more arduous and demanding than for a woman, and he must follow the dieta more rigorously. Women can diet for a year and experience what a man has learned in six; if a woman follows the dieta for longer, she holds sway over men.

When a woman takes a *baño floral* (bath infused with flowers), her sensitive skin absorbs the essence of the flowers more effectively than a man's skin does. She has empathy with the consciousness of flowers and the immaculate way they unfold.

On the left are wise sovereigns known as the *a'tun mauca runa,* "the great ancient ones" who are the bringers of harmony. They watch over the women ascending the celestial temples to worship. They are the guardians of space, time, and the stars and galaxies, and they bring unity. If the elemental forces of earth, air, fire, and water were not in equilibrium, life would be inconceivable. We see harmony everywhere in nature, as in the water cycle: how it forms into clouds, rain, rivers, lakes, and oceans, and how this nurtures life.

Women are the creators and preservers of life. The man provides his sperm and kindles new life, but the woman is the creator; life flourishes within her. If women did not preserve and nurture this embryonic life, we would not be here.

When the man wants more offspring, he impregnates the woman, each time giving her more

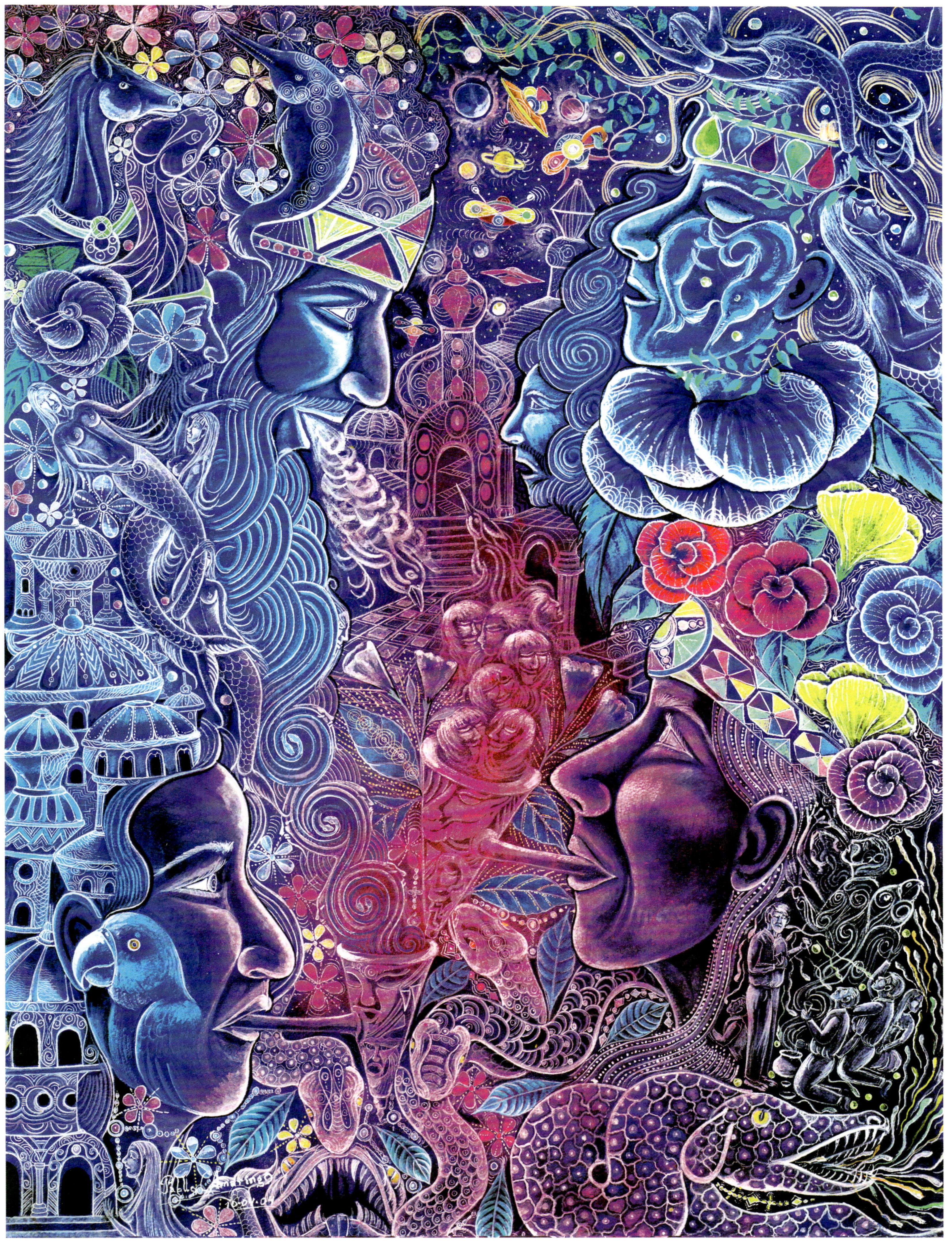

AYARI WARMI
Vestido de mujer elegante
2004, Gouache on Arches Paper
57 x 76 cm.

children. However, when a woman understands the “ways of the flower” inside her, she has control over her reproductive process. The egg opens like a flower to allow the sperm to enter, and then it is closed, never to open again. The egg faces forward for two hours and then turns around. During this time the woman can remove the sperm by first making sure her nails are short to avoid hurting herself, and then washing thoroughly using water and lemon juice to flush the sperm out of her body.

Many women in the Amazon avoid getting pregnant in this way. The flowers around her pipe represent her awareness of the reproductive function of her body. People who do not know this must use contraceptives, some of which contain chemicals that prejudice health and well-being. Natural methods are harmless.

Like a queen at her coronation, she wears a floral crown to symbolize the wisdom she receives at the celestial palace. The energy and aptitude of a woman has an inner focus; her talent as a homemaker and for bringing up children is innate. The precious stones in her crown represent the philosopher’s stone, her spiritual alchemy.

Men and women are very different; their roles differ yet they function in relationship and help and teach each other. Women are able to sense danger well before men do. This is suggested in the upper right side of the painting where the ayahuasca vine touches her temples and crown.

A woman wins the right to wear this crown when she truly fulfills her earthly and divine role as a woman, mother, and partner. It is through her that the man receives his crown. Men should reflect on and appreciate the spiritual endowment of the ayari warmi, a woman of both inner and outer beauty.

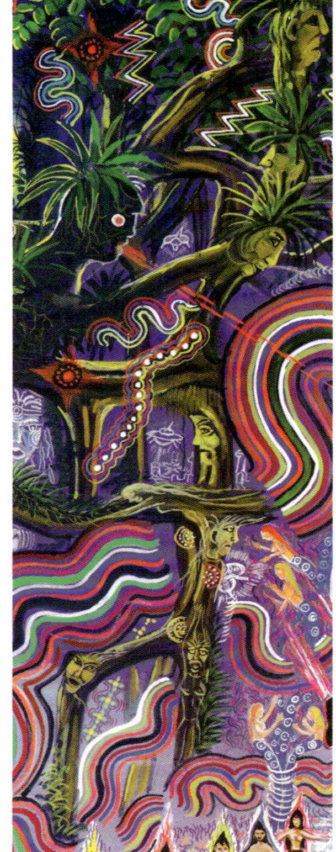

A'TUN SUPAY LANCHA

LANCHA FANTASMA

The ship represents man's divinity, along with fortune, wisdom, and good use of our talents.

In this vision the shamans in front sing the ícaro of the *lancha fantasma* (phantom boat) and a strong mareación soon starts to take hold of them all. Hidden places in the earth open and spirits arise from caves to celebrate with circle dances the arrival of the great phantom ship. Ayahuasca is the sacrament of this joyful festivity.

You can sense the exhilaration and ecstasy of the mareación—dryads and nymphs work while animal spirits dance to help the plants to flourish. On board are ayahuasqueros as strong as caimans. On the decks are warriors, sylphs, musicians, revered gurus from India, and the great teachers from ancient China. This is how the great masters travel outside finite time and space. They all move like ships and roar like thunder when they journey to another dimension, celestial realm, or another place on earth. This is the wonderful gift of the a'tun supay lancha.

In this painting the lancha represents the *huairamama* (mother of the air), or cosmic serpent, a being that adopts the appearance of a ship. She is the manifestation of the cosmic vibration that creates all matter. She is the mother of all angels, cherubim, and seraphim.

The huairamama arrives with a great whirlwind and energy from outer space, which you can see as the multicolored waves to its side. This whirlwind uncovers the pot of ayahuasca, and the spirits and muses appear in the flames to meet the arrival of the a'tun supay lancha. They hold musical instruments from which blissful transcendent melodies emerge, both in sound and vision. Emerging from the top of the flames is the *huarmi del cushqui* (queen of money), whose name is *Chai Cullkimama*.

To the left of the lancha you see the *machaco sirenas* with blue snake bodies emerging from the river. *Huarmi murayas* (female shamans) escort the lancha with ropes of white flowers. Their incandescent auras show that they are doctoras who heal with pink, yellow, and white flowers.

Above is a woman with a beautiful crown and snakes instead of arms; she is Queen Safila (venerable woman). She teaches the shamans how to defend themselves against sorcery, and protects the lancha from a *puma machaco* (a snakelike puma) on a branch of the renaco tree that attacks the lancha by projecting its red *mariri* (magical phlegm). The puma machaco obeys malicious sorcerers and has the capacity to cause *daño* (harm) or even death to its victims.

To her right you see the *chaicunis* hiding around the renaco tree. They are the spirits of the ancient Shipibo who have emerged from secret places to witness the arrival of the lancha.

The anguilamamas discharge electromagnetic rays to defend the lancha from enemies seen to the right: brightly colored *chiripa machacos* (rainbow snakes), one with a red horn and the other with a crest; and the *shitanero* (malevolent sorcerer) with red eyes, smoking his pipe. At the top right a puma banco has transformed himself into a jaguar. To his left is a *yana machin* (black monkey) leaping

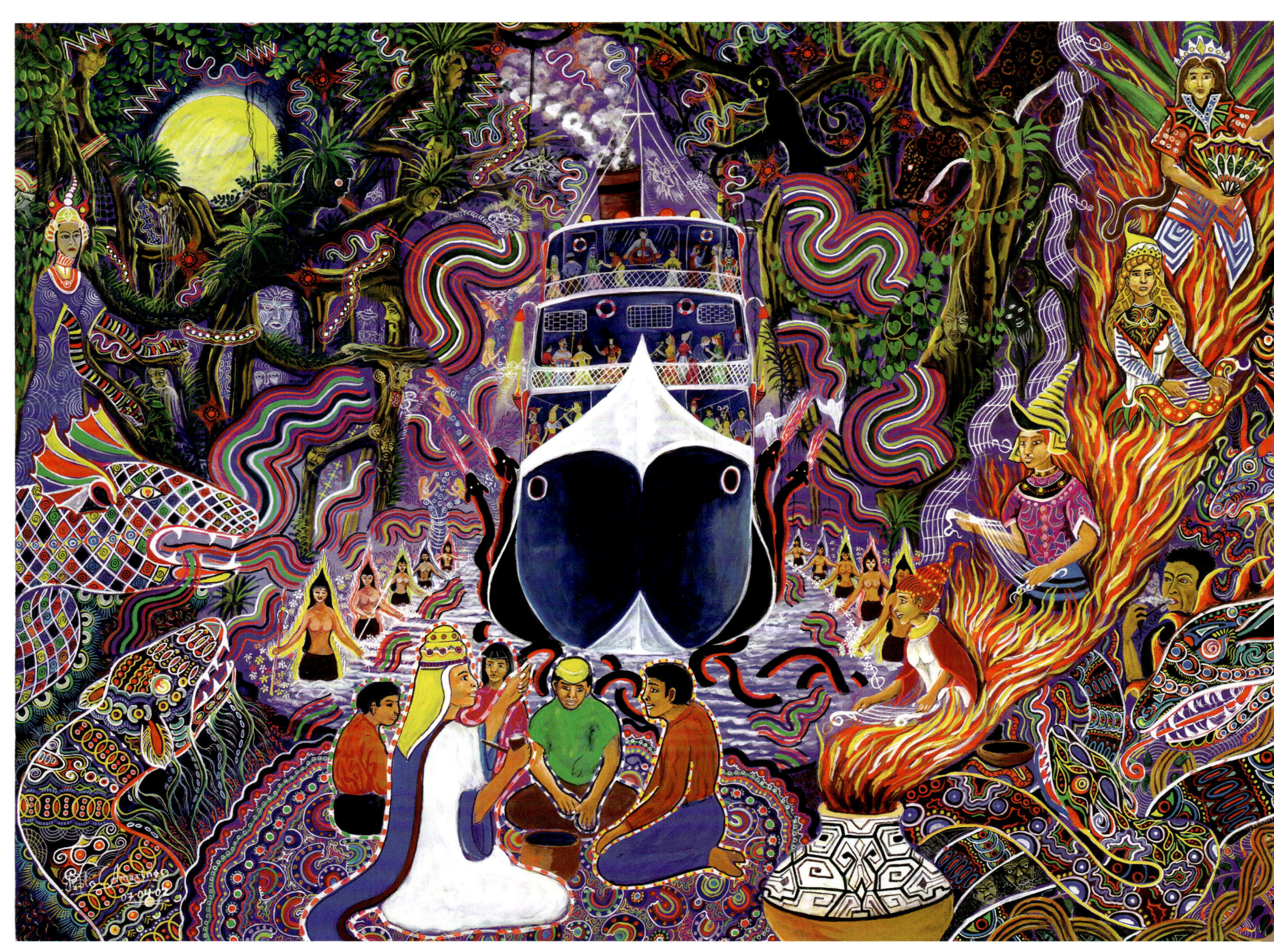

A'TUN SUPAY LANCHA
Lancha Fantasma
2002, Gouache on Arches Paper
57 x 76 cm.

through the branches. This animal is brave and agile and can intercept an enemy's virotes and *marupa* sorcery—the use of insects, snakes, or scorpions that are retained in the mariri of the hechicero, who sends them to cause serious or fatal harm to his victims. When a shaman learns the ícaro of the yana machin, he can defend himself against marupa sorcery.

The shamans sit on a carpet of tingunas, ever-changing patterns that characterize ecstatic ayahuasca visions. Tingunas are made of primordial energy and can materialize into a shrine, a palace, or an animal.

To their left the sachamamas are projecting waves of electromagnetic radiation in the form of arkanas that protect the lancha from harm.

The a'tun supay lancha appears in your vision to help you evolve spiritually and teach you the importance of conserving the rain forest. The lancha also gives you a strong, clear, and truthful mareación, as its boiler is an ayahuasca cauldron.

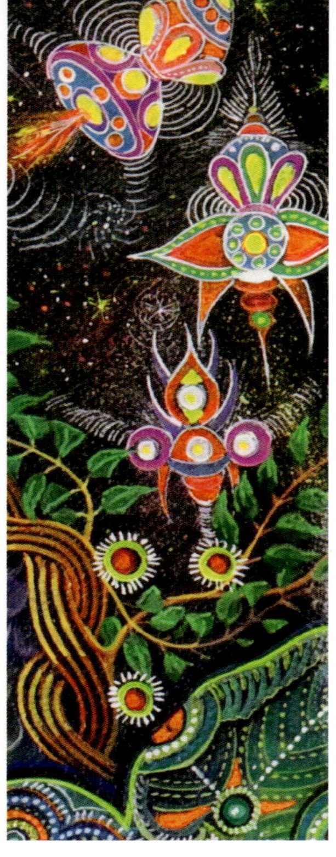

VUELAN VERSUCUM

CANCIÓN DE VOLAR

From time to time a shaman needs to rehearse his ícaros so he will not forget them when healing. *Vuelan versucum,* which means "songs that fly," is a solitary practice requiring a free day so that he can become fully conversant with his ícaros. The shaman finds a remote place where no one will bother him and runs through the ícaros of all the plants, trees, barks, roots, insects, and birds. The ícaros come back to him as one by one the plants make themselves heard through him.

Performing this ceremony is a sumiruna at the bottom left, a muraya (a level of vegetalista) at the bottom right, and banco sumi above. Each one is bathing in the eternal fire while celestial beings, known as *seraphs,* charge their pipes with healing energy. The shaman imparts this energy to his patients when performing sopladas: that is, healing with tobacco smoke. They learn the ícaro of the ocelot, *sajino* (peccary), guacamayo, *pucacunga* bird (*Penelope jacquacu,* Spix's guan), *trompetero* bird (*Psophia crepitans,* gray-winged trumpeter), and *paujil* (*Crax rubra,* curassow).

The eyes of the green jaguar have a hypnotic power that prevents it from being seen. The power in his eyes is concentrated through the rhythmic movement of his tail.

The green temple on the right is where sumirunas and banco sumis study healing at a distance, and receive energy for transforming themselves into animals and for entering trees. They learn the language of trees, plants, moss, and humus in the soil. When the earth is ravaged and polluted, even the soil cries. The ancient sages understood that our physical body is made from the earth's humus. This is why we are called humans; the words for "man" and "soil" derive from the same linguistic root.*

The *gaita del ayatuyo,* or *aya gaita,* is a wind instrument made from the bone of a dead person, usually an arm bone. Its sound is so intense that it fills one with sorrow or makes people faint. I used to feel only slightly perturbed when I heard it as a child, but my brothers would go crazy and fall out of bed. It was once a common instrument on the River Ucayali but has now all but disappeared.

Shamans learned to play the aya gaita to keep evil away from their villages. It can also be used to pacify wars and has been used to abate terrorism, but you must play it well. People coming down the river on rafts also used to play these instruments. My papa would always listen. Sometimes it was so beautiful it stunned people and made them tremble. When delivering news of some grave misfortune, like a death in the family, the aya gaita can be very useful to stop people from breaking down with sorrow.

In vuelan versucum, the shaman also learns to communicate with animals. He learns how to call boas and snakes from their hiding places with their ícaros; dozens of them collect underneath the house to listen. Snakes are very sensitive to music. He also needs to know the ícaro to make them go

*This etymology appears to be accurate.

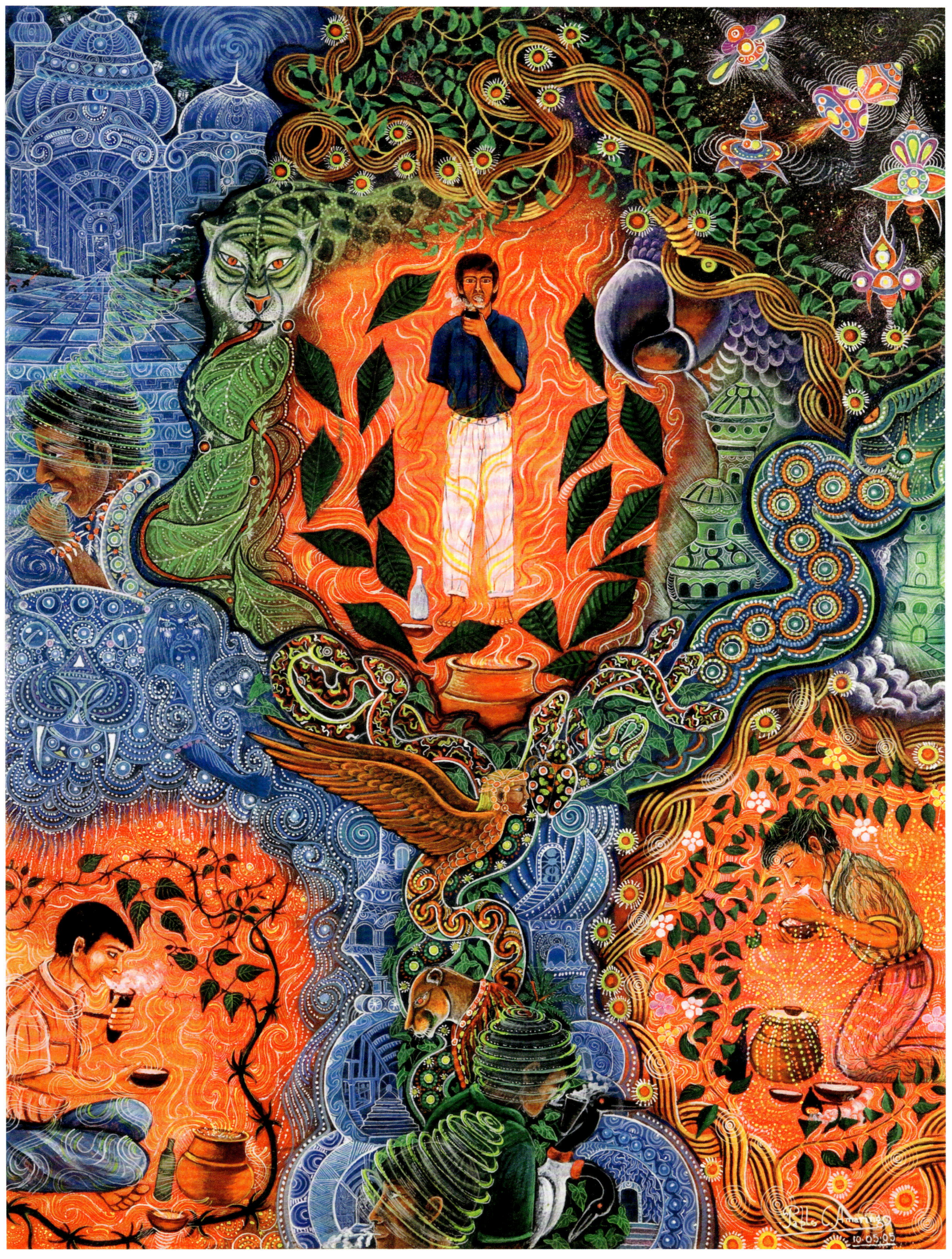

VUELAN VERSUCUM
Canción de Volar
2005, Gouache on Arches Paper
57 x 77 cm.

away again; otherwise they stay around the house and bite people. The ícaro for healing snakebite is also learned.

The blue areas of the picture show the way to celestial wisdom. The spirits encountered by the vegetalista on this journey are his teachers, and from them he gains entrance into the spiritual temple, which is composed of living pearls and precious gems. Its chambers and hallways have columns made from flawless diamonds that can never be desecrated. Only the pure of heart illuminated in love, humility, and wisdom may enter the magnificent and sacrosanct temple.

The blue spiral above the temple symbolizes the movement of spirit and matter from solar systems and galaxies to subatomic particles.

In the water in front of the temple are the anguilamamas, who discharge electromagnetic rays that protect the sanctity of the temple. Behind the temple (very small) you can see the indigenous warriors who also act as guardians.

The extraterrestrial ships in the corner are from another galaxy and have traveled for thousands of years and visited many worlds to extract minerals and come to the Amazon jungle to receive life energy.

The spiral waves encircling heads like hats are their secret learning, which should not be revealed to others unless you are a teacher. Secret knowledge is what you discover for yourself, and you should submit to it. A ritual precedes every activity, as, for example, rubbing your hands or preparing ayahuasca; they do not need a reason. When secrets are kept they accumulate power, and when divulged, they lose power. It is like a house that, if broken into, loses its integrity.

There is also a banco puma with the face of a puma, dressed in his ceremonial garments. The *ishkay tuyuyo* (two-headed Jabiru stork) protects the shamans and has twice the normal vision to warn of approaching perils. The winged beings like snakes are *rikramachaco sirena*—a sirena of the subaquatic realms with the ability to fly like a bird.

This is a powerful picture with teaching and healing contained in it. I chant ícaros when I paint, so if ever a person wishes to receive teaching or healing, they should cover the painting with a cloth for two or three months. On the day they remove the cover, they should prepare themselves by bathing and meditating. When it is uncovered they will receive the power and knowledge of the ícaros that were sung into it. These paintings are special and I will not be painting pictures like this again.

YACU CABALLO

Water horses live around cliff edges and large pools on certain rivers where people rarely venture. They come in many colors—black, red, white, and pink—and are inclined to jump and skip around restlessly.

The yacu caballos are employed by shamans to journey under water, reaching great depths and passing through tunnels to where the pucabufeo lives.

These highly intelligent horses can give warning when a river is going to change its course and possibly flood a village. This happened in the case of Caballococha, a town on the Amazon near the Colombian border, which has since disappeared. Many people lived there, and every evening a black horse used to emerge from the river and run around the streets and in the plaza. Children would follow without fear because they were used to seeing it each night, but soon the land on which the town stood began to sink little by little. One day the horse was seen running about at midday. That night, Caballococha was flooded and disappeared.

Beware if while you are sleeping you hear a horse shrieking and no horse is actually there. It is a warning that you are about to be flooded by the river. Some say the sounds are made by *runamulas* (mule people). These are people who have been transformed by a brujo or sorcerer. Young women who go to bed with clergymen are also likely to be turned into runamulas. They can be very disruptive creatures. I once saw one pass by my mother's house, breathing fire and steam from its mouth and defecating everywhere in the village.

The yacu caballos are useful for maintaining the proper level of the rivers and for making journeys. However, you must not fear them or strike them, as they are sacred; if you do not bother them, they will not harm you. You should pass them quietly when navigating the river because they may cause whirlpools that can easily sink your boat.

Many yacu caballos used to live a little downriver from Contamana on the River Ucayali, and a number of boats have sunk there. The yacu toro is similar, only wilder. If you molest or anger a yacu toro, it starts pulling at your boat. Sometimes they can be seen going in front of a phantom ship.

Some hechiceros in remote places use the yacu caballo to attack their victims. They lead the yacu caballo screaming from the water and into the wilderness. Later they approach the victim in his sleep, biting and dragging him away. Sometimes they can kill.

At first I didn't believe these things but one day I was coming home with some people and we saw a big boat on the river and a huge gray horse leading it. We startled it and it went away.

The *unicornio* emerging from the *mahuete* (large earthenware jar) is a transformed sumiruna who has undergone his dieta inside there. He has lived inside for the period of his dieta, leaving only for his necessities.

The two sirenas in the waterfall are *yacu huarmi* (water women). They symbolize the sacred purity of the water flowing from the temple at the top. Water is a vital element for all life. In my

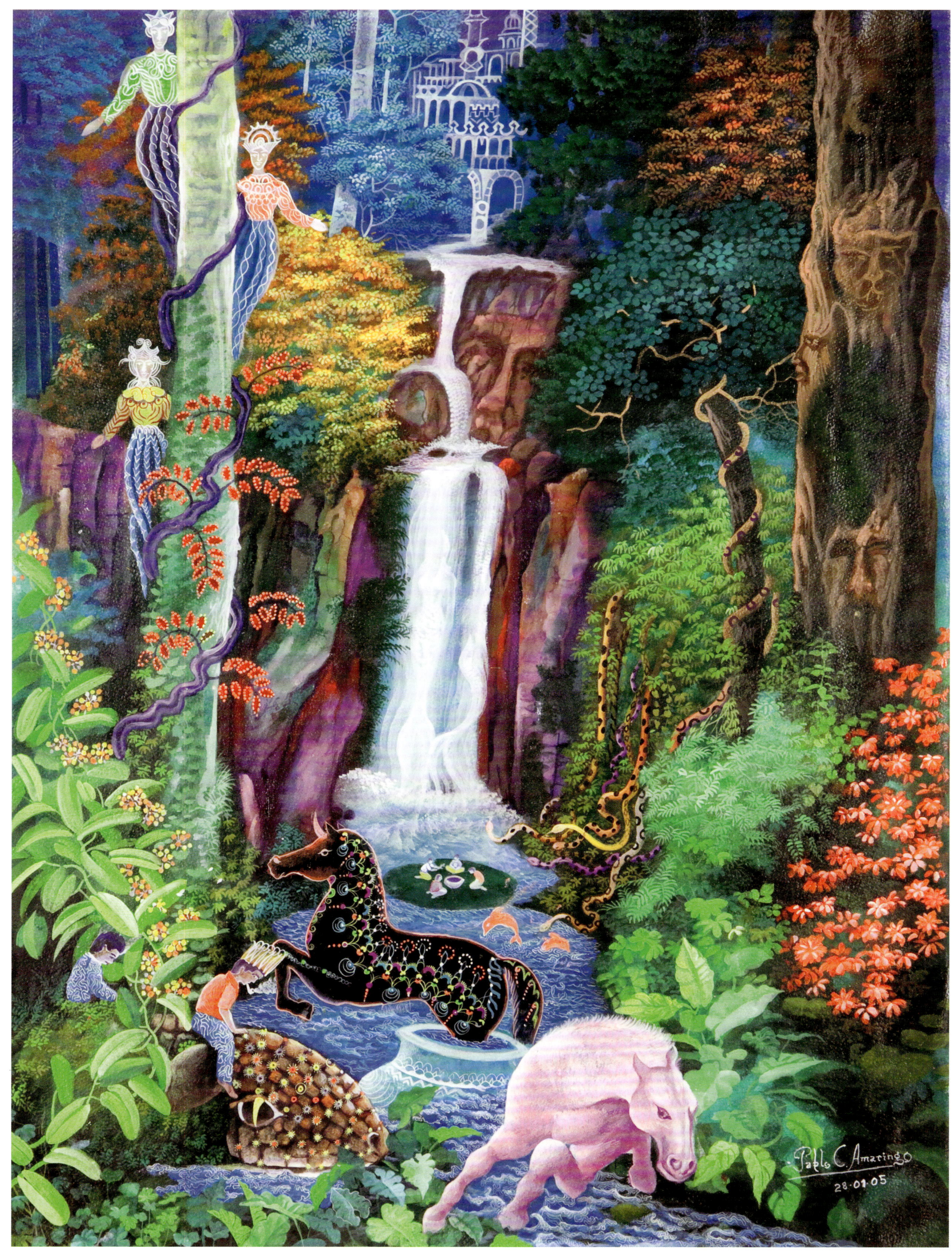

YACU CABALLO
2005, Gouache on Arches Paper
57 x 77 cm.

visions the spirits have shown me how important it is to use pure water to bathe, drink, and prepare medicines. When you take a bath with spring water you feel happy, younger, and calmer. There are many flowers and leaves that you can add to pure spring water for baños florales, or to make potions such as *misquipanga* (*Renealmia alpinia*), which protects you from attack by animals.

The yacu caballo is the genio of the *piri piri* plant (*Cyperus articulates*), used for healing pregnant mothers and newborn babies. The seeds are crushed to obtain a juice that is rubbed over the baby's face and legs so that it grows strong and graceful and will not be lazy. The ícaro of the caballo piri piri is used by the Shipibo for hunting and fishing, and for catching *paiche* fish (*Arapaima gigas*), which lays its eggs in the piri piri.

The word *ícaro* comes from the Quechua word *icarai,* meaning "to blow." Ícaros can be used for attraction or for obtaining justice, love, or visions of patterns for painting on textiles and ceramics. These ícaros are generically called *tayas* and include *pusangas* (spells) for enchanting a partner, *arrullos* (lullabies) for putting a child to sleep, *aires* for creating a festive atmosphere, *coros* for stirring or calming spirits, *hymnos* for defense, and *taquinas* for protection or killing. The *huaquanqui* is for making a woman cry and is derived from a rock that looks like a vulva.

Below the waterfall, a shaman is holding an ayahuasca session on top of a giant Amazonian water lily (*Victoria amazonica*).

To the left you see the *lupuna blanca* (*Ceiba pentandra*). This is one of the tallest trees in the Amazon; its guardians are the three sylphs who are entwined around its trunk.

The tree with red flowers behind the lupuna is the *tahuari* (*Tabebuia serratifolia*), also a large canopy tree and more widely known as *pau d'arco.* It has a wide range of medicinal properties and there are many well-documented studies on it.

The tree with yellow flowers to the side of the lupuna is *tinta caspi* (*Haematoxylum campechianum,* or logwood); the scientific name means "blood wood." The bark and leaves are used medicinally for their antibacterial and anti-inflammatory properties. The resin is used as a natural dye and is similar to brazilwood. Below and to the left is the *renaquilla* (*Clusia rosea*) bush.

On the right-hand side is the *shihuahuaco* tree (*Dipteryx* sp.), wherein you see the *hamadryades,* nymphs that enter the tree and live there. As with the *huacapú* tree (*Minquartia guianensis*) nearby, the wood is very hard, and when it dies, it eventually petrifies. The hamadryades turn into the rocks and cliffs that you can see overlooking the spring.

The resins of trees such as the *tahuari, remocaspi* (*Aspidosperma excelsum*), *tinta caspi,* and *copal* (*Protium grandifolium*) are the blood of the hamadryades. Hence, their resins and barks are powerful medicine for us.

The *huanarpo macho* (*Jatropha macrantha*) tree on the right displays its bright red flowers; they are widespread in South America. The powdered bark is used widely in Peru as an aphrodisiac and natural libido enhancer, and as a sexual stimulant for men.

In the foreground a sumiruna wearing a crown of white feathers is smoking his pipe while riding the yacumama. Mounted behind him is a muraya; these shamans can summon and control the yacumama with their ícaros.

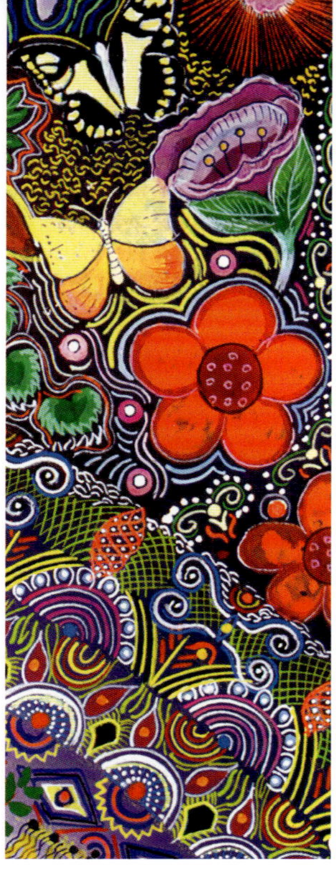

ENCANTO RUMI

PIEDRA ENCANTO

This stone is forged in space and brought down to earth when summoned by the sumiruna for initiating his disciples in voyaging to other galaxies, and diving underwater or into the earth. A sumiruna is not harmed by fire and can spend years away on his journeys after taking large amounts of ayahuasca.

The *encanto rumi* is like a flower that opens its knowledge to us. The sumirunas below are learning how to receive spiritual fire and how to withstand the extreme conditions that they will experience on their lone voyages. The sumiruna who has ascended to the rock in the sky has received his staff, crown, and belt. I was given my staff and belt but did not ascend to the rock. Had I done that I might have reached the level of sumiruna.

The eagle represents the sublime beauty of the stone, the jaguar its magnetic power, and the bull its soul. The stone rises to the clouds where you see the *puya runas* (cloud people) and the *guacamayo runa:* people with the head of a guacamayo (macaw) and the body of a man. The guacamayo runa teach the shaman how to know when it is going to rain and how to make it rain. I have talked with them and know they can direct the rain precisely to any desired location.

In the interwoven geometric form above you can look through windows into the vastness of space. Some galaxies have spiral-shaped patterns and others are elliptical. This geometric lattice is like an observatory into intergalactic space.

The animals you see below the stone are the spirit allies of the curandero; the *venado* (deer) shows the healer the source of his patient's pain, and the ícaro of the sachavaca strengthens them. The toucan is summoned if the person is sad or depressed; its "tuqui, tuqui" sound lifts the person's sadness. The bat pursues insects that have been despatched by other shamans to spy on what is happening. Some shamans direct insects, such as wasps, dragonflies, and butterflies, to act as informers. The *tibemama* (sparrow hawk) is an ally that has the power to look into the depths of rivers and lakes.

The *papastrueno* (*Dioscorea* sp.) is a creeper plant with a tuber, similar to that of a sweet potato or yam. Its genio looks like a little old man and lives in caverns on hillsides. When indigenous people diet with this plant it makes them invisible, and while asleep the papastrueno genio teaches them the secrets of how to master storms and lightning. Using this energy he can topple trees or fertilize their orchards and fields with the power of the storm. A sorcerer can use lightning to kill people and animals instantly from a distance.

Among the flowers you see the five petals of the *sanango* (*Brunfelsia grandiflora*), the *tahuarí* (*Tabebuia impetiginosa*), and ayahuasca vine (*Banisteriopsis caapi*). The maestros below are preparing crowns of leaves and flowers for bringing positive energy to their ceremony. The ancients understood their value for venerating their gods, kings, and emperors.

Shamans use magical stones for healing. These *encantos,* as they are called, possess hidden powers

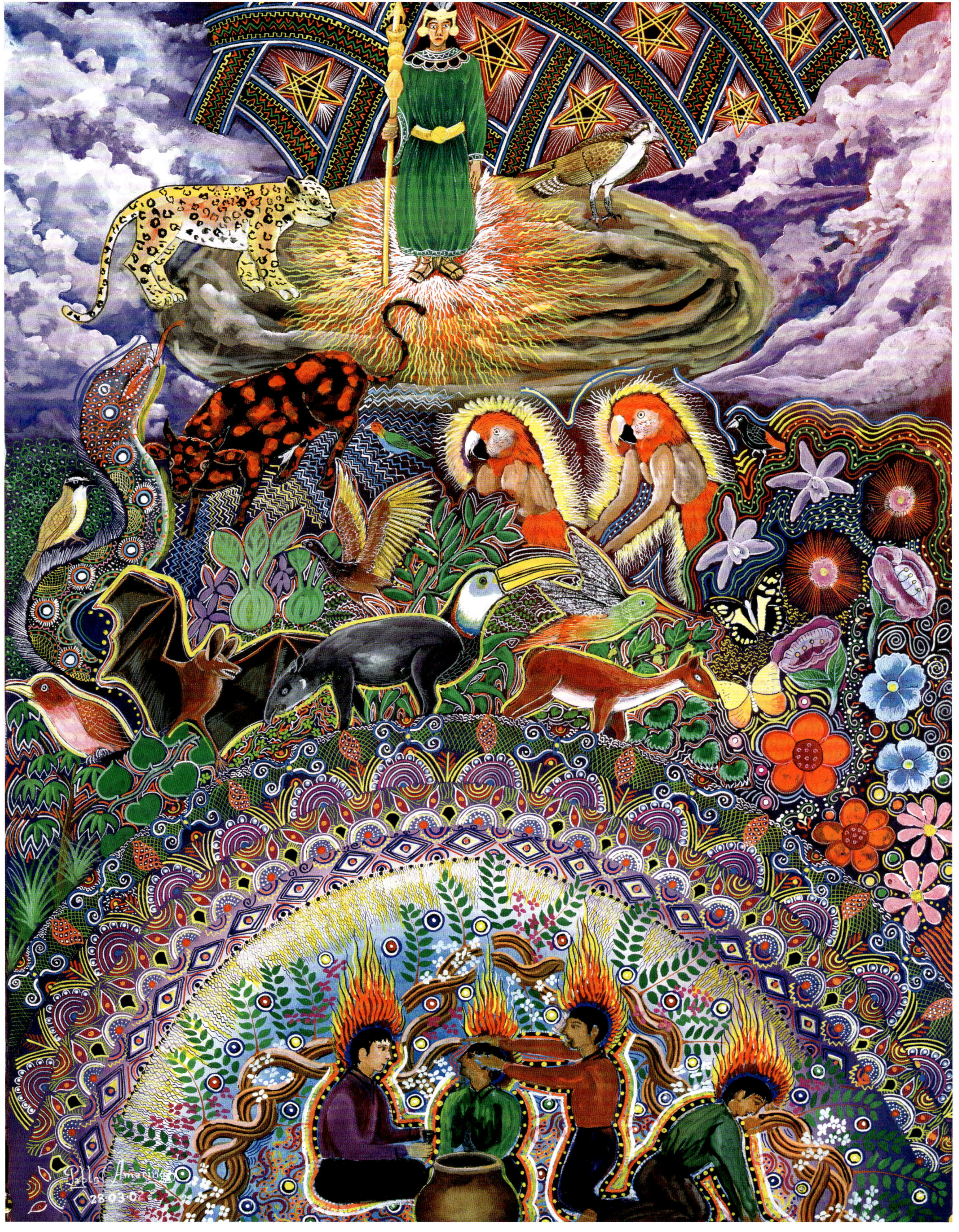

ENCANTO RUMI
Piedra Encanto
2002, Gouache on Arches Paper
57 x 76 cm.

that can be combined with ícaros to heal. However, they must be kept hidden as the spirits can harm people who see them and cause vomiting, diarrhea, and headaches.

These stones were formed when the earth was still hot from volcanic activity and the primordial energy was locked away into the rocks and minerals as they cooled. Thanks to these elements, life evolved and spirit was introduced into humanity so that we would know light from darkness, and of the existence of death. When we die we turn into unconscious energy without knowledge of any previous existence.

In everyday life we may not fully realize our human potential, but when we drink ayahuasca we can explore unused neural pathways. The learning capacity of the human mind, although limited, is the most outstanding phenomenon of the universe; it stores and retrieves information, and possesses the power of imagination, art, and logic. Ayahuasca can show us many things that are normally unfathomable and imperceptible in ordinary consciousness. The plant seems to have a consciousness with which we can only fleetingly become acquainted.

There are also stones known as "lightning stones" that are formed when a bolt of lightning strikes a tree, creating a stone inside its trunk or roots. Sometimes they are puma-, snake-, or toad-shaped and are found in hardwoods and palm trees, such as *shebón* (*Attalea butyracea*), *pifayo* (*Bactris gasipaes*), and *chonta* (*Aiphanes aculeate*).

These stones are also called *encantos,* and can be used as a medium for apprenticeship to lightning. The stone is placed in a bowl with some water, covered, and left in a cool, dry place for eight days. Early on the ninth day the apprentice drinks the water and begins a monthlong dieta. You learn to heal in your sleep, and not through visions, as is the case with ayahuasca. Shamans who learn in this way can be very powerful. Some diviners and mediums make the stones into figurines with penises; they are called *huacanqui* here in the selva, and are used as love charms and amulets.

Stones are a living record of the earth's history. Our ancestors who worked with stone and lived in caves communicated with them. There are still primitive people who practice this. You should be careful when encountering encantos in an ayahuasca vision because their esoteric powers cannot be received by a person who has not first dieted and purged with ayahuasca.

The ayahuasca vines around the maestros sprout strings of pearls and form a splendid jeweled dome of amethyst, agate, onyx, emerald, turquoise, sapphire, and ruby. A shaman on his way to becoming a banco sumi is given this in his vision and will never forget the joy of perceiving such beauty.

Precious stones can be used in many ways. Alcoholism can be cured with amethyst. Put it in a bowl of water and leave it standing for a week, then drink half a glass of the water twice a day and diet on salt, sugar, oil, and lemon for a week. Carrying it in your pocket strengthens resolve to defeat alcoholism.

Emeralds in necklaces or rings can heal tuberculosis and protect against snakebites, and turquoise cures liver and kidney diseases. For two months, put it in water in the evening and drink the water the following morning. Keeping one in your pocket helps to reduce nightmares and prevent headaches.

Stones can also be used as charms to protect against such things as intrigue, hostility, or envy. The stone is put in a bowl with water, covered, and left for eight days in a cool, dry place. Then you drink a glass of this water a day to relieve discomfort, bad temper, or grief. It can also be useful when dieting to reduce hunger or avoid gluttony.

The shamans have a corona of fire because they are masters and teachers. It gives them euphoria, bliss, and a great desire to live every moment happily.

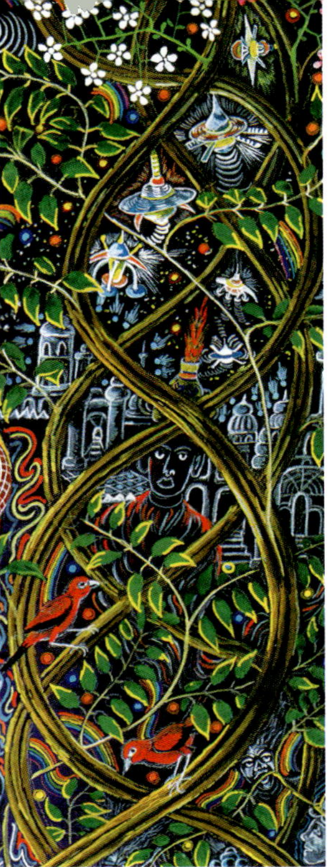

UNAI SHIPASH

MUSAS DEL TIEMPO Y ESPACIO

The muses of time can be seen in the upper sphere, and the accompanying muses of space in the lower sphere. The winged beings on either side of the celestial palace in the upper sphere are *aralim* (thrones). They maintain the cosmic forces that govern the physical universe, nuclear particles, and electromagnetic and gravitational fields.

The two divinities in yellow are *virtudes* (virtues) who represent elevated qualities of love, compassion, and kindness. There are also two seraphim and a cherub with many arms. The celestial palace is the heaven of the Supreme Being.

The muses in the upper sphere order time, while below they use their time to work on earth, watching over the entire biosphere from the ozone layer down to the depths of the ocean. This is the work they have been ordained to carry out by decree of the Supreme Being.

Time and space appear united to us and we are a part of them, but an alternate time and space also exist beyond our everyday experience, which we can perceive through the eye of ayahuasca.

The eyes are the windows through which the world attracts us, through which we choose colors, shapes, and sizes. It is possible for us to lose all this at any moment; if we go blind, there will be no use for our eyes. Space will continue to exist in our hearts and minds but no longer in our vision.

They say time is worth silver or gold, but in fact it has no material equivalent. In spiritual terms, time is life and not to be wasted, so we should take what is offered and learn what we can. Everything has a purpose.

We learn to sing just by listening to a song, but studying the song is a different matter; there is an important distinction here. We start learning through an action, so we start by humming the song, but this is followed by study and analysis. This is valid for all studies, including spiritual studies. If you do not analyze and synthesize during your apprenticeship, something is missing.

Each of the sublime beings in the picture has a different job to do. Some make the plants flourish while others look after the fertility of the soil, or watch over the energy coming from the sun, passing through microscopic pores in plants' leaves to produce food.

As they work and oversee every detail, they sing to raise their spirits and are never pessimistic. The whole universe is in constant resonance. Their songs are very beautiful and further our spiritual and material well-being. That is why I sing, whistle, or hum while painting. Music encourages me, makes me happy doing what I am doing, just as the muses do while working on each of their creations.

I have seen how the earth was once a burning star in movement, a fluorescent blue-green. Then beings appeared and put clouds in the sky and a dark powder on the earth's surface—the soil. I have seen what we now know about the origin of life on earth; water condensing from gases, creating seas, allowing aquatic plants to evolve. That is what the volcanoes below represent.

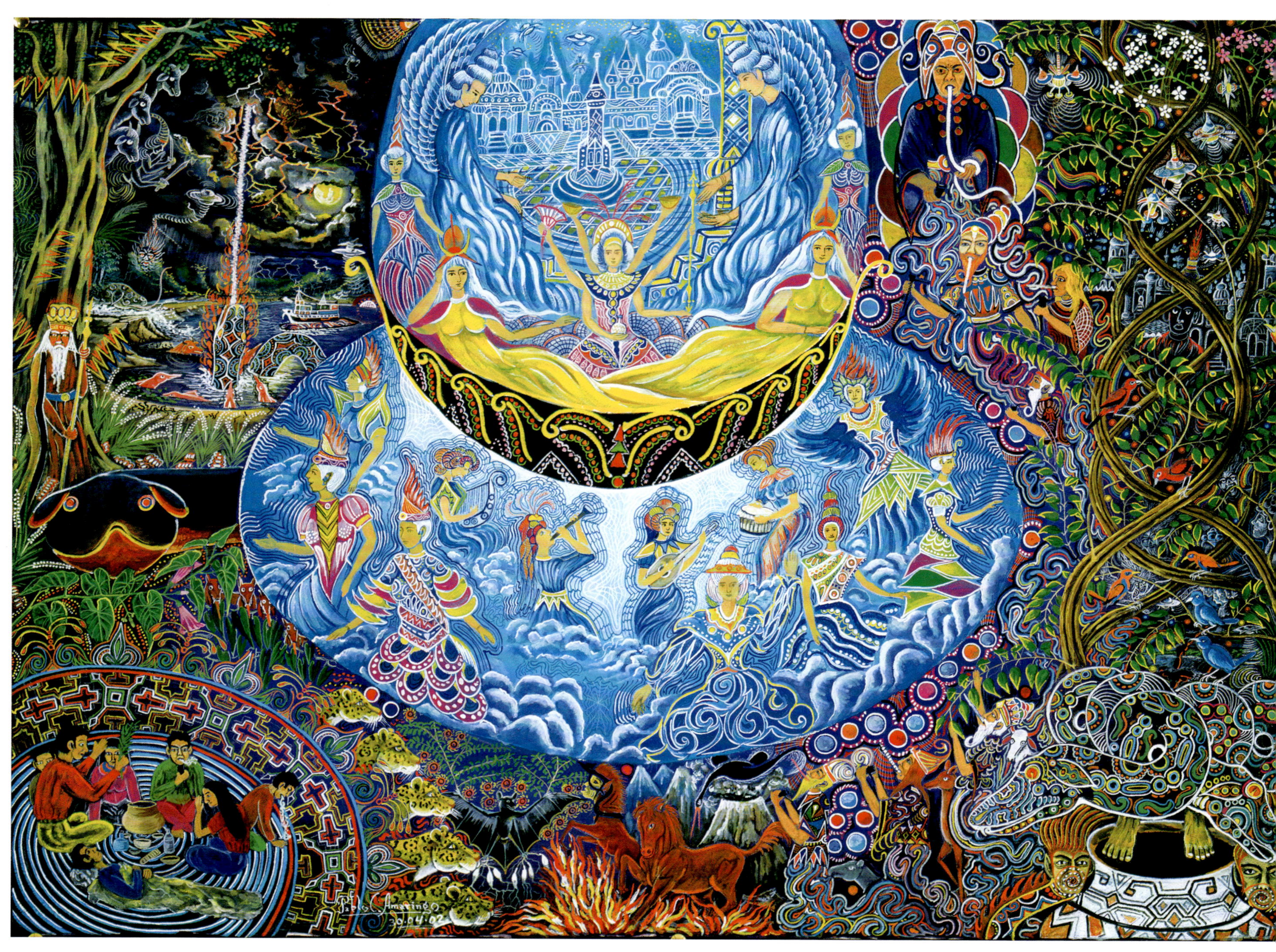

UNAI SHIPASH
Musas del Tiempo y Espacio
2006, Gouache on Arches Paper
57 x 76 cm.

On the right you see the feet of an ancient Shipibo woman who has been transformed into an anaconda, from which the spirit of ayahuasca emerges with her guardians. All of this comes out of a *tinaja* (ceramic vessel). It is time to explore the outer world; the snake coiling out of that tinaja is the mother of ayahuasca, and the feet are for exploring many new places.

A person's eyes, ears, and hair help you to diagnose their sickness, and the feet reveal their state of health. If you look at them while chanting ícaros, the knowledge comes to you.

The red birds that you see in the ayahuasca vine are *chicua*. They are the prescient, wise guardians of ayahuasca. They appear at critical moments, such as when someone is cutting down ayahuasca. They warn the shaman that someone may fall or that some other danger is afoot.

When I was only seven years old, someone told my father I was intelligent and that he should give me the brains of the chicua. The bird was killed and immediately I had to eat its brains, wash them down with warm water, and then diet for eight days. Thus, I received the intelligence of the animal, which made me a seer and a man of vision.

The horses you see at the bottom of the picture can take you to enchanted pagodas and other secret places, which you could never reach on foot, nor even by flying. Many people would like to go but do not know how, and neither do sorcerers. The horses fly with you so far, and from there the spirits escort you to sacred temples made from crystals and precious stones. It is only possible to see them using ayahuasca.

First you must purify your heart and soul, otherwise you cannot go in. You must learn how to see with love, justice, and goodness. If you are just, they let you see a little way, but if you have goodness you can see places where only a select few are allowed.

People will often claim to carry out justice, but usually it is little more than an agreed boundary, one side of which belongs to you, the other to your neighbor. Goodness, on the other hand, is having just enough food for yourself, but still you share it with your neighbor. Goodness is greater than justice; you give of yourself. It makes demands on your heart but you feel happy.

Suppose I am your servant and do everything for you, and I want something that you are not willing to give me. You are not doing wrong, because you are the owner and can give to whom you wish. I cannot complain that you are unjust or bad, but there is no compassion. This justice is simply holding on to property jealously.

Many people complain that others are bad, even though they know that they have a positive side, too. Understanding spirituality is realizing that the negative side is there to show you the positive side.

If you have many possessions but are careless and do not look after them, someone will come and help himself. The thief teaches us to look after our things; he does you harm but he also does good. You need both light and dark to be illuminated—both polarities must be present.

The great masters wearing crowns are the mystic teachers of the vegetalista in the art of mariri. The mariri is the magical phlegm they emit from their mouths; *yura-mariri* (white mariri) gives health, *ancas-mariri* (blue mariri) bestows extrasensory wisdom, and *puka-mariri* (red mariri) is used by sorcerers to harm. The high master above wearing the blue *cushma* is chanting the ícaro of the mariri.

Below you see a sachavaca, a deer, and a goat with red horns. The black bird with the red beak is the *yaku-sarara,* a combination of a bird and a river ray that can fly and dive deep into the water. It protects the shaman from enemies.

On the top left is the *remo caspi* tree (*Aspidosperma excelsum*, or *Pithecellobium laetumj*). The guardian of the tree is a sublime Oriental king of great virtue who wears a gold crown and carries a golden scepter. He grants permission for dieta with this tree only to *paleros* (vegetalistas) willing to follow the strict demands of the diet.

In the cocha there are several bufeocolorado, a puka toro, and a yakumama (mother of the waters) that is projecting electromagnetic radiation to fertilize the plants and bring rain. The flames around its head signify that there will be a storm. The yacumama accompanies the supay lancha, carrying murayas and sumirunas. In the sky you can see the sylphs of thunder and lightning.

This lake is a mystical cocha brava. These cochas are protected from hunters and fishermen by the anguilamama; consequently, they are always alive with fish and animals. The anguilamama is the mother of the cocha brava—a large one can be seen lurking underneath. It can transform itself into a *yakutoro* or a giant *supay paiche* (a supernatural South American freshwater fish, which is a living fossil and one of the largest freshwater fishes in the world).

On the bottom left are crosses as the Shipibo draw them; they have nothing to do with Christ's cross. The Shipibo cross represents the bow and arrow when it is fired and denotes being a good hunter, people who achieve their aims, and good medicine.

Above is a plant called *lengua de perro* (*Cynoglossum officinale,* or dog's tongue). Behind this are Shipibo dogs with their tongues hanging out.

The jaguar is sovereign of the jungle, and a shaman who acquires its feline alertness, strength, and hypnotic power becomes an expert healer, able to uncover malevolent enemies.

The *masho* (bat) at the bottom represents the vibrations that we hear as sound. When a shaman transforms himself into a masho he can feel, see, and hear what is happening around him without being detected.

At the top right are the flowers of ayahuasca. There are several types: ayahuasca *cielo* (sky) has white flowers, ayahuasca *trueno* has yellow flowers, ayahuasca *lucero* pink, and ayahuasca *cascabel* red.

Ayahuasca cielo can give visions of angels, *arcontes* (spirit priests), divine *aralim* (celestial beings), and celestial palaces. A *maestro vegetalista* is able to draw in the sublime powers of these divine beings.

Ayahuasca *cascabel* (rattle) is a rare variety with very powerful effects; it gives visions in red and is used by shamans to heal and cleanse a person suffering from hechicería.

Ayahuasca *trueno* (thunder) allows you to hear the voices of sylphs, *napeas* (nymphs), and dryads. The thunder refers to the deep sound that originates in the stomach, not in the chest. This ayahuasca helps you to hear the words of the celestial masters, who speak through thunder.

Ayahuasca *lucero* (illuminated) gives beautiful visions of celestial palaces and brilliant colors. It also allows you to see within yourself, into your body.

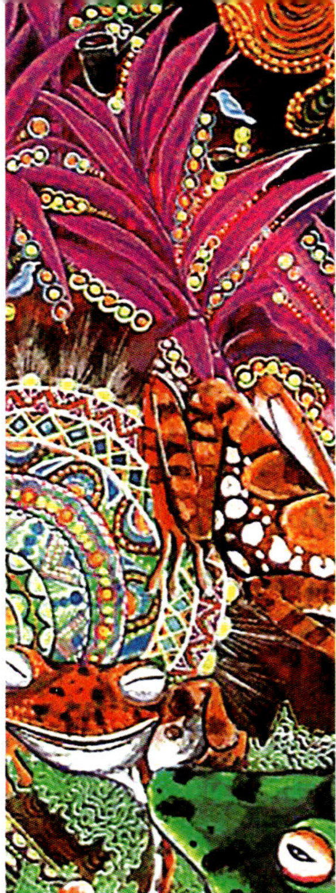

CASPI SHUNGU

CORAZÓN DEL ÁRBOL

In this painting we see the spirits materializing into earthly existence through the *puca lupuna* tree (*Cavanillesia hylogeiton*), which is a threshold between the two worlds. It is not easy for the spirits to materialize into physical form. If they cannot take on human appearance, they manifest as animals, since they are the spirits of animals. If they appear as humans, they can procreate with women. This is what you discover through the visions of ayahuasca and other plants like toé, *chric sanango,* and *ajo sacha*.

If you diet correctly, the invisible world becomes manifest. We have evolved the ability to access this alternate world using plants, to discover inspiration and meaning in our lives. Each of us has a unique role to play in protecting Mother Nature, furthering the spiritual evolution of humanity.

The spirits work untiringly to preserve life, but we humans cause ever more damage to nature as our civilization progresses. It is due to our lack of imagination above all; we think we are the only beings here on earth. We should all work like scientists, teachers, and composers so that we can creatively engage in the world, so that it continues. By playing a part in its functioning, we will not die. When I am old and cannot see well enough to paint, I will be doing other things instead, but I can still paint now and I am seventy-one.

Two shamans are sitting at the foot of the puca lupuna tree, smoking their pipes. They chant the ícaro of the tree and liberate diverse spirits through the *shungu,* or heart of the tree. Some go out to do benevolent deeds, and some are wayward or harmful.

You can see a host of animal spirits emerge from the tree: the sachavaca, *sapo* (frog), *lagartos* (lizards), and the *unicornio dorado* (golden unicorn), which represents the source waters of life—water that preserves life and which we drink.

For the shaman to benefit from the power and knowledge of the released spirits, he must gain mastery over them. The relationship with a spirit ally is a reciprocal one, as the spirits benefit from the shaman's companionship.

To seek out his allied spirits the shaman must prevail over and tame the spirit of the sachamama, mother of the selva, and the yacumama, mother of the water. He must possess the attributes of the anaconda and the caiman; the strength of the eagle, the boa, and the bull; and the colors of the guacamayo. If he cannot exercise mastery, he will not be a powerful shaman. A muraya can enter into the tree or into the waters and dive into the depths of the earth, but does not have the ability to go into space.

The shamans below are learning to impart energy to their breath so that the spirit of an animal infuses each soplo. The tobacco smoke or perfume in the soplo conveys their power when blown correctly from your chest and head.

The apprentice develops his ability to communicate with the spirits through his thoughts and

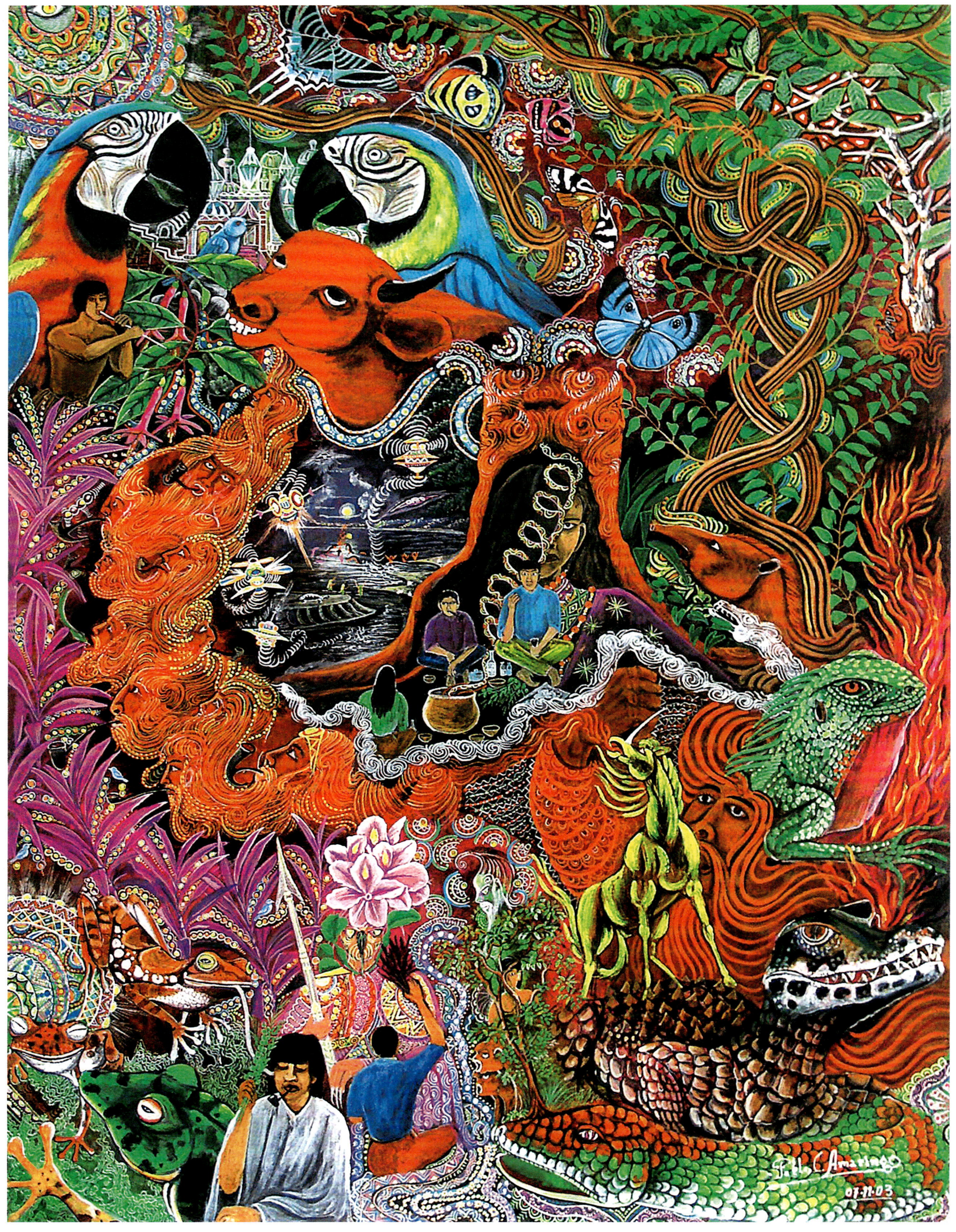

CASPI SHUNGU
Corazón del Árbol
2002, Gouache on Arches Paper
57 x 77 cm.

chanting ícaros. While he concentrates on receiving the power of the released spirits, the maestro by the tree is working to liberate them.

The sirenas and the bufeo colorado come to the surface of the cocha, bringing specimens from the depths to be taken into space. The extraterrestrial vessels have arrived to take the plants to the farthest reaches of outer space. Many kinds of plants flourish and bear greater yields when taken to other planets. This is what is taught here, and it is an exciting prospect. The extraterrestrials bring vapors to release to the plants and waters. This makes water turn deliciously fresh and crystalline overnight, so you can drink this water the next day.

The pucatoro is very difficult to control, but knowing its ícaro, you can make it come to you and stand still so that you can mount it. All the animals here—including the alligator and the giant toads—are for riding and mastering.

Above the pucatoro is the blue-and-yellow guacamayo, who guards over the ayahuasca ceremony to maintain spiritual order and support the shaman's work. He uses the guacamayo's ícaro to drive evil spirits away from his home. The *blue morpho* butterfly (*Morpho menelaus*), also seen in several other pictures, has special significance. Being of the sky, it represents our higher purpose and destiny. A shaman with a true calling as a healer and teacher wears the butterfly like a tie for all to see the knowledge he possesses.

The helical form of the ayahuasca vine indicates that it can reveal the DNA of living things and embody their vibrations and ícaros. The DNA of animals and plants has much in common with our own; this makes it possible for us to have empathy with a tree or an animal. Through our imagination we can contact the consciousness of the plant and animal world.

To the lower left you see the cascading purple leaves of *Tradescantia pallida,* and to its right, the pink flowers of the putu putu.

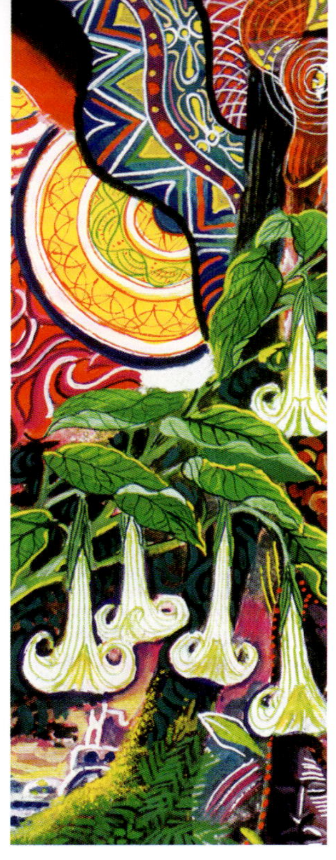

EL ENCANTO DE LAS PIEDRAS

Human beings have always understood the value of precious stones—ruby, topaz, amethyst, jade, onyx, beryl, and others. This is why in ancient times shamans wore necklaces of precious stones, and the kings and priests of ancient Persia, Sumeria, and Babylonia could believe in their divinity. Prognosticators and fortune-tellers wore them so that their readings would be more illuminated. The stones connected them with the formation of the stars and primordial creation; they were sacred.

These mystic qualities are wasted without proper understanding. It would be like placing a gold necklace around a dog's neck; a dog cannot appreciate its value. Stones and minerals are the foundation of all plant, animal, and human life. The magnificent bejewelled sachamama (mother of the forest) represents the mineral origin of life on earth.

At the top left there are two sumirunas; the one on the left has a shining corona that is symbolic of his sublime power. He holds a lustrous encanto that radiates incandescent light for healing deadly diseases. It is so bright that he needs to hide it in his clothing, because if these stones are seen by a person who has not dieted properly, they can cause *daño* (harm and illness). On the other hand, diviners can display their stones and embellish their bodies with them like magicians. To his right, the sumiruna with a pipe heals by singing the encantos' ícaros.

Once when I was ill, I remembered that I had a ring with a very precious stone that I should have put on sooner; stones can heal without the need for soplos. Even artificial stones can still have a degree of power. To benefit from a stone's power, you fold it into a cloth or tea towel like a rosary and carry it around in your pocket or under your belt.

To the right of the sumirunas is a *lobo marino* (*Otaria flavescens,* or sea lion), a *yangunturo* (*Priodontes maximus,* or giant armadillo), a bufeo colorado, a scarlet macaw (*Ara macao*), and an anguilamama (electric eel). Like the sachavaca, *paujil* (curassow), pumas, and jaguars, these animals carry stones inside their stomachs for digestion. Below you can see the black *sachavaca macho* (male tapir) and the patterned sachavaca (female).

Guacamayo and other birds that visit *colpas* (salt licks) often swallow small stones or grit that are mixed into the clay. Colpas are mines for these birds, as grit is essential for their digestion and help break down seeds in the absence of heavy teeth that would upset the balance of a flying bird. These gizzard stones are usually smooth and round and are used to heal hemorrhages after they have first been removed from the animal and smoked. The *ruro* (gizzard) of the paujil can also be used to heal oral and vaginal hemorrhages; it is removed and dried in a rag. When required, it is boiled for five minutes with the paujil's liver, and the water is drunk.

Stones can also be found in certain kinds of fish, and these bring good fortune to the finder. If you find one, you should wrap it in a red or blue cloth and keep it safe. Stones found inside plants can also bring good luck, so be careful when cutting plants down, in case they contain one.

We can use stones as charms to protect ourselves against such evils as intrigue, hostility, and

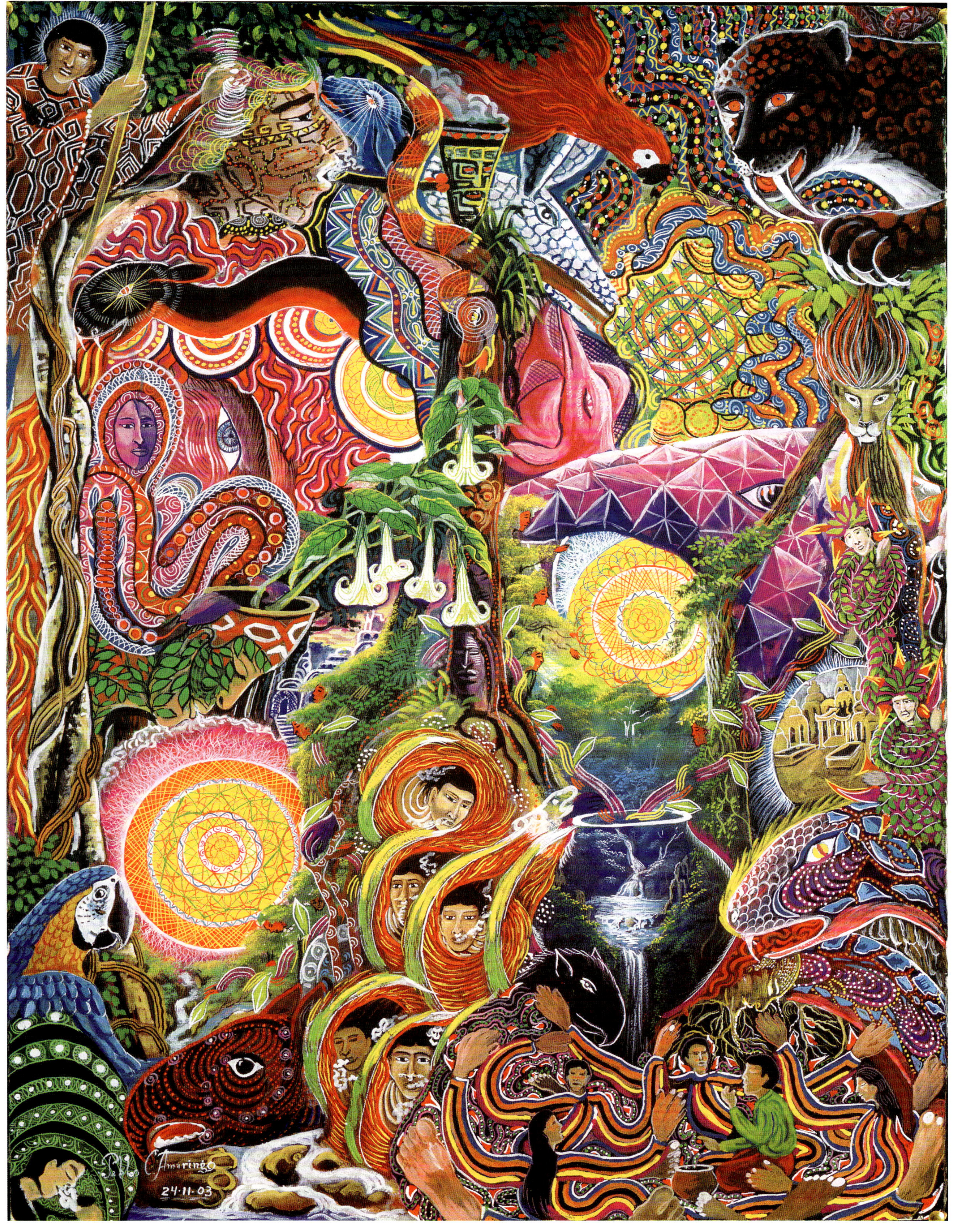

EL ENCANTO DE LAS PIEDRAS
2003, Gouache on Arches Paper
57 x 76 cm.

envy. The stones are placed in a bowl with water, covered, and left for eight days in a cool, dry place. One glass of this water is drunk each day to relieve discomfort, rage, and sadness. It also kills hunger so it can be useful when dieting or to avoid gluttony.

Above you see the sabre-toothed jaguar, which attacks enemy sorcery with its long teeth. Beneath its paw the *nina puma* (fire puma) emerges from a tree that has been struck by lightning and broken. This can leave a stone inside its trunk or roots, and what is left is called an *ila,* a Quechua term for a tree or rock that has been struck by lightning. They are highly revered and much care should be taken with them. They come from lightning and, seen in the state of mareación, they are magical and full of esoteric powers. One cannot receive them without proper dieting and purging with ayahuasca.

Shamans seek these ila and use them to learn about lightning. The stone is placed in a bowl with some water, covered, and left in a cool, dry place for eight days. Early on the ninth day, the water is drunk and a monthlong dieta begins. The learning takes place during sleep, unlike ayahuasca, which teaches through visions.

Nina puma is the personification of air and wind that gives shape and sanctity to the mountains, deserts, rivers, and lakes; the sanctuary of spirits who teach us their natural wisdom. This feline nina puma transforms itself into the king of the spirit world.

Below, you see shamans surrounded by elemental fire, which teaches the esoteric mysteries of the encantos. The two gold spheres, with the matrix of living crystalline energy, show the nuclear forces inside the encantos.

The spiral on the interlocking grid shows that creation has a spiral form, which we see on every level from the DNA helix to the spiral-shaped galaxies. You can look through the spaces in the grid and see other worlds.

Winding around the grid, you see blue and red spirals and whorls symbolic of the brain. They reassure you of the possibility of reaching your maximum potential by opening the parts of your brain that are closed. Your capacity to learn, store, and retrieve information is the most outstanding phenomenon of the universe. This opening of the mind occurs in the ayahuasca mareación, when the mind opens like the pages of a book and you can witness and gain insight into many complex things that are normally hidden in waking consciousness.

When the brain is not used sufficiently, it goes soft, just as when the pages of a book are exposed to humidity they stick together and will not open. The brain needs to be exercised and sometimes we must refresh our knowledge. I do this every year and this is when the stones are useful; they help one to rediscover.

Growing from the pipe is the visionary plant toé. The flower of the toé is called an angel's trumpet, as this is what the angels play to infuse the forest with celestial music. Also emerging from the pipe is a snake with very fine threads like the legs of a centipede, but so fine that they are scarcely visible. You can hear the hissing sound it makes as it glides through the jungle, with a sensual rippling along its length. The threads are sensory antennae that perceive the vibrations caused by other creatures, and can even hear movements deep within the earth.

Every encanto possesses an individual vibration or ícaro. It is very beautiful to hear them when placed inside tinajas from which they impart ícaros never before heard. When you hear ícaros emanating from the tinajas, you may even hear your own ícaros that are still to be learned, yet are already in existence. The modern world does not have the sound it used to have, the sound of the primordial world. We experience discordance; nature's rhythm, so essential to humanity, has been disrupted, and the spirit beings are not happy.

The landscape depicted on the tinaja symbolizes the sublime element of water, which is essential to all living things. The ancient Temple of Pachamama (Mother Earth) to the right is where you learn how the diverse forms of life on earth have evolved to be completely interconnected.

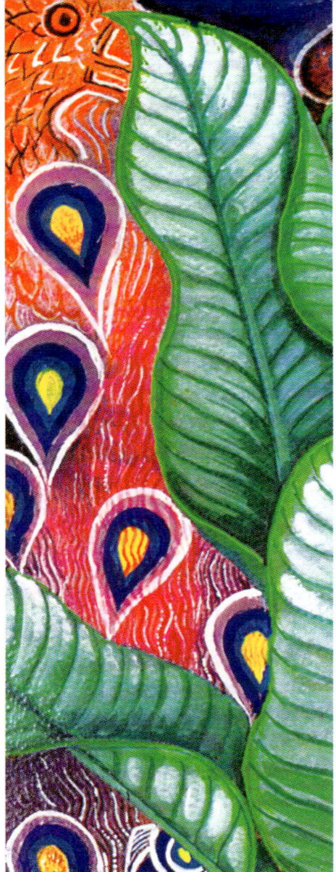

PATIQUINA SAMAI

ALIENTO DE LAS PATIQUINA

The *patiquina* (*Dieffenbachia* sp.) is widely used in Peru in baños florales for counteracting *brujeria* (witchcraft) and attracting positive energy. You can also simply chant its ícaro to summon its powerful spirit and impart good health. The four varieties of patiquina seen here are *verde, blanco, negro,* and *pintado* (green, white, black, and mottled), each with its own spirit or guardian that you can see beside each of the plants.

The patiquina verde on the top right is used to represent the lungs of a person; the different shades of green ranging from the edge of the leaf to its center indicate the state of the person's lungs. In this case you can see a good state of health.

As breath is the embodiment of spirit, the leaf indicates the essence of a person's being, while the heart is symbolized by the roots and veins of the plant. When the lungs are unwell, the heart fails as well, because it cannot do its proper job of circulating the essence of life to enable us to live harmoniously.

To heal a person of tuberculosis a curandero will chant the ícaro of the patiquina and administer baths of patiquina leaves as part of the diet.

The patiquina blanca on the upper left is used in floral baths so that your work or business flourishes, or for good luck. It has the power to elevate your consciousness. It is also used for guarding against brujeria and if grown in your garden or carried on your person, it protects you from bad intentions, envy, or *mal de ojo* (evil eye).

You can heal sorcery in just two or three days with the patiquina blanca, but you must know how. It will not be effective on criminals, murderers, or people who have performed abortions or used enchantment to get their own way. If the person has a good heart, then the plant heals; otherwise it will do more harm to the sick person.

The patiquina negra seen below right is used for protection against *hechicería* or brujeria and acts like a shield. Brujeria does not normally kill the victim unless the sickness has persisted for a long time. Hechicería, however, does kill and this is the main use of patiquina negra and patiquina pintada.

The blue rings ascending from the curandero's forehead shows his power to heal. Chanting the ícaro of one of these patiquinas gives immense power to a curandero's sopladas and to his ayahuasca ceremonies.

If you focus on your breath while thinking of something important to you, such as asking for a remedy or advice, the patiquina will show you. The curanderos in the ceremony below intend to use the knowledge for virtuous purposes. They receive this wisdom with appreciation, love, and humility, and the plant is showing them the six-pointed star (hexagram).

The six-pointed star confers understanding of what you are really asking. This is very important

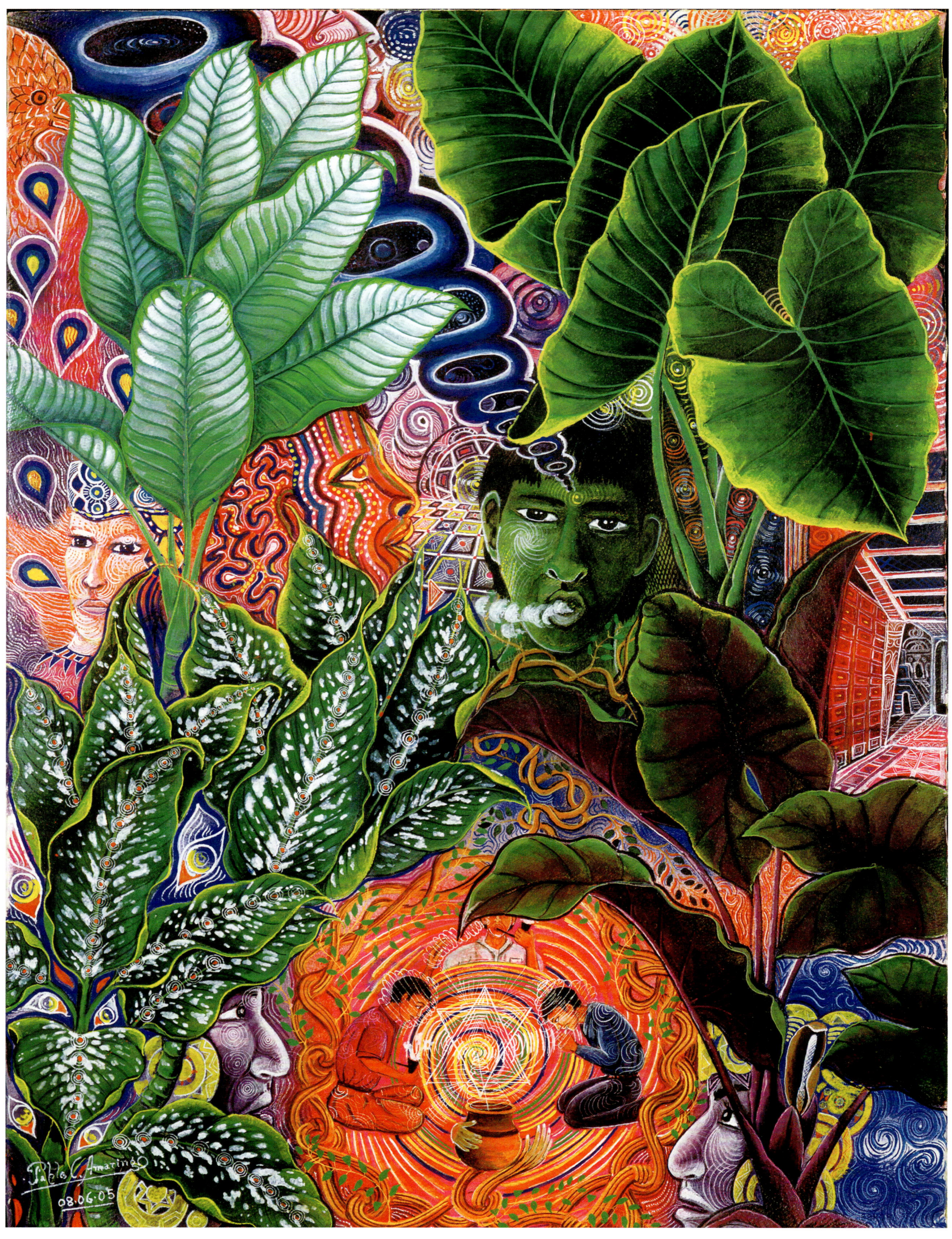

PATIQUINA SAMAI
Aliento de las Patiquina
2005, Gouache on Arches Paper
57 x 76 cm.

when drinking ayahuasca; you should ask as though addressing your grandfather or however you wish, but ask to be taught what you need to know. "I am drinking you so that you teach me something." Then you will receive.

In our ignorance we make errors, but when we have learned, we no longer do so. If you are going to heal somebody, you should understand your motivation, that you are doing it from the goodness of your heart. In this way you will be successful. If there is any reluctance, the energy will not get through to them because our cells and auras function according to the openness of the heart.

Our efforts will always bring progress unless there is inner contradiction. Often our plans do not work out because a part of us is saying no, feeling doubt or fear, and this prevents the realization of our plans. We must be in the flow and project the outcome we desire. We must understand that the focus of our mind is a part of the force that makes our plans successful.

The temple on the right is where a vegetalista learns about healing with flowers, roots, bark, and branches; with perfumes and smells, and with the claws of the sachavaca and the *sajino* (collared peccary). The claws break off the animal naturally, then the shaman heats them and inserts them in his nostrils. It does not cause bleeding. He then diets for four hours while smelling the burnt claws to absorb their healing power.

On the lower right you see copal smoke, which is used to cure ear infections. The smoke of copal is like a fumigant that kills bacteria inside the ear.

The ayahuasca twisting and forming a circle around the ceremony symbolizes an all-seeing eye for perceiving both physical reality and the spirit world. Some plants show you in your dreams, but ayahuasca teaches while you are fully conscious. The star in the center of the ceremony is formed of two overlaid triangles and symbolizes humanity and divine perfection.

Above is an entrance to a temple, like a crown. Here sublime spirits teach shamans the mystic nature and workings of plant cells. God has made humans reliant on the oxygen produced by plants.

The red circles on the ridges of the patiquina pintada leaves represent the breath of the plant cells producing oxygen. We must protect plants for the sake of our children, as man is turning the earth into a desert. The survival of animal and human life depends on plants so we must protect and love them if we are to live in peace.

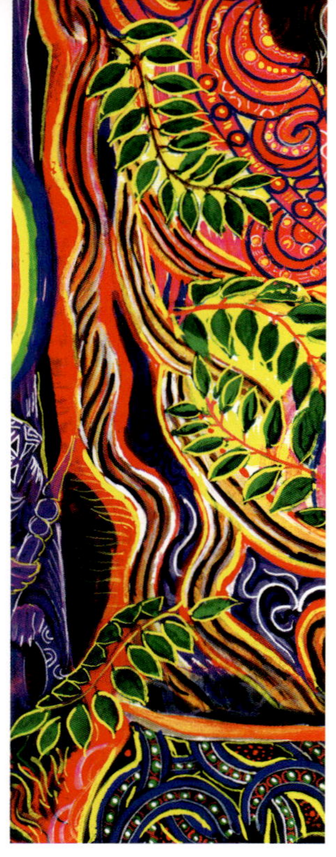

AYAHUASCA CHAYANA

LLEGADA DE LA AYAHUASCA

Ayahuasca chayana means "the arrival of ayahuasca," and refers to the onset of colorful visions—mareación—that this medicine provokes. At this time elemental spirits, *napeae,* and *camenae* arrive singing and orchestrating the mystical setting of the ceremony. They are seen here emerging from the tinaja with chacruna leaves.

The spirits bring perfumes and balms to prepare and protect the maestros; the *onaya,* sumiruna, banco puma, and banco sumi. They must also dress in brilliant vests made of scales like armor, to shield them from virotes and the *sacrataquina* (malignant chants) of sorcerers.

The camenae bring electromagnetic nets to capture and entangle the sorcery. They teach the maestro other evasive skills, such as how to foresee where he will be attacked. The maestro learns from the jaguar how to mesmerize enemies who want to kill him.

I remember one day I was taking care of a shop in the market by the harbor in Pucallpa, and I heard someone chanting a sacrataquina inside a nearby house. I understood because he was singing in Quechua, and wondered who he wanted to kill. The words described the funeral mass of his victim and his shroud, the people who would cry for him, and the cemetery where he would be buried. He sang to a bird called the *huancahui* (*Herpetotheres cachinnans,* laughing falcon), which cried bitterly as the man's family would cry for him when he was dead. I felt quite awful and outraged. I have never done work like this. He was a cruel and malevolent sorcerer and I could tell by the way he sang that he was getting pleasure from it. The next day I no longer wanted to take care of the shop, because of the sorcery that had taken place next door.

The *puma machacos* (snakes with the skin of a jaguar) emit rainbow-colored arkanas that encircle the ayahuasca ceremony and deflect any sorcery. They allow the maestros to study the ícaros, suck out illness with their mariri (magical phlegm), and perform other healing arts in safety. The hide of jaguar is thick, so the snake's vest is very strong and impenetrable.

The sublime master wearing a blue-scaled vest is a sumiruna from ancient Atlantis. He is here to teach the wisdom of the esoteric sciences that originated in Lemuria and were later brought to Atlantis.

On either side of the painting are magnificent beings known as the *sylphidae.* In the trees on the left are the spirits of the earth. They are called *refadim.* You can see the *yana yakumama* (black anaconda), which is the mother of the waters. The yana yakumama serves and guards the maestros with its great mesmeric power, so they can accomplish their good works.

The sumiruna holding his scepter is dressed in a protective purple robe made of the cells of mariris. The armored scales of the *pucaboa* (red boa) beneath him also protect him.

The ayahuasca vine on the left branches several times, and the offshoots are like its children. That is why, when you cut ayahuasca, you avoid cutting where there are many offshoots. If you wish you can

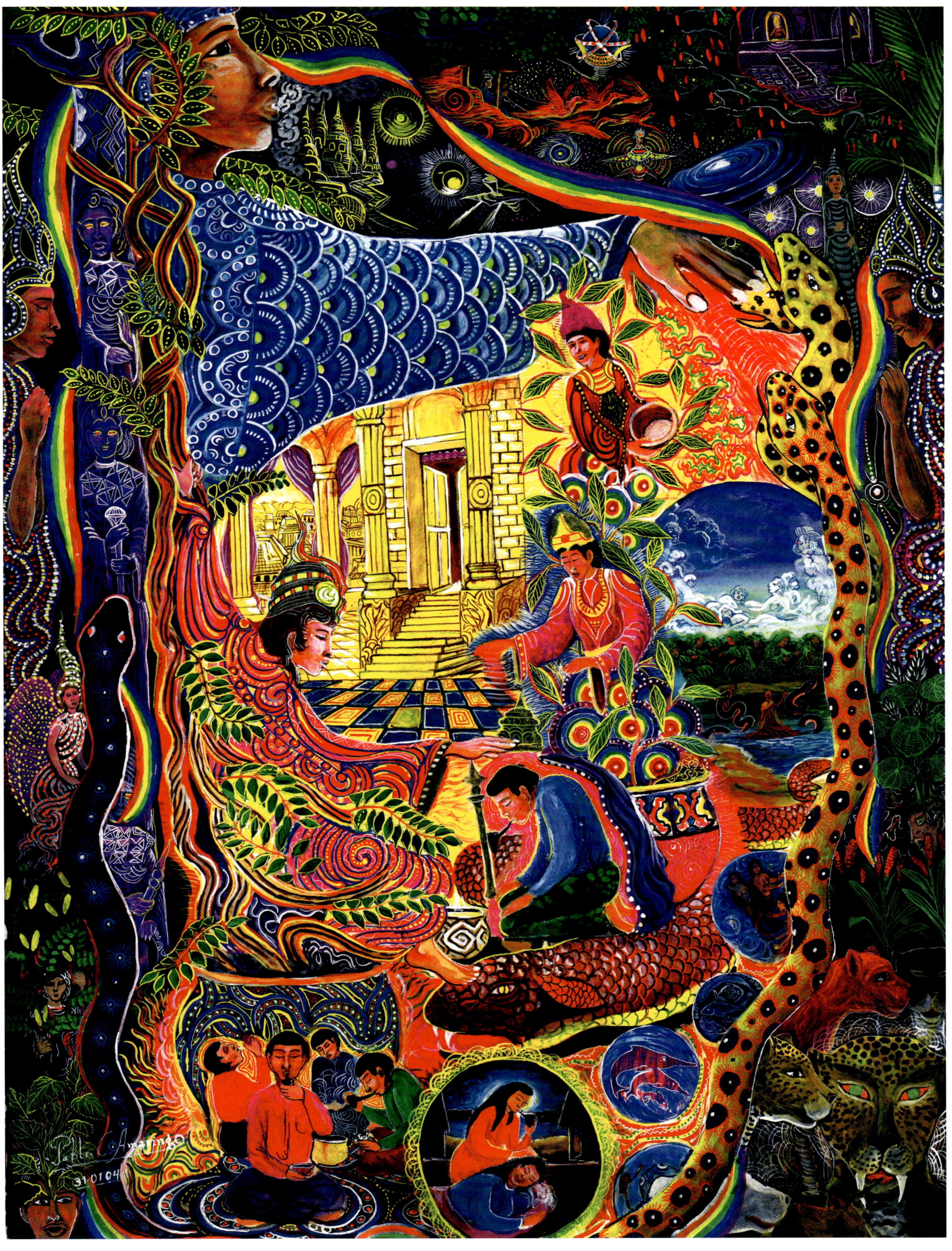

AYAHUASCA CHAYANA
Llegada de la Ayahuasca
2004, Gouache on Arches Paper
57 x 76 cm.

replant any surplus to your needs, as it will grow again. In the golden temple the ayahuasca teaches about the upbringing and care of children. There must be love between the father and his children; he must not be withdrawn. When the child is a baby, the father should hold it in his arms and cuddle it, and later hold its little hands to help it walk.

The experience of ayahuasca is similar to being taught by your own grandfather. Here it teaches that children should respect and not play with sacred objects, such as the shaman's bag, his tobacco, pipes, and ceremonial garb. In front of the golden temple is an exalted master, a prince or *ayar* from Atlantis who teaches about the spiritual conception and development of children, that it requires justice, discipline, love, and wisdom. This ayar wears a turban, which signifies his nobility and majestic authority.

He teaches how you should raise your child—not just from birth, but from the time of conception. You should conceive a child only when you are in good health, and preferably be in retreat for a period of three or four months before conceiving. This way the baby will be born strong and healthy. You should never conceive a child while you are drunk or seriously ill.

In the temple you are taught to nurture your home and family. You learn to care for the structure of your home and to inspect the drains, roof, and gutters, to be ready for days such as the one we experienced yesterday, when the rain poured and the streets became rivers of mud. Even the dogs took shelter anywhere they could and the noise was so loud we could not hear ourselves speak; all we could do was watch the spectacle and chew coca.

People seldom maintain their homes properly anymore. A woman who does so is not only taking care of her house, she is a good mother and wife, and serves her family. She has an attentive eye, sees everything, and watches out for danger. She is hardworking and takes care of family possessions and pets.

At the top of the painting, the tree with red fruit is the *punga* (*Bombax munguba*); it grows near water and in swamps. It reaches thirty meters, and from its soft wood a medicinal phlegmlike resin is secreted. A vegetalista chants the ícaro of this tree when he extracts virotes; his *llausa* (saliva or mucus) retains the virote. The palace by the punga is where the mysteries of the mariri and the soplo are taught.

Next to the punga tree you see a powerful vegetalista soaring on his flaming chariot, which is pulled by the *puca tibemamas* (sparrow hawk).

Leaves of ayahuasca, seen lower left, are rubbed under children's armpits to make them grow up to be decent, reliable, conscientious adults. Three leaves are rubbed on the sweat glands of the armpits, where it is absorbed more quickly.

The formidable banco puma, lower right corner, is smoking his pipe. This knowledgeable master is accompanied by his feline spirit allies, the *yanapuma* (black puma), and the *lluichopuma* (red puma), who protect the vegetalistas healing here.

TRUENO AYAHUASCA

This variety of ayahuasca normally has yellow flowers, but here they appear white because yacu toé has been mixed into the brew, coloring the vision white. The ayahuasca liana can be seen growing from two Shipibo tinajas and forms two pillars that support a splendid palace of learning. People who learn here open their arms and say, "Blessed ayahuasca, you are my teacher," and that is why you are here.

The genios (guardian spirits) in this palace maintain vegetation in all its diversity, including its most luscious verdant forms. Drinking *trueno* (thunder) ayahuasca with a knowledgeable shaman can be an overwhelming experience, causing thunder and torrential rain to fall, but it integrates you strongly with the biological cycle of the Amazon.

Vegetalistas who learn from trueno ayahuasca specialize in the sonorous, resonant sound of thunder and its power to command respect. The power of this sound comes not from the throat, the source of our logical expression, but from deep within the body, from the *shungu,* a Quechua word meaning "stomach and heart." This is where our strength is; for example when we eat well, we speak louder. These shamans can hear the voices of sylphs, napeas, and dryads; that is air, water, and plant spirits, respectively.

On either side of the palace are towers. The one on the right is the tower of knowledge, where they teach people how to prepare the land for growing crops, and to sow seeds and nurture plants until harvest. It is important not to exhaust the soil, so the ayahuasca tells people what the next crop should be to replenish the nutrients in the soil. They learn how to nurture human beings, and to feed and care for a baby and guide its development.

When building a house, you learn how important your intention is. You learn where to locate it and how to orient it, using a compass to face the northeast so that it is protected from the prevailing winds.

Also in the tower of knowledge you learn the layout of gardens; where each plant will flourish to protect your house and give it a warm ambience. This applies to domestic plants. Wild plants are for protecting the natural environment.

The spirits construct their temples and palaces from precious stones encrusted with pearls and diamonds. All these have specific qualities and energies. Even if a house is humble it can still be a jewel, offering sanctuary and protection. The materials used in buildings have an influence on those who live and work in them. For example, you should never lay floor tiles made from black stone; this should be reserved for places of power—courthouses or government institutions.

In the tower of knowledge an apprentice learns how to approach his work, whether as a tradesman, architect, carpenter, or potter. A jeweler learns how to craft the best and most exquisite necklaces, a cook learns how to prepare food from many different cuisines, and a doctor learns how to prepare effective medicines.

Ayahuasca teaches you that no one job is greater or more important than another, just as no one

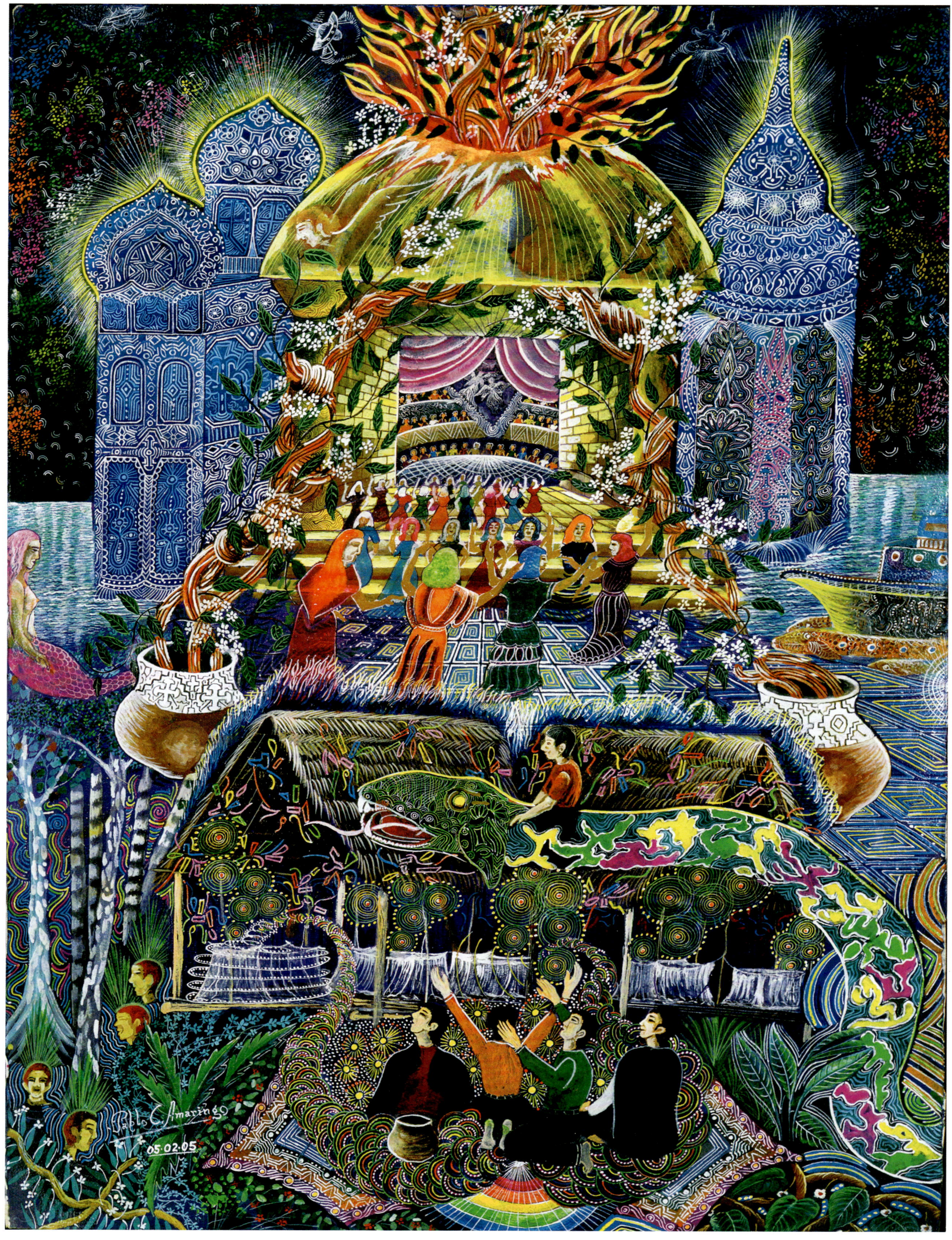

TRUENO AYAHUASCA
2005, Gouache on Arches Paper
57 x 77 cm.

plant is more important than another. Everything depends on growth and development, and each one is the right size to grow and flourish in its environment. Each of us has the potential to learn and develop our talents.

In the center of the palace the spirits are gathering on terraces to teach the sumirunas, onayas, bancos, and banco pumas (vegetalistas with varying powers) who are assembled inside.

In the tower on the left the apprentice learns the wisdom of his body and soul. Left in solitude and darkness without any distractions, your inner eye opens. You learn the language of your cells so you can control the natural processes of your physical body. This affects the aging process by instructing the cells not to deteriorate. If we could do this, we would not age or die and would always have the physical bodies of young people.

We must all learn how to educate and develop ourselves; it is important to start this before reaching the age of thirty-five. Whether you want to be a maestro or a man of worth and education, you should sow the seeds of your aspirations as early as you can. After the age of thirty-five you should be satisfied with what you have achieved in your life, because from then on our cells and vitality start to decline.

In this place of darkness you can understand your physical transience, your mortality, and even though you may despair when you see yourself in old age, you also understand that life is a continuum and that you will become another form of life. It is an important spiritual teaching that the apprentice receives here.

The spiritual beings have a project for us; paradise is not just in heaven, as religion has it. There is a place for us here on earth and we can be happy here. This is the secret knowledge of the beings that live in darkness.

In the lower part of the painting, vegetalistas are healing sorcery. The nets looking like *mosquiteros* trap the malignant sorcery. The sumiruna riding the snake defends the vegetalistas from sorcery. The snake forms a great protective circle around them, which is not completely visible in the painting. Lower right are patiquina verde (*Dieffenbachia* spp.) The trees on the left are *guacamayo caspi* (*Andira inermis*), and the beings with them are the *suni guacamayo caspi,* who nurture and protect the trees. The mermaid with the pink hair and tail is a *puca sirena* (pink mermaids who enchant men with song); on the right-hand side you can see the barco fantasma with the yacumama.

The flames blazing from the top of the cupola, intertwined with the ayahuasca vines, represent the energy. The palace itself symbolizes the shungu of ayahuasca trueno. In the cupola there are beings with wings preparing to fly to other places, other sanctuaries.

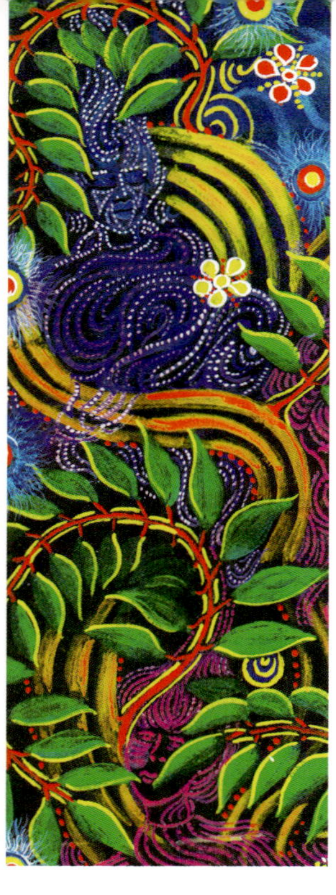

AUCA YACHAI
SABIDURÍA INDIGENA

This picture conveys the diverse knowledge that Amazonian people have of plants— not only their medicinal properties, but their value as a food resource. This has accumulated over centuries through communing with plant spirits, drinking ayahuasca, and following a dieta. A dieta is a discipline intended to bring about quiescence of our animal appetites and desires, so that we become more plantlike and receive teaching directly from the plant spirits. This goes beyond discovering a plant's pharmaceutical and healing properties. In a dieta, the personality of the shaman and the plant meet in a magical world.

It is essential that a shaman healing with ayahuasca be pure and impeccable; otherwise negative energies may ruin the ceremony. To achieve this, he retreats into a dieta lasting up to six months, which includes scrupulous hygiene, sexual abstinence, and eating simple food from the forest. The purification allows healing energy to flow from his body to his patient without any harmful elements.

He chants the ícaro of the correct plant to summon the appropriate wisdom for healing his patient. For example, to heal an external wound he might chant the ícaro of *caña de azúcar* (*Saccharum officinarum*). The sugar cane juice effectively cauterizes the wound by sealing the skin.

The shaman employs the rhythms of nature to his advantage. Three days after his initial healing, the sick person may be exposed to the rising and setting sun. The side of a tree trunk facing the sunrise has thinner bark than the side facing the sunset. Following the flow of nature, healing begins at sunrise and is completed when the sun goes down. At sunset the shaman chants and sweeps his *shapaca* (see glossary) over the patient's body to complete the healing.

Our hands correspond to the leaves of a tree, our arms to its branches, our legs to its trunk, and our feet to its roots. By seeing his patient as a plant, the shaman knows how to heal him with plant wisdom.

Many Indian healing practices are little known. For example, aching or bruised limbs are dressed with a paste made from the ash of the *pájaro bobo* or *sauco* (*Alchornea castaneifolia*). The wood of these trees is also used for magical ceremonies. In the picture the leaves of the pájaro bobo tree are red and green, and the long yellow leaves are sauco leaves.

The *troncomoro* (a beaded strand) is worn by indigenous Amazonian people around the waist or neck as adornment. It is made of the nuts and seeds of the *pashaca* (*Microlobium acaciifolium*), and *sacha* (*Virola calophylla*) trees, each of which has a different property. To speed recovery, troncomoros are placed around the patient, but first they are sanctified by being buried in the earth. After they have been washed, the same water is used to wash the patient's feet. In this way the patient is protected from a relapse.

Belts and bracelets made from *ampi huasca* (*Chondredendron tomentosum,* curare) protect from

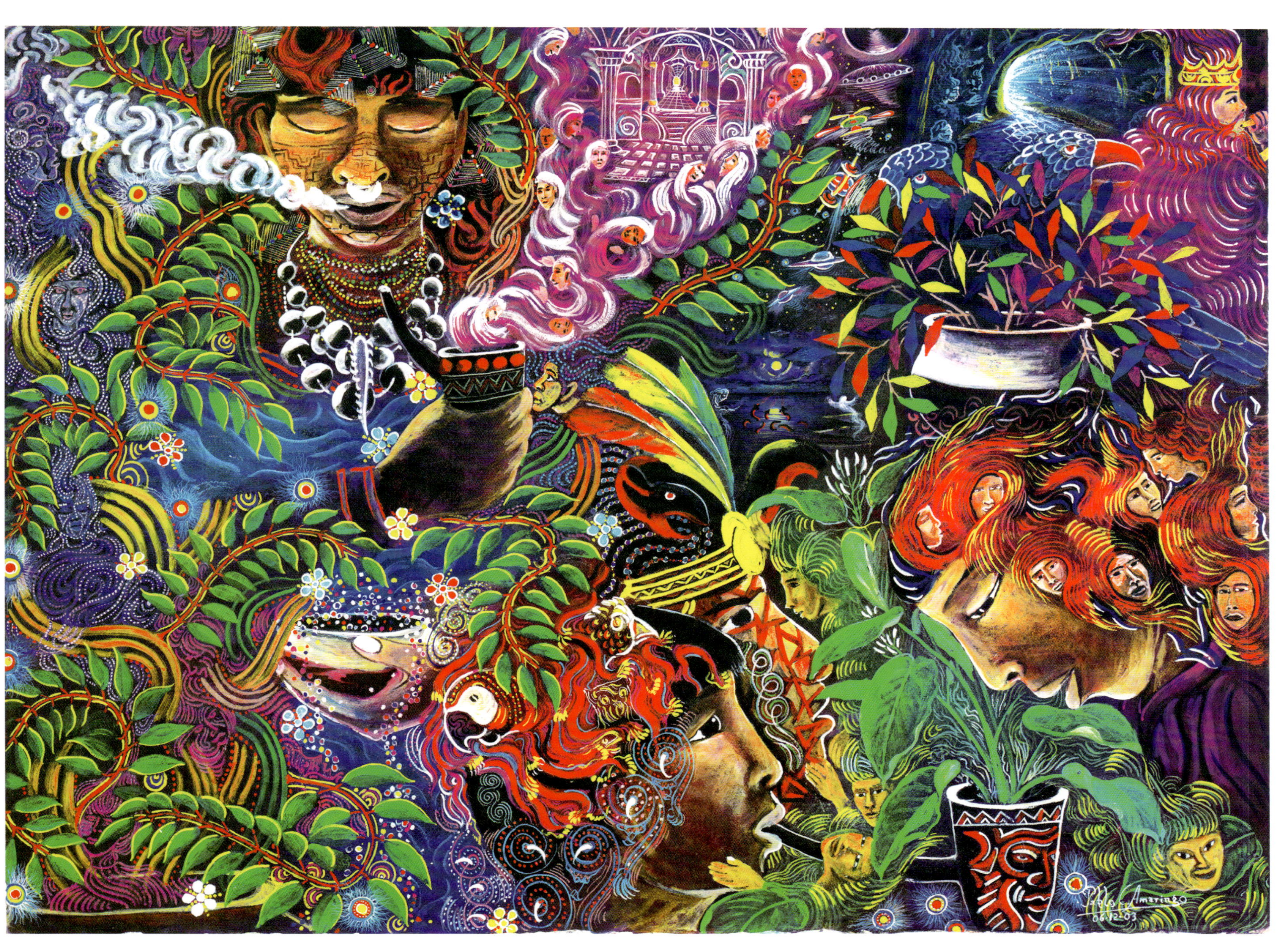

AUCA YACHAI
Sabiduría Indígena
2003, Gouache on Arches Paper
56 x 76 cm.

ingested poison and reduce the effect of the venom of a snakebite. *Carahuasca* (*Guatteria modesta*) is woven with ayahuasca vine to make bracelets that keep the heart strong. Both of these plants are visible in the painting.

Children are encouraged to chew *tamshi* (*Heteropsis jenmanii*) fibers to keep their teeth healthy and prevent decay. The juice of *yumanasa* (*Mutinga calabulal*) and *guayusa* (*Piper callosum*) leaves are mixed to make an eye ointment for maintaining good eyesight and preventing infection. Guayusa can also be taken as tea for its stimulating effect and for keeping people awake.

Medicinal baths are prepared by boiling black stones from the riverbed with the bark of *huacapú* (*Minquartia guianensis*), *tahuarí*, *cumaceba* (*Swartzia polyphylla*), and *capirona* (*Calycophyllum spruceanum*) leaves. They are cooked in an enormous earthenware pot for a day. Five days before the new moon, the person bathes. It gives immunity to many diseases and was the secret of my father's continued good health; he became ill only when he was about to die.

Indigenous people often have strict prohibitions about dealing with the dead. After contact, people must purify themselves with strong-smelling leaves and exclude themselves from the community for the next eight days. Houses are built directly on the ground, with the earth as floor, so the dead are often buried in their houses and their spirits prevented from returning home by blocking the grave with netting. After three attempts the spirit will no longer try to return, as by then it will have entered the spirit world.

The yellow feathers in the crown of the *nativo* (native) attract jaguars. A wide headband denotes his greater skill and status as a hunter. Colored resins from the barks of the *cumaca* (*Licania* sp.) and *remocaspi* (*Aspidosperma excelsum*) trees are used for painting the body before hunting. The camouflage protects the hunter from dangerous animals and enables him to avoid frightening the prey.

The perceptions of an indigenous Amazonian are different from ours. They can see from the perspective of an animal and from this they understand how the jaguar or puma lives, how its markings and stripes protect it. This knowledge enables them to protect themselves by using the animal's markings.

They do not identify their understanding of the world as a system of belief. If something is held sacred, it can be relied upon as a reality. For example, they can make you retrace your steps by looking for your footprint and carefully removing the ground around it. It is then hidden under *huito* (in glossary). This compels you, as though spellbound, to go back.

The size of a vegetalista's pipe indicates his level of mastery and rank. The pipes of the bancos are not as large as those of the murayas, while the sumiruna's pipe is the largest. The sumiruna in the painting is smoking his pipe to take out mariri.

When the vegetalista prepares you for a diet, he blows tobacco smoke over your body and chants the ícaro of salt to cleanse your skin of salty impurities. After this you no longer crave salt, sugar, or alcohol, and can diet for long periods desiring only bland foods.

In the lower part of the picture they are learning how to divine using pipe smoke. In it they see everything, whether things are well at home or if anybody wants to harm you.

Having no written language, much is communicated in symbolic ways. When a man loves a woman he will know from the way she ties her ribbon whether she loves him, too. A plant or animal will often be identified by saying what it does or what it is used for, not by its name.

If you are robbed, the shaman gathers the *maramara* plant (*Urea baccifera*) and *catahua* (*Hura crepitans*). Then he carefully wraps them with the leaves of the *piñón colorado* (*Jatropha gossypifolia*, the type that has five lobes) and ties the bundle. He then hits it repeatedly with his shacapa while blowing sopladas. This makes the thief become very ill with fever so that finally he confesses his crime and returns the stolen property.

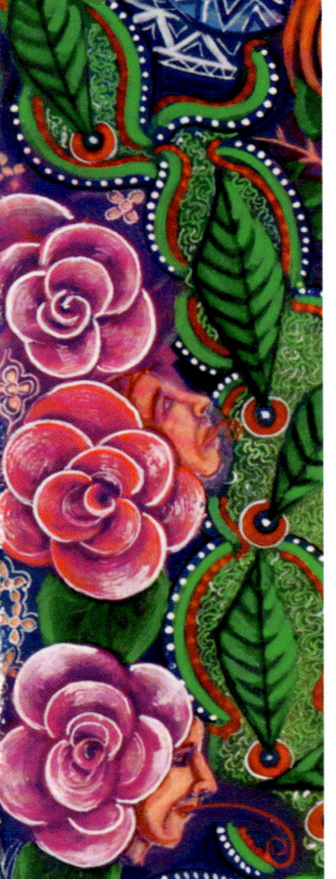

ALLPA MANCHARI

ELEMENTOS DE LA TIERRA

Allpa manchari is guardian of the heart of the earth. He connects us with the earth that nurtures us. *Manchari* means "feared and respected"; allpa manchari is lord of the earth. He has magnificently curved horns, which symbolize the elements of the earth that support life and metabolic processes necessary for growth.

Here the spirits are communing with the spirit of ayahuasca and the *ashpa runa* (earth people) who serve allpa manchari. They do not suffer from the intense heat and fire in the heart of the earth, because it is their domain.

A human being cannot grow and fully develop if he lives in the same place all his life; it is like always eating the same food. For this reason, allpa manchari teaches that it is natural to look for varied experiences in life, and that you should allow others to do the same if they wish. Staying in one place can lead to boredom and possibly depression. This is why I enjoy staying in new places for a few days or months—it makes me feel alive. When you return home you are not the same as before. If you travel you can see things from a different perspective, talk about different issues, and change your views.

Smoking his pipe on the upper left is a sumiruna who has attained esoteric mastery. He can perceive extrasensory dimensions and travel to unknown realms.

The allpa manchari ingests combustible gases produced by the earth, drinks petroleum, and eats carboniferous substances. The ashpa runa also consume combustible materials to feed their alchemical fires that produce spiritual energy, which is released through volcanic eruptions. When a volcano erupts we feel changed because we are part of their alchemical process.

Plants and flowers are the foundation of life on earth. Using energy from the sun they grow and blossom in the spring, giving us vitality through their flowers, even before yielding any fruit. Similarly, young men and women keep the secret of life. When a man is young and beautiful and a woman is young and lovely, they are flowering too. But little by little they start to decay; the flower loses form until it is no longer a flower. This is part of life.

We take pleasure from watching the changing cycles of nature—it gives us a kind of nourishment. If the plants die due to our destructive activities, we will have to hide in caves or retreat into holes because the world will be a desert.

At the bottom of the picture among the flowers is the face of a woman. She is an elemental being, a diva, and a connoisseur of floral perfumes, aromatic essences, incense, and ointments for healing and purifying.

The flowers have five petals, incorporating the geometry of a pentagram. Each petal represents the entire plant: the leaf, root, flower, fruit, and seed. The fuchsia color represents purposeful activity and teaches us to be helpful and warm to others. The flowers are held in the hands of his servants,

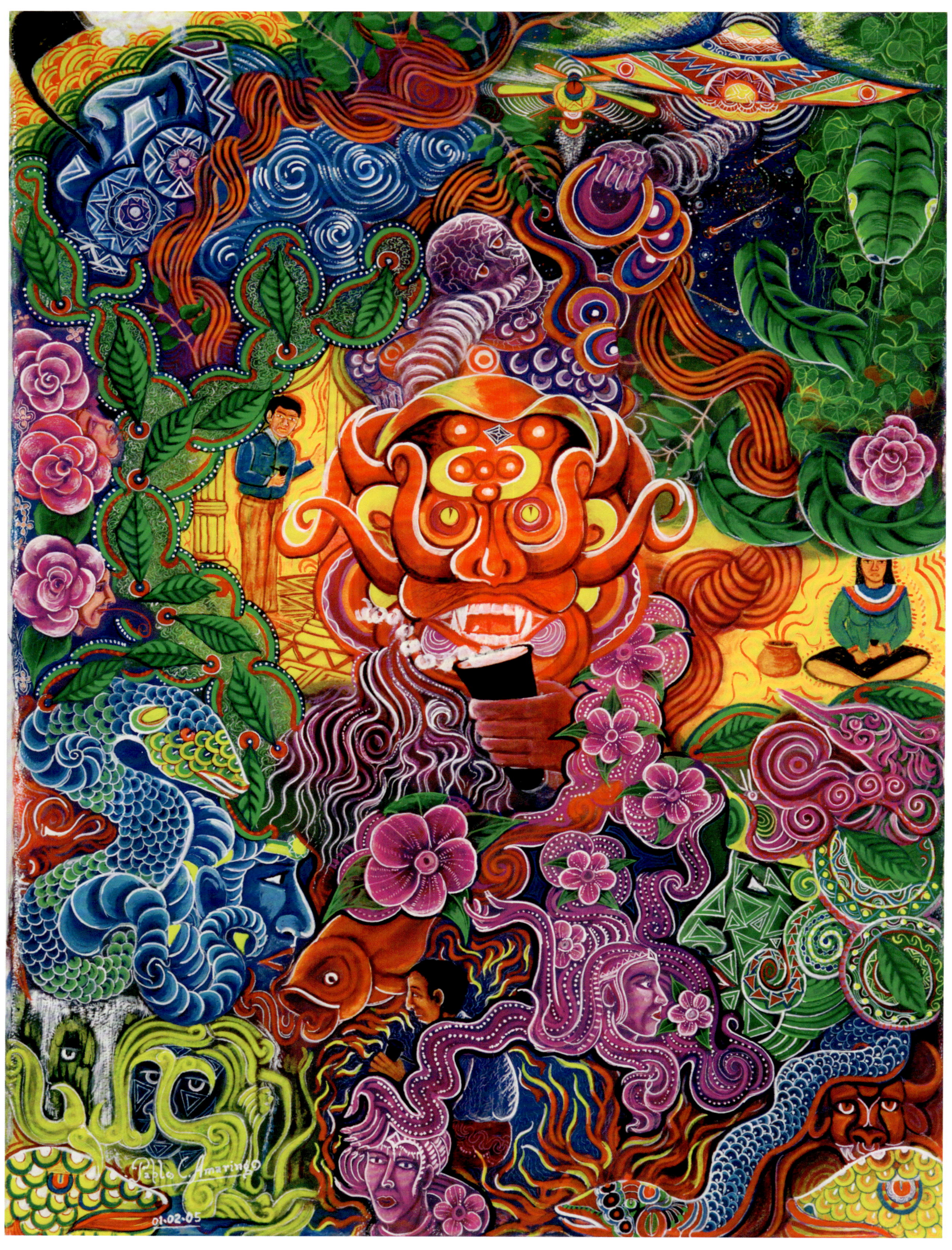

ALLPA MANCHARI
Elementos de la Tierra
2005, Gouache on Arches Paper
57 x 76 cm.

the *mamaicunas* and the *tataicunas*. These teach us to look at different ways of transforming our lives, to be cocreators, and to fully participate in the unfolding of our lives.

On the left are the red and black seeds of the *huayruro* tree (*Ormosia amazónica*). The brightly colored huayruro seeds are widely used in Amazonian jewelry and craft work; they protect travelers and attract good fortune. The green and red aura around the vegetation shows the spiritual energy that enables it to grow, reproduce, and flourish.

For a shaman to heal people from outside his community, it helps if he understands the cultural background of the person. This is particularly important when he comes from another continent, which is happening increasingly today. When he knows this he can heal wherever they are from.

The blue *huacras* (horns) are the cornucopia that symbolize abundance and nurturing of the earth, and are part of the Peruvian coat of arms. When something is going well they say, *"Huacra sumaq talac talac,"* which means, "The horn is moving magnificently."

If the allpa manchari does not keep you in his grasp, journeying to other worlds can be very dangerous. He gives us a vital connection with the earth, without which we would die, as life in other realms has a different manifestation. Even the moon has a different form of life from here on earth. If the allpa manchari blows on you with *ashpa manchari sisa,* which is the flowers of the allpa manchari, you are bonded to this being in the heart of the earth and you can travel safely to anywhere in the universe. This flower is seen on the upper right with a giant green snake coiled around it, together with the ayahuasca vine.

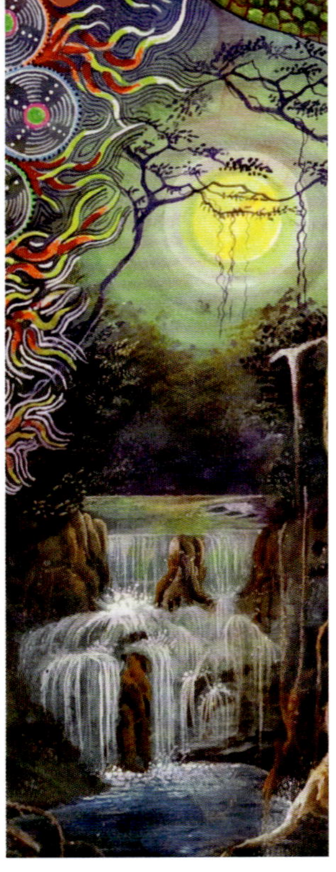

LLULLO MACHACO

SERPIENTE VERDE

Llullo means "green, tender, and young" in Quechua. In the Peruvian selva, people call babies *llullos.* The idea expressed in this picture is that however our life unfolds and whatever our destiny might be, we are all born in absolute perfection. We are innocent when we come into the world and have no guile or deceit—like an immaculate book in which nothing has yet been written, a *tabula rasa* ("blank slate" in Latin). As we grow we learn imperfection from our perceptions, experience, and upbringing, but when we are born we are pure and unsullied.

The llullo machaco symbolizes this purity and its verdant color is like the virgin forest—uncultivated and uncontaminated—yet our religion teaches us that the purity of our soul is already tainted at birth by "original sin." This doctrine stems from Adam and Eve's disobedience of God, so even a newborn baby who has never done anything evil is flawed and sinful. The serpent has long been regarded as the evil that tempted them into eating the fruit of the Tree of Knowledge. Religions have used these guilty feelings to manipulate and control us, and no good has come of it. The llullo machaco, however, teaches us that the serpent was also a redeemer who brought knowledge to Adam and Eve so that they could understand good and evil and thereby develop their humanity and morality.

The birds are messengers from the celestial temples and palaces seen above. The macaw, the fuchsia-colored *yahuar garza* (*Platalea ajaja,* roseate spoonbill), the red-feathered bird with the yellow beak is the *chicua* (*Piaya cayana,* squirrel cuckoo), the *chicuro* (*Eubucco bourcierii,* redheaded barbet), the *yana pishco* (*Cotinga cayana,* spangled cotinga), and the *suisui* (scarlet tanager). All these birds possess much esoteric wisdom; they warn of danger, reveal secrets, and teach the sublime wisdom of love.

We need love from the moment we are born until we die—it is perfection. Without love you can have justice, but justice without love is mere power and arrogance. Power without love eventually corrupts, whether you are a chief, a father, a mayor, or a president. You do things that you should not do because you believe that you are superior and that no one can teach you anything. You do not realize that even an ant that knows nothing can still teach you something.

We must allow ourselves our mistakes and faults because we know that no one is perfect. We need to accept that each of us has different beliefs, values, and ideals. Some confuse love with overbearing concern, and the result is disastrous. Problems need to be talked about at the right time and instead of shouting, you should speak nicely. My son Juan is like this when directing his workers, and encourages them to live and feel good about themselves.

You need love to have faith in life right up to the moment of your death. It does not fail us; it cannot. The llullo machaco teaches that there are four types of love: *agape, eros, philia,* and *storge.* The most sublime and heavenly expression of love is agape, which is based on the principle of unconditional love toward others. Eros, philia, and storge are the three aspects of love that can fail, but

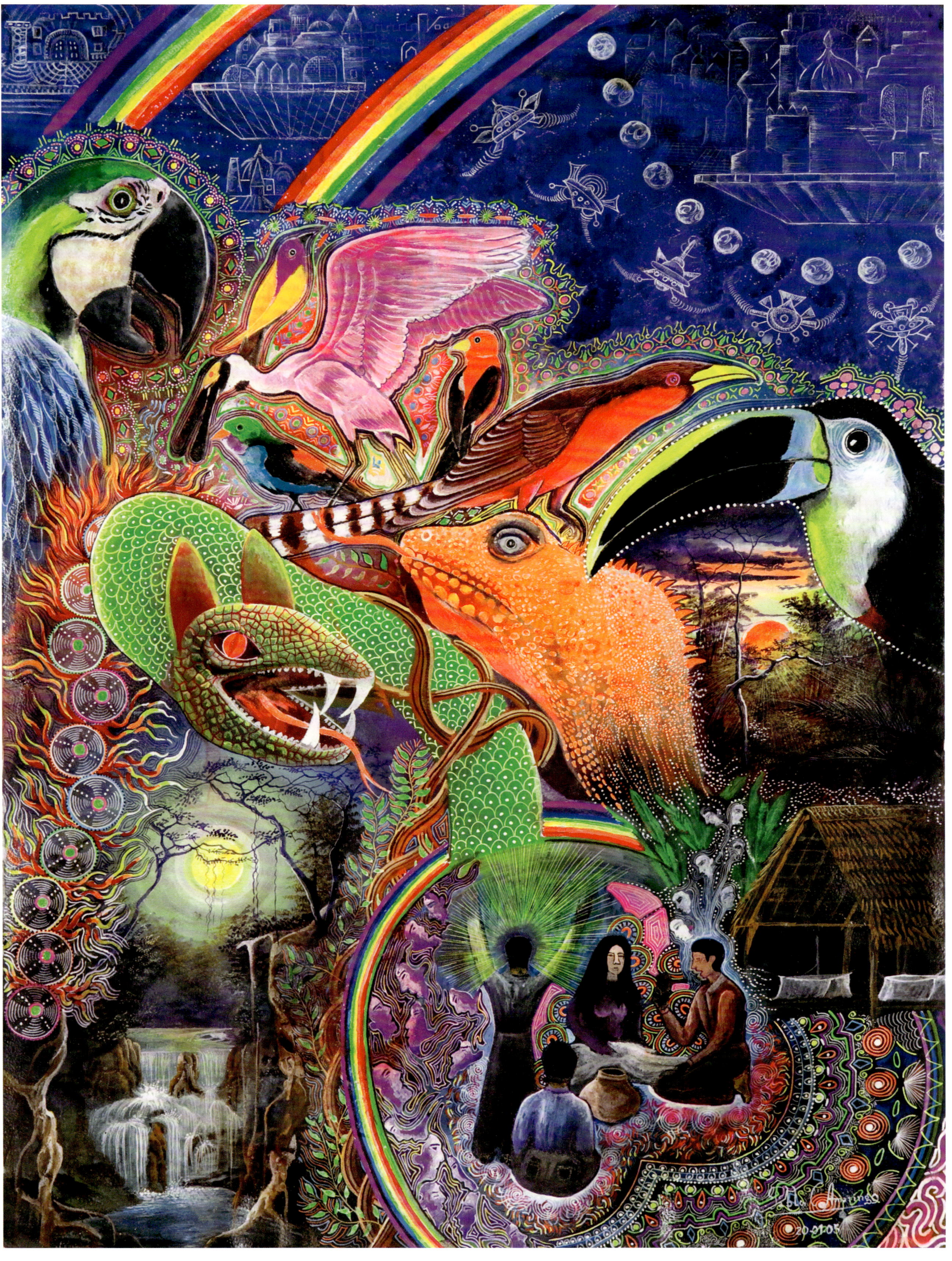

LLULLO MACHACO
Serpiente Verde
2005, Gouache on Arches Paper
57 x 77 cm.

agape is immutable, as it is based on the divine grace of the spirits that cannot be broken. It is altruism, selfless service to all humanity.

Storge is the natural love and affection between a parent and child; philia is the love and loyalty that we have for friends, family, and community; and eros is the passion and sensual desire between a man and a woman. Love is not *gnosis* (knowledge), but *epignosis* (above knowledge). You can read all the literature about ayahuasca, understand its chemical composition and so on—this is gnosis; but only when you drink it is there the possibility of realization of this knowledge, or epignosis.

The orange *caballo machaco* is an aquatic iguana not often seen these days. It inhabits the undergrowth near cochas bravas. Just to its right is the sunset, heralding the transformation that occurs at nightfall when the moon rises, left, and all the animals in the forest move to different locations. The moon has an important influence on the metabolism of plants and animals, and affects the minds of humans.

To the lower right are the white-faced *tunchis* (ghosts); and below, the shamans in their ayahuasca ceremony learn the divine knowledge of love. The shaman with outstretched arms is receiving power and wisdom from the llullu machaco.

To the left are traces of neutrinos and electromagnetic fields, the basis of all physical matter that creates the splendor of terrestrial and aquatic life.

The toucan is a metaphor for suffering. When he lacks water, he opens his beak and squawks to plead for rain. Love is like water; we cannot live without either. When we have love, seeing others suffer is unbearable but we must not be depressed. An open heart gives us energy to work for others so that they feel free to live life to the fullest. When someone is sad we can help by offering advice, making jokes, or giving consolation.

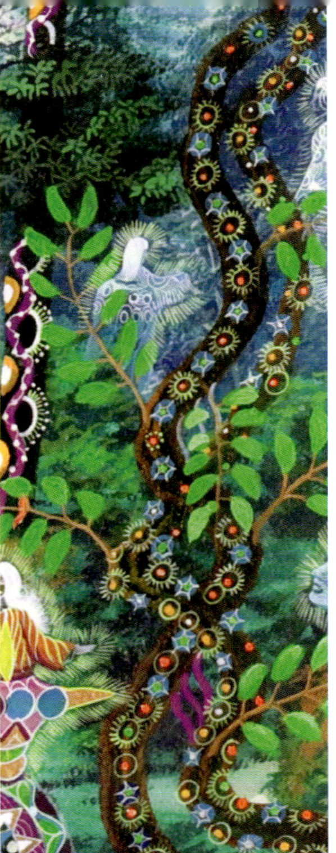

HUARMI TAQUINA

ÍCARO DE MUJER

Huarmi taquina is the ícaro for drawing in feminine creative energy to an ayahuasca ceremony. It is a very powerful ícaro that connects us to Mother Earth, the Pachamama—the principle that brings new life to the world. When the huarmi taquina is sung you feel a vibration flowing through you, harmonizing you with the great rhythm of the cosmos. The song of creation reverberates with all life and the earth itself.

Feminine energy is universal and part of the fabric of the cosmos. Just as a woman spins and weaves textiles to produce clothes, so this divine force spins and weaves cosmic particles into the fabric of life. When a woman works with spiritual awareness she communes with an unfathomable force and her cloth has no beginning or end. Wearing a cloak woven in one piece without any seams connects you with the source of cosmic life, so you flourish and evolve a higher state of consciousness. It makes you wise in matters of divinity and you live an enlightened life.

The stars and planets in the top left corner show that this ícaro originates in the galaxies near the center of the universe. The mask of flowers next to it symbolizes the hidden power of a woman; she has more will power, blood, and passion than a man. A woman who is a mother represents Mother Earth. The spirals at the top denote the nurturing love that a mother has for her children, and men should also have this. As long as the feminine force is present, there is respect for life. If men are left on their own they can be very destructive.

When the huarmi taquina is sung it bestows feminine powers of intuition, creativity, love, and patience. The water at the lower right represents the eternal source of life from which the DNA spiral helixes grow upward. Life on earth emerged from the seas and oceans, and we emerge from the amniotic fluid of our mother's womb when we are born. The women here have merged with the rocks and trees in the landscape, showing that the feminine force is the omnipresent source of nourishment and abundance. The angelic beings above enjoy the earth as a mystical garden filled with luscious plants and exquisitely fragrant flowers.

The lianas and flowers to the right show how nature delights us with her beauty. The shapes, colors, and scents of the flowers are invitations to love and harmony. When you give yourself a floral bath, these flowers attract taquinas that penetrate your skin. When my sister was seriously ill, the curandera performed ícaros and sopladas while she slept; this alone healed her.

Beauty in any of its forms is an expression of the feminine essence, and we naturally respond with love and admiration. For many people today the absence of beauty causes separation from the feminine principle and leads to unhappiness and spiritual deprivation. The beautiful women and sirenas seen below near the waters represent divine union and beauty. The horse symbolizes the burdens that people carry in their lives, but despite the suffering, we persevere, give birth to new life, and nurture our children.

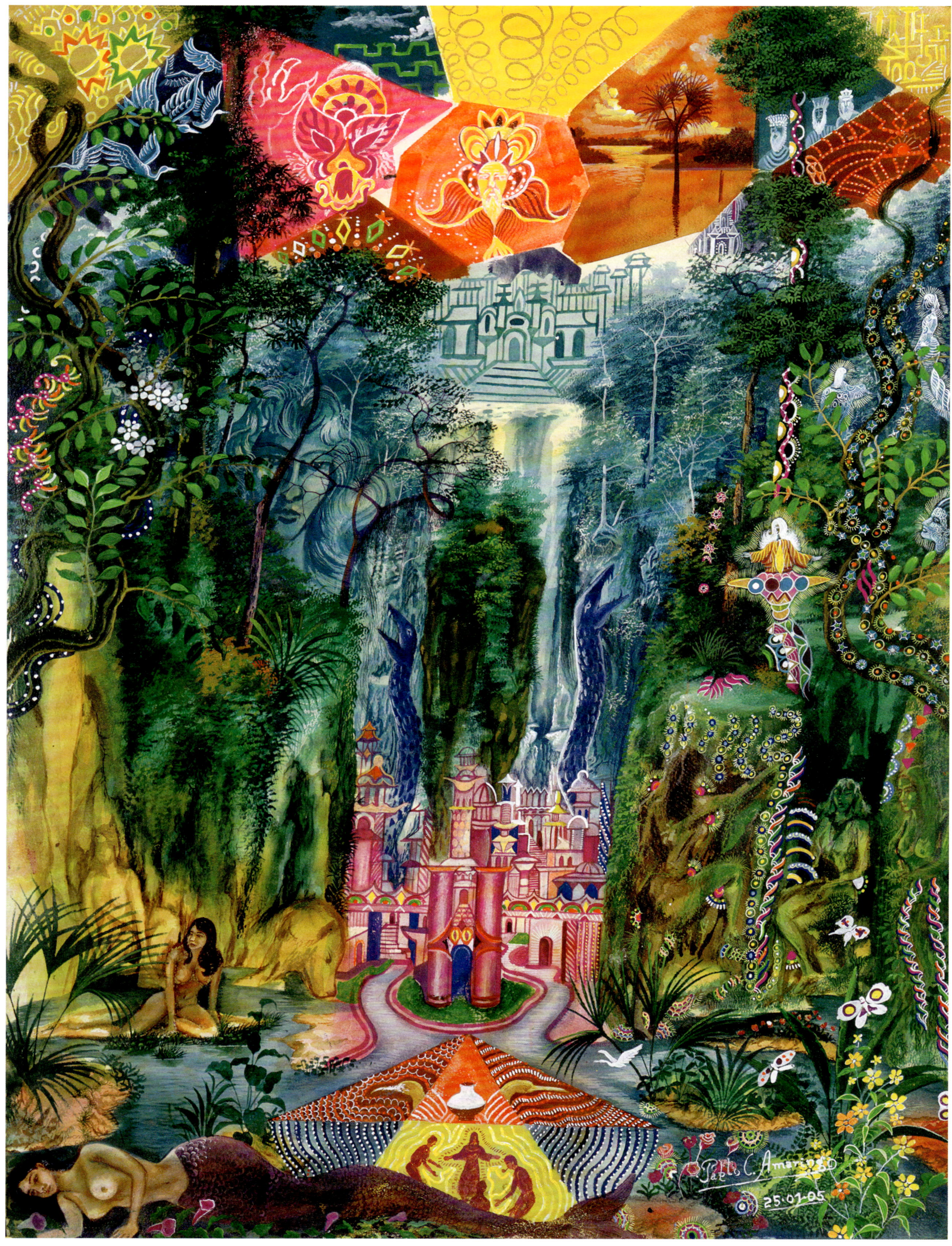

HUARMI TAQUINA
Ícaro de Mujer
2005, Gouache on Arches Paper
57 x 77 cm.

The celestial masters created the palace and temples seen in the center, which represent the mystical feminine soul that informs and brings life into existence on the earth. The blue temple above symbolizes purity and spiritual love, and the water that flows from there down to the lower temple baptizes and purifies the earth. In the waterfall are yacumama *llipian,* which means "brilliant" or "shining" yacumama; they can fly between realms. To the left you see the form of a naked man symbolizing the sacred union between man and woman that is needed in order to create life and form a family.

Left of the temple, the face of the woman in blue represents the sacred feminine force. This is eternal and we live within the unknowable mystery of her being.

The ark at the bottom of the painting represents the sacrosanct. Within the ark is a pyramid in which a princess brings understanding of the mystic origins of cosmic life to the sumiruna and his apprentices. In the upper part of the pyramid is a tinaja used by indigenous women for carrying water on their heads for their families. To either side are birds who sing songs of the river, the forest, and the universe.

At the bottom is the shapely figure of a sirena from the depths of the water. She has evolved from the element of water, and we are made of the same water as she. Water is the fountain of life that renews and vitalizes us so we can flourish. That is why a woman's tears refresh, cleanse, and transform her.

Wearing silk helps maintain good health, and particularly when unwell, wearing silk pajamas at night is very healing. A woman's taquina is like silk woven into a textile as smooth as her beautiful skin. We should always take good care of our skin. It is where our cosmic nature resides and if you look after it, your house will remain in good repair.

We are made of music. Artists do well to whistle or chant, as I do when I paint, much as a little bird sings to protect the forest. The huarmi taquina is the vibration of the spirit that accompanies creation; everyone feels happy when they hear it. The woman represents beauty and her chant is an exquisite birdsong lifting your spirits like lianas twisting up into the sky.

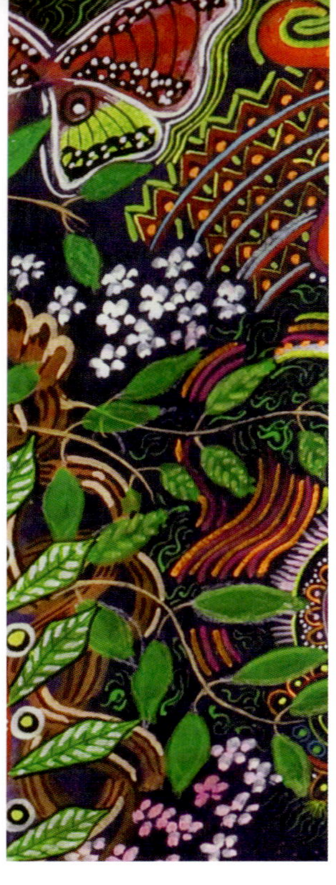

CHACRUNA VERSUCUM

CANCIÓN DE LA CHACRUNA (2003 VERSION)

Two versions of this painting are presented in this book. We originally had *Chacruna Versucum* professionally photographed in 2007. The following year Pablo showed us a revised version of this work (the second version). This was an exception, as he had painted over the original canvas, something he does not usually do. He commented that on reflection, he regretted repainting the canvas, and this is one of the reasons we felt it important to include both versions. We talked with him to understand his thinking and development between the two paintings. *Versucum* is a Latin word meaning "verse" or "canto." (Note that both versions are dated 2003 on the paintings.)

The five dryads sing gently to heal through the circle of chacruna leaves; they transmit love and healing energy. These special fairies accompany the plants of the rain forest and, in particular, the tree canopy. They represent the five points of the human body, the five outer senses, and the many inner faculties that are derived from them: intelligence, consideration, knowledge, discernment, spiritual perception, and wisdom.

In the central circle the celestial aspects of chacruna are represented by the circle of leaves, while the ayahuasca vine represents the earth. Combining the two plants is a symbolic union between heaven and earth. In the center is the origin of chemicals and the biological beginnings of life. The circle also symbolizes the sections of the earth, which you see in the center: north, south, east, and west. Between the leaves of the chacruna are the eyes through which we perceive the world; however, they are not entirely physical.

The circle at the bottom left is where the chacruna versucum chants enter and leave the underworld of the yacurunas (water people), seen on the right hand side through the *chomos* (small earthen pots) of the indigenous Amazonian Indians.

To the upper right is the banco puma in his terrestrial form when dieting in the forest, while below is how he appears when healing people—as a puma with a man's head. He can also transform himself into a monkey and ride the yakumama. The man fallen from the capsized boat is being taken by the yacurunas to their underwater realm. Looking on is the *nitimushcanpoma,* or "crushing tiger"—a jaguar with a human head with serpents growing out of it.

The hummingbirds are like messengers. Their sweet trills are the most delicate and sublime ícaros for chanting to people looking for new strength or suffering dreadful illnesses. However, they must be sung with utmost precision.

These celestial spirits dwell in the palaces and temples at the top, where they gather to sing songs of adoration. This is a very different concept from the kind of worship you find in today's religions. We have been brought up to have the same religion as our parents and grandparents, but there are

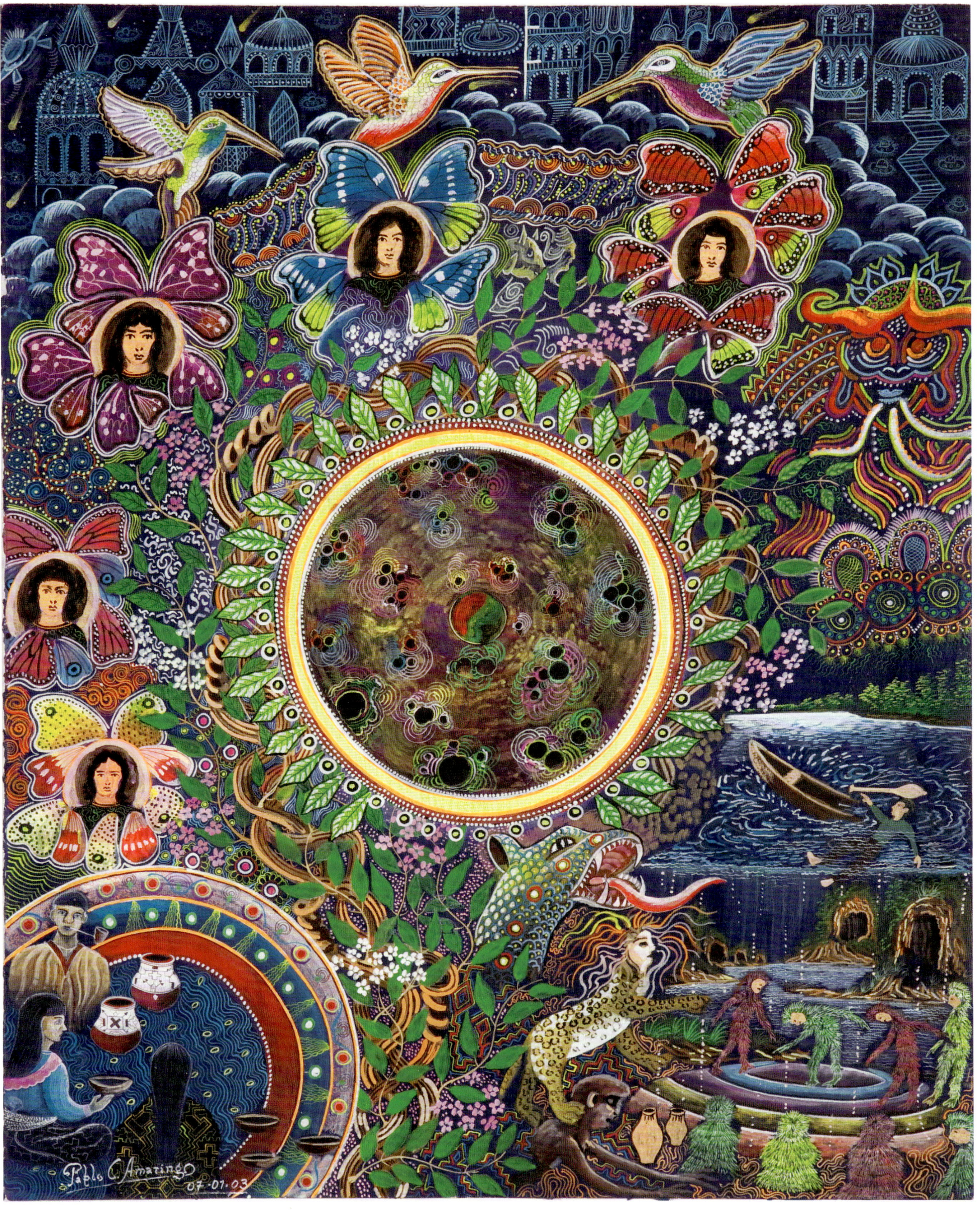

CHACRUNA VERSUCUM
Canción de la Chacruna
2003, Gouache on Arches Paper
51 x 64 cm.

many forms of religion. For example, art is a form of religion and each of us needs to explore and consider religion for ourselves.

This has been an important quest in my life. My parents and grandparents were strict Catholics, but I have always looked for a different religion for my equilibrium. If you belong to a religion that claims it owns the truth, you can become hateful or disrespectful to persons of a different religion, because your beliefs differ. This creates discord and separation among people and is mistaken. I see religion as something that is open and free, just as one has the freedom to choose the color of one's clothes. No one should tell you what to wear, and this is how religion should be.

In this respect, in compiling this book we share a facet of religion, because we endeavor to understand each other. What we are doing together here is like a religion—it is something we are determined to do, and it liberates us.

This is a book of freedom, faith, and loyalty to the imagination, and it will be a treasure for the world. This is what the painting teaches here, to know how to share with respect and honor for the other person. If, for example, the other person has a different form of belief, a different way of dressing, this should not seem bad to you because this is what he likes; this is what brings him happiness.

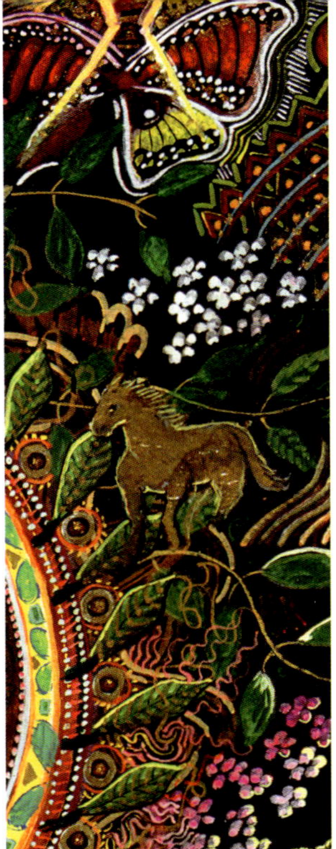

CHACRUNA VERSUCUM

CANCIÓN DE LA CHACRUNA (2007 VERSION)

After I had painted the earlier version, I realized that chacruna has many other attributes and I wanted to emphasise its celestial aspects. This is the reason why I have painted this second version.

In the center is the triangle of life representing body, soul, and spirit—the geometry of the human body, which has many triangular shapes. The triangle with an eye on each corner symbolizes intelligence, wisdom, and the merging of wisdom and ignorance. This is what we call the nucleus of the mirror. Our inner depths are reflected through our eyes. In the circle are all the constituents of life, the patterns that form our bodies, limbs, and organs, as well as our mental faculties and our intelligence; everything is blended together here.

The triangle of life is the golden symbol of the plants. It shows how life is created from biochemical activity forming plant cells, rocks, and minerals. All of these have combined to create life; our bodies and those of animals contain minerals and metals. In my visions I have seen eighteen metals in the body. The golden horses around the circle represent the energy that a person can receive from working with ayahuasca.

In this painting I have elaborated on how the yacuruna kidnap the man fishing from his canoe in the cocha: first the sirena lures him by her song, then the yakumama creates a whirlpool to capsize his canoe. Finally, the yacuruna drag him down to their world with a rope.

Surveying the scene is the *nitimushcanpoma* (a crushing tiger). It looks on with its finely tuned feline senses.

In the subaquatic world the yacuruna emerge from blue, purple, and yellow concentric tunnels. These tunnels lead to the city of the *hitrodos;* these beings never surface as the yacuruna do. Behind is the red yaku toro (water bull).

I repainted the dryads to show their forms of energy and geometry. Starting from the lower left, this first dryad radiates golden points that form a pentagram for healing sorcery and evil. The dryad above shows his golden points as a heart within a triangle. This is to relieve those who are unwell and suffer pain and stress. With this, the person becomes calm and blood circulation returns to normal.

The next dryad has triangles directed up and down to illustrate the connection between the spirit and the physical. We need to know that we have been created from spiritual matter; without spirit there would be no physical matter.

The next dryad shows us the importance of hope for love, for an exciting life. This teaching will come to us in our hour of need.

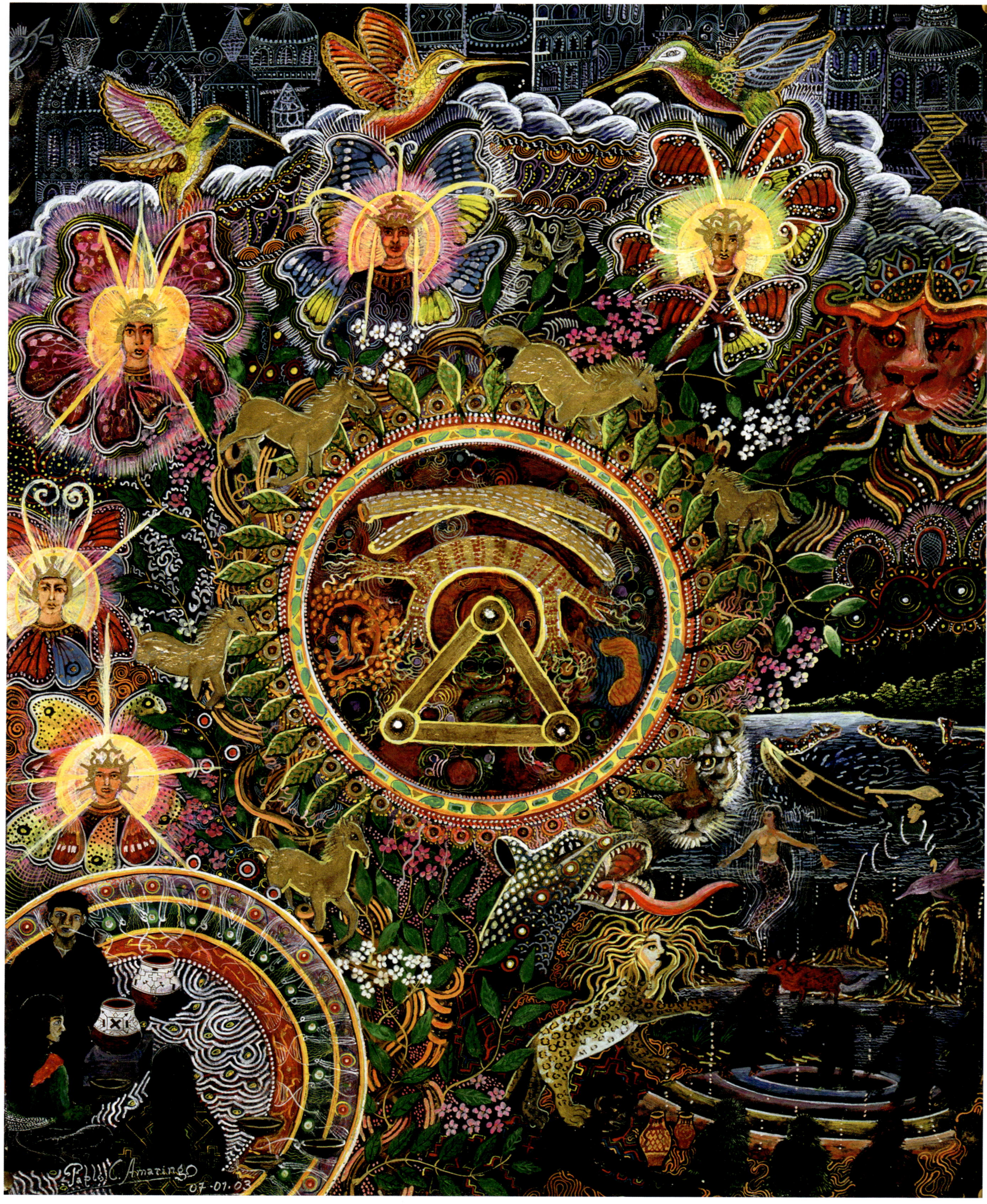

CHACRUNA VERSUCUM
Canción de la Chacruna
2007, Gouache on Arches Paper
51 x 64 cm.

The last dryad represents the acquisition of sacred teachings, holiness, and cleanliness of mind and body. This dryad shows how one should act to cultivate reason and be able to relate to people of all walks of life.

The banco puma was repainted to show that he has the ability to travel to other dimensions and galaxies; here he is no longer earthbound.

The empty chomos are repositories that receive the sounds of the rain forest, the rivers, plants, and animals. These have sounds and vibrations that are outside the range of human audibility and resonate from pole to pole.

When someone acts compassionately it uplifts the soul, increases the vibration of peace, love, and repose, and betters us all. Malevolent thoughts, pessimism, and harmful actions create dissonance in the soul, and these detrimental vibrations affect other people.

The current world does not have the sound it used to have. In the primordial era stones could speak and communicate with people. Now we suffer from contaminated sound that is mechanical and discordant. The spirit beings are not happy because the natural rhythmic sounds and harmonic vibrations that humanity needs have been changed.

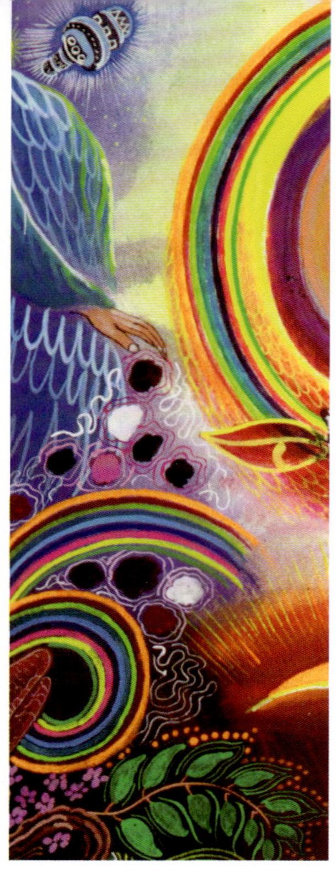

AYAHUASCA RAURA

LUZ DE LA AYAHUASCA

In this painting we see the changing influence emanating from the celestial bodies on our future, showing us that our destiny is not static; it is in constant flux and that we need to actively seek our future.

The sun, the moon, and the earth influence our lives. The waxing and waning of the moon is symbolic of our birth, death, and reincarnation. As the moon wanes, fades from sight, and emerges again, so do we. The moon also sets gently into the ocean, just as we descend into the depths of the earth when we die, but then, like the moon, we rise again. People should not believe that when we die we cease to exist. That is not the case, for each of us will emerge and rise again as a new person.

The earth in the picture is enveloped in a luminous rainbow, which represents the celestial influence of the huairamama, the cosmic serpent. We are taught that everything in the cosmos is subject to change and transformation. So it is with us. We need change, and that is just what is happening; many things in our lives are changing.

On the left we see Queen Samhadi, "the illuminated one," presenting to King Kundal a golden vessel containing a balsam prepared from the most fragrant plants and resins. It is a symbol of the natural world that surrounds us, all that we sense and perceive. The balsam represents the sun, the moon, and the earth, and is an instrument of our transformation, our path, our skills, and our intuition. Below the king you see the divine Shiva, who is symbolized by a skull. He represents the death of the physical and its subsequent spiritual transformation; he is both creator and destroyer.

The winged beings are the *angeles avatares,* the spiritual guardians who control the rotational, orbiting, and swaying movements of the earth.

On the right are the *huiririmas,* native spirits holding spears who are employed by sorcerers. Below them is the *camungo* bird (*Anhima cornuta,* horned screamer). It is alert, can hear the faintest sound, and warns vegetalistas of impending danger. Beside the camungo is the spirit guardian of the *tamshi* plant (*Carludovica divergens*), which is used to make rope, here growing out of the top of his head.

Much of life's rhythm is due to the influence of the moon. Without it, birds cannot procreate; they cannot give birth or incubate their fledglings. Fish cannot procreate and neither can we. The moon affects our moods and character. Not everyone is affected in the same way; it depends on our individual metabolism, our blood, and our spirit. This is why some people become disordered when the moon is full.

You see this with children who are especially susceptible to lunar influence. At the full moon they become angry and do not want to eat, drink, or even have anyone speak to them. These children should be protected with sopladas and chanted the ícaro of the moon. Although the moon is much

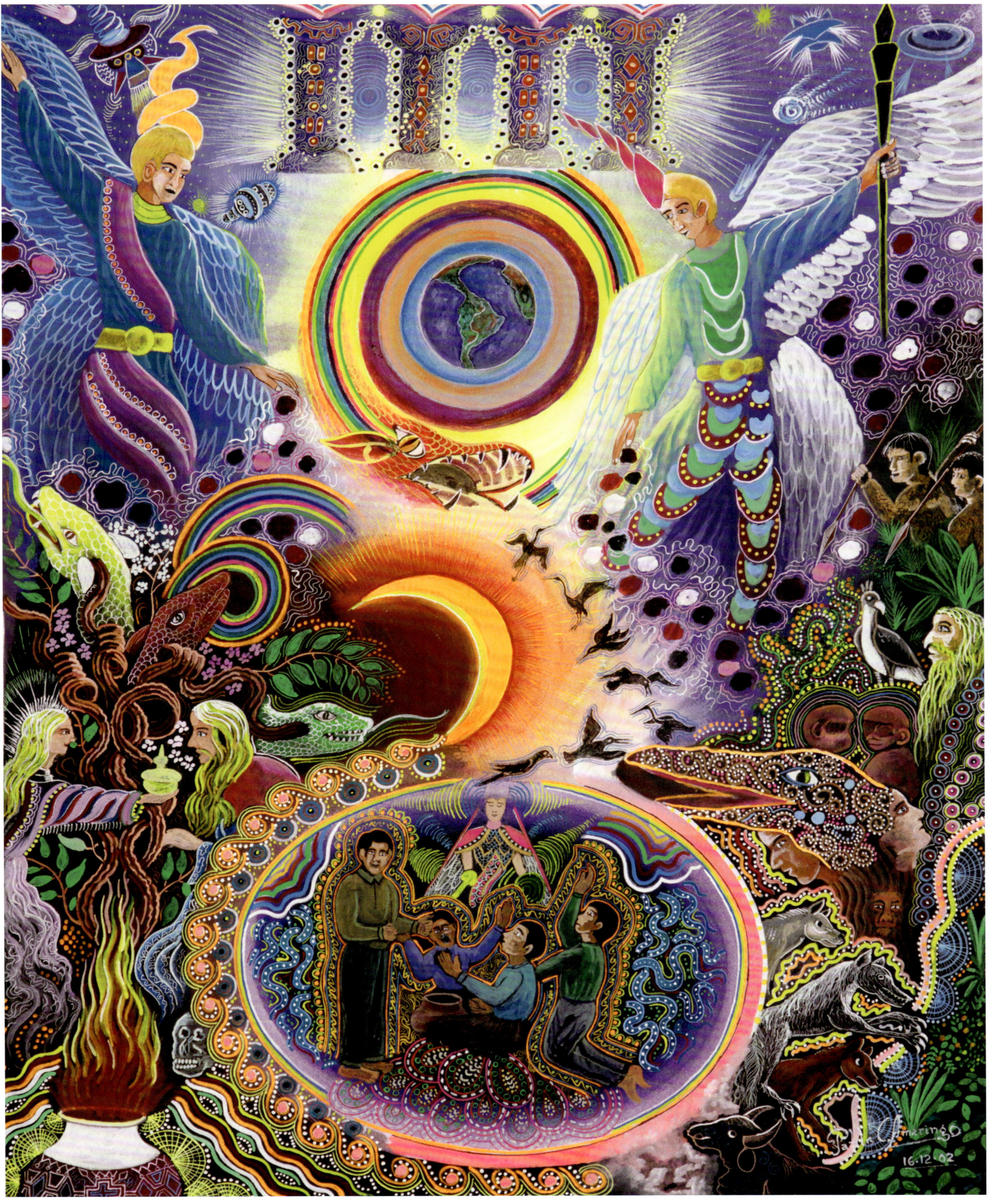

AYAHUASCA RAURA
Luz de la Ayahuasca
2002, Gouache on Arches Paper
51 x 64 cm.

smaller than the earth or the sun, it can influence both. This is what the eclipse of the sun in the painting is saying.

The ícaro is the sound of the universe, planets, stars, comets, and supernovas. Everything is created by music, by vibration, by sound. When the celestial spirits enlighten us with their wisdom, we receive the ability to sing ícaros and we become part of a divine choir. Music is universal, and we are made of primordial vibration. Ícaros are the music of creation.

Above you can see the Temple of the Three Windows, where you learn the ícaros of the celestial bodies and how the stars and planets die. The only way to get in is by flying and soaring in through a window.

You learn that you are tied to Mother Earth through your navel, as you were once tied to your mother. The ayahuasca vine represents the umbilical cord that bonds you to Mother Earth. There is an electromagnetic influence from the great mothers: the huairamama, yacumama, and sachamama, of the sky, the waters, and the land respectively. You can feel this much better walking barefoot, as the Indians do. Doing so gives us peace and reminds us that we too are indigenous beings.

The painting shows us that this knowledge is based on intuition. We see the birds flying and they represent the potential future that awaits us. Our future is not static or predestined. It is dynamic; our future changes according to our emotions, attitudes, and actions, whether they are positive or negative. We are the cocreators of our destiny. If we do not undertake constructive actions toward the future we want, it will not come and our lives will take a different direction. We risk going astray and as a result, having nothing. The birds are flying, exploring, and seeking their destiny, just as we should.

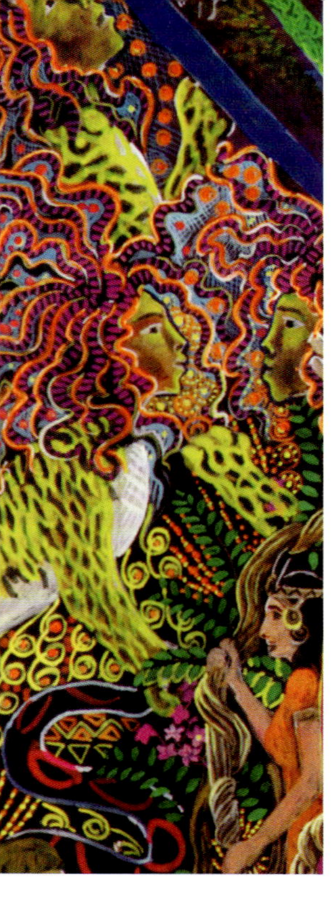

NUKÑO MASCHASHKA

DULCE VISIÓN

Here you can see pure joy emanating from a chant below, and the effect it has in other spiritual dimensions is shown in the spheres above. When the spirits begin to chant, it is not only audible in one place; their song is heard throughout creation.

Music is very special; it is the expression of joy, and it can imbue you with the flame of passion. All that has been brought into existence, the stars and the cosmos, is created by music and sound. Since it deeply influences our thinking and emotions, we should listen to music that inspires our highest humanity.

Because we are created from spirit we possess divine essence, and although we have many diverse religions, we have a single innate desire to venerate that which is sacred.

If you want to learn to play music, find a cross and practice standing in the middle after midnight. This is of more benefit than spending weeks in music school, because you will be helped by genios who will give you intuition, a well-tuned ear, and even a good voice.

If you want to chant well, you must go to a place where no one will hear you. You are not like a singer who learns a song that has previously been sung by others. A chant must be learned from the spirits, treated as sacred, and kept secret if it is to have power. Great onayas chant to call spirits into a ceremony and to strengthen their concentration. Although they are sublimely beautiful, they are not intended for entertainment. When used for healing, they are sung very quietly.

My uncle chanted so well that people were in awe of him. He was a good uncle to me and the only one with whom I could laugh. Once we went fishing in a very remote place and on the way back he asked me if I wanted to hear the ícaro of the *murohuayra* (spirit of the whirlwind), which, he informed me, was about to blow over the water in front of us. Then he sang. What a haunting sound! We were both stunned and a moment later the whirlwind started up, right in front of us. It was very strong.

Behind the spheres are the immaculate *arcontes* who generate life force from the sleeves of their robes. These waves originate in the mind of the divinity.

In the spheres are the seven divine muses, or *kunan versucum,* here represented by the seven colors of the rainbow and also contained in the seven notes of the diatonic scale. They resonate within us, as we are made from the pure energy of spirit. We are made of music, the vibrations of the spirit.

Each color inspires a different faculty to enable us to live in harmony with the natural world. The color red represents love, justice, and power; yellow, intelligence; green, life force and aura; orange represents knowledge; blue, spiritual wisdom and discernment; azure understanding; and violet, spirituality.

The vocation of a curandero is to serve ayahuasca and to receive the ícaros of the great arcontes. This is the aspiration of the onaya, muraya, banco puma, sumiruna, and, most powerful of them all, banco sumi. When you hear these ícaros you are left in a state of awe and wonder.

The ícaro of the ancient city of Pahuahuan, out of which the waterfall is pouring, opens the

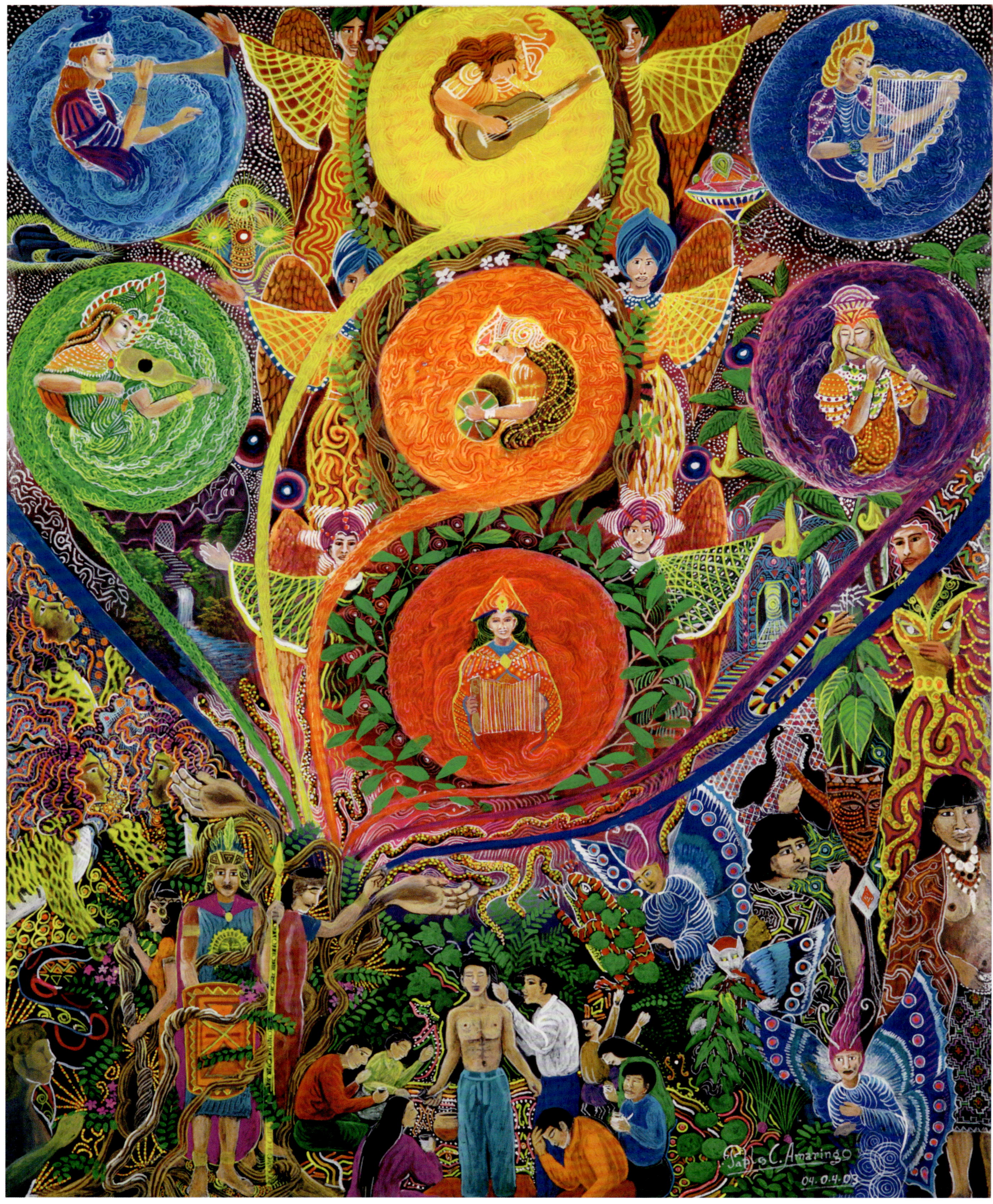

NUKÑO MASCHASHKA
Dulce Visión
2003, Gouache on Arches Paper
52 x 65 cm.

gateway into the mountain realm where the grand masters of the pyramids dwell. They revealed the secret science of pyramid building to the ancient Egyptians, Toltec, Maya, and Inca. Few can sing this ícaro, as it opens one's consciousness to these masters' esoteric influences and brings strange dreams. Mountains are spiritual pyramids, so they should never be destroyed.

The curandero at the bottom is chanting an ícaro to heal an ear infection that has caused pain and deafness. He is chewing *pichana albahaca* (*Ocimum micranthum*), and using *agua florida* to give a soplada to the patient's ears. His ícaro places an arkana around the patient's head, like a protective hat. The tip of the tail of a *carachupa* (armadillo) is used to prevent foreign bodies from entering the ear.

Nearby the curanderos are healing other patients of headaches, or what shamans call *pulsarios* (pulsations or throbbing aches). This cure can be performed by chanting alone, without the need for medicine. Only water that has been treated with sopladas and ícaros is required.

To the right you see the illustrious princess *Sumaq Shipash* (beautiful maiden) wearing her exquisite robes of red, gold, and green. Her dress is brocaded with golden serpents, symbolizing the power she gives to the vegetalistas to diagnose the pulsations and heal.

Growing out of the pipe is *toé amarillo* (*Brugmansia* sp., yellow toé); next to it are two *camungo* birds (*Anhima cornuta,* horned screamer). They are guardians possessing finely tuned senses and can warn of any approaching danger.

In ancient times, Inca nobles and princesses used to meet tribal people of the upper jungle at a place called El Encuentro on the River Urubamba. Similarly, on the River Yanatile the Shipibo, Conibo, Shetagua, Arahuac, Amahuaca, and Mashcopiro people met the Incas and the people from the Sierra to barter their products. This trade took place annually in June, when they would exchange exotic birds and animals such as parrots, *guacamayos,* cock of the rock (*Rupicola peruvianus*), and monkeys, as well as embroidered clothes, feathered cloaks, and jewelry. This contact through trade explains the presence of so many Quechua words in the language of these Páno peoples.

Although these meetings were primarily for trade, the people also exchanged knowledge and ideas. The Shipibo say they taught the mysteries of ayahuasca to the Incas, and that is how Inca priests at the Temple of the Sun (Coricancha) made their discoveries in esoteric and astronomical knowledge. This association also explains why many people have Inca-related visions when they drink ayahuasca.

Below, the Inca holding the gold spear and shield is Auca Inca, one of the four brothers who founded the Inca empire. Behind him are sublime masters who taught the use of plants and shared this knowledge with the Inca, the Maya, and other ancient civilizations. When the Spanish arrived they joined the indigenous peoples in the selva. You see an indigenous man standing on their left. The extended arm with outsized hands projecting from the vine symbolizes the ability of ayahuasca to reach through distance and time.

Next on the left you see the nitimushcanpoma, the *otorongos* (jaguars) with human heads and serpents growing from them.

In the bottom right are two Shipibo dressed in exquisitely embroidered clothes. In olden days the women were taught by spirits how to paint these complex geometric patterns. They used brushes made from the hair of maidens, which is more pure than the hair of a woman who has known a man. These Shipibo women are powerful curanderas with immense knowledge of healing, especially healing of women. Shipibo curanderas cover their patients with water from a pure secret source and extract the illness by sucking.

Piñon blanco (*Jatropha curcas*) is growing above the shamans healing in the picture below. The large seeds of this plant are rich in oil, which is used for making many products, such as soap and candles. The oil can also be extracted for use as biodiesel fuel. *Chanca piedra* (*Phyllanthus nirur*) also grows above the shamans and is used widely in Peru to eliminate kidney stones, gallstones, and urinary tract infections.

Lengua de perro (*Cynoglossum officinale*), to the right of the shamans, is also known as *cinoglosa.* It is used medicinally as an astringent and antiseptic. *Pichana albahaca* (*Ocimum micranthum,* or wild basil), bottom right, has antibacterial, antiseptic, and antifungal properties. To the left you see a being with wings like a butterfly who teaches vegetalistas how to communicate telepathically.

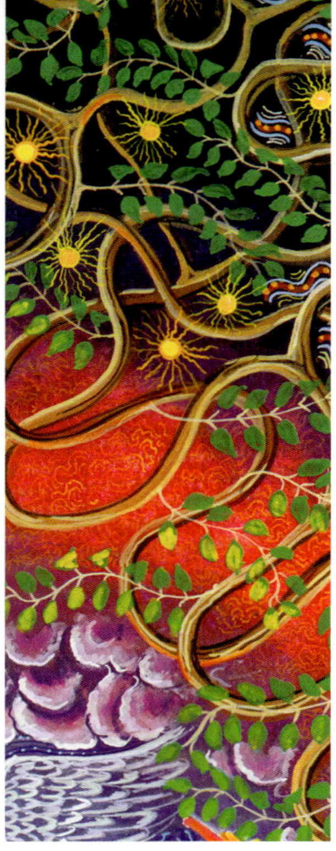

ALLI MARIRI

An important moment for a shaman's apprentice is when this magical phlegm is received from the maestro. It can be obtained by chanting the ícaro of the *punga* tree (*Bombax munguba*), which produces a fatty, phlegmlike resin, although there are fish and snails that have it as well. Snakes are great teachers of intelligence and sensitivity and there are certain kinds that transmit the mariri: green, blue, black, white, red, and sky blue. However, if you swallow the mariri of the black snake, you are taking in death and pain, so this is what hechiceros, or sorcerers, use for killing people. The apprentice opens his mouth and the snake goes into him. The next day his back burns badly and hurts a lot; then the pain goes to his head before reaching his stomach. To get it out, the apprentice smokes tobacco in a pipe and swallows the smoke. The snake of his vision has become phlegm and it comes out as a completely intact snake.

When night falls, the vengeful apprentice begin to swallow needles, spines, and nails, while making sure the needles are aligned vertically, not horizontally; otherwise they get stuck in the throat, causing death. They also swallow broken glass and other horrible things with which to harm people by blowing them into their shoulder, arm, stomach, or head. This can be done from afar or, if the victims are present, when they are not looking and they feel nothing. This is hechicería, which is for killing people; brujeria is different and is for causing accidents and illness.

The red snake can be used for both killing and healing, but the white snake is just for healing. It is during the ayahuasca session that the snake enters in the vision. The green snakes know all about plants. Yellow snakes are for knowing about rocks, precious stones, and minerals, and what they contain. Blue snakes are for becoming wise and very intelligent. White is for speaking well.

In the picture you see the arcontes giving strength to the mariri. Arcontes are angels whose wings join together when they are working, and when they finish they come unstuck again. Whenever I saw them I felt reverence for them, as they came out of their tunnel from the depths of another world.

In the top left-hand corner you can see a banco puma who has lived but is now sleeping. He will one day return to earth and is just waiting for a cataclysm to awaken humanity; then he will return to earth. He was once flesh so he must return as flesh.

Unlike hechiceros, brujos make concoctions that are secretly put into their victims' food or drink, or spilled on the path leading to their houses, making their lives full of obstacles and frustrations. The effect is like a curse that causes unhappiness, but does not kill as a hechicero does. Amulets and talismans can protect you from brujeria but there is no protection or cure for hechicería, unless your heart is connected with the dynamic energy that religious people call God. I call it that because when I found it, I remained permanently connected.

I first took ayahuasca because I did not believe in God, I did not want to believe, but several times I was attacked and became so ill as to be on the verge of death. That is how I found God and that saved me. If you react strongly or try to resist when someone behaves badly toward you, instead of making peace, you make more war and misfortune. But if you show love it all dissolves. Love is

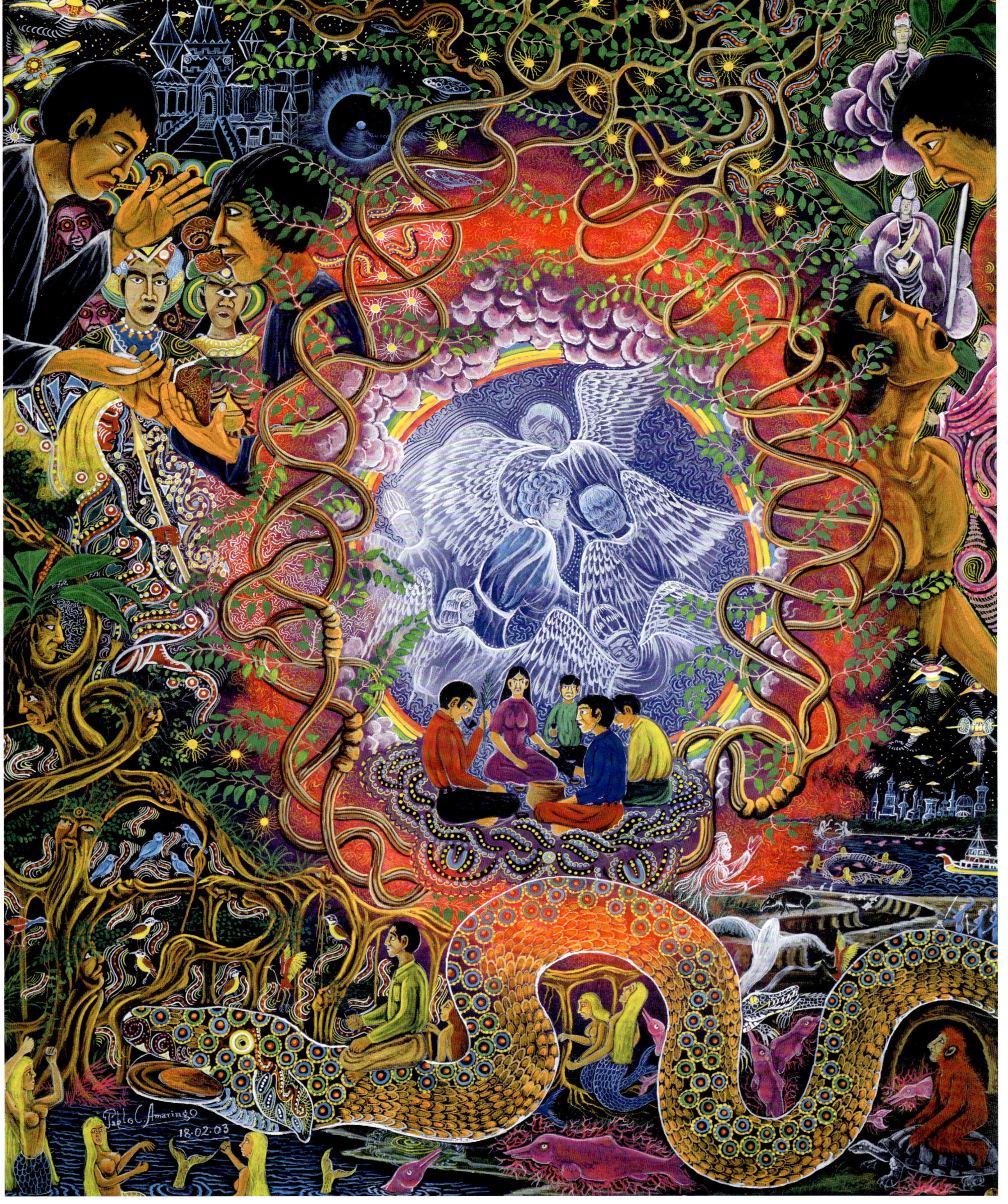

ALLI MARIRI
2003, Gouache on Arches Paper
52 x 64 cm.

big, we need it, and it is with us from birth to death. It gives us peace and consolation.

You can see the renaco tree in the picture's lower left. It is the mystic house of aquatic spirits—yacurunas, sirenas, bufeos, and sachamamas. Yacurunas are hairy beings that live in the underwater realm. They use charapas as a means of transport, like a canoe, as seen in the bottom right corner.

You can also see a tunnel that connects with other universes. As you go down the tunnel it widens until you can see a cupola. Some people cannot understand these things; their capacity is limited by their fear of losing their sanity for what could await them at the end of the tunnel. Here the dynamic energy is flowing like streamers of beautiful colors, but without an open heart and mind you will not be able to enter.

I have entered here. It is a dark black universe, but when it is inside your mind you can see in that darkness if your heart is pure. We see thanks to the light of the sun, but if the sun were extinguished we would be plunged into darkness. You can drown in darkness. It is like water; you cannot breathe in it.

If we had expanded senses, everything around us could be seen in the dark and all the spirits would be visible, but because we do not have this, we see just darkness. We say we are alone, but the spirits are always there. We can feel ashamed because the spirits can see us and when we do not see them, they laugh at us. When you see them you will laugh, too!

"How does Pablo know so many things? Where does he read them?" people ask. But they are from my experiences and things I have seen for myself. If we could use this knowledge in our lives we would have peace and joy and the world would be so beautiful. Those beautiful temples I paint cannot easily be entered; first you must take the *aya catuca* or *bano de los muertos* (bath of the dead) to purify you. Then the spirits put *aji* (Peruvian hot pepper) on your tongue; it burns but it purifies you. They put eye drops prepared from strange plants into your eyes, and put other plants into your ears so that you can hear properly. The lowest beings receive nutrition from the vapor of the plants, which smell wonderful. That is why flying saucers visit us from other planets to get energy from plants, water, and animals.

In our lives we are have little understanding or awareness of the microscopic beings around us trying to put our minds and bodies right. The world is very complex and we cannot yet fully understand our role in it, only little by little. These paintings are an instrument of teaching to give us skills and mental faculties so we can live better. In the painting you see that the ayahuasca liana intertwines in a spiral helix, as it is like the DNA of the spiritual realm.

BARCO FANTASMA

Manuel Huaya was a sumiruna who lived by the River Inomapuya, a tributary of the River Tamaya, which runs into the River Ucayali. He was a contemporary of my great grandfather, Joaquin Amaringo Vasquez, who died in 1939 at a ripe old age. Huaya dieted and drank ayahuasca, gradually moving up the grades from onaya to banco puma and muraya, and finally became a great sumiruna.

He traveled about in his boat covering a territory as far as Santoa, a long way up the Ucayali from Tamanco. He was a great doctor and healed people everywhere using ayahuasca and medicinal plants. With his knowledge of the supernatural, he had command of the earth, water, sky, and fire. A sumiruna cannot suffer from burning because he has an invisible protective aura that would probably be detected only by sophisticated technology.

He inhabited a world of great masters from Atlantis, China, the Ashanti people of Africa, and palmists from Eastern Europe. He lived with the fairies, sylphs, and muses who guarded the forests, rivers, and plants. These beings and all of life had a role to play in his world, even the termites and roots under the soil.

In order to make contact with people on the earthly plane, these beings sometimes incarnate into humans. Such were the people of Atlantis until it was submerged under the ocean.

Our earth is inhabited by a diversity of life forms, and every species has a different ecological purpose. They support each other and support us as well if we can learn to open ourselves to them. In the spirit world plants sing and dance as they grow, and we too can experience this feeling of life flowing. Millions of spirits surround us all the time, since every plant or animal has a spirit. They come to us when we are born and give us intelligence and understanding. It would take us thousands of years to discover everything for ourselves; learning from spirits is quicker.

Manuel Huaya transformed a huge anaconda into the boat you see here with two huge eyes, which is why it is called a phantom boat. It has several floors, each representing a level of life's evolution, but also functioning as a level of social hierarchy. Our problem in the world today has come about because we have disrupted the natural order of things. The power of the anaconda, for instance, comes from its position high up in the food chain; it incorporates the intelligence and energy of all the levels of life underneath it.

This boat is alive and has a steel horn on its forehead, like a rhino, for defending itself from danger. It also works like an antenna for communicating, and enables the boat to move around unnoticed. Some spiritual things need to be invisible to humans. Electricity exists but cannot be seen, and in the same way sacred things cannot be easily noticed. The boat of this famous shaman healed people and taught disciples. It had a magical song called "Acero Punta," meaning "steel point."

People boarded the boat for healing sessions and would be taken anywhere they wanted, but it could not exist in the daylight, only at night. With his crew and full complement of passengers, he would spend weeks going from pueblo to pueblo. When people heard the gurgling of whirlpools, they

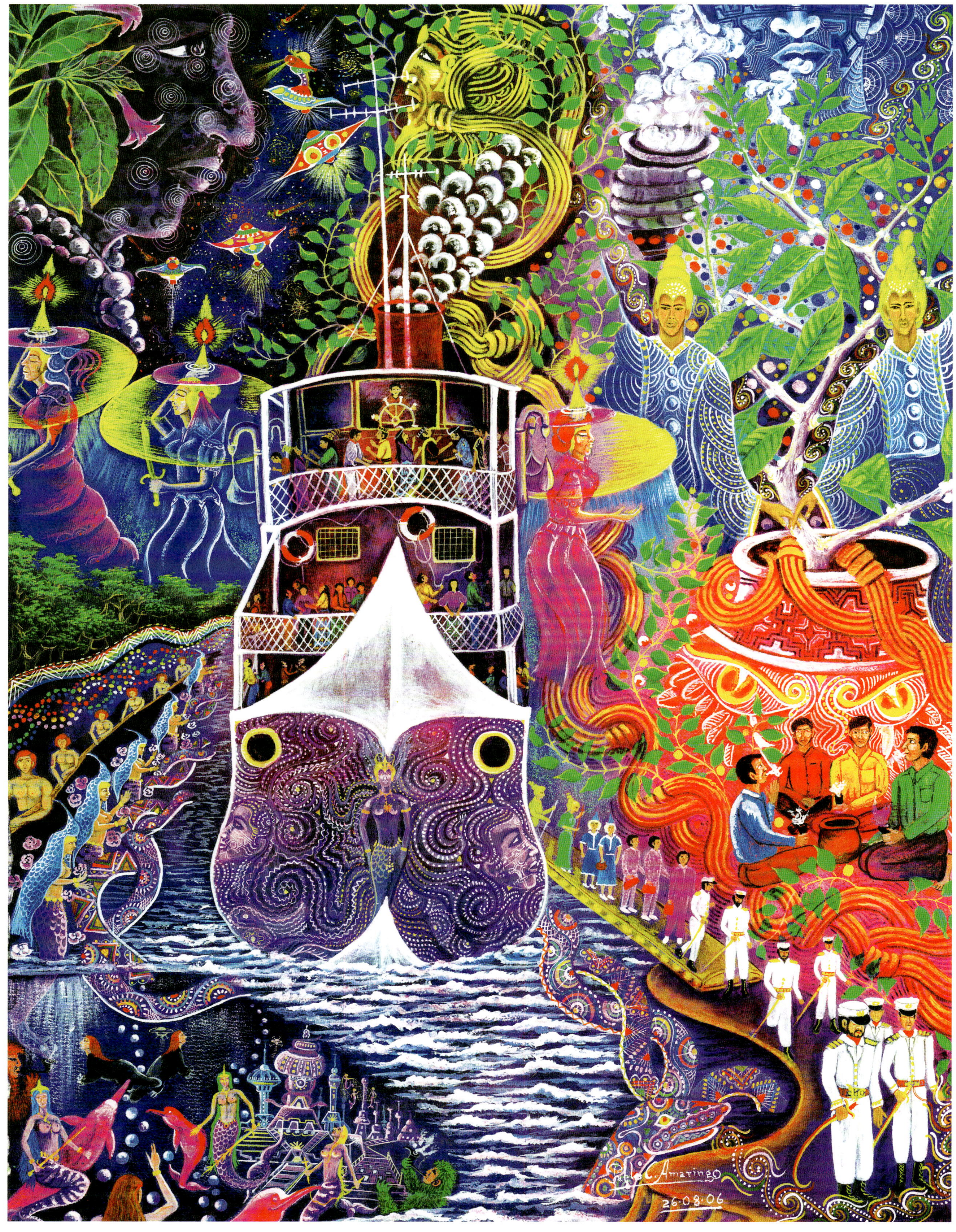

BARCO FANTASMA
2006, Gouache on Arches Paper
57 x 77 cm.

used to say, "Ah, that's Manuel Huaya's boat." You can see large anacondas in the water guarding the important society people on board, and the marines disembarking.

The ícaro *de los cantaros* can be used for enchanting a person for either good or bad. When it is for good, you are protected like a well-situated fortress; but when it is for bad, you cannot get up again, and you die. The shamans seen here are good, unlike some whose love is conditional on how much money you give them. As ever, there are good shamans and bad ones.

I was a shaman dedicated to creating well-being and I learned how to overcome the bad. Here in the Amazon you must always prove that you are stronger than the other shamans; otherwise you will be attacked. Let us say a patient comes to me for protection from attack by a brujo. If I undo that spell, the evil goes back to its source and the frustrated brujo now wants to harm *me*! It is a dirty world and the easiest solution is to also be evil and kill the other brujo. The world is like this to teach us to know good from bad. There cannot be one without the other, or positive without negative. However, it is always easier to be bad and destructive than to work on the side of good.

I rose to the grade of muraya, one short of the highest rank of sumiruna. Later I got out of shamanism altogether and never wanted to drink ayahuasca again. Many shamans find it impossible to quit. If they do, they fear being killed, and if they practice as shamans again, they probably will be. Some are tempted to kill the first time to save themselves, then bit by bit it gets easier to kill again. I used to drink ayahuasca every night to find solutions for me and people around me; I never got ill during all that time.

The largest size of tinaja is called a *mahuete,* and one is seen on the right. They are important for archiving chants, which are stored inside like a computer. As with all sound, the things we say do not fade into nothing, but are immediately transmitted to another place. The voice is like a telephone; it captures something and deposits it in another place. This should remind us that our words have consequences and power, so we should be more conscious when we speak.

We will understand this better as the situation worsens. I am saying this as clearly as I can now: The world cannot continue anymore the way we are. Some people are honest, loving, and charitable, and want the best for others; while many are thinking only of who has the most power or possessions. These people are deceived and asleep.

As Paolo Coelho's *Alchemist* says, some people are like the dawn; they get up early to see the sunrise, while the rest are sleeping. You can have all the wealth in the world; what is bad is not to know how to share it. We come into the world with nothing and we leave with nothing because in the spiritual world we do not need material things. The world will be ruined if we sleep in ignorance of this; those of us who have woken up are already working for a better world.

Scientists say the world is going to collapse soon and no one knows how to stop violence and corruption; in fact, there are more crimes and murders every day. This is a very crucial time for the world and humanity does not know what to do.

Will it really end in forest fires, floods, tornadoes, and climate change? We know we cannot survive this, and if we do not change, we will die. So we are trying to say something that will wake people up. Many think they are doing their best for their children by giving them money, food, clothes, and a home, yet the children still turn out badly. What they really need is teaching. It does not matter where they study, but if they do not cleanse their hearts and minds first, they will be thinking badly and not awaken. Parents need to teach their children by example; it is not good enough to work like a slave to pay for their private education. This is what I have learned from plants and spirits, which some call the voice of God. We are gods too, but we do not know how to take our proper place as gods.

Look how plants are greater than we are; animals eat them and then are eaten by other animals. All life eventually goes back to plants, whether we are vegetarian or not. Plants made life possible. They began the task of embodying the invisible spirit that later gave us spirit. This is why we love plants and will always need them around us.

In the background you see the *llimpiq atun huarmis* (the grand shining women). They are sylphs with golden swords and powerful energy lamps above their heads to guard the boat against threats from above.

To the left of the boat are the *huarmi murayas* who, like mermaids, wear the armor of celestial fish. They are tending pink and white flowers for use in alchemical healing.

Behind them are the *pukachukcha* (the red-haired ones). These are the men who attend to the ayahuasca ropes so that those on board can perform their healing arts in safety.

Guarding the entrance to the subaquatic realm you see the *huarmi vaca marina* (woman manatee), bufeo colorado, and sirenas with golden scepters, the underwater guides of the murayas. There is a green-haired yakuruna, or *taksa yakuruna* (small yakuruna), smoking his pipe. The yakuruna on the left is a *pukaninaruna* (people of the red flame) smoking his pipe. Behind them is a magnificent city protected by sirenas with magic nets that prevent spells from passing through.

On the side of the mahuete is the face of the *pukaurcutucu* (red owl) with bright fiery eyes, guarding the shamans while they drink ayahuasca.

The beings at the top right are the arcontes of ayahuasca; they are sky blue because this color inspires courage. Their crests indicate their rank and job. Behind them a sumiruna smokes his pipe.

Growing at the top left is toé with its pink flower, sometimes added to ayahuasca to intensify the visions. A piece of flower mixed with your ayahuasca brew can enable you to see a person clearly. Smoking a dried flower like tobacco also gives hallucinatory dreams. What remains can be put under your pillow at night to give you dreams of spirit beings.

When Manuel Huaya wanted to get married he visited the mermaids and pink dolphins living under water. Sumirunas use dolphins as seats and giant lizards as benches. Their sun hats are *rayas* (stingrays) and their shoes are *carachamas* (*P. Genibarbis,* armored catfish). In the old days people were so involved with the mythic world that they interchanged these words; *rayas* for hats, and *carachamas* for shoes.

The muses swimming around at the bottom of the picture go everywhere with the boat. There is a muse for each secret teaching given by the plants; for example, the whistle to attract the particular bird you wish to hunt. Other muses appear in ayahuasca visions to teach the whistle for attracting the *huangana* (*Tayassu pecari,* white-lipped peccary), *carachupa* (*Priodontes Maximus,* giant armadillo), or deer. Some muses like the *shapishico* (a kind of *chullachaqui*). *Sacharuna* or *surichaqui* will help you hunt if you leave them matches and tobacco to smoke. The yacuruna with green hair is there, too.

You can see the mermaids pulling the boat along with ropes of ayahuasca, singing to drown out the noise of motors. The engine room of the boat is a huge vessel of ayahuasca cooking; it produces the steam that you see emerging from the funnel.

You see the flying saucers coming in to land under water. The world is full of mysteries and we will never finish the task of studying them.

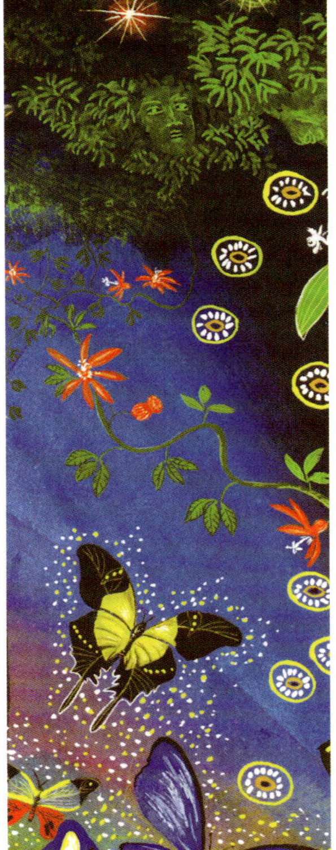

CONCENTRACIÓN PALISTICA

Ayahuasqueros gain their knowledge from visions, whereas *paleros,* who diet with the roots, bark, and branches of certain trees, obtain their knowledge through dreams. Only a few select murayas and sumirunas learn to be paleros. The apprenticeship, or dieta, is stricter and longer than for an ayahuasquero, and can last from three to six years, during which time the apprentice may not see anyone other than his own maestro. He should on no account have any contact with women.

The maestro's job is not to teach, but to provide the right food and conditions for his apprentice to follow the dieta. First, he must build his *tambo* (see glossary) in the forest, at least a hundred meters (328 feet) away from his maestro. The apprentice cooks or macerates his chosen *palo* (the roots, bark, and resins of trees). When the mareación starts to take effect, he meditates in solitude with the spirits of animals, gnomes, sylphs, and sibyls, and moves up to the tree canopy, where they concentrate with him. When the wind blows, the foliage moves, allowing them to visit other stellar fields and explore lives that we have never known, and be with extraterrestrials. Later, while asleep, he receives the ícaros of each animal.

Initially he takes the palos one at a time, gradually increasing to five at a time if he can manage it. The two trees you see in upper part of the painting guard the door through which he enters to learn. On the left is the *remocaspi* tree (*Aspidosperma excelsum*), and on the right is the *huairacaspi* (*Cedrelinga catenaeformis*).

Between these trees you can see the temple of *alquimia palistica*, which is made from a variety of trees and is very beautiful. I have been there without taking any *palos maestros* (only medicinal palos), as it is possible to go there in an ayahuasca vision and still be received.

When a palero is healing a sick person, the genios of the trees appear to him one by one and indicate whether or not they can heal. If not, they disappear without saying anything, until finally one appears who is willing to heal the patient. They are very jealous and will not heal just anybody. The job of a palero is to make a bridge with a spirit able to heal his patient; this is why the faces look at him. The genios will teach their enigmatic wisdom and cooperate only if the palero has the self-discipline to follow the rigors of the dieta.

Palo spirits are pure, like priests, and cannot be combined with ayahuasca. Each one has a specific purpose in the temple of alquimia palistica.

There are many palos. Some of the most important ones are *remocaspi,* which teach the customs of the indigenous people in dreams and will be your companion for the rest of your life. Others include *ajosquiro* (*Cordia alliodora*), *cumaceba* (*Swartzia polyphylla*), and *puca lupuna,* which can also teach hechicería. The leaves of *shihuahuaco* (*Dipteryx* sp.) and *itauba* (*Mezilaurus* sp.) are mixed with ayahuasca to intensify visions. *Abuta* (*Abuta grandifolia*) cures drug addiction and alcoholism, while *alcanfor caspi* (*Cinnamomum camphora*) gives you a strong sense of smell to diagnose patients. *Bobinsana* (*Calliandra angustifolia*) is a cure for arthritis and gout, and provokes beautiful dreams.

In the upper left of the picture are two celestial beings known as the *principado*s (principalities). Their assigned task from the supreme divinity is to inspire humanity in the arts and sciences. The

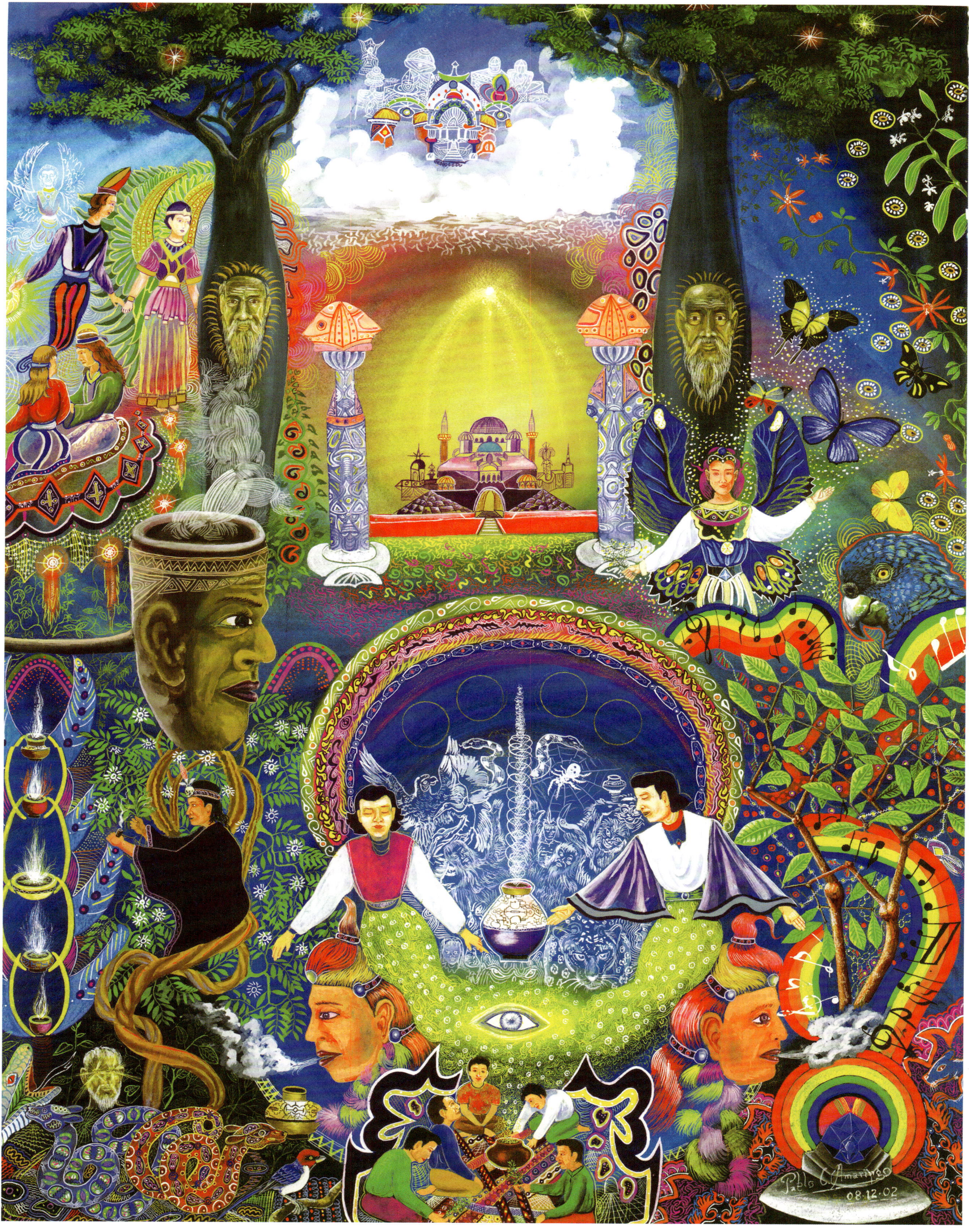

CONCENTRACIÓN PALISTICA
2002, Gouache on Arches Paper
57 x 76 cm.

principado holding the horn is called Ada Morgana and is a master of divination. Below them are the *jura plata*, majestic spirits known as *camenae*.

A palero should be treated with utmost care and respect, as the spirits of palos can be very severe and overpowering. A palero usually has a little bag for keeping tobacco and other personal things, which no one else should touch, as it could interfere with his experience.

Palo spirits teach an apprentice how to journey, how to chant and blow sopladas, and how to transform into trees or animals. When the apprentice returns home after his long diet, people fear him as though he were a master of martial arts and look at him in trepidation and are unable to speak. Paleros can heal very effectively but if you annoy them they can be dangerous. Ayahuasca *sumis* are powerful but humble, but these paleros are not. A palero will take his apprentice's power away if the apprentice lies to him.

You can see the palo spirits below in the painting. The ornate daggers on either side are their feet: dagger-shaped boots that stick into the ground when they touch it. They serve as secret weapons and can help in climbing trees when needing to make a quick escape. If you strike their feet with a machete it will not harm them. Not surprisingly, no one dares to provoke a palero!

My grandfather, Ambrosio Amaringo Vazquez, was a palero. He would never eat with us; his food was prepared for him under water by the yacuruna. They served him chicha, masato, and even roasted fish, all of which he consumed alone in the water, where no one could bother him. He also ate exotic creatures that you do not normally see on the earth.

As a sign of a good shaman, he was competent in managing his day-to-day business. Dozens of employees worked under him, fishing and collecting products from the forest, such as *chambira* (*Astrocaryum chambira*) and *tamshi* (*Heteropsis jenmanii*). The former is a fiber twisted from the leaf of a palm and used for weaving very fine bags and hammocks. Tamshi is a long aerial root (above the ground) split into fibers and used as rope in roof construction or for weaving baskets.

He was able to look at people and tell them how many years they would live, and it would all be true! When my sister was only eighteen, he told her she would live twenty-one years, and that is what happened.

In his bag lived *jergones* and *cascabeles* (small poisonous snakes) and scorpions. No one dared interfere with or steal from his bag.

He was quite miraculous when healing people. They would lie on a bed for him to diagnose the illness, and he would pull out worms, placing them in a jar for all to see. When people came with splinters or bones stuck inside them, he would pull them out without cutting or using instruments. People came to see him from great distances.

He called the spirit that helped him *papa tua* (father of the palo), which means "genio dedicated to saving the sick." You cannot find people working with such spirits anymore. No one is prepared to devote so many years to dieting and self-denial.

On the left a sumiruna in black lies in a hammock made of ayahuasca rope, which vibrates in the wind, making sounds like a musical instrument. They live very singular lives and can live underwater with great ease. They understand how energy manifests into matter and can pull out gold, silver, and diamonds from under the earth, just by touching the ground.

To his left the hierarchy of grades of shaman is symbolized by the winged vessels with fires burning in them. Going from bottom to top, the onaya, banco puma, muraya, sumiruna, and banco sumi are represented. As stated earlier, the banco sumi is the highest grade achievable. The winged vessels symbolize that those who embark on the path of learning from ayahuasca and palos are all moving toward higher levels of knowledge and wisdom.

Below the ayahuasca vine there are two horned snakes; the blue one gives spiritual knowledge and the red one determines your gender at the moment of your conception. These snakes with deer heads are called *sacra machaco* (trickster devil snake). You also see the *caspi runa* (spirit of the trees) and the *chicua* bird (*Piaya cayana,* squirrel cuckoo). These beings protect the palero apprentices while they are preparing plant medicines.

Paleros are so strong they can pull up any creature from a river or cocha. Once an employee of my grandfather was fishing in a favorite place and was nearly dragged under water by a yacumama. Furious, my grandfather pulled it out of the water. He said for six years no one would be able to fish there, and it was true; he had rooted out the anaconda mother spirit, the yacumama, from the water. These yacumamas attract fish, which is why they call them "mother of the water."

Sometimes several meters of riverbank can be eaten away by the river in one season. My grandfather used an anteater's claw to draw a line near the bank of the river to limit how far the river would erode when it was high. The river never passed the mark made by this specially prepared claw.

To the right you see mounted on a stone pedestal a brilliant multifaceted sapphire with rainbow emanations forming a harp. This represents the blissful and harmonious ícaros within the sapphire.

The chacruna leaves seen on the right are not for making ayahuasca, but in this case for the palero to chew. Chacruna can be chewed in this way with mandarin or coca leaves, and it will give you a short-lived mareación.* The chacruna should be dry, not fresh.

The butterflies are not for guarding over distant places, in the way ayahuasqueros use them. Paleros send them out as emissaries to survey and locate people from the past, and later explore in their dreams. This is how they learn from the wisdom of ancient prophets, kings, and queens.

Below is the *ojo del entendimiento* (eye of understanding). A person's eyes are a window to their emotional nature and a mirror of the soul. They reflect love and compassion, but can also reveal a lack of feelings. A person who sees and understands with the eyes of the heart can enjoy life unselfishly and with consideration for plants, animals, and all beings.

On either side of the ojo del entendimiento is an *ishkay* sumiruna. *Ishkay* means "two" in Quechua. This is a twin sumiruna; the left side is female and the right, male, a reminder that we have both male and female in us. Behind them is the large tunnel that leads to the underworld realm of the tunchis. You see the great teachers called the *sinchi yachai* with their braided, colored hair. They are masters of the cleansing and protective powers of mapacho smoke.

*This suggests the leaves could contain some kind of inhibitor, although the authors can find no evidence or information to indicate this.

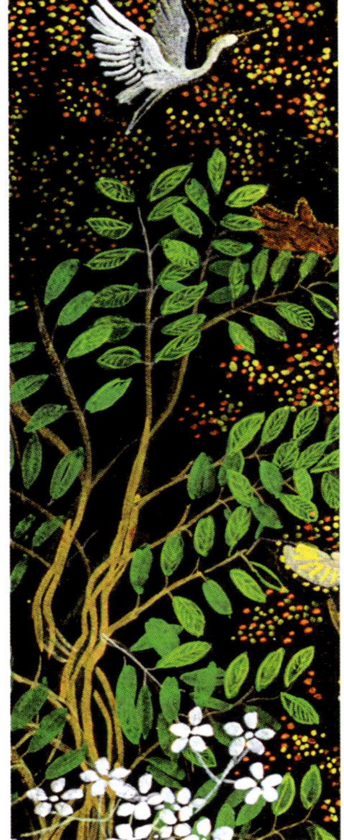

LAS NALPEAS DEL RENACO

The renaco tree you see growing here by a waterfall is guarded over by napeas—nymphs who look like mermaids. The renaco is their temple, palace, and sanctuary, where they dance and sing the ícaro of the ayahuasca mariri, the magical phlegm of ayahuasca. This phlegm gives a shaman the power to cure any sickness and remove virotes (poison darts), and thus heal sorcery.

The napeas sing enchanting ícaros of the renaco tree and *santa maria* or *matico* (*Piper* sp.) plant, which grows nearby. Shamans use the matico leaves to craft *shacapas,* or fans, which they shake like rattles to accompany their ícaros and assist concentration. Matico can also be used to heal machete wounds, and for coughs. The leaves are crushed and boiled in water, then the lukewarm liquid is used to bathe the wound.

Apprentice shamans gather in the palace to learn how to heal marupa sorcery and receive the powers of different kinds of mariri. There is mariri from the *punga tree* (*Bombax munguba*), the *setico* or *imbauba* tree (*Cecropia* sp.), the *congompe* snail (*Megalobulimus maximus*), the *shuyo* fish (*Hoplerythrinus unitaeniatus*), and the *ilausa-machaco,* or boa phlegm; all of these produce a natural phlegm. The apprentices learn to chant the ícaros of these mariris to extract the virote.

An important time for an apprentice is when he receives the mariris from his maestro. They appear as long colored threads just behind where they are seated. The maestro keeps his mariri in his stomach and allows it to come out when he is healing. The group has already taken ayahuasca and the maestro is smoking mapacho to intensify the mareación, or visionary effects of ayahuasca. This is shown by the radiant electromagnetic patterns around them. To either side are the spirits of the *naupa yana runa,* legendary black beings who inhabited the earth before humans.

The wheel at the upper right has circles of vibrating molecules and depicts the structure of an ethereal mariri cell. The nucleus of the cell is a four-pointed star representing the dimensions of time and space. If a maestro shaman has followed the dieta properly and impeccably, he can use the mariri to counteract sorcery and malign forces.

To the left of the mariri cell are *ilausa machacos,* or phlegm boas. Flying below is a *tibemama* in the form of a sparrow hawk; its acute vision can penetrate to the depths of rivers and cochas. Below, looking like plants, are the forest spirits known as the *allpa supai runa.*

In the palace they teach shamans the importance of butterflies, lizards, and the *huasi ukulluco,* or house lizard. When I was a shaman, I used to have a huasi ukulluco to protect my house from sorcery. The mariri of a sorcerer holds virotes that enable him to cast deadly spells. The mariri contains needles, razor blades, and the poisons of snakes, wasps, and other insects. All of this is retained in his stomach and he must not eat anything. Unless he follows his diet properly, the needles will not align and he will choke on his own evil and the poisons will kill him.

The huasi ukulluco lives among the roots and undergrowth of the renaco. Below the shamans, a multicolored jaguar defends the spiritual sanctuary.

The *puca sararas* (*anhinga anhinga,* red herons) flying out of the yacumama's mouth assist shamans

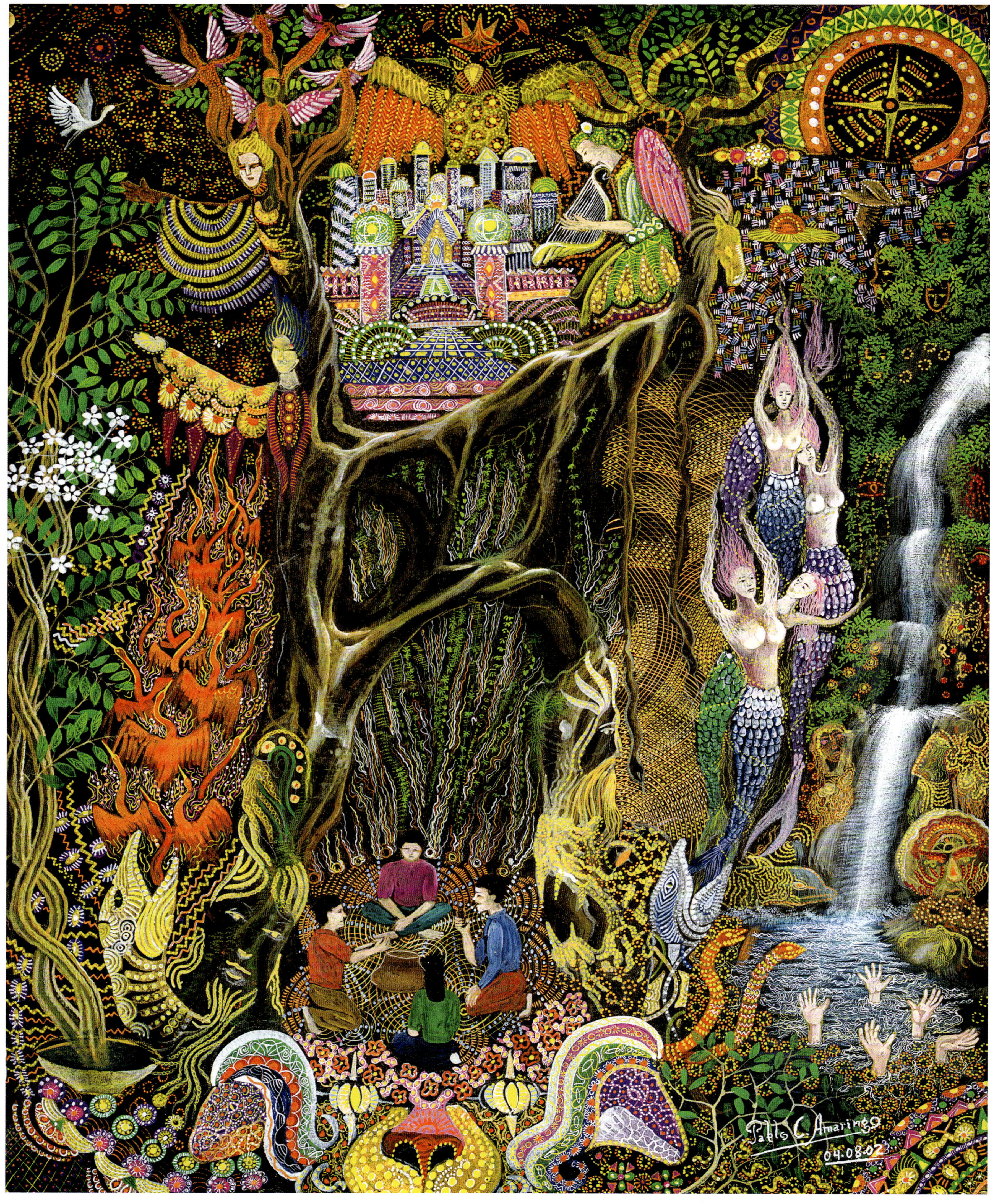

LAS NALPEAS DEL RENACO
2002, Gouache on Arches Paper
54 x 61 cm.

by catching the perilous virotes sent by sorcerers. The yacumama emerges from the water at midnight, raises its head, and breathes in with such force that birds are irresistibly drawn into her stomach, where they continue to live until released by shamans to heal marupa sorcery. Usually these birds are tibemama (osprey), the *yana tibe* (black tibe), sararas, and owls.

Above the branches of the renaco tree appear spirits known as *a'tun runa* (great people)—warriors who defend the renaco tree as though it were a castle. Thanks to them, animals can live safely in the labyrinthine roots of the renaco tree, concealed from predators.

Spirits and beings who have come from other worlds in extraterrestrial crafts gather here at night to make music, play games, and celebrate in the spirit of a fiesta.

If you sleep under a renaco tree, you will have enigmatic and mystical dreams. However, it is not advised to sleep there alone, because living in the branches above are the guardian spirits known as *supai-ñambi,* who will not allow you to sleep, so you might be in for a surprise.

If alone, you should climb the renaco tree and tie yourself to a high branch. From this vantage point you can watch the festivities without any need for ayahuasca. All this takes place in the darkest part of the night; just before daybreak they are all gone.

Above, the a'tun runa play the harp and other musical instruments, and sing ícaros. The spirits keep the renaco tree and the surrounding area pure and immaculate as a magical palace should be. Animals and insects do not defecate in the vicinity, and even remove fallen leaves.

The a'tun runa live in accordance with the celestial laws and understand the imperfections of humans. The earth need not be harmed if humans can accept that they do not govern the planet but are a part of the biosphere. The a'tun runa despair at the destruction of nature caused by humans through ignorance and material desire. We must evolve and realize we have a role to play in bringing the ecological system into balance, and discover the well-being and health offered to us by nature.

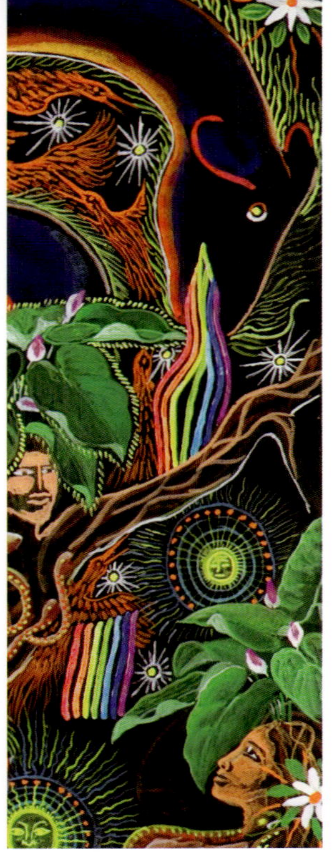

CASPI MAMAN

MADRE DEL ÁRBOL

When you go into the selva, whether or not it is flooded, you will see the immense caspi maman looking at you. She has created this magnificent green temple in which you find yourself, and she will show you that the selva consists of a multitude of levels starting underground, going through the forest floor, and up into the tree canopy.

She will reveal herself little by little to be a source of immense knowledge of plants and spirits living within her embrace. You will notice that one of her guardians is observing your activity night and day, in the form of birds, snakes, and monkeys; they know exactly where you are from your sound, and are conscious of your smell. As you move about, each one is intelligently looking after its domain as you pass from one to another. That is why when you go wandering in the selva, sometimes you meet with a nasty surprise because you have unwittingly crossed a boundary. You have gone too far!

That is why when you explore the selva you should restrict yourself to an area not more than twenty to thirty hectares (fifty to seventy-five acres). In the morning you prepare yourself for the day with the leaves of the *mishquipanga* (*Renealmia alpinia*). When rubbed over your face, arms, and legs, this plant will give you protection for a whole day. The next day you should use *huancahuisacha* (*Aristolochia pilosa*), which has a bad smell and keeps away snakes, spiders, scorpions, salamanders (some of which are poisonous), and *ronsapas* (*Apismellifera scutellata,* or African honeybees), whose sting is worse than a wasp and makes your body erupt in spots. Later you can cover yourself with half-rotten *zurrapa* (humus from the forest floor) mixed with earth, to protect you from harm from falling branches.

There are other secrets and rituals that allow you to wander freely in the forest without misfortune. When a shaman wants to learn, he concentrates on the plants of one area—the roots, bark, and peelings that drop from trees. These tree parts, called *ritidomas,* are often good for the skin and are produced by *caoba* (*Swietenia macrophylla,* or mahogany), *cedro* (*Cedrus* sp., or cedar), *capirona* (*Calycophyllum spruceanum*), and many others.

The mother herself teaches you how to make a hat or crown using different leaves that protect you, while others are poisonous or sting you. If your crown is taken away from you on a journey, you will lose all your accumulated knowledge. You must protect yourself by applying *agua florida* (see glossary) to the crown of your head and performing sopladas with tobacco smoke.

To enhance your mareación, the mother asks you for an offering of tobacco and a pipe, which she smokes with you.

On the left of the picture you can see a powerful sumiruna and palero smoking a cashimbo. His ornate crown is formed by two blue-and-yellow guacamayos who watch over the shaman when he drinks ayahuasca. Behind them is the transcendent Queen Devaki, wearing an iridescent, spiral-patterned

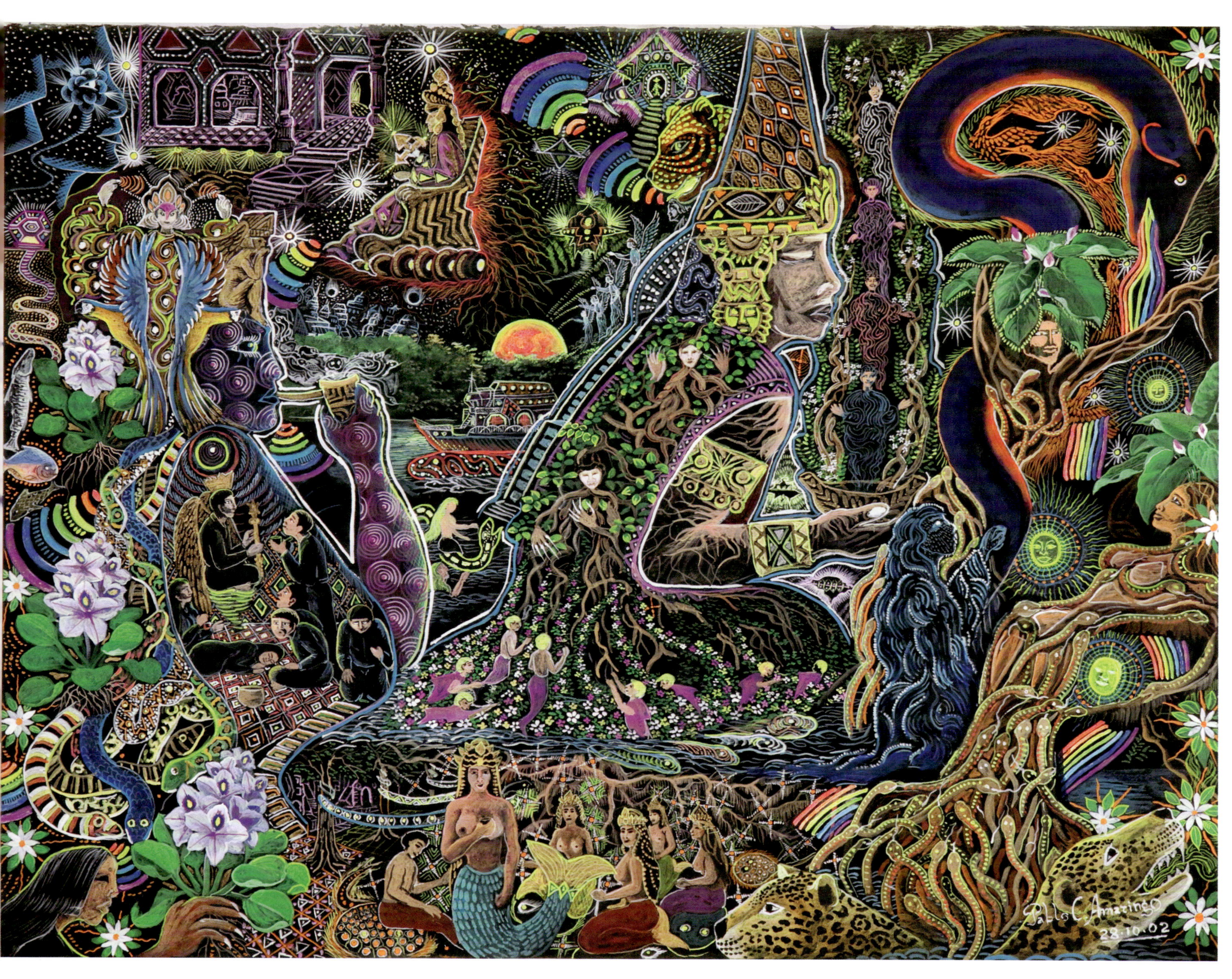

CASPI MAMAN
Madre del Árbol
2002, Gouache on Arches Paper
51 x 64 cm.

garment. She can appear to a shaman in physical form as a human teacher of esoteric knowledge. She teaches the ícaros of formidable palos, such as *remo caspi* (*Aspidosperma excelsum*), *ajosquiro* (*Gallizia corazema*), *alcanfor caspi* (*Cinnamomum camphora*), *huairacaspi* (*Cedrelinga cataneiformis*), and *lupuna colorado*, or *pukalupuna* (*Cavanillesia hylogeiton*). All these trees are grand teachers that can cure as well as harm or kill. The spiral waves radiating from the queen's hands illustrate her healing energy, which helps the shaman.

Sitting to the right is a winged dryad wearing her crown; she is the guardian of the palos. Apprentices of alquimia palistica who specialize in palos can gain mastery of them only after several years of strict dieting helped by these dryads.

Just below, a group of maestro shamans are practicing alquimia palistica. The levitating maestro with wings, crown, and palo scepter is a banco sumi who, having reached the highest degree that a human can achieve, is akin to an angel. With him are an onaya, a muraya, and a banco puma. The stairway and tunnel represent the initiation with ayahuasca and other teacher plants to evolve higher states of consciousness.

The setting sun signifies that plant diets should begin at night. Direct sunlight is harmful when undergoing a plant diet, and detracts from its benefits; the moon's rays, however, are auspicious.

Above, sitting in her exquisitely carved throne, is Camena Hagata. She defends the shamans from sorcery while they are healing in their ceremony. Her magic wand radiates ultrasonic beams to disorient sorcerers so that curanderos can prevail over them. She also accompanies the shamans when they fly into the astral temple next to her.

Below her, in the cocha, the yacumama is transforming into a magnificent a'tun supay lancha. The shaman travels on the lancha to visit the subaquatic realm of the sirenas.

The lilac flowers on the left are putu putu, also known as *wamaruiro*. These flowers are mixed with *chapo* (a sweet drink made from bananas) and taken in the context of a diet to help women's menstrual pains. The ícaro of the putu putu can heal a person suffering mental disturbance. The mother of the putu putu is the yacumama, and when she navigates along the waters, the dense, floating mass of putu putu opens for her and closes again afterward to impede fishermen's access to cochas. A wonderful characteristic of this plant is that its fibrous roots cleanse dirty water.

To the right, the Caspi Maman is wearing her illustrious and richly ornamented conical crown. She has adopted the form of a great renaco tree, which is a spiritual temple and sanctuary in the cosmology of the Amazon. Her many-tiered temple unites the underwater realm of sirenas and yacurunas with the celestial realm, where you see angels descending the temple stairway. Among the roots of the renaco are *sirenos* (mermen) gathering aromatic flowers. Sirenos are rarely seen because unlike sirenas, they never leave the subaquatic realm.

In her hand she holds a wooden bowl with ayahuasca lianas growing up in double helixes. In their midst, rising like smoke, are sylphs who help shamans to heal with ícaros and sopladas.

In the subaquatic realm there are *sirenas coyas* (mermaid princesses) wearing golden headdresses as a sign of their purity and nobility. The sirena queen holding her cashimbo is an *intisirena* (sirena of the sun). She is guardian of the four cardinal points of the underwater realm.

To her left is a sireno seated on a huge stingray. These stingrays are known as *pambamuri* or *rayamama*. To the right of the sirena coyas are two *yaku pumas*—great cats of the underwater realm. Just above is a female yana yacuruna surfacing and touching the anguilamama. Her long tresses have the appearance of flowing water.

On the right a woman is formed of the renaco tree. The pleats of her dress are like snakes, which gives a palero working with renaco the sensitivity of a snake and an understanding of its characteristics. Through his ícaros he can attract snakes. The *loro machaco* (*Bothrops bilineatus*), literally "parrot snake" (because of its parrot-green color), climbs trees to catch and eat small birds using hypnosis.

For this reason, if you wish to catch a young loro to keep as a pet, first you fell the tree where the young are being raised in their nest. Then you go away for a day and a night to avoid being bitten by the loro machaco. When you return, the young loros will be there waiting for you.

At the top right-hand corner is the anguilamama, who is discharging electromagnetic rays from her mouth. The upper part of her body circles around a cluster of puca sararas that form the shape of a brain and spinal cord. This is to illustrate that the brain exercises precise control of the discharge of this lethal electrical energy.

After reaching old age, the anguilamamas become the mothers of *cochas bravas* (enchanted lakes) and *aguajales*—flooded areas where the aguaje palm (*Mauritia flexuosa*) grows. They also guard *pirales* (tangled vegetation), formed from densely growing putu putu that blocks the entrance to a cocha from the river. This makes it difficult for fishermen to come in to fish. When a cocha is protected by the anguilamama, you cannot bathe there because it can easily kill you.

Just below are the leaves and flowers of the *ajo sacha* (*Mansoa alliacea*), important as a teacher plant and for its pharmaceutical properties.

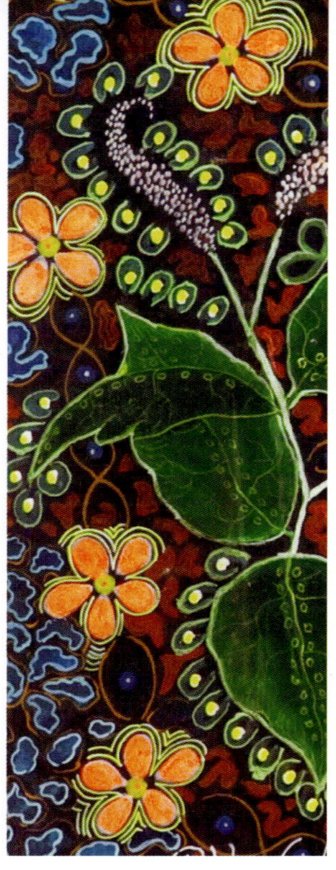

CHASHNAMANCHO UMANKI

ASÍ ES MI CABEZA

This picture is about how a shaman heals people by transforming his head into the head of an animal. Whether this is a horse, snake, bird, dog, bull, or stork, the secret of this practice is that the maestro learns to think like the animal and share its instincts. If he is a *sachaperro* (wild dog) he will be able to heal like a dog. If he is a jaguar he will be able to heal like a jaguar, and as a bird, he can understand the thinking of a bird.

Intelligence and education enable human beings to reach greater perfection and learn more from their experiences. Animals are also highly intelligent, but do not have the consciousness to distinguish good from bad. To communicate with an animal and draw in its spirit a shaman must chant its ícaro and experience the animal's hypnotism, concentration, and instinct.

To heal a baby, a shaman might call the horse. As his thoughts change, his face and head change too. When he performs a soplada on the baby, the baby receives the horse's strength to struggle with its illness, and will not give up. In another case, the agility of a bird may be called for.

If the shaman transforms himself into a monkey before performing a soplada on a fidgety, restless boy, this will prevent the boy from falling ill.

A soplada from the head of a boa would help a girl grow her hair long and beautiful like a boa. They healed my mother like this, and that is how she grew hair down to her waist.

Above you see the yangunturo (giant armadillo), which has armored scales that shield it from harm. When a shaman performs soplos with the power of this animal, a person can fall from a high tree without injury and have protection from fire.

I saw this when I was a boy in Tamanco. My grandfather, Ambrosio Amaringo Vasquez, was a powerful palero and held in awe by people who dared not speak in his presence. Once he gave a soplada of the yangunturo to a man who was later thrown off a precipice without suffering any harm.

Above is the bufeo colorado, whose body parts are used as ingredients in pusanga to magically attract the opposite sex. Sometimes people are strongly affected by this power, which can lead to their becoming emotionally overwhelmed and even losing their sanity. If a shaman chants the ícaro of the bufeo and gives soplos to the affected person, this will restore emotional and mental equilibrium. Such a thing happened to my sister, who, as stated in the commentary for the painting *Supai Pucabufeo,* was so powerfully overcome that she had to be restrained by seven men.

The sachavaca (tapir) is mainly nocturnal and has few natural predators due to its bulk and thick protective skin. They find shelter in the undergrowth or in water, as they can remain submerged in rivers for long periods of time. A person imbued with the energy of the sachavaca can venture deep into the jungle without fear, knowing he will be safe and not get lost.

The huangana (white-lipped peccary) has a rank and penetrating odor produced by its scent glands. It has a very acute sense of smell, and despite its poor eyesight, it is adroit at finding its way through

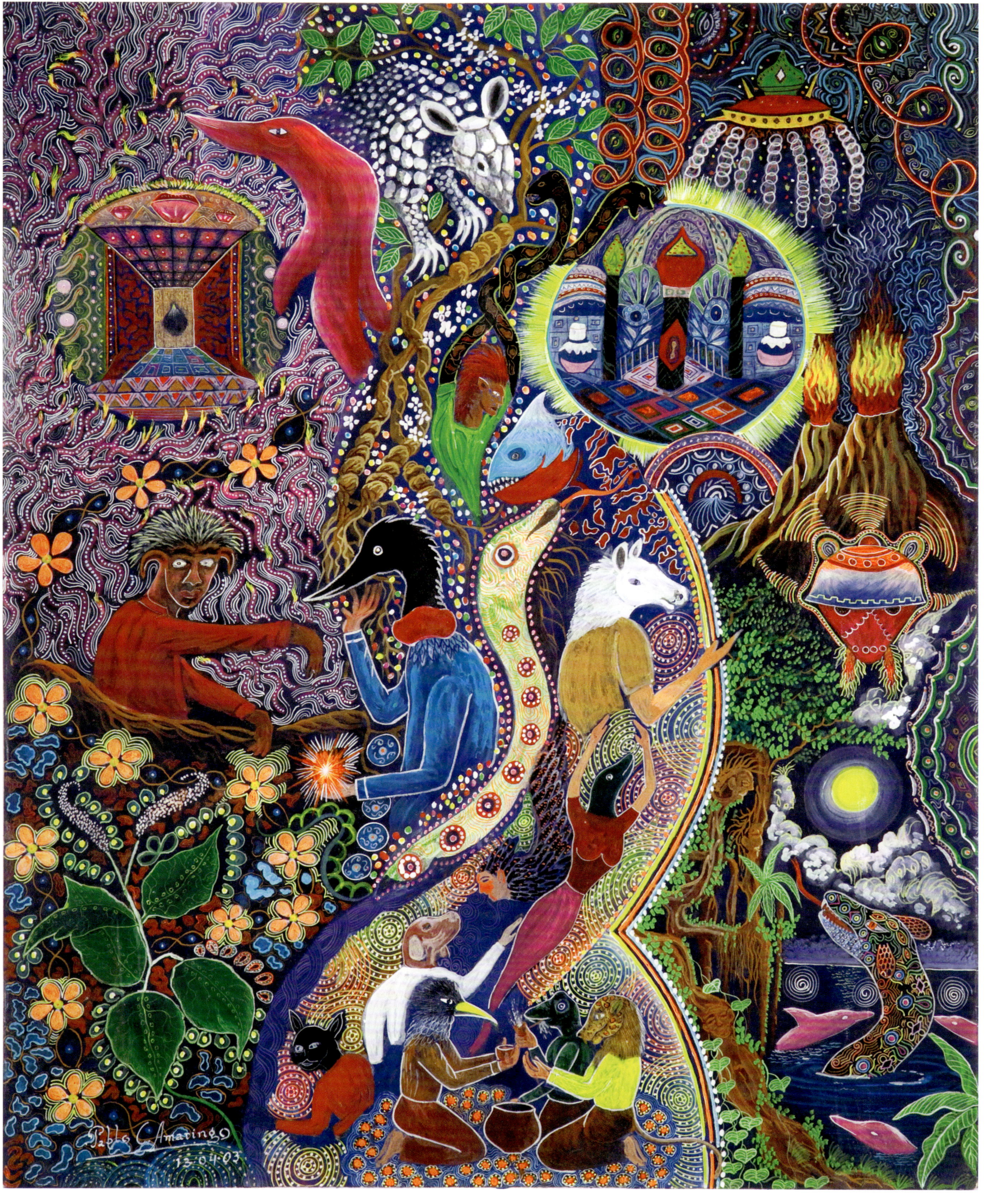

CHASHNAMANCHO UMANKI
Así es mi cabeza
2003, Gouache on Arches Paper
51 x 64 cm.

the jungle by tracking scent trails. When a shaman makes a soplada with the head of a huangana, the person never needs a compass or map and will always find his way.

To the right you see a cocha and in the clouds above are the *puyurunas* (cloud people). By learning their ícaro a shaman can heal with the power of the rain and static electricity in the sky. In the cocha is a sachamama, which embodies the vital force of the earth and preserves the rain forest. Extraterrestrial ships constantly visit us and bring beings from unknown dimensions to inspire and encourage humanity using ultrasound ícaros.

On the right-hand edge of the painting you can see neutrinos (nuclear particles) and electromagnetic energy, which is the foundation of physical matter and the splendor of terrestrial life.

A sumiruna who has mastery of the four elements can sing the ícaro of the volcano, which imbues him with spiritual and imaginative fire, and with his soplo he can harness the power of an erupting volcano to cure any illness.

A great radiant light like the sun encircles the temple to the left. The purpose of this illumination is to celebrate the divine energy that forms our physical bodies. The human body is a sacred temple that is like a universe in itself, with the physical organs and glands performing different functions. The body consists of trillions of cells, and each individual cell has an incalculable number of constituent elements; all these work in total unison and harmony.

To the lower left are the sweet-smelling leaves and flowers of the *albaquita* (*Ocimum micranthum*), also called *huacrasisa* (horn flower). The uplifting aroma intensifies the concentration and perception of the shamans as they undergo their transformation.

Plants have evolved to produce nectar that entices birds and insects to propagate their pollen and seeds. Amazonian shamans learn the ícaro of the albaquita to bring separated couples back together, a practice that is called *amarres amorosos* (love magic, or "ties").

These methods of healing require the maestro to follow the dieta. You can also use the energy of flowers for a soplada to bring out the grace and charm of a woman so that people love her.

On the upper left, surrounded by tingunas (electromagnetic patterns), is a door to the temple of alquimia palistica. This door is hidden from most people and only those who have been purified by their deeds and courage are allowed to enter the temple.

Chanasmancho umanki implies that the way my head looks determines how I think, because it is the same thing. A soplada with the moon will make a woman very beautiful and people will love her because she is like the moon. It is best to wait for a full moon and sing *quilla sumac* (beautiful moon) to her while she receives the gentle rays. The ícaro ties the moon's energy into her body as spirals, and makes her like a mother, or a queen. When the moon rises, everything in the jungle transforms, all the animals move to different locations. The moon has an important influence on the metabolism of plants and animals, and affects the minds of humans.

In this painting the maestro transforms himself through his mind and heart, using the ícaros of the animals, plants, clouds, and heavenly bodies.

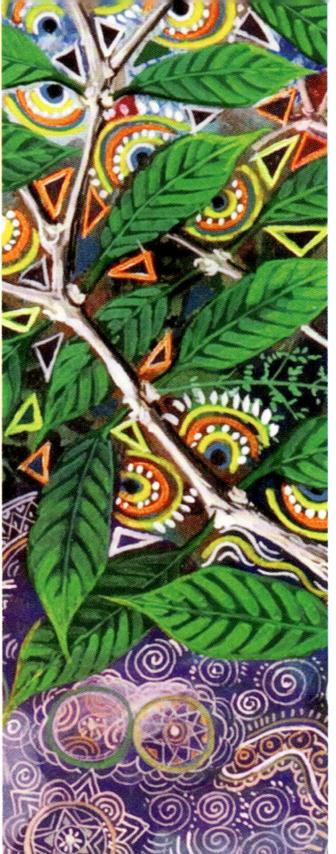

YANA HUÁMAN

AGUILA NEGRA

Yana huáman means "black eagle" in Quechua, and refers to a powerful maestro with the innate gift of a benevolent teacher who cares for his apprentices as though they were his own blood.

The black eagle does not fly like other birds, as it has specialized *remiges* (flight feathers) on its wings that enable it to soar very high. Its phenomenal eyesight can distinguish small details from a great distance, thus a *yana huáman* possesses the gifts of insight and discernment known as *huáman ñahui* (eagle eye). With the eye of insight a person can add new information to what is already known. With the eye of discernment a person recognizes an issue and assesses its components.

This noble maestro stands in front of the illuminated temple of the *huáman poma* (eagle tiger), an enchanted place for learning the ícaros of plants and animals.

The yana huáman teaches his apprentices in the ways of the *wani* (dark) sorcerers who use hechicería marupa. Then there are *chonteros,* who fire virotes with the same malevolent intentions. An apprentice must be fully conversant with all these evil practices to be able to heal the daño they cause.

The apprentice learns how to perform soplos to protect his homes and clothes, especially before eating, so that enemy demons cannot invade and kill, and to prevent tunchis from frightening or molesting him. He teaches them to chant ícaros to stop snakes and toads from entering the house. This is common when the surrounding vegetation is very thick.

The yana huáman teaches his apprentices to emulate respectful Indians who do not touch other people's possessions imprudently or thoughtlessly, in case they have been used in a ritual. Neither should they wear other people's clothes, because through contact you can pick up another person's bad luck or negative energy.

The wings of the black eagle in the picture symbolize the protection the maestro gives to his apprentices, just as a father places his children under his wing so they can develop their skills and knowledge safely. Without him they are vulnerable and susceptible to the machinations of wani sorcerers.

Above to the left you see the *punga* tree (*Bombax munguba*), which secretes a phlegmlike resin from its soft wood. Using the ícaro of this tree, a maestro extracts a maleficent intrusion, such as a virote or marupa. The mariri absorbs virotes and poisons and renders them harmless.

Below is the *yahuar mono coto* (*Alouatta seniculus,* blood howler monkey) whose ícaro cures infected blood caused by daño.

The *yahuar toro* (blood bull) eats herbs and plants used by sorcerers, and its ícaro heals *manchari*—a state of trauma or fright caused by tunchis and malignos. The ícaro also heals mal aire, an illness caused by bad or cold air.

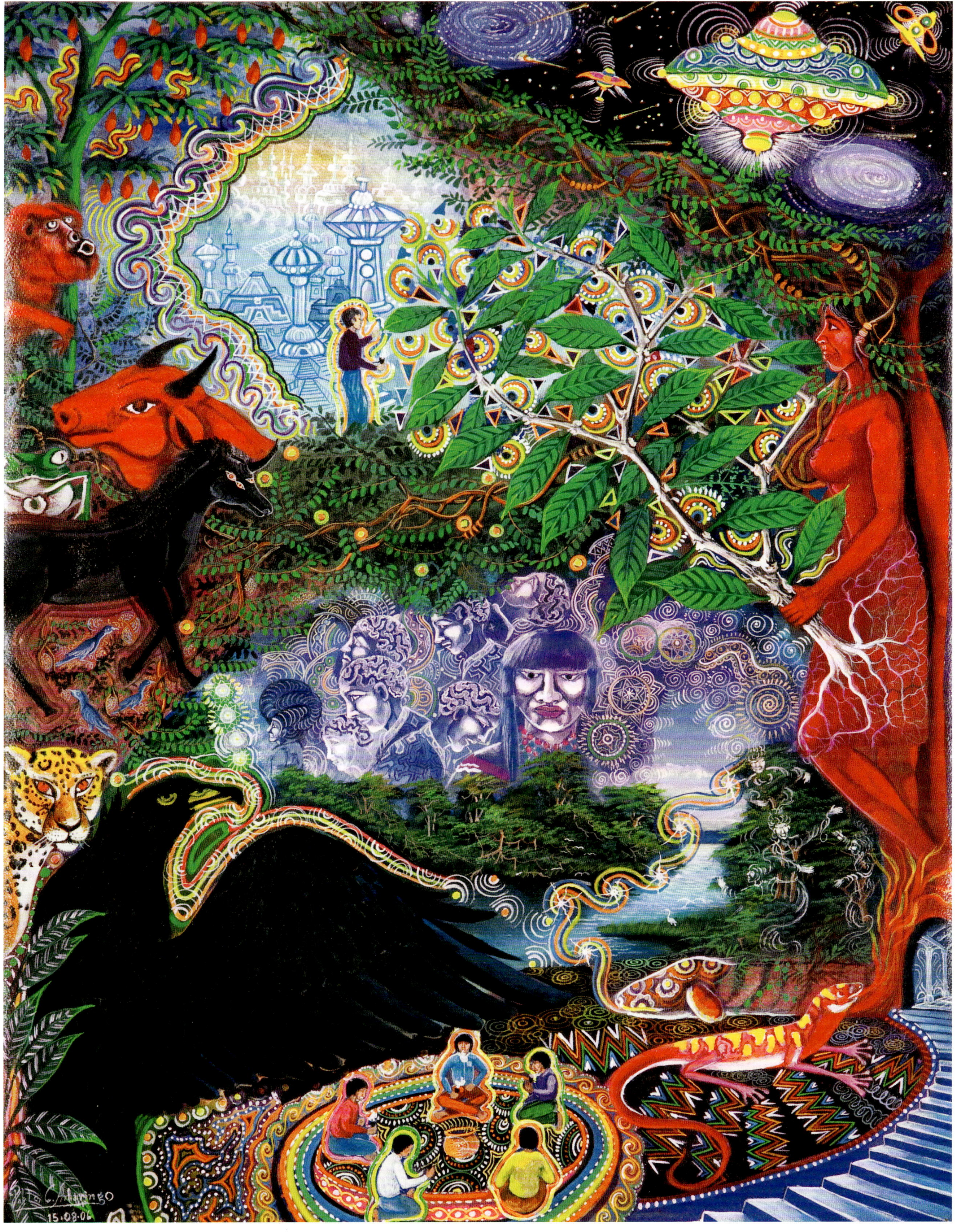

YANA HUÁMAN

Aguila Negra

2006, Gouache on Arches Paper

46 x 61 cm.

To the left is the venomous *sapo* (*Phyllomedusa bicolor,* giant leaf frog) used in marupa sorcery, whose ícaro also heals the victims of this type of sorcery. The maestro removes the toad's poison with his mariri. The horned horse with five eyes is a *supaycaballo* (phantom horse); this ferocious creature is used by sorcerers for stealing a person's soul. The curandero controls this beast through its ícaro, and with his soplo of mapacho smoke, reincorporates the victim's soul.

The blue birds below are called *montetes* (*Nothocrax urumutum,* nocturnal curassow). The ícaro of this bird enables a maestro to discover other people's secret intentions, thus the bird is his guardian.

The apprentice learns the mysterious ways of the *yahuar puma* (blood jaguar), which, unlike the *otorongo* (tawny jaguar), will track and hunt you if it sees you. It is a dangerous and savage animal and moves without making any sound, not even the slightest rustle. It can pounce and kill you without warning.

The otorongo in the painting is the feline king of the jungle. The hypnotic power of its eyes may be harnessed by a master shaman who knows its ícaro, so his enemy will think he is a cunning and savage otorongo.

Below are the leaves of the patiquina pintada, which are used in floral baths to protect against hechicería. The ícaro of this plant also protects against sorcery.

The yana huáman teaches the mysteries of the *supay gato* (phantom black cat) and the *yana allco* (black dog). The ícaros of these animals enable you to see good and bad spirits, and they sharpen your sense of smell and hearing so you can detect your enemies. The ícaro of the *yana huallpa* (black hen) is effective at curing depression and mal aire.

When the fat of a black hen is mixed with the excrement of a black dog and daubed around the eyes, whether it is day or night you see ghosts, demons, and gnomes. To see normally again you must use the fat of a white hen mixed with the excrement of a white dog.

To the lower right is the iridescent *nina ukulluco* (fire lizard) projecting flames from its mouth. The ícaro of this magical animal is used to cure burns, inflammations, and wounds caused by stinging insects, scorpions, and snakes.

The yana huáman uses the spirit of the aquatic lizard for frightening enemies. A soplada for instance, will cause a snake to fall on the enemy, warning him not to attack. The lizard with a black back, however, is for killing.

Just behind is the sachamama (mother of the forest), with trees and plants growing on her. She projects an electromagnetic rainbow that symbolizes the elements that fertilize plants. The curanderos in the ceremony are singing the ícaro of the sachamama to prevent sorcerers from thwarting their work.

The woman on the right edge of the picture is the mother of the puca lupuna tree. A disciplined maestro who has undertaken the rigorous dieta demanded by this powerful palo climbs the stairway (bottom right) to her temple. She is the "tree of the red moon" and teaches the mysteries of the lunar rhythm that influence women's ovulation.

A shaman calls on the mother of the puca lupuna for assistance when healing, and chants the ícaro of her sap. Here she is holding a chacruna plant, the leaves of which are used to make ayahuasca. The addition of puca lupuna sap to the brew enables you to you to physically see and talk to her in your mareación. The sap is her blood and it bestows the gifts of healing and self-defense.

Another way to ingest puca lupuna is by cutting into the bark to obtain the resin, which is then mixed with tobacco and left for a week, until it becomes more fluid. After drinking this you sleep for twenty-four hours, and the next day you remember all your visions perfectly.

The mother of the puca lupuna takes you back to the primeval origins of the Amazonian Indians, a people with no language at all who made only grunts and guttural sounds. You see many nations: Jibaro, Huambisa, Machiguenga, Puca Chaqui or Huaorani, Amahuacas, and Mashcopiro. The latter three remain isolated and refuse to this day to wear clothes. Some of these are depicted in the middle of the picture.

With puca lupuna you travel with the clouds and discover distant islands. The Indians examine you, open your mouth, lift your eyelids, and look inside your head to examine your brain. You are completely exposed and frightened.

Their hair is coiled like snakes. They call you to eat but the spirit tells you that you should not. They teach you to throw a spear, use the *pucuna* (blow pipe), speak many languages, and mimic with expressions and thoughts.

When you wake up you feel good. You go into the forest after blowing mapacho smoke on your body and rubbing tobacco on your shoes to keep the snakes away. She shows you how every tree has an emotion that affects all life around it. You become very sensitive to smells. Flying saucers are always around when you make ceremonies with lupuna.

VARIOPINTO DE LA CHACRUNA

In the upper part of the painting is the crucible of alchemical transformation representing the genesis of ayahuasca mareación. On each side are magnificent sylphs; on the left is Mesafel and on the right is Resfenel. They are the guardians of the two plants, chacruna and ayahuasca, that combine to form the mystic brew—ayahuasca. The chacruna induces colorful visions, while the ayahuasca liana promotes insight. If you drink pure ayahuasca—the liana without chacruna, perhaps some mapacho tobacco—your visions are only in black and white.

The shamans in the ceremony below are receiving knowledge of the union of opposites from these celestial beings. On the right one learns about black and white. The source of all life and unmanifest energy is darkness, so when you are meditating or looking for inspiration you must do this in a dark place.

On the upper part is the palace of *onánti,* a Shipibo word that means "knowledge." Here sublime teachers show you who you really are and where you are going with your life. They let you see the truth about your nature and personality without arousing aversions or fears of a reprimand. You realize that all things have two sides: life has two directions, positive and negative, light and dark, and we must know both.

To be good you need to know its opposite within you, otherwise evil will pull you in. It is only by entering into the depths of the soul and striving to synthesize our opposing dispositions that we can transform ourselves. The two sides exist to show us good and evil. In the palace you choose whether to follow the path of evil or good. They let you choose the path you want to take.

The face with the luminescent eyes on the right shows that to receive insight, ayahuasca should be taken in darkness. We think we can see ourselves, but our inner self remains hidden in the darkness. We normally see from the outside; our clothes, for example, are merely part of our outer appearance, which we use to present ourselves while disguising the quality of the heart and our real concerns. This is why the Indians say that they are the truly open ones, and that we are hypocrites because we wear clothes and seem to be other than what we really are.

Darkness increases sensitivity and inner awareness; even the pupil of your eye dilates. In darkness is found the energy of life; it is where we receive enlightenment and the illumination of our darkness. The erupting volcano represents the power of this radiant fire, which brings enlightenment.

If you look at everything around you and then close your eyes for five minutes, you will start to see with your mind, not with your eyes. Through practicing this you can develop a very powerful mind. The cyclops teaches the strength of inner vision; the single eye in his forehead symbolizes the power of the third eye that illuminates the mind. That is why I can retain so much detail of the visions I have seen.

There is a distinction between wisdom and knowledge. You can have great knowledge but it is useless if you lack the wisdom to use it. Knowledge can be great, but wisdom is challenging.

The spirits teach that in order to cultivate our mind, we need to develop our perception; that is, to

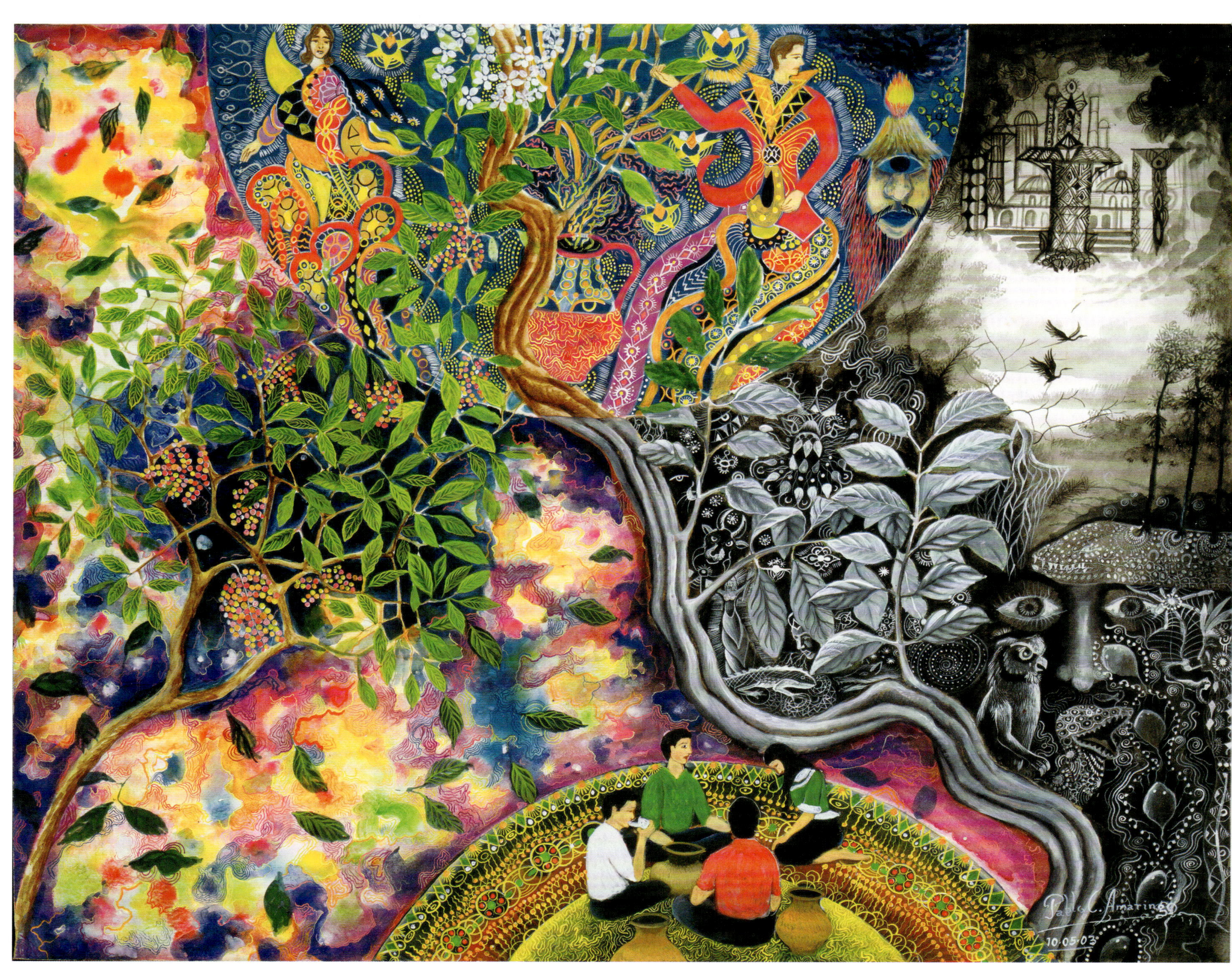

VARIOPINTO DE LA CHACRUNA
2003, Gouache on Arches Paper
48 x 62 cm.

see things from a different perspective. If we look at an object from another viewpoint we gain a broader understanding. We can look at something both upside down and the right way up.

You must read words differently; this enables both sides of your mind to work. For example, let's read this note here: It says, "Inventory of Paintings." But looking at it the other way around it says, "Paintings of Inventory," which has another meaning. One then has another perspective. This is how you should read, both ways.

Sometimes when we learn more and expand our minds, the brain chemistry alters and we become hyperchemical, which means you can metamorphose at will. For example, I could transform into a hawk, a large owl, or a *rompe-mortaja,* seen below.

On the right is the sachamama, with trees growing from its back. After hundreds of years without moving it has become part of the forest. If it sees you first, it becomes invisible to you and will come directly at you with an open mouth to ingest you.

This creature is supernatural because you can see the trees standing there normally, but not the mother underneath. If you follow the proper diet and take ayahuasca she teaches you her ícaro, so you can develop hyperchemical abilities. When you are a powerful curandero you can transform yourself into an animal or become invisible to brujos wanting to harm you while healing. This ícaro has to be sung deep in the rainforest where no one can overhear; otherwise those hearing it get sick.

Lower down is the yacumama (mother of the water). To its side are stingrays, which grow to be huge after forty years. These giant fish, known as *rayamamas* or *pambamuri,* may surface near the banks of rivers looking exactly like beaches. They are covered with sand and you can tread on them normally.

To the right, wearing his crown is an *ayar,* an Incan sumiruna able to transform himself into animals and trees to explore their elemental nature. Here he has transformed himself into a *machaco runa,* a being with the head of a human and the body of a snake, in whose body you can see shapes representing hyperchemical particles.

Science can teach us much about food and nutrition. A diet purifies the body; excessive salt and sugar corrupts the body, while the spirits stay away from people who eat salt in particular. This is why the shaman's diet prohibits salt and sugar. Through our diet we can learn to be closer to the spirit world.

On the left we see clouds and waves of chromatic energy. Colors symbolize a person's knowledge, insight, and discernment. The aura can be perceived as emanations of color, and a maestro with an awakened third eye understands the aura's importance in revealing our inner nature and how we conduct our lives. Bright colors are an indication of perfection, and soft colors, sublime beauty and purity.

We see the ayahuasca ceremony surrounded by tingunas, indicating that transformation is taking place. These electromagnetic emanations can materialize into trees, clouds, plants, or animals. A good shaman will see many colors because he is knowledgeable.

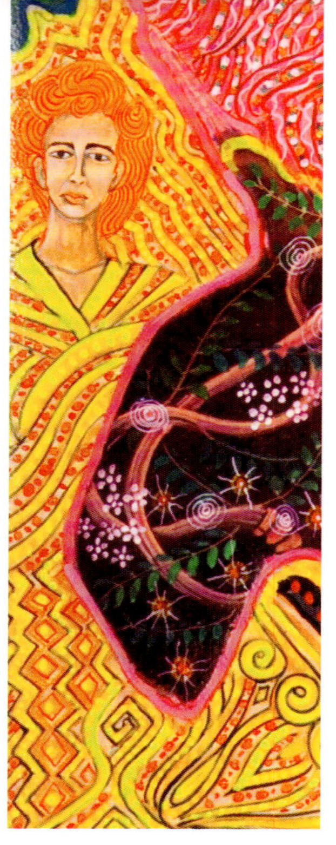

ANGELES AVATARES

ESPÍRITUS PERSONIFICADOS

This painting depicts the transcendent nature of the gravitational forces that control the rotational, orbital, and swaying movements of the earth.

As in antiquity, the indigenous people of the Amazon see natural forces as having a spiritual personification. Avatar angels are the guardians of the earth—cherubim that reside at its four corners. In the painting these angels are aligned with the four directions: north, south, east, and west. The fuchsia angels are in the west, the yellow to the east, the green to the south, and the blue to the north. These cherubim hold the earth within an electromagnetic field that manifests as a gravitational force. This field keeps the oceans and seas from overflowing as Earth spins on its axis. The immense mass of water rotating with the earth would spill over if the spiritual forces of the angelic powers did not maintain it.

In the upper left you see the avatar angels in their celestial realms holding the gravitational forces precisely, and thereby safeguarding the planetary biosphere. No one can say this all happens by chance or accident.

The ocean currents circulate in long cycles due to varying salinity and temperature. They maintain the global climate system, which enables the rain to fall on the rain forest and flow back to the ocean through rivers. Avatar angels watch over the opposing centrifugal and centripetal forces that result in the circular movement of Earth, and prevent it from spinning out of control.

The ayahuasca vine and chacruna plants growing from the Shipibo tinajas with geometric patterns are boiled together to make the mystic brew ayahuasca. The avatar angels transmit spiritual energy to plants so that maestro shamans can see in their visions the angelic powers at work.

The colors of the avatar angels have significance: green represents the principle of life, blue stands for zest and energetic strength, and the yellow to the east represents morning freshness and joy. In the west, the color fuchsia represents the satisfaction of a productive day.

There are ícaros for the rotation of the earth and they can be very effective for healing. In the session below, three sumirunas wear their feathered crowns and smoke their pipes while singing the ícaro of the green cherubim to cure a patient suffering daño. Pulsarios are leaving his body in spiral waves. After healing they sing the ícaro of the blue cherubim so that he gains strength. The ícaro of the fuchsia cherubim prevents boredom and inactivity, and the ícaro of the yellow cherubim will make a person happy.

Around them you see *sacha chikuri* (*Cichorium intybus*) leaves, which are used as a compress to reduce skin inflammations and infections. At the lower left are the leaves of *lengua* (*Cynoglossum officinale*), used medicinally as an astringent and antiseptic.

Extraterrestrial ships visit Earth frequently. They come from parallel universes and sumirunas board them to understand the mysterious forces of electromagnetism and gravity that maintain the cosmos. To the right you see a giant neutrino that has manifested and will transmute into physical matter.

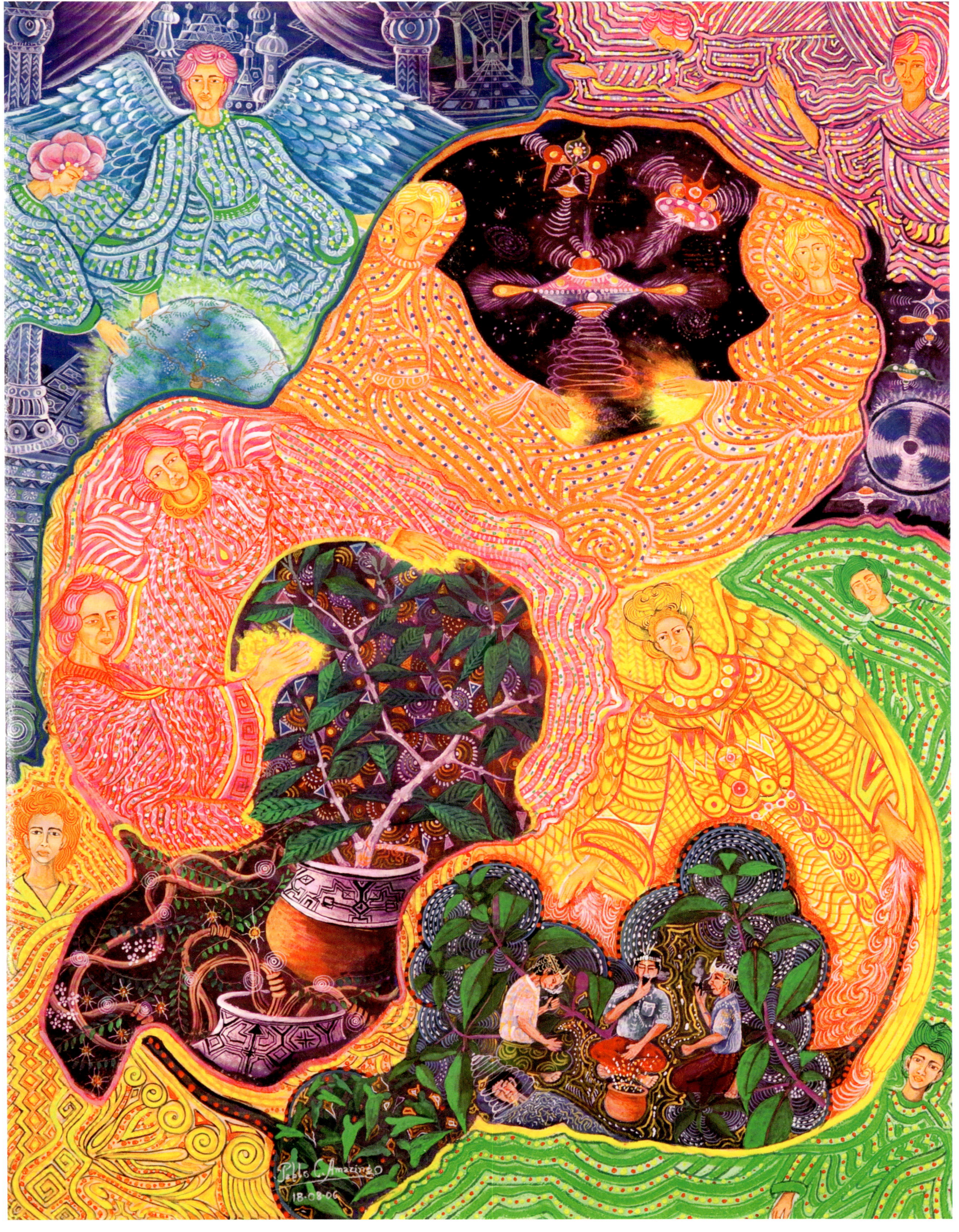

ANGELES AVATARES
Espíritus Personificados
2006, Gouache on Arches Paper
46 x 61 cm.

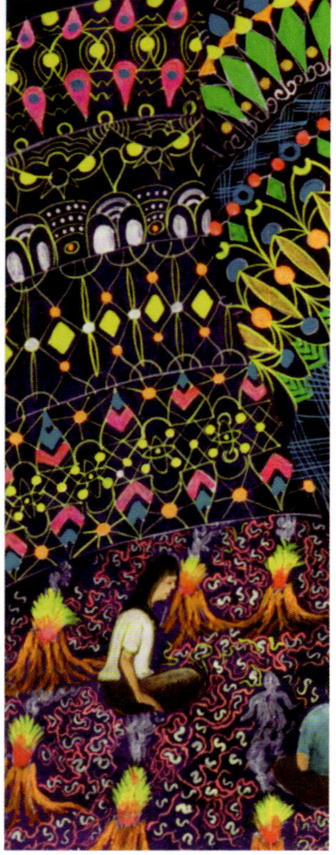

UNICORNIO DORADO

Here we can see two ceremonies, one on each side of the picture. The ceremony on the left is with indigenous and *mestizo* people (of mixed ancestry), and on the right there are highly educated, cultivated people—scholars and priests.

The time it takes for an educated person to learn and gain wisdom and discernment is dependent on his training and the manner of his education. Indigenous peoples who have not been educated are, however, closer to the natural world and in contact with the domain of spirit. You find the spirits where there are forests, rivers, and cochas; in nature you can enjoy the silent whisper of the wind and even the sound of plants. This communion with the natural world forms the basis of growth and development for native people.

Spirits have the potential to learn and carry out fruitful actions, but they do not have a soul like ours. This is why they are guardians of living beings, plants, and trees. When trees are cut down you can see their spirits rising from them.

The *huacras* (horns) represent the different paths of evolution and knowledge; the native people and the educated people evolve in different directions according to their customs and culture. The huacra on the left shows the path of the native traditions, while the right one indicates the path of modern civilization. Those that follow the path of indigenous people arrive more quickly at the sacred temple. This shining temple is illuminated with the colors of freedom, peace, and beauty. It is a shrine of spiritual luminance and everlasting radiance. Those who are bathed in its light enjoy freedom of spirit, peace, and happiness.

The temple is guarded by cherubim, not angels, and they allow only those who are pure and virtuous to enter. If granted permission to enter the temple you are announced by the ringing of melodious bells and chimes. These bells range from tiny to massive in size and are made from different metals, crystals, and precious stones. Each of these bells has a unique timbre, and together they produce an enchanting and harmonious resonance. When you hear the sound of these bells you are uplifted and filled with the fire of vigor and vitality.

Inside the temple the sublime divinities are making plans and diagrams for a material world capable of limitless expansion for life to proliferate. To the right side of this magnificent temple is the entrance to a universe inhabited by spirit beings with eternal life.

In modern urban cultures everybody receives an education—people study at schools, colleges, and universities. This is organized in a formal and structured way, and although you are taught many facts and techniques of classification and analysis, you are not taught how to understand or discern. Often what we study creates confusion and delays the acquisition of natural wisdom. Indigenous people are not educated in this sense, but are taught through ceremony to be aware of environmental and spiritual forces.

The destiny of humanity is to live in harmony with nature, to seek mastery of a spiritual life without exploitation or greed. Indigenous peoples, when left alone, live in balance with nature and

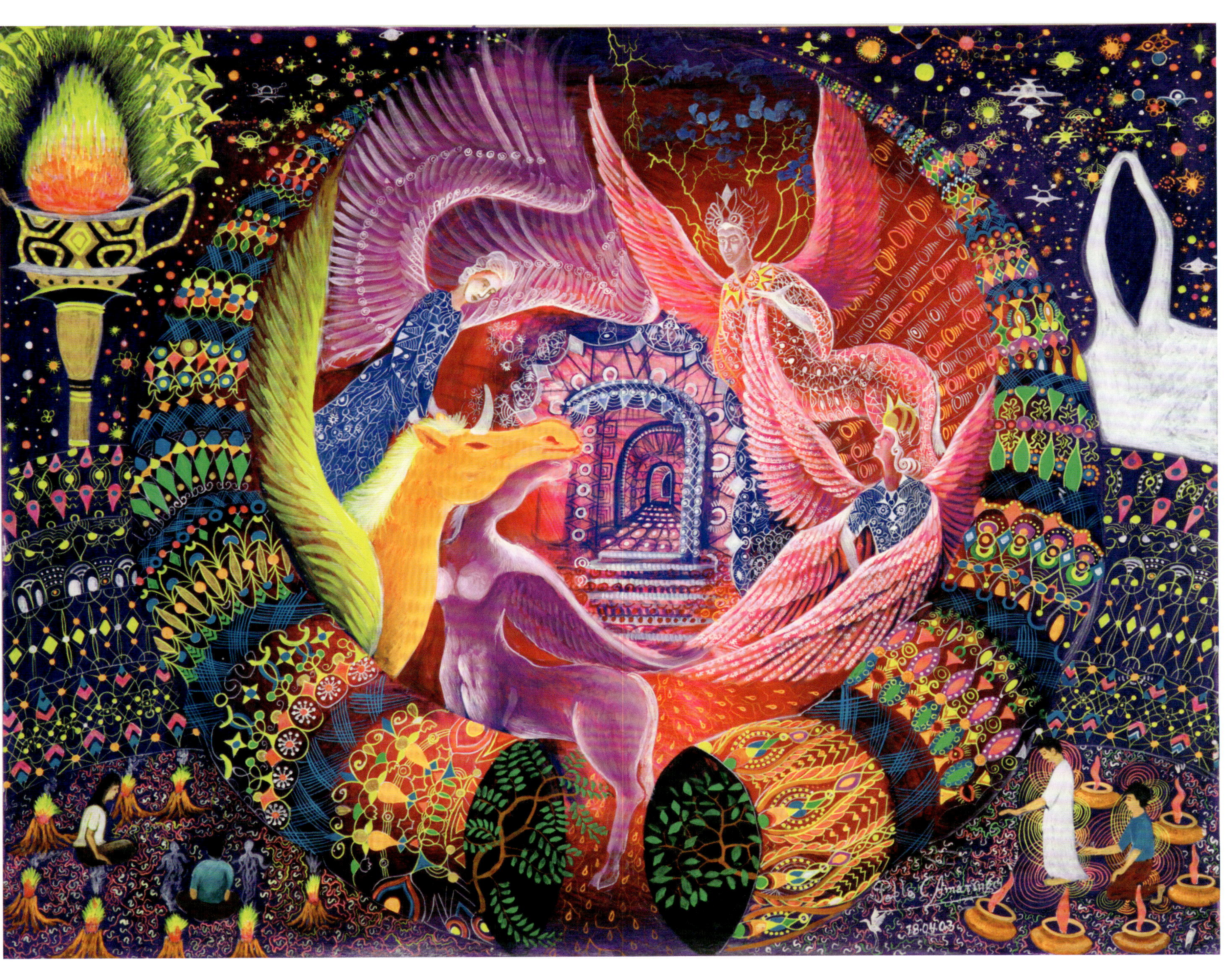

UNICORNIO DORADO
2003, Gouache on Arches Paper
48 x 61 cm.

possess an awareness of spiritual realms. To us they may appear primitive and naive but that is not true; they have wisdom that recognizes and respects the beliefs and views of all people. They have a reverence for the sacredness of plants and animals; their devotion is to preserve life. This is the teaching that is gained by the huacra on the left.

When learning with ayahuasca we can choose which of the two huacras we wish to follow. We can decide on the spiritual knowledge of indigenous people—the tried and tested way of natural wisdom; or the way of Western society, which explains the world using science. Our civilization has much knowledge and material wealth but does not have the spiritual knowledge and wisdom that brings true happiness, which comes with living in harmony with the earth.

I have been taken through both of these huacras. In the temple they told me that I was a penitent, respectful man and they taught me to be confident in my human form and respect all other humans. After I accepted this they sent me back on the violet mare seen here: a female unicorn (the male unicorn is gold). Riding the unicorn brings you back to the place they took you from; however, you return changed, revitalized, and awakened with knowledge, intuition, and creativity. They give you a new understanding of life. This is where you learn about justice and compassion.

This painting shows that there are many possibilities. You see that the mareación is resplendent with tingunas, which grow like colorful plants into diverse shapes.

The blazing torch on the left is a symbol of both spiritual protection and your own inner fire. The cherubim give you this in the luminescent temple and it makes you fully alive, and gives you peace and wisdom to teach this to others.

This painting is good for contemplation. When you look at it carefully and reflect on it, you receive wisdom. All the paintings in this book can be used for contemplation; the colors and forms are interrelated. If you find this difficult you should cover the painting for two or three months with a cloth of the same color as the painting. After this time prepare yourself with a cleansing bath, then dress in your best and brightest clothes with adornments and flowers. When you are ready to uncover the painting, concentrate and meditate on an important matter; then wisdom and good things will come to you.

The three of us are drawing from the essence of this painting while we have this conversation. I easily forget things when writing about a picture, but speaking the words brings out the depth and meaning. When writing about a painting, I usually write a few paragraphs to give the basic theme. But with this book we have followed a path of learning. It is a complete book and I believe people will be able to take much pleasure from it and contemplate many matters.

When a person laden with knowledge has the opportunity of speaking and teaching others, it is as though he discharges a great weight. I am very happy when I explain and teach these things. I feel happy because I am unburdening myself by what I give to you. By giving that knowledge I feel relieved, as if I were fulfilling a mission. I am very happy working with you, happier than I have ever been working with anybody before; it comforts me, makes me feel alive.

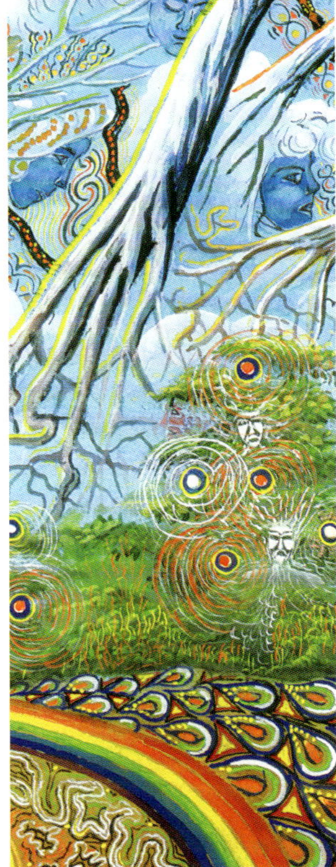

ILA

ÁRBOL MAGICO

Ila is the name given to magical trees that uproot themselves and fly up into the sky. As they go they become steamships like the acero punta or the *manchay buque* (splendid ship) from space.

When shamans walk along a tree, as you see them doing here, they can defy the restraints of physical laws, such as gravity. Thus they are able to visit other worlds, galaxies, and constellations. As the ila flies away it makes a terrific thundering noise that many find unbearable. After drinking ayahuasca the shaman begins his journey on the ila, causing more noise as other trees shoot out of the ground, roots and all. If he is not prepared for the noise, he could go mad.

See what happens to the earth when the trees take off? It is like an earthquake! What is left behind is pasture with a few little trees. The disciples and their maestro in the middle know that they are protected by the rainbow-colored arkanas that surround them, but others are frightened.

The man on the left is sick and the man on the right is being healed by a curandera using a *shacapa*. Below are the animals that have also been uprooted from the ground—anacondas, insects, and spiders—all caught up in the whirlwind and flying with the trees. The trees and plants are also entangled and even the stout renaco trees cannot resist the storm.

A tree has been transformed into a manchay buque in the middle of the picture and the maestros board it with the puyurunas. The most prestigious maestros wear tunics, mantles, or cloaks, and travel to the fifth galaxy in a tremendous asphyxiating heat. They must tolerate this until they get out and can breathe again. One maestro takes his bow and quiver of magical arrows for protection; another carries a shield. A third carries an earthenware pot of burning aromatic plants and resins; the smoke offers protection.

In the boat the apprentices sing and drink water only. It is rough but there is always something to learn from a difficult journey. When you are sick the ayahuasca is purifying you; that does not make it a bad journey. For an apprentice, however, it may be unbearable and the maestro should know how to apply a soplo to reduce his mareación, not on the crown of his head, but on one side and from the bottom up, not the head down.

My brother, Manuel Amaringo Shuna, was holding an ayahuasca ceremony for some people and he performed a soplada of the ila. Suddenly they saw trees falling and flying, and they ran away in fear because they had not been properly warned. Fortunately they were at their chacra, not in the city. You can see the serpents flying in the wind; they are cosmic serpents.

Flying saucers fly in front like guides shining a rainbow light. This is a beautiful painting if you can understand all that it says, not in words, but in colors and forms.

Just above the prow of the manchay buque are the mysterious regions of space called black holes. Although they cannot be seen they can effectively draw in celestial bodies. Inside the black holes

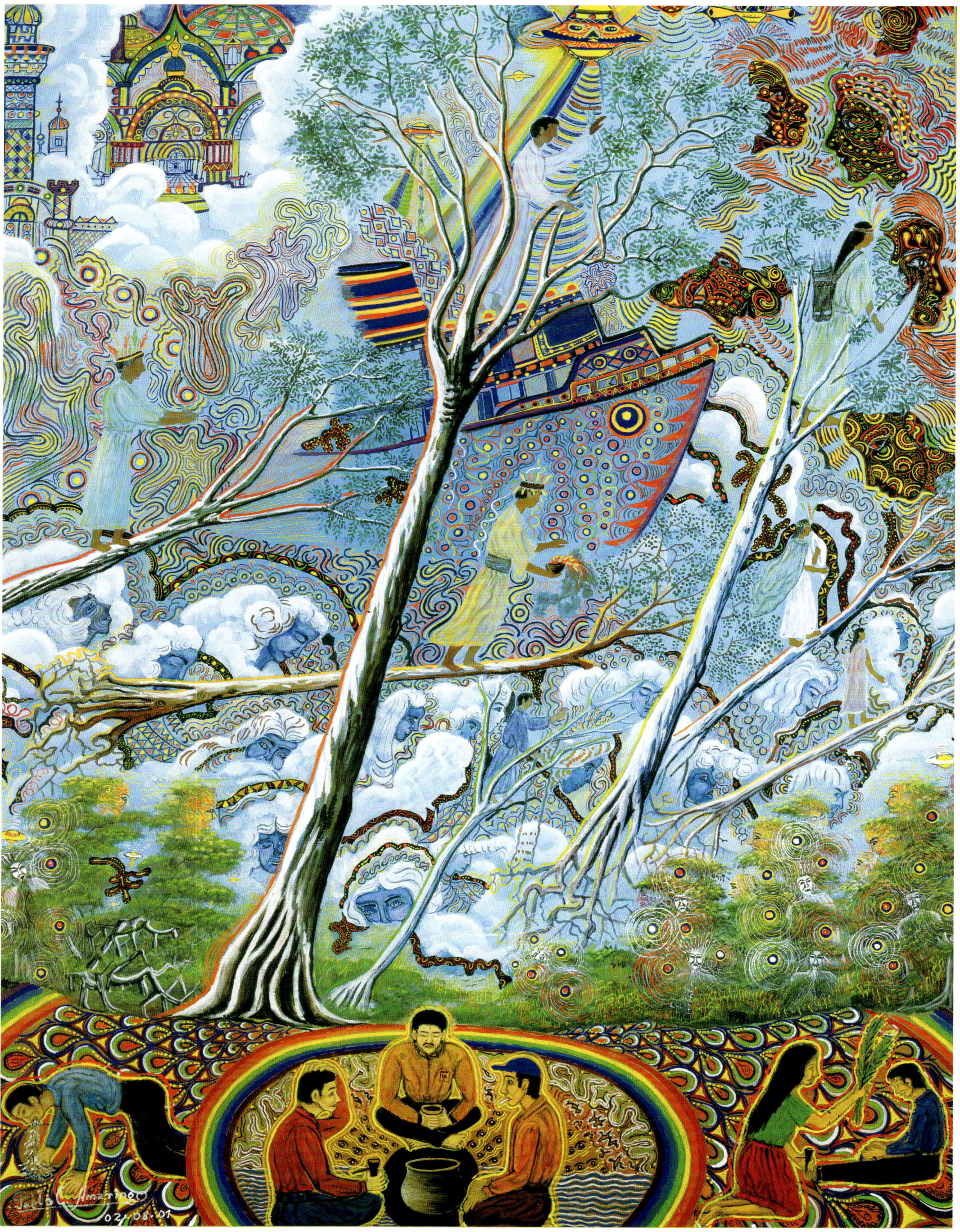

ILA
Árbol Magico
2001, Gouache on Arches Paper
57 x 76 cm.

you see the spiral galaxies and primordial material that has disappeared there. This is similar to when anacondas grow so big that they can eat logs, leaving their *mapirui* (snake excrement) on the beaches in the selva. Sitting near the mapirui is dangerous and can cause fevers and urinary infections. Shamans fly their ilas right into the black holes, using them as a conduit to other galaxies.

Here they travel to Orion to learn from the advanced civilizations that live there. The celestial temples of Orion seen at the top are where the masters of Atlantis learned their esoteric sciences, agriculture, and occult wisdom. The knowledge of Atlantis passed to the ancient Babylonians and Egyptians. The great pyramids of Giza are laid out as a mirror of the stars of Orion. The patterns on the beings with black faces represent astral forces; they are guardians of the black holes. These spiral and wavelike patterns show that the geometry of life uses curves, waves, and helixes; this is the form of the natural world. Only artificial, mechanical forms are made with straight lines.

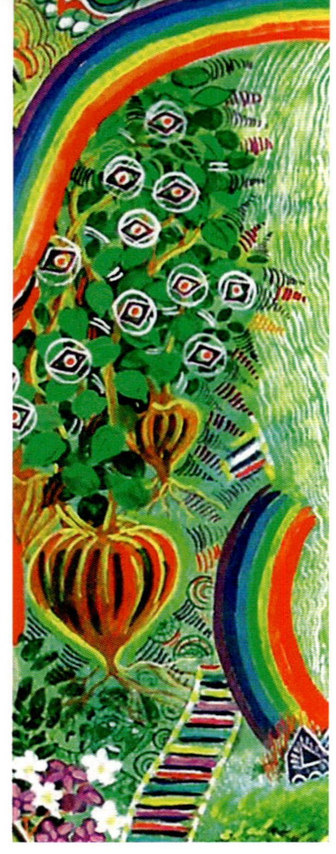

SINCHI PUCA LUPUNA

The most formidable tree a palero apprentice can work with is the puca lupuna (*Cavanillesia umbellata*). After a lengthy journey beset with trials, he reaches the splendid palaces and temples above made from precious stones and crystals. He must be well prepared for the strict diet required by this palo, which will test his resilience and character. If he fails he could lose his sanity, or even face death.

The mother of this tree does not distinguish between good and evil, thus both curanderos and hechiceros can learn to heal or to harm. A sorcerer learns to murder without any qualms, and can kill his own father or son without feeling shame. A curandero, on the other hand, can learn to heal this kind of sorcery. On the right edge of the picture is the mother of the puca lupuna, which is the great temple of alquimia palistica.

Many of the birds nesting in the canopy of the tree are useful to both curanderos and hechiceros: the *tuyuyo* (Jabiru stork), the *chicua* (*Piaya cayana*), the *suisui* (*Thraupis* sp., tanager), the *ayapollito,* and the *yacu pato* or *pompom* (water duck). The *sarara* (*anhinga anhinga,* heron), the *quilla sarara* (moon heron), *pucasarara* (red heron), and *yana sarara* (black heron) also live here.

Below you see the paleros in their ceremony concentrating intensely on their visions. If distracted, they could lose control and be overwhelmed by a tempest of elemental powers. At the bottom left the sachamama and the huairamama emerge from a tinaja with Shipibo designs. The sachamama is the mother of the jungle. When she moves the ground quakes and trees are uprooted, and she causes strong winds and lightning.

The huairamama is the mother of the sky and moves like a whirlwind, creating rainstorms and rainbows that project from her mouth. She has dominion over the atmosphere and requires the palero to stand firm while attempting to master her until the storm passes.

In the top left is the *yana machin* (black monkey) leaping between the branches. It is a brave and agile creature, and can intercept enemy virotes and marupa sorcery. Through learning the ícaro of the yana machin, a shaman can defend himself against these perilous threats so even a sorcerer with a command of wasps, scorpions, *ronsapas* (African honeybees), and poisonous *isula* ants (*Paraponera clavata*) will not be able to inflict too much harm. The nests of these wasps and ronsapas are just to the right.

To the left is the *yana puma* (black puma), whose ícaro is used by the shaman to acquire the puma's agility and speed to deceive his enemies. The ícaro is also used for counteracting fear, while a soplada with mapacho smoke creates an arkana around a person so that nobody can harm him.

On his journey with puca lupuna the palero learns from great spirits and wise teachers from other dimensions. To the right is an Amahuaca sumiruna, smoking his cashimbo in order to learn about a person and see his future. Just to his right, protruding from the puca lupuna, is a banco puma of the Wari people, and just above, a palero of the Chancas. The Chancas were powerful vegetalistas and that is why their descendants, the Ashaninka, have so much knowledge about plants. From the

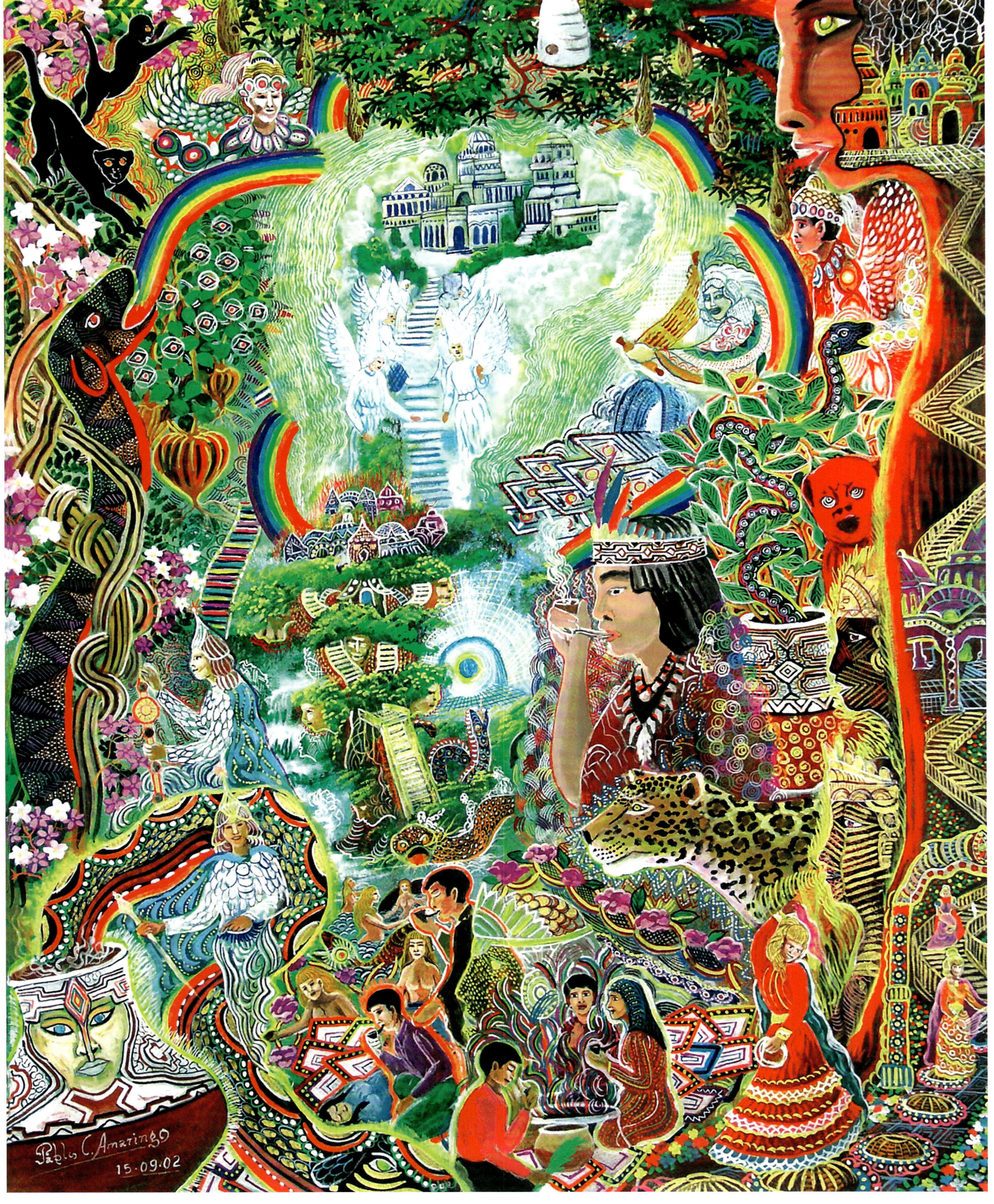

SINCHI PUCA LUPUNA
2001, Gouache on Arches Paper
57 x 77 cm.

Waris came the Panoan speaking peoples: the Amahuaca, Shipibo, Conibo, and Shetebo. Below is an Achuar sumiruna teaching his apprentices the ícaros for neutralizing harmful virotes.

To the left holding spears are dryads who teach the shamans the ícaros of the puca lupuna and other powerful palos, such as *ajosquiro* (*Cordia alliodora*) and *catahua* (*Hura crepitans*).

To the right you see the golden-haired sibyl known as Floripes. She is a princess from the galaxy of Andromeda who teaches the paleros the arts of divination: cartomancy, chiromancy, and scrying with crystals or water. The shamans can be seen divining with cards to discover hidden knowledge.

She rubs aromatic balsams onto the foreheads of the paleros to help them become clairvoyant. My grandfather, who was a powerful palero, could see the future and would tell people the date they would die.

Above her is the jaguar. A shaman who knows the ícaro of the jaguar is able to use the mesmeric power of its eyes to hypnotize his enemies.

Above and to the right is the *yahuar pelejo* (blood sloth). Sorcerers use the ícaro of this animal to harm their enemies. A curandero who knows the ícaro can take his revenge on the sorcerer. However, he too will then become a sorcerer.

Above you see Solomon, the king of ancient Israel. He had mastery over the elements and knew ayahuasca. Next to him is Atamat, the deity of wisdom, and in her papyrus scroll she shows the sublime power of words to inspire an entire new world. During Solomon's reign, many kings, queens, and princes sought audience with him to hear his parables, proverbs, and judgments. His people enjoyed peace and prosperity because of the knowledge and wisdom he received through dreams and meditation.

In the center are the steps that an apprentice must ascend in order to achieve higher states of consciousness. At the middle temple he will learn the mastery of spiritual forces and pythonism, or the art of predicting events. To reach the middle temple is a great challenge, as the steps fall away, so he must tread with care and agility. The yacumama is the guardian of the middle temple and if the apprentice can learn her ícaro, he will gain the power to dive into the depths of rivers and oceans.

On the way he will encounter the hypnotic eye. If the apprentice blinks or glances aside for a moment he will fail; without total concentration he will not arrive. He learns from the *papastrueno* (*Dioscorea* sp.) seen to the left. This powerful plant, when carefully used in a dieta, will grant the power of an electric storm. However, a sorcerer using the energy of lightning can kill a person or animal in an instant, wherever that person may be.

The celestial dome above is located beyond the ionosphere, and this is where the sublime ícaros of the atmosphere and the firmament are sung by avatar angels who are the guardians of the biosphere of the earth. A maestro reaching this exalted temple gains extrasensory knowledge and the ability to travel through space to visit other galaxies, such as Andromeda, and giant stars, such as Antares.

YACURUNA HUASI

Here we see the yacuruna living beneath a renaco tree with the *chaicuni.* The chaicuni are the ancestral spirits of the Shipibo; they dress like them and even have bells hanging from their noses. The yacuruna and the chaicuni live in the *shebónal*—seasonally inundated areas where *shebón* (*Attalea* sp.) palms grow. They hide amidst these tall palms that produce dense hanging fronds like thick ropes, called *maromas.* The chaicuni avoid contact with humans, and when surprised they immediately plunge into the water and disappear to avoid talking with us.

The roots of the renaco tree extend deep into the water, where they are home for the yacuruna. Those with green hair are called *taksha yacuruna* (small yacuruna); others are black, brown, blue, white, or multicolored. According to their color they go down holes covered by large colored stones. The holes are guarded by *yana cocodrilos* (black crocodiles).

The yacuruna come out of their tunnels to fish but their eating habits are different from ours. They drink *chapo* made from fish, and also enjoy the fruit inside the large seedpods of the *guama* (*Inga edulis*). They also eat the seeds of an aquatic grass called *gramalote* (*Brachiaria mutica*). Gramalote is protected by large black lizards that rarely allow anybody to go near because this plant is also used by curanderos to heal sorcery and *saladera,* a pervasive period of bad luck.

Puca gramalote is a variety used for healing. Curanderos make a poultice of it mixed with camphor resin (*Cinnamomum camphora, Alcanfor caspi*) and *Thimolina.* The poultice is placed on the body, where it draws out the sorcery.

What you see here is a yacuruna's house. I have seen how comfortably these *señores* live in their well-appointed houses. All their furniture is alive and moves; if you sit on a chair, it trembles under you, and worse! Animals of every kind are used as props for living; they are a part of the yacuruna huasi.

Yacuruna often kidnap people to reproduce with them under water. If you are a man, you may be taken for the husband of one of their daughters; similarly, a woman may be taken as a wife for one of their sons. They pull you into their world so you no longer recognize your own human world. You see people distantly, as we see a plane in the sky full of people.

After living with the yacuruna for a time you can no longer leave and you are no longer normal. For example, your foot might be twisted backward; it is very strange, but you can still walk perfectly well. Your face is twisted to the back of your head, your eyes go all white, you cannot see well, and you are completely changed. You forget all about your family and you no longer recognize people who live on the land; they have altered your brain.

The sumiruna in the picture is riding on the back of a boa to where the yacuruna live. A muraya with dominion of the underwater realm is riding on a *yana charapa* (*Podocnemis expansa,* black turtle). On the occasion I visited the yacuruna I was well prepared and rode in on the back of a charapa. There used to be many yana charapas on the River Ucayali in the old days; they climbed up the riverbanks and you could ride them.

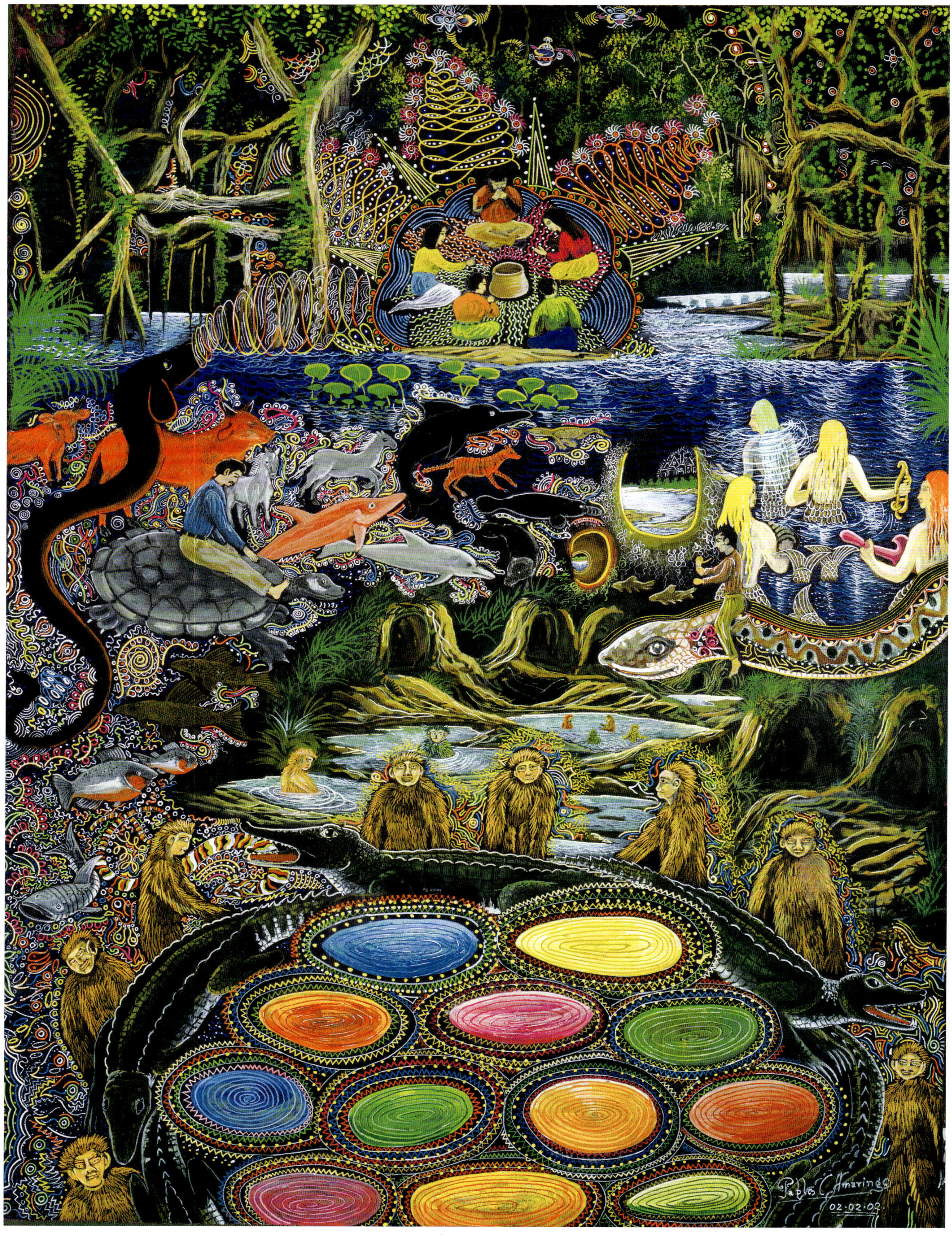

YACURUNA HUASI
2001, Gouache on Arches Paper
57 x 77 cm.

On the left is the anguilamama. She radiates spirals of electromagnetic rays that protect the shamans during their session. The blue waves surrounding the shamans keep them completely dry, even though they are seated in the water. This is the sign of a powerful shaman; he can be in the water without getting wet. The luminous spirals emanating from the renaco can heal hechicería and more complicated illnesses.

The red-bellied piranha (*Pygocentrus nattereri*) serve as defense against sorcery, and their ícaro can heal *mal aire del agua* (sickness from cold air). Large aquatic mammals, such as *vacamarina* (*Trichechus inunguis,* Amazonian manatee), pucabufeo, *yanabufeo* (black dolphin), and gray dolphin (*Sotalia fluviatilis*) are powerful allies to shamans who sing their ícaros to neutralize harm from sorcery, or when people lose their senses from pusangas (ícaros of enchantment).

In the cocha are *yacu caballos* (water horses), which sumirunas and murayas ride through subaquatic tunnels leading to other cochas and rivers. Also found in these tunnels are sirenas, bufeos, and many animals seen in the picture: yacu toro, *yacu ailco* (water dog), *paiche machaco* (*Arapaima gigas,* snake paiche), and the highly venomous *nacanaca* (*Micrurus* sp., coral snake).

Only people who have been taken by force can enter the tunnels where the most powerful yacurunas live. After eight months it is too late to rescue them.

When I was a boy I saw my grandfather, Ambrosio Amaringo Vazquez, rescue a person who had been missing for months. He was brought into the house looking half-dead, followed by several yacuruna. I was not allowed to look, but I was curious so I climbed up to the roof of the house and lifted the palm leaves to look into the room. There I saw the yacurunas with their faces hidden under their sunhats surrounding the rescued man. The padre on the veranda afterward said it was too late; the man was already transformed into a different shape. He said nothing could be done, the man would have to go back to live with the yacuruna.

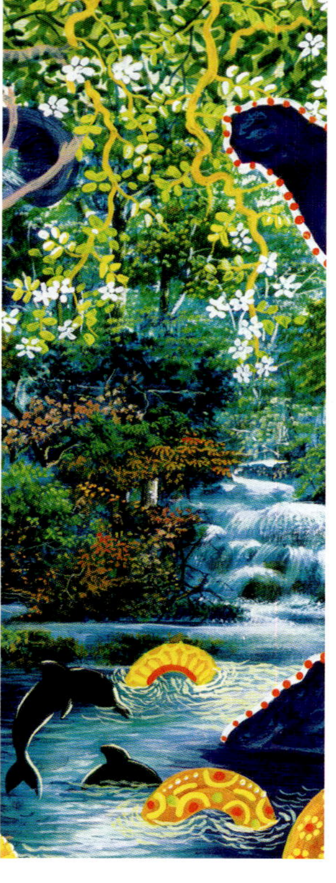

LLULLUN LLAKI SUPAI

AMOR FRESCO DE LOS ESPIRITUS

This picture represents the sublime mystery inherent in the plant kingdom, which produces the food and oxygen that animals and humans require.

The luscious rain forest and waterfall symbolize the primacy of water for life. The anacondas in the water warn us of the dangerous degradation of our rivers, lakes, and forests, and of destroying what is for our benefit. Seeing it makes you cry; people should not destroy the rain forest. When the spirits walk there they do not trample and crush the vegetation, they walk lightly, and we should learn how to do the same.

The sumiruna is horrified to see the destruction caused by humans who treat the forest as though it were worthless. He cries at the disorder in the world because he knows what is happening and can foresee everything that will happen. The cadaverous coral-colored people emerging from the mouth of the sachamama echo this tormented vision.

In the upper left are the maestro's bird allies: the tibemama and the sarara. They plead with us not to mistreat plants and trees, and to use only fast-growing trees for timber, not productive trees that fertilize the atmosphere. These mystical birds are sad at the way humans desecrate and squander their resources.

The anacondas are confused by our ignorance when they see the depredation of the natural world. We build densely populated cities, cover the land with concrete, and pollute the soil and water. Our buildings should be spread out to conserve the environment and not encase it in cement. That is why the *a'tun yana caballo* (great black horse) rises from the subaquatic tunnels that lead to the submerged Atlantis to warn us. We too could easily be annihilated, just as Atlantis was, by the terrifying destructive power of earthquakes, volcanoes, floods, and storms.

At the top of the painting are the huge eyes of the sachamama. She is sad and furious as she surveys the destruction of her habitat. What will become of all the animals of the rain forest without a place to live?

The bufeos have aligned themselves on the left to look like a plant, to illustrate their reciprocity with aquatic plants through their breath. Life spirit moves through respiration and inspiration, and bufeos give color and strength to the plants.

At the lower center is the a'tun yacuruna, the great master of the yacurunas. Luminous particles of ethereal matter flow through his body and give the sumiruna his extrasensory powers. The colors of the particles symbolize divine virtues: magenta teaches selfless love and altruism, ochre represents self-reliance and trust, and white gives integrity and purity. The yacuruna guard the underwater kingdom where they live and come out only late at night to survey humans on the land.

To the right are magnificent queens and kings: great teachers from the ancient Persian, Sumerian, and Indian civilizations. These venerated beings are wise and their knowledge profound. They remind

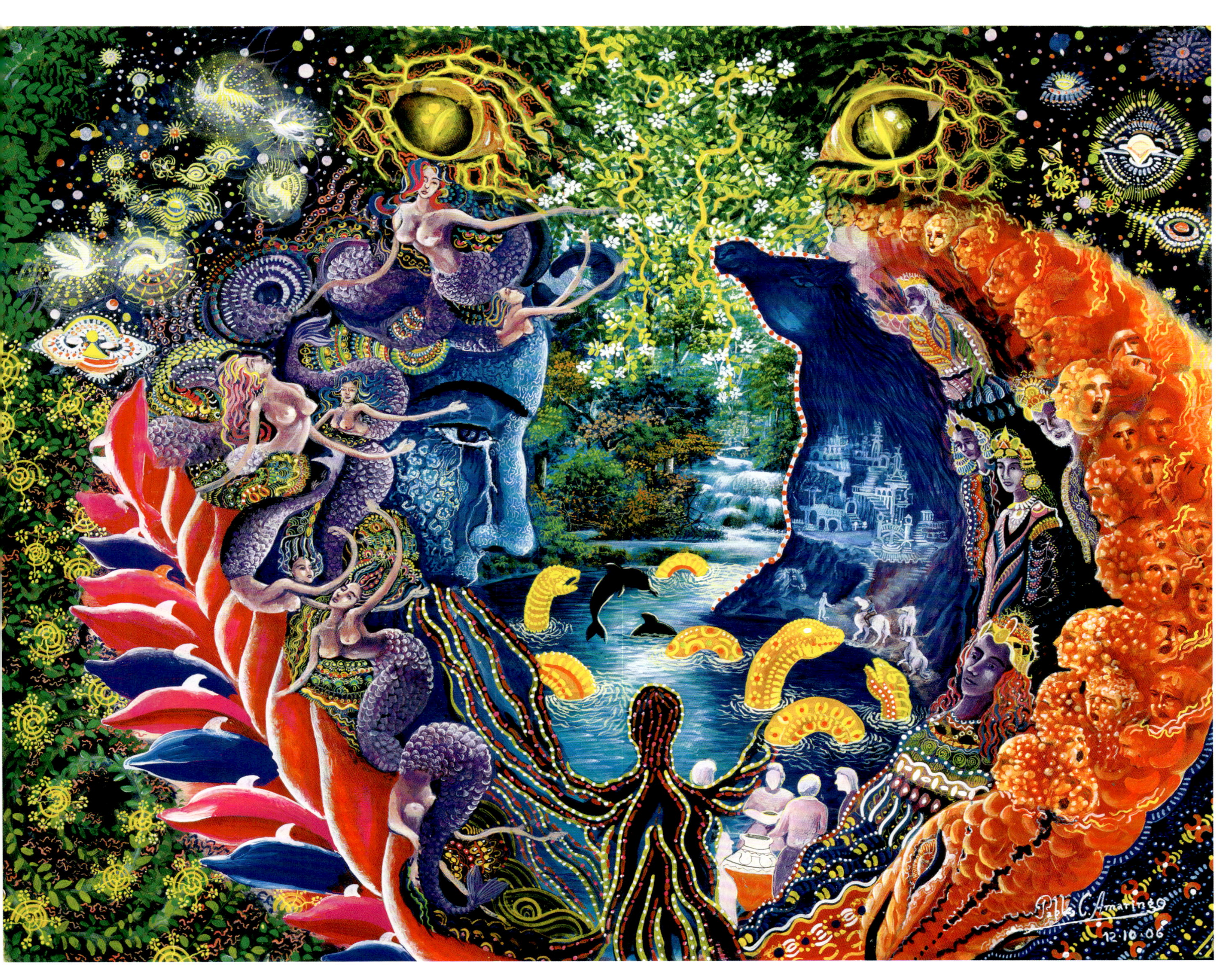

LLULLUN LLAKI SUPAI
Amor Fresco de los Espiritus
2006, Gouache on Arches Paper
48 x 61 cm.

us of the primal covenant between humanity and Mother Earth that gives nourishment and life. They teach us to care for trees, animals, the soil, and our water resources. If we do not regenerate and decontaminate the natural world, we will inevitably perish.

The sirenas here are *oceanides,* who preside over the freshwater sources of the earth, from subterranean springs to rivers. They have hyperchemical abilities and when visiting other galaxies, take off their fishtail-like trousers and soar into space. When a shaman sees the oceanides, he experiences his knowledge expanding and realizes how much he has yet to learn from life.

Some of the flying saucers here live inside the earth; others under water. Some spirit beings live on earth, others come from outer space, but all live as one. When they join together they appear like a plant.

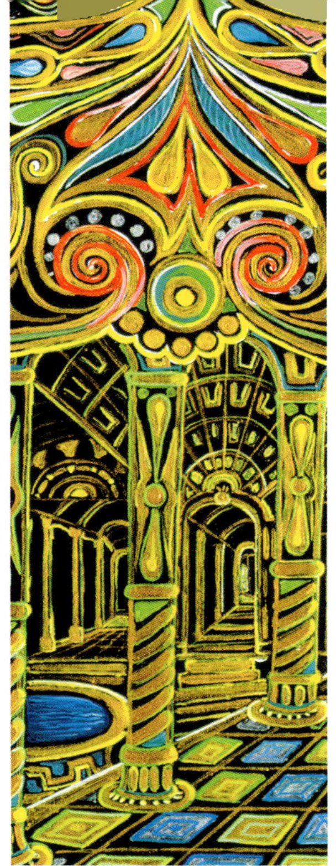

PAGODA DORADA

At the upper left of the picture is the huairamama (mother of the sky), who has dominion of the atmosphere. She moves like a whirlwind and creates storms; her rain fertilizes the rain forest and makes the plants flourish.

Just below the huairamama are circles with the shamans smoking tobacco in their cashimbos. From left to right they are onaya, muraya, sumiruna, and banco sumi. The hierarchy of these shamans also corresponds to the higher levels of consciousness to which an apprentice strives.

The sirens here are oceanides, who have dominion over wells, rivers, and subterranean springs. At the lower left is the sachamama (mother of the forest), who manifests the vital force of the earth and preserves the rain forest. To the right we see a sumiruna in a yellow shirt curing his apprentice of mal aire with a soplo of mapacho smoke. Below is an onaya healing a patient suffering from daño caused by malevolent sorcery. The spirals around them are caused by energy flowing into the shamans' hearts and minds as they make their diagnosis and concentrate on healing the illness. The curandera in blue is using this energy to sing the appropriate ícaros. In the midst of the fire are elemental spirits known as *seraphs.* A banco puma in a blue shirt and a curandera in a white dress are charging themselves with this energy so their sopladas of tobacco smoke will heal effectively.

In the center is the Pagoda Dorada, a temple where shamans learn the geometric architecture and physiology of the human body. They study the body's organs—the nervous, circulatory, respiratory, and digestive systems. These systems are more sophisticated than any manmade machine. The stomach and intestines are called the *cuenco de oro* (golden bowl). In Quechua the word *shungu* encompasses the combined function of the heart and stomach that keeps the body in precise balance.

The Pagoda Dorada is an occult temple that no one sees, like the soul of a person. Inside is perfect harmony; it is the optimal place for life to function. The distance between Earth and the sun gives rise to the exact temperatures and conditions for life to flourish on Earth. If the distance were any different, life on Earth would not be possible.

The five doors inside the Pagoda Dorada correspond to the five senses: sight, hearing, smell, touch, and taste. Without our senses we would be unable to perceive the physical world.

In the dome of the Pagoda you can see eyes, nose, ears, and a mouth. The red and blue semicircles symbolize respectively the blood and the oxygen essential to the body. The power of speech comes not from the throat, but from deep within the body, from the shungu.

Vegetalistas use trueno ayahuasca, seen on the right, to work with the resonant power of thunder to command respect. In the Pagoda Dorada the shamans learn the power of words to influence our thoughts. Badly chosen words can cause harm, so when you speak about people you must be conscious of your words to avoid defiling anybody. The two angels on either side of the Pagoda Dorada, with their trumpet and horn, represent the spiritual power of sound.

Above, wearing his gold crown, is an ayar who is a grand Inca sumiruna. The waves spiraling around him indicate his mastery of transformation into other living beings. Above you see the wise

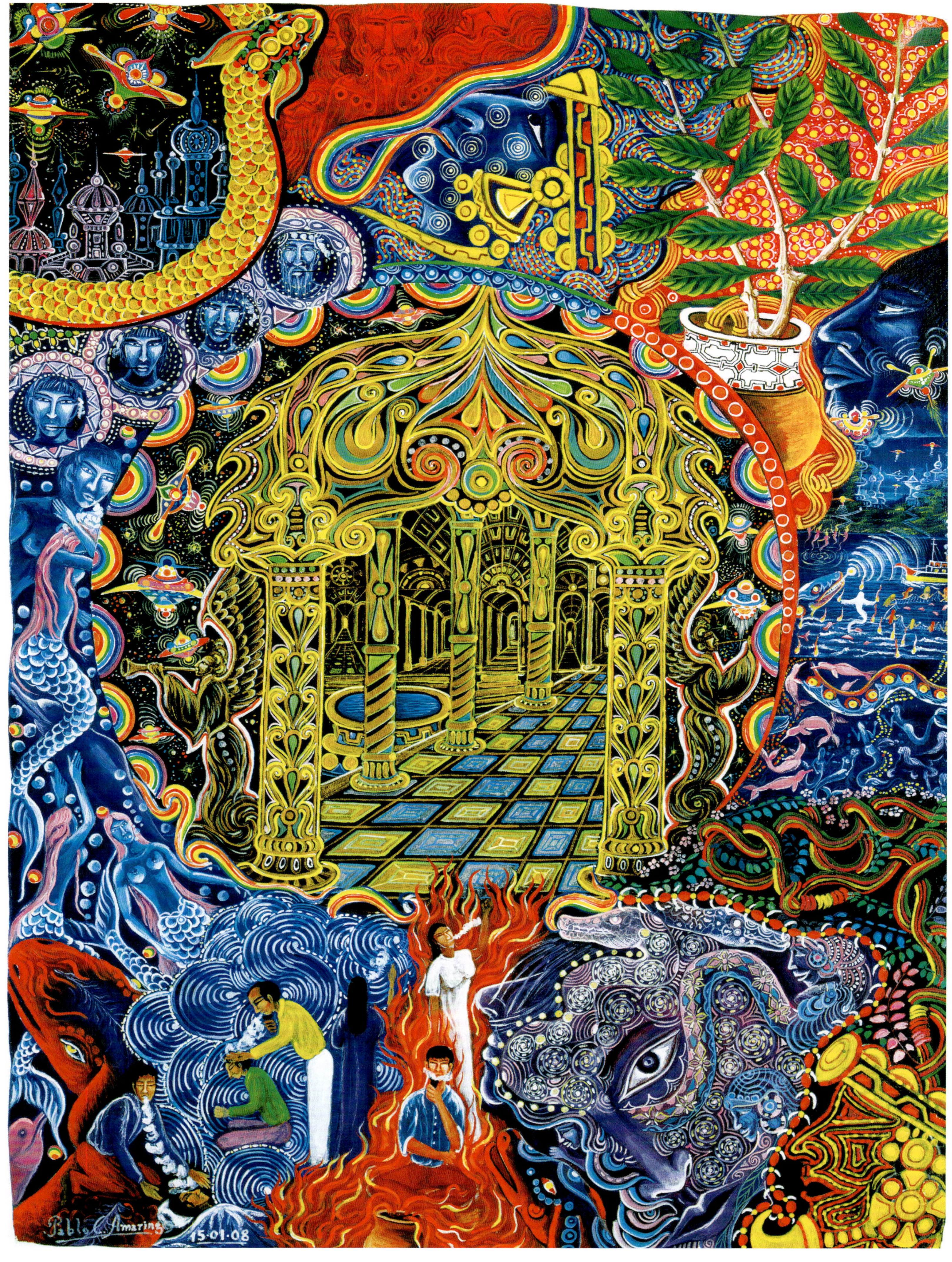

PAGODA DORADA
2008, Oil on Canvas
50 x 70 cm.

sovereigns known as the *a'tun mauca runa,* who are bringers of harmony. *A'tun mauca runa* means "the great ancient ones." They are the guardians of space, time, stars, and galaxies.

At the top is a Shipibo tinaja with a chacruna plant and an ayahuasca vine growing out of it. These plants combine to form the mystic brew ayahuasca. To the right is the face of an aborigine with a bone through his nose. In front is an extraterrestrial ship carrying beings who visited primitive peoples on earth in prehistoric times, and gave them laws and spiritual teachings.

Below you see a cocha brava with the barco fantasma, and the yacumama projecting electromagnetic radiation from its mouth. Sirenas are there with their magic nets for ensnaring enemies. In the cocha are the *nina chukchas*—beings with flames instead of hair; they are *malignos,* or evil spirits. The white-shrouded tunchi is a wandering human spirit, and is a common cause of mal aire and *susto,* or fright.

At the bottom right is an Incan ayar, a mighty sumiruna who is in the process of transforming himself into a *machaco runa*, a being with the head of a human and the body of a snake. Just to his left, in the composite face, you see the machaco runa and the spiral shapes of hyperchemical particles called *espiritones* that form the underlying composition of physical matter. The Incan masters transformed themselves into machaco runas with ease, and in this form were able to traverse the great distances between the galaxies at the speed of thought. These great maestros developed extrasensory abilities that allowed them to explore other dimensions and celestial realms.

In the upper left you see extraterrestrial ships arriving from a celestial city to teach sumirunas and banco sumis the science of transformation of physical matter.

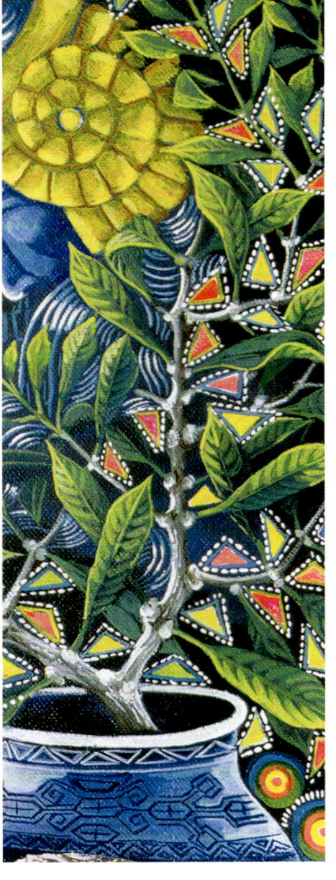

SOPLO DEL BANCO PUMA

The banco puma is a master shaman who transforms himself into a puma to go hunting or to hide from an enemy. In the old days when people in the Ucayali region did not have firearms to kill large animals, the banco puma would use his ability to bring back food for his family.

Magnificent cats, such as the puma, are rulers of the jungle on account of their strength, fierceness, and intelligence. When the shaman transforms himself into a puma he acquires its attributes; in particular a keen sense of smell and *sinchi-ahui* (strong eyes), which can mesmerize an enemy. A banco puma is a skilled healer with great knowledge of medicinal plants. He can also travel to other galaxies and dimensions.

A banco puma combines his ayahuasca with *bijahuillo* (*Stromanthe stromanthoides*), a plant that has the coloration of a puma and heals leprosy and skin diseases in the most mysterious way. It enables the banco puma to transform himself into a puma by making five somersaults.

In many parts of the world, including the Amazon, dogs were once used for healing by allowing them to lick a patient's body all over. The saliva contains antibacterial and antiviral compounds, together with enzymes that are able to cure many illnesses. In ancient Greece dogs were trained to lick diseased people at the temple of Aesculapius. It is common to see animals licking their wounds, which accelerates the healing of burns and sores.

The great master Jesus, who was a sumiruna, used his saliva to cure blindness by licking a man's eyes. Indigenous shamans are also aware of this treatment. There are many more esoteric healing methods using flowers, bones, stones, roots, and leaves.

To absorb feline wisdom, the banco puma sleeps with a cat lying at his feet. Cats are mysterious creatures with much wisdom and knowledge of plants. This close contact with the cat creates a telepathic communion.

Banco pumas like the one seen here were once highly honored as princes, and had crowns of gold embedded with precious stones and brightly colored feathers. Among their allies are nocturnal birds, such as the *ataulero* or screech-owl (*Megascops choliba*). The ataulero makes loud and strident calls, letting people know if anybody is approaching and whether they harbor good intentions.

When the banco puma ventures out on his pursuits, the ataulero accompanies him and because of its stealthy manner, does not betray his whereabouts. Other allies include the dove and the enigmatic bird flying in the top left, which symbolizes the mysterious nature of birds.

He wears a *troncomoro* around his neck; indigenous people also wear them around the waist. Troncomoros are made from the nuts and seeds of trees, and large beads carved from the *topa* and *cetico* trees. The one here is made from the male *huayruro macho* (*Ormosia* sp.), and the "female" *huayruro hembra*. The male huayruro seeds are black and red, while the female seeds are all red. Wearing them gives protection against the *mal de ojo* (evil eye). Adding the rib bones of small anacondas to the troncomoro, as seen here, gives added strength.

He also wears a troncomoro on his shoulder made from crystal, beryl, amethyst, jade, diamond,

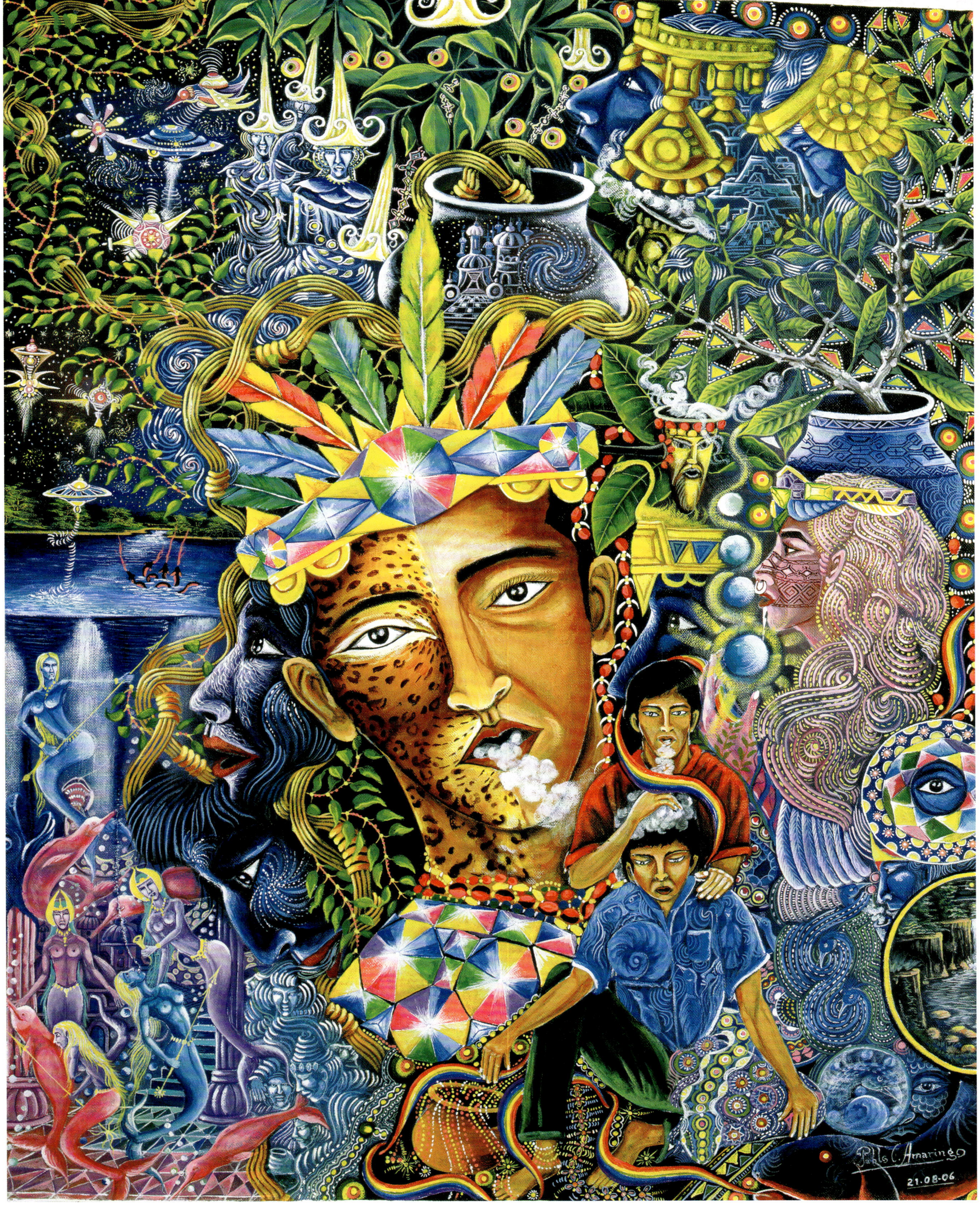

SOPLO DEL BANCO PUMA
2006, Oil on Canvas
72 x 91 cm.

sapphire, and emeralds that he uses for healing and protection. Emeralds protect against snakebite, and can help to cure tuberculosis.

On the upper right are women wearing gold crowns with *orejeras* (ear pendants). They are spiritual masters of the mysterious *chachapoyas* (cloud people) who were never entirely subdued by the Incas. Below them you see their magnificent city and citadel of Kuelap, one of the most impressive pre-Columbian ruins in South America, set on a mountain with immense walls, splendid palaces, and huacas (shrines) shrouded with secrets and mystery.

To the left an ayahuasca vine is growing out of a *mahuete,* decorated with a celestial palace and spiral galaxy indicating that the sacred vine is the *puncucamac* (gateway) to these esoteric realms. The mahuete to the right holds a chacruna plant.

The pipe below is carved with the face of an ancient Oriental doctor whose knowledge of the occult sciences imbues the pipe with spiritual power.

To the right of the banco puma is a Shipibo sumiruna; these were often women, as is the case here. Her arm is entwined with plants and radiant spheres are rising from her hand, representing other worlds like the earth. The spiral luminescence symbolizes the flow of life force throughout the universe.

Below her are two protective birds, the *trompetero* (*Psophia leucoptera*), and the *ishkay tuyuyo* (two-headed Jabiru stork), whose two heads provide superlative observational and listening abilities to warn of enemies.

In the lower left, subaquatic realms abound with sirenas and bufeo colorado. They inhabit the deepest parts of rivers and cochas, and as with the yacuruna, can travel from one river to another through extensive networks of underwater tunnels. The sirenas have sovereignty in this domain; they are guardians of esoteric knowledge and defend the secrets of their underwater kingdom with gold spears and belts. On the surface of the cocha brava, anguilamamas are emitting electromagnetic rays to prevent people from going there to fish or hunt. As the madre of the cocha brava, the anguilamama projects a powerful rainbow arkana, and this protects the banco puma who is healing with his soplo.

A soplo from a banco puma gives sustenance, strength, and vision to his patient. By concentrating on his soplo, allied with the spirits of the entire plant kingdom, he can heal his patient in as little as an hour. Just to the right, the banco puma's apprentices are practicing healing with soplos.

On the crown of the banco puma is the jeweled eye of the anaconda, which gives him prudence and insight into the future. The maestro receiving the soplo wears a blue shirt in which his allies appear: spirit beings, birds, stones, and pearlescent shells from the sea.

Above you see the flower of toé, a plant sometimes combined with ayahuasca to intensify your visions. With toé you can learn what a person is thinking, and it can enable you to see spirit beings as they are in their natural form. Shamans use toé to help them delve into profound mysteries. They may be assisted by extraterrestrials, seen here coming from Mars and Jupiter, and from other galaxies.

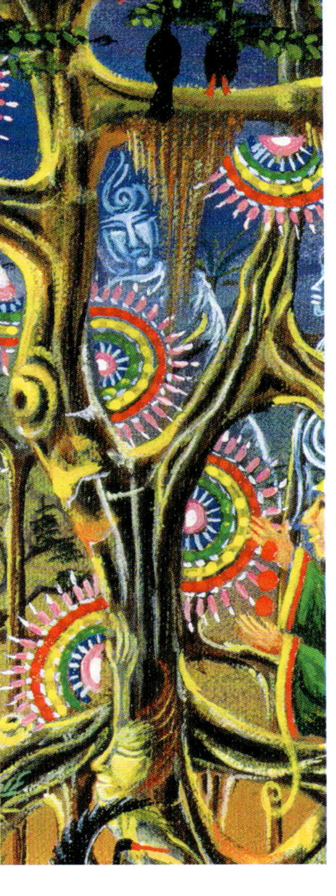

SUMAC ÍCARO

Sumac means "beautiful" in Quechua. Shamans sing sumac ícaros to call malign spirits to discover the cause of the sickness of their patient. These spirits, or tunchis, can be seen in the painting in their white shrouds with red-eyed supay tuyuyos. Tuyuyos are used by sorcerers for evil purposes so should never be eaten, as they can make you evil and savage when angered. Flying close to the renaco tree on the right are *yana sararas* (black herons). A curandero can use the ícaro of these birds to cure infectious diseases, such as measles and whooping cough. They can also be used for marupa sorcery.

The stars, galaxies, and all of creation are made from spiritual particles or vibrations that we perceive as sound or music. Ícaros are waves of resonating energy used by shamans to call in spirits for healing patients. To heal daño (harm caused by sorcery), the shaman calls the malignant spirit with a sumac ícaro to make his diagnosis.

As he sings, he calls in the *olor del monte* (odor of the jungle) and the air of the water; everything has its own distinctive scent. A powerful maestro who has sharpened his sense of smell through undergoing a diet with *ajo sacha* (*Mansoa alliacea*) can detect the sorcery in his patient's body, and discover the cause of the daño.

Encantos (magical stones) have hidden powers that can cause illness. Tobacco smoke can also cause illness if a brujo has imparted an evil energy to the tobacco through his soplo. The shaman sings the sublime sumac ícaro to attract the evil spirit or energy causing the daño.

The spirits always accept the invitation, which is why you see the tunchi, the *chullachaqui* (legendary beings), and the yacuruna in the lower right. Elsewhere there are nymphs, dryads, fairies, and hamadryads who live in the trees, and elves and sibyls who have all come to listen to the sumac ícaro.

The renaco tree is known as the temple of the waters, as it attracts many magical beings, animals, insects, and birds to live safely in its entangled branches and aerial roots.

When the sumac ícaro is sung in ceremonies it brings visions of palaces, pagodas, and temples, and touches the hearts and minds of everyone. The spirits do not have a physical body like us; they have cells made of hyperchemical particles called *espiritones*—waves that originate in the mind of God and permeate the fabric of multidimensional reality. When the shaman sings the sumac ícaro, spirits arrive in space ships from faraway galaxies to see if someone needs them.

Lower down is the sachamama (mother of the forest) entering the water where she transforms into the yacumama (mother of the waters). From there she transmutes into vapor and rises to the clouds, which are made from purified water, where she becomes the huairamama (mother of the air) and with her rain, fertilizes the rain forest. They are hyperchemical beings with the power of transmutation and symbolize the life cycle of the rain forest.

Riding the huairamama is a muraya, whose spirit can unite with the great anacondas: the sachamama and the yacumama.

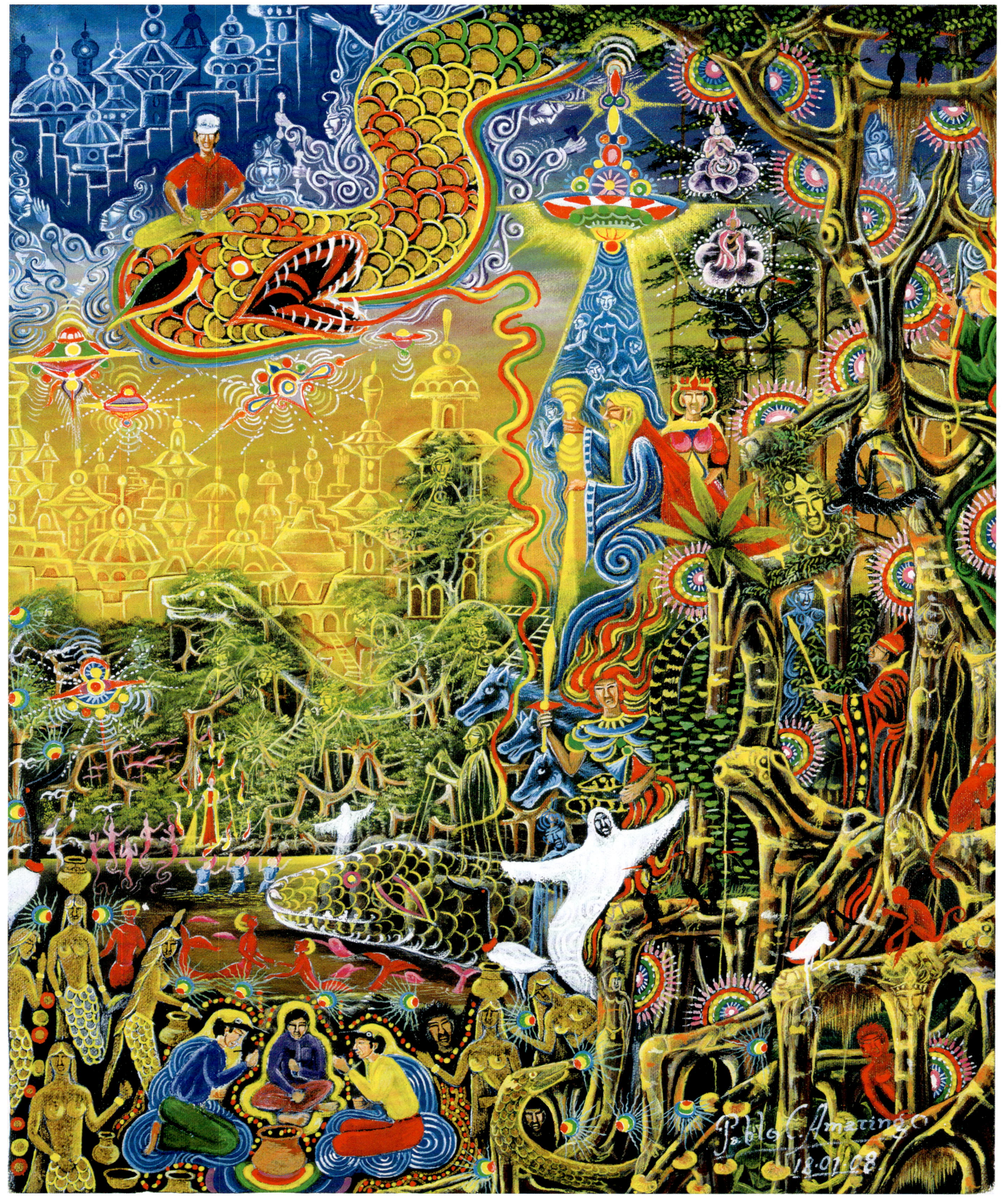

SUMAC ÍCARO
2008, Oil on Canvas
40 x 50 cm.

On the right-hand side is a prince, a master of love charms who teaches the ícaro of the renaco to shamans for making *amarres amorosos*—ties for bringing couples together.

In the renaco tree to the lower right are red monkeys, which have such courage and agility that they can intercept virotes sent by sorcerers. They also warn of approaching danger with their piercing screams.

To the left, holding his wand, is the *varayoc runa:* the authority who rewards shamans for their achievement and mastery of the healing arts.

Above to the left is the great King Cundaline, monarch of the celestial palace. His golden scepter symbolizes his extensive knowledge of ayahuasca and alquimia palistica. Above him is an extraterrestrial craft radiating a blue beam, which transmits knowledge from other dimensions. Next to the king is the majestic fairy queen Lola Baluarte, an affectionate and communicative teacher of the art of healing with balsam, resins, and plants.

Just below is Queen Nefina, with her long hair of fire. She uses her golden sword to protect curanderos from sorcery. Next to her are yana caballos, used by sorcerers for attacking their victims. Curanderos learn the yana caballo's ícaro for healing the daño caused by these sorcerers.

In the cocha are blond-haired red sirenos, or *yacupucarunas,* who are the guardians of the *tamimuri* tree (*Brosimum acutifolium*). They assist the sumirunas in front of them in their ceremony to cure malignant wounds and *huicsa nanay* (painful stomach afflictions) using the bark of the tamimuri. The shaman sings the ícaro of this powerful tree and performs soplos with tobacco smoke, which acts as an antiseptic. Cloaked around the shamans are the spirits of *guacamayos* (macaws), which form an arkana to protect them from the noxious projectiles: the infamous virotes of evil chonteros.

On either side of the sumirunas are sirenas called *yacu warmi* (women of the waters), who have been called by the sumac ícaro to take the maestros to visit the subaquatic realms of brujos, necromancers, and hechiceros. The yacu warmi defend them from the dangers of this realm. This is the sublime quality of the sumac ícaro.

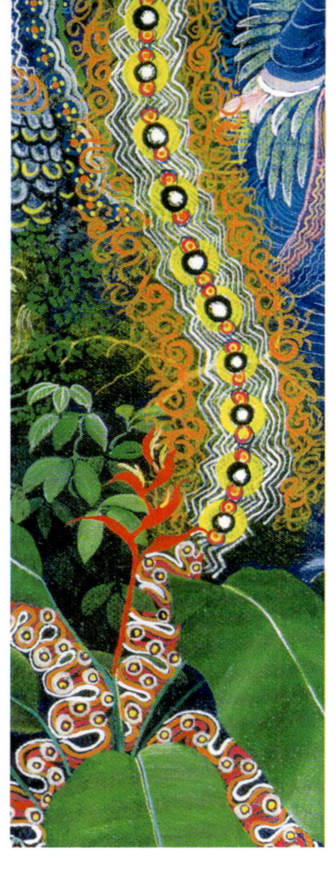

HADA DE PERONUGÁ

MAESTRA DE LAS ARTES

Nuga was a queen from the court of ancient Mesopotamia, also known as Naqi'a. Mesopotamia was the cradle of civilization and it was here that writing, mathematics, and geometry first evolved. The ancients understood the influence of celestial bodies on people and events. The Mesopotamians calculated the movements of celestial bodies, measured time using minutes and hours, and divided the circle into 360 degrees.

Nuga had complete mastery of the healing arts. Here she is teaching shamans to use colors, shapes, and sounds—all of which are symmetrical patterns of energy—for healing. She is cloaked in chacruna leaves. Flowing from her hand are luminescent gemstones, pearls, and crystals representing the great teachings of antiquity that still inform and shape our culture. She shows us how the shape and use of our hands underpins civilization and distinguishes us from the other primates. With our hands we write, paint, heal, and build our homes. We should always take care to keep our hands clean, so as not to taint the food we eat or the things we do.

Below her is the great nymph Xilánster, who heals with perfumes and aromas, and teaches self-hypnosis and meditation to maintain a healthy mental and emotional state. She knows the secret location of the black rose, a mysterious flower used for divination and hypnosis.

Just below is a priest and priestess of the Chanca people, who were contemporary with the Inca. They had extensive knowledge of plant medicine, which is why their descendants, the Ashaninka (seen above and to the left of them), are highly respected even today.

Below is the *machipuri sacha* (spider plant), which is difficult to find, like the black rose. The *flautero* is a mysterious bird whose song you can never hear. It is said that if you once hear the beautiful song of this bird, you will live an extraordinary life. Many years ago when I was a curandero, I heard one and offered to pay eighty thousand soles for it so I could listen to its enchanting songs.

At the top left are the flowers of the *floripondio* (*Brugmansia suaveolens*), whose spiral waves and luminous serpentine patterns represent the power of this plant to expand and illuminate the unconscious mind.

Below, sitting on the ayahuasca vine, is an Ashaninka muraya wearing a black *cushma* (cotton tunic) and holding chacruna leaves in his hands. These are the two plants that are boiled together to make the brew ayahuasca. His body is enveloped by white mariri coming from the sylph Queen Kilga and the nymphs to the left and just below her. Queen Kilga was an ancient Sumerian priestess, and here she teaches the muraya the art of clairvoyance and spiritual perception, seen as the luminescent blue spirals around the Ashaninka muraya. Just below her is the "eye of mystical knowledge."

Circling down is the *marupa machaco* (marupa serpent) projecting waves of brightly colored sapphires, rubies, and onyxes into the crown of the *macua runa* (wise elder), called Yachay Sapa. He is a master of divine inspiration, and his name means "incomparable in knowledge." Yachay Sapa teaches

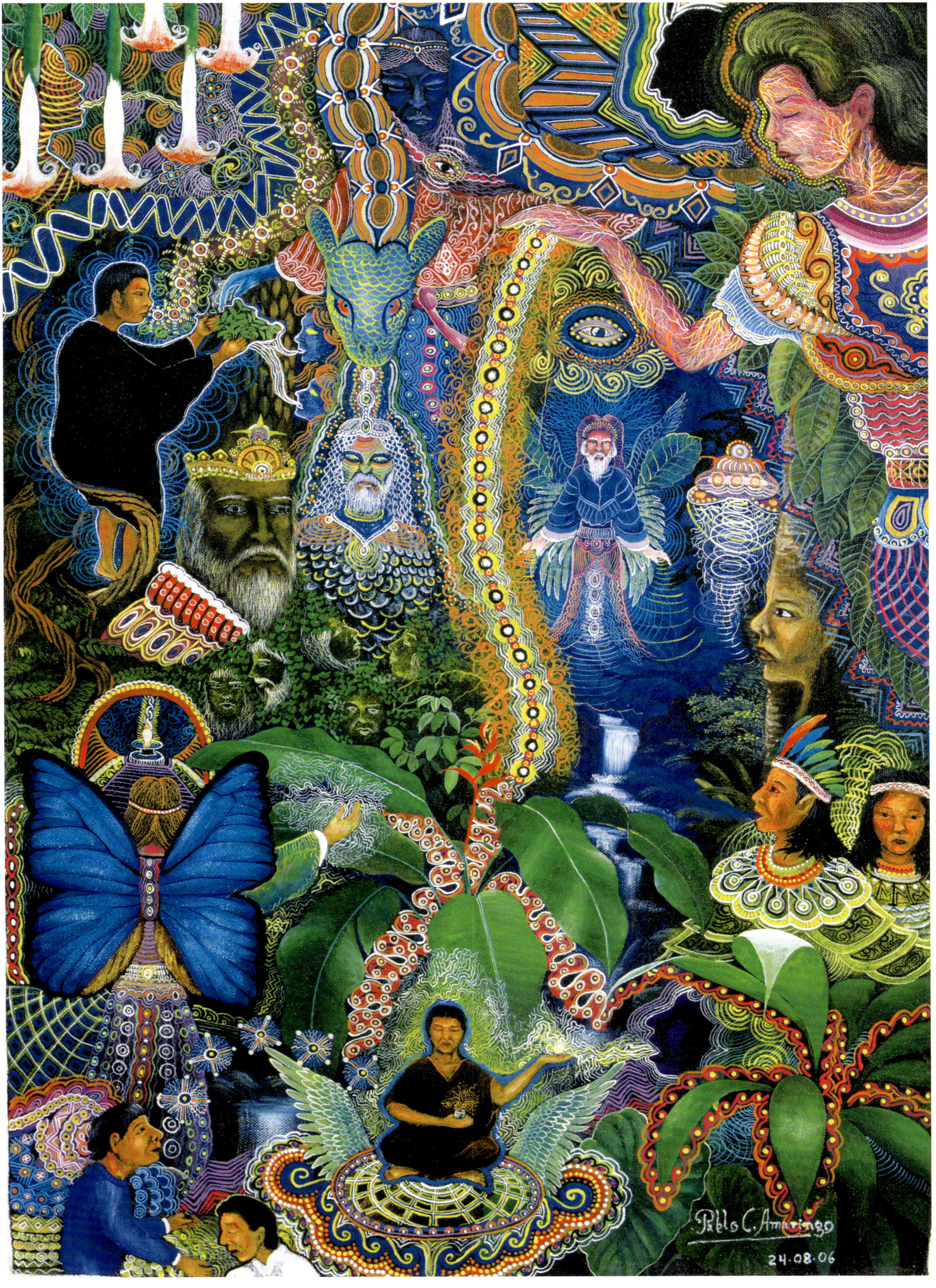

HADA DE PERONUGÁ
Maestra de las Artes
2006, Acrylic on Canvas
44 x 64 cm.

the ícaro of the marupa machaco to curanderos for extracting virotes and marupa sorcery from victims of hechicería.

Just below and to the left is the wise Oriental king, Maucanuelotz. His gold-jeweled crown and ermine-trimmed gown are evidence of his majestic authority to instruct in the principles of justice, discipline, and the development of virtuous conscience.

Below, with her iridescent blue wings, is the *sumac ñusta,* which in Quechua means "beautiful princess." She is a fairy from the Aquarius constellation and she stands in front of a sanctuary inspiring love, beauty, and gentleness. Flowing from her hands are iridescent waves that transmit the sublime fragrance of flowers. She is a specialist in the extraction and distillation of balsams, scents, and incenses from flowering plants found only on earth. Her delightful perfumes are a source of joy and contentment for these extraterrestrial beings.

The muraya sitting on the winged flower is singing the *sacha yana versucum sisa* (the song of the wild black flower) to call the medicinal powers of the plants and intensify his mareación. To his right is the spirit of the *sacha yana sisa* who has responded to the song.

The muraya is an accomplished *perfumero.* The flower with wings symbolizes the subtle powers of floral perfumes. Plants have evolved these attributes to attract insects and birds to drink their nectar for their fertilization. Underneath are the leaves of the patiquina verde, which are used in baños florales to attract good fortune, love, and success.

Just above is the *mishquipanga* (*Renealmia alpinia*), which in Quechua means "sweet leaf." The fragrant leaves of this plant are also used in floral baths for making your life flourish. The chromatic spiral patterns are radiating exquisite scents to inspire the spirit and senses.

Above is Nabu, the magnificent winged deity from ancient Mesopotamia, also known as Hermes Trismegistus, who is a master of magic, science, and prophecy. Above him is the "eye of understanding" that penetrates infinite space and time. When humanity realizes its potential, it will begin to use this eye to help the biosphere survive the coming calamities of climate change and extinction of countless species.

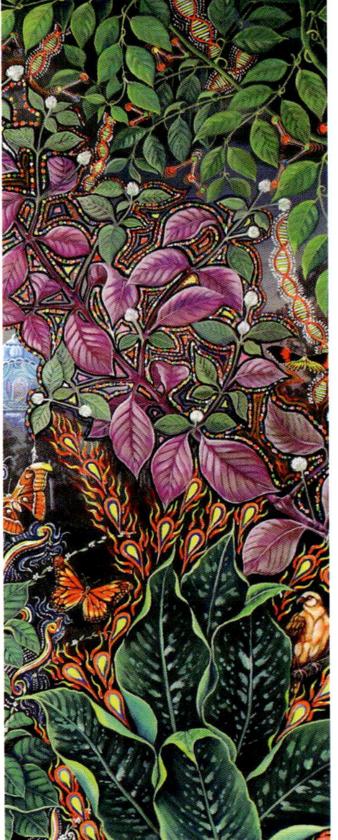

MISTERIO PROFUNDO

This picture embraces all the wisdom and all the plants used by a vegetalista. Without *el vegetal* we would not be able to discover hidden knowledge of the earth or the spiritual realms beyond.

The sacramental and religious use of plants goes back to antiquity. The Greek philosophers—Plato, Aristotle, and Sophocles—were initiates of the ancient mysteries of plants. The teachings and wisdom of these sages has influenced our understanding of metaphysics and science to the present day.

The celestial cities, palaces, and temples beyond the river are not usually visible; however, in an ayahuasca mareación we are gifted with the ability to see them. In these esoteric schools and temples the ancient sages and shamans learned of the *misterio profundo:* the sacred mystery of the plants.

I have been to these temples and seen beings of great intelligence, beautiful appearance, and luminescent attire. The walls are a lacework of glittering precious stones. There are hanging gardens of multicolored aromatic flowers, and circular gardens filled with an abundance of towering trees. I saw birds of chromatic plumage singing songs so delightful that they captivate the soul. I was shown the spiritual origin of this wisdom and learned that a plant can show its spirit, speak to us, and teach us.

Plants are a key to the mystery of life; they provide food and oxygen essential to animals and humans. All life is dependent on plants. Without them we cannot survive.

Plants have compassion for all life and teach us how to preserve our health and combat disease. To the lower right is the patiquina, which protects against sorcery and daño—sickness caused in the spirit world through negative emotions, such as envy. It is surrounded by esoteric flames indicating the cleansing and protective powers of this plant. The *ishanga* or *maramara* (*Urea baccifera*) seen to the left with thorns on its stem is a nettle with many healing properties. The leaves can heal burns, wounds, tuberculosis, and venomous bites.

To its right is the *mucura* (*Petiveria alliacea*), which can cure infections and respiratory diseases. The roots are boiled and the decocted liquid can be used for healing cancer. The leaves are also used in baños de flores to heal saladera and mal aire.

Above you see the purple leaves of the *lancetilla* (*Alternanthera* sp.), whose flowers and leaves are used to heal arthritis, alleviate stress and gastric problems, and treat wounds. The plant can also cure diabetes, as it contains proteins required by the pancreas to synthesize insulin. To the left is a fairy known as Dari, a doctora of plant medicine. Around her are astral particles that form protein molecules and hormones necessary for health and well-being.

Just above the fairy you can see the *retama* (*Cassia alata*) showing its leaves and beautiful yellow flowers resembling a candle flame. This is a powerful medicinal plant whose flowers are used to cure burns and also infections of the gallbladder, kidneys, and liver. The leaves have antibacterial and antiviral properties, and are used to cleanse intestinal parasites.

In the top right you see the branches of *uña de gato* or cat's claw (*Uncaria tormentosa*). The bark and roots of this plant are used to heal infections, tumors, arthritis, and rheumatism, and to enhance the immune system. It also strengthens bone marrow.

To the left are purple flowers and leaves of the *aire sacha* (*Kalanchoe pinnata*), which has many

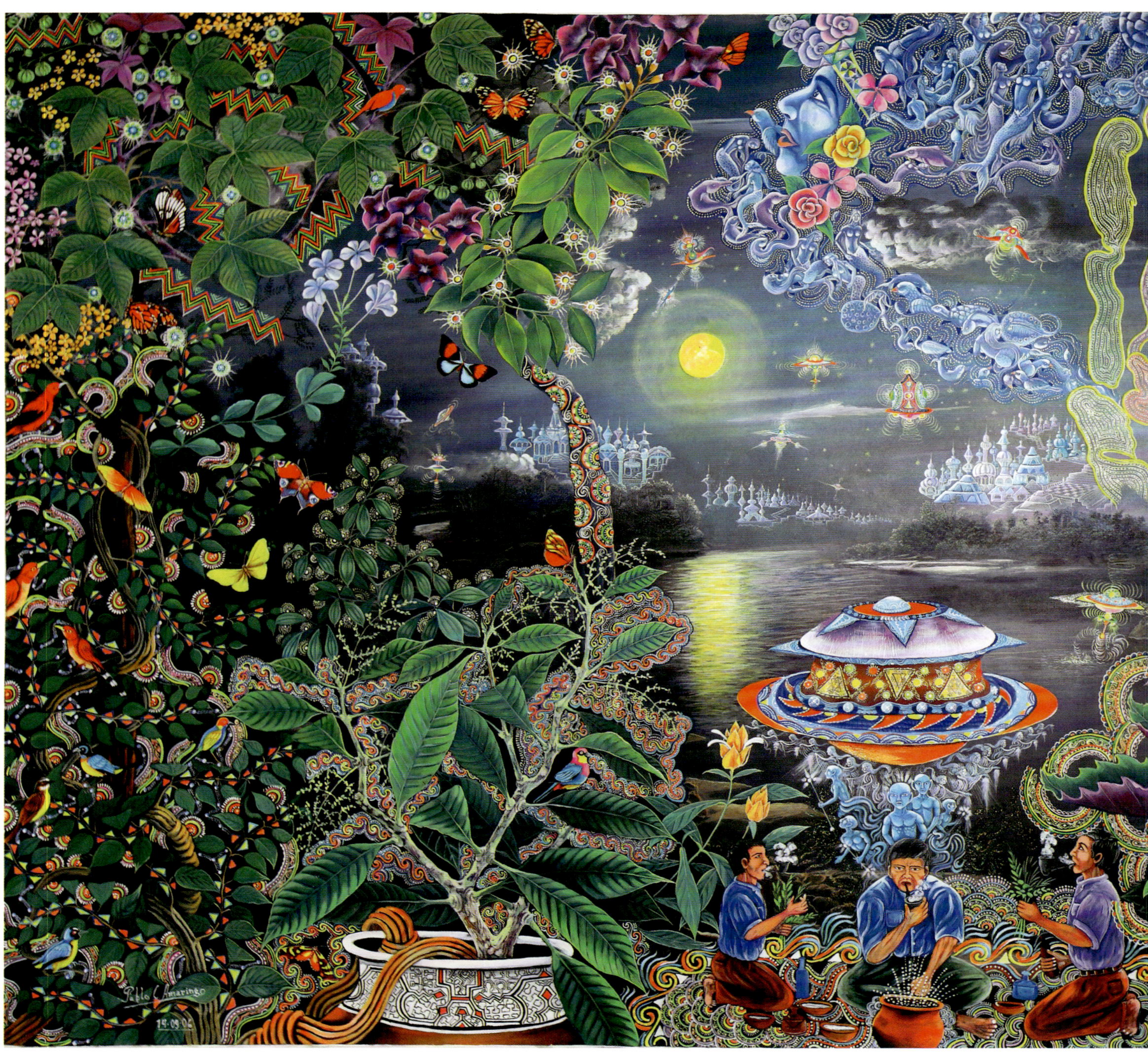

healing properties; it is used for bacterial infections, migraines, liver diseases, kidney infections, and fevers. Above the flowers is a butterfly. Butterflies are the shaman's messengers and give him vital information. At the top left is *piñon colorado* (*Jatropha gossypifolia*) used in baños de flores to treat daño and saladera. It is also a purgative for intestinal parasites, and heals wounds.

Just above the tinaja is the *matico* (*Piper aduncum*), used as an antiseptic for healing wounds and inflammations. An infusion of this plant is used to cure respiratory, stomach, and kidney infections, and to clear parasites.

The rainbow patterns symbolize the sublime curative properties of palos that heal the lungs, heart, and mind. The trees in the background produce powerful palos: *remo caspi* (*Aspidosperma excelsum*), *huairacaspi* (*Cedrelinga cataneiformis*), and *pucalupuna* (*Cavanillesia hylogeiton*).

In his mareación, the shaman sees multicolored spiral patterns on the tree bark indicating the medicinal powers of the palo, and how they fortify the body and blood. Medicinal plants can also be recognized by their guardian birds: the ayapollito, the chicua, and the suisui.

Amazonia is home to a host of plants with the potential to be the salvation of humanity. Many others remain to be discovered that could help cure devastating diseases. The helixes in the painting tell us that the proteins of plant and animal DNA are identical, which is why they can affect our bodies and our minds at a profound level.

Above the clouds is a sumiruna, a shaman with mastery over the elements: earth, air, fire, and

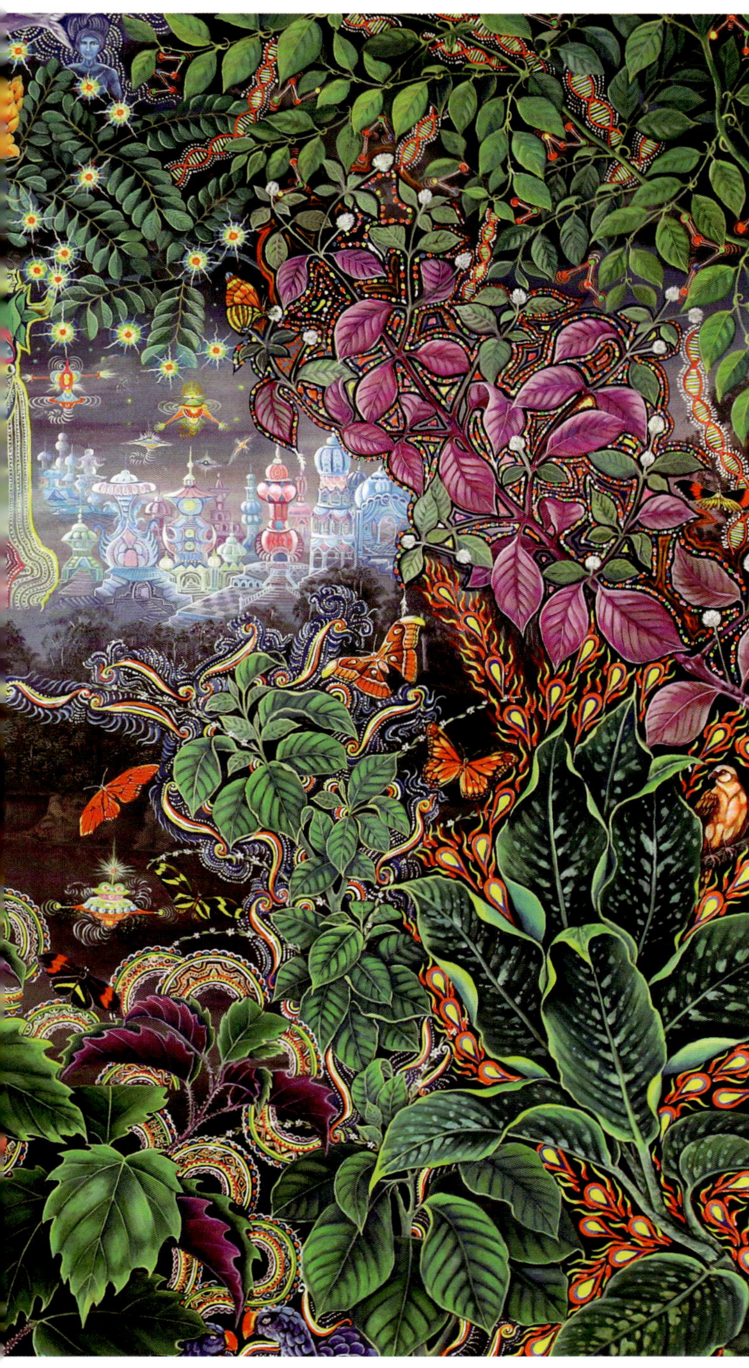

MISTERIO PROFUNDO
2002, Acrylic on Canvas
250 x 150 cm.

water. Around him in waves are enigmatic beings: the pambamuri (stingray), sirenas, bufeos, charapas (river turtles), and sararas (herons). The sumiruna has mastered their ícaros, and can call upon these beings to help him heal.

Water is a vital life-giving element for plants, animals, and humans. I was shown that the orbit of the moon regulates nature's fecundity and influences the atmosphere, producing rain and wind. Neither the sun nor the stars reflect in the water when the luminance of the moon is present. The full moon seen here with its shining halo is in the strongest phase.

The spaceship that has arrived from a distant galaxy brings spiritual beings to teach the sumiruna, muraya, and banco sumi in their ceremony below. They warn of the imbalance of the biosphere caused by man's destruction of the rain forest. Through negligence, ignorance, and greed, humans have prejudiced the delicate web of life on which we depend. The beings are giving shamans energy to heal the planet with ícaros and soplos. The pipes of such powerful maestros should never be touched by anybody, as they are immensely powerful.

Beside the maestros in their ceremony, chacruna and ayahuasca grow from a Shipibo tinaja. They are enveloped in the luminous patterns of tingunas, which are manifestations of sacred life force.

This painting—its colors and forms—brings to our hearts and minds the importance of caring for plants. We need to love and appreciate them, not just use them for our gain. We also need to work with them to study the sublime truth of what they are showing and telling us.

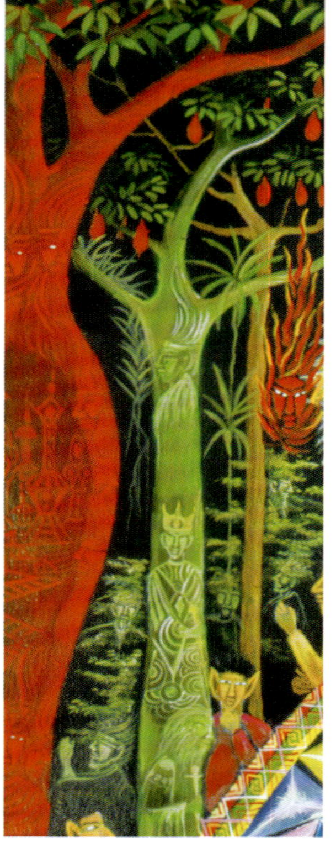

LOS GRADOS DEL CURANDERO

The concentric wheels in the center correspond to the levels of esoteric knowledge of a curandero: Beginning from the outside they are onaya, banco puma, muraya, sumiruna, and the innermost, banco sumi. The wheels also represent the varied levels of higher consciousness that drinkers of ayahuasca seek.

The red tree to the left is the puca lupuna. Inside its trunk is a temple where the shaman learns while dieting this formidable tree. Puca lupuna is also used by sorcerers, so a curandero must diet this tree to be able to heal this type of sorcery.

Below the tree is a chullachaqui riding a giant charapa. The chullachaqui is a mischievous, gnomelike being who protects the animals of the rain forest. Many innocent people have gone missing after going out alone in the forest. After walking some distance they are relieved when they run into a beloved old friend or family member who cleverly tempts them down the wrong path and promptly disappears after they are thoroughly lost. Only then is it clear that this was no friend or relative, but the menacing chullachaqui, who is a highly skilled impersonator.

Chulla means "unequal" in Quechua, and *chaqui* means "foot," because one of his feet is twisted back on itself, or is the foot of a beast. If you should find yourself in these circumstances you must remember to look down to check that both feet of your familiar friend are the same. This trickster will always try to hide or cover his bad foot, and if deceived, you may never be found again or you too will become a chullachaqui!

To its right is the green *punga* tree (*Bombax munguba*), whose fatty, phlegmlike resin is secreted from its soft wood. The curandero diets this tree to learn its ícaro, which he sings to extract deadly virotes or marupas sent by malevolent sorcerers. The magical phlegm, or mariri, of the curandero absorbs these intrusions.

All around are beings called the *ultratumba,* literally "beyond the grave," which refers to the spiritual realm of deceased people. Between the trees are the *chaicuni,* the hidden ancestors of the Shipibo. There are *manes* and tunchis, which are also spirits of the dead. The manes standing among the shrubs are "blessed" spirits who received proper funeral rites but return to earth to help curanderos and protect plants and animals. The white-shrouded tunchis are the forgotten spirits of humans who wander the earth. They are common in the jungle and frighten people, causing the illness known as mal aire.

The *nina chukcha* is a kind of maligno or evil spirit, with hair of flame. They are used by sorcerers to harm their victims, and unless the person is healed quickly he will be consumed by fever and die.

At the top is a *guacamayo runa* with the head of a guacamayo (macaw) and body of a man. The guacamayo runa teaches the shaman to interpret features in the sky to predict when it is going to rain and, if necessary, to create rainfall. In the guacamayo runa's soplo you see gnomos, caretakers of the earth's minerals. To the right is a banco puma teaching the mysteries of the soplo with which a curandero invokes the energy of a plant or animal to heal his patient.

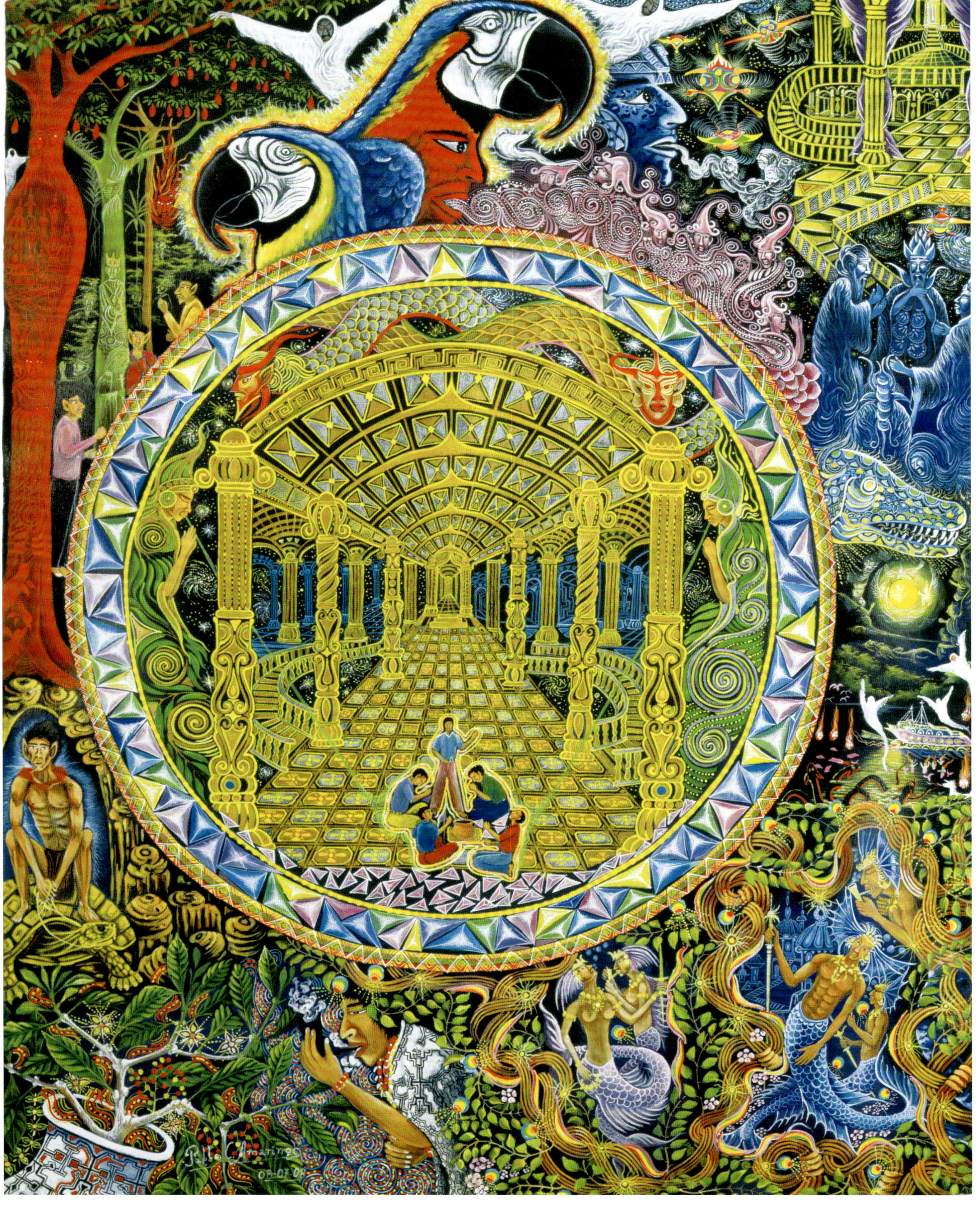

LOS GRADOS DEL CURANDERO
2008, Oil on Canvas
72 x 91 cm.

To the right is the golden *palacio de descanso* (palace of rest), a sanctuary of peace and tranquillity where curanderos learn to illuminate the heart with love, justice, humility, and truth. At the foot of the steps are great masters of philosophy and occult wisdom.

On the top of the pagoda inside the circle are the *machacho runas* with a human head and the body of a serpent. They are sumirunas with hyperchemical abilities that allow them to transform their physical bodies at will. These masters can travel to other galaxies and visit celestial kingdoms governed by angelic beings.

Inside the innermost wheel, to either side of the celestial pagoda, are enigmatic *metatrones,* angelic powers that sharpen the shaman's imagination in a ceremony. Human achievements are first created in the mind. The geometric pattern of the pagoda symbolizes the mathematical structure of the universe first formed in the mind of the Divine Creator.

To the right is a cocha brava. These cochas are protected from hunters and fishermen by the mother of the cocha brava: the anguilamama. The barco fantasma or supay lancha is a manifestation of the yacumama (mother of the waters). In the cocha are puca sirenas (pink mermaids) who in the old days seduced men with their bewitching songs and took them to live in their underwater palaces. You used to see many of them on the banks of the River Ucayali.

At the bottom right are the *sireno machaco* (snake mermen), powerful allies of murayas and sumirunas who have gained mastery of the underwater realms. Such maestros can draw upon the powers of this domain when chanting their ícaros. Next to them are the *angash sirenas*, mermaids who guard aquatic plants and teach curanderos about their medicinal properties and the ícaros that accompany them.

To the left a Shipibo curandero smokes his cashimbo next to a tinaja (earthen jar) where the chacruna grows. Around the chacruna are tingunas—colored astral waves and particles. The tingunas have hyperchemical properties that can transform them into plants, clouds, or birds.

The geometric designs on the Shipibo tinaja represent the luminous vibration of the cosmos and are depicted here as chromatic spirals known as "neutrinos." Neutrinos transmute into physical matter when their ícaro is sung. The outer rings of the circle revolve like a karmic wheel. The curandero in his mareación will move clockwise around the wheel to the top, and then enter the circle in a spiral.

The picture is intended for meditation and contemplation of inner peace and harmony. When you look in the center, you should not blink or glance away; this process purifies your mind and reveals your spiritual light.

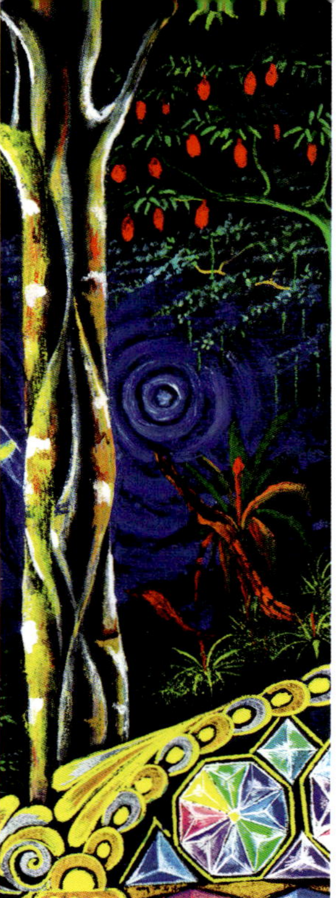

PUÑUSCA MUSCUNA

REVELACIÓN PROFUNDA

This picture shows the profound revelation given by ayahuasca to heal *daño* (see glossary) caused by *hechiceros* (see glossary) and *brujos*. These unscrupulous shamans secretly harm their victims with black magic, using the same plants that can otherwise perform wonders for our physical and spiritual health.

The red tree to the upper right is the *puca lupuna* (*Cavanillesia hylogeiton*), which is like a forest temple. Within its trunk you can see the grand maestro that instructs any aspiring apprentice with the discipline to follow a very exacting diet. The *puca lupuna* does not distinguish between good and evil, and is used by sorcerers to inflict harm, so a *curandero* must undergo a diet with this tree in order to heal the victims of this type of sorcery.

To the left of the *puca lupuna* there is a tree with red fruit, the *punga* (*Bombax munguba*), which grows near water and in swamps. It reaches thirty meters, and from its soft wood it secretes a phlegmlike resin. Shamans chant the icaro of this tree when they extract *virotes* (deadly darts from the spirit world) using their *mariri,* or magical phlegm that retains the *virote* and makes it harmless.

To the left of the punga tree is the *ajosquiro* (*Cordia alliodora*), a tree that can be used for malevolent sorcery. A *curandero* must diet with this tree to learn its ícaro in order to heal daño caused by sorcery.

The blue spiral behind the punga tree symbolizes the eternal movement of spirit and matter inside solar systems and galaxies. Ayahuasca has revealed to me that you need both light and darkness to be illuminated. In order to appreciate the spiritual nature of humanity and the prevalent cosmic forces, you must understand that the negative side is there to show you the positive side.

When I was a shaman, I dedicated myself to creating well-being and I learned how to overcome evil intentions. The unfortunate reality here in the Amazon is that you must prove that you are stronger than the other shamans; otherwise they will attack you. If a patient comes to me for protection from attack by a brujo and I undo that spell, the evil goes back to its source and the frustrated brujo will want to harm me. For many, the easiest solution is to be evil too and kill the other brujo. The world is like this to teach us to distinguish good from bad, as there cannot be one without the other. However, it is always easier to be bad and destructive than to work on the side of good.

Just to the left of the ajosquiro are two Inca sumirunas wearing their golden crowns; they are male and female. They teach shamans the importance of harmonizing feminine and masculine forces, which are an integral part of creation.

To the left are celestial guardians bearing a sword, shield, and scepter; they are known as the *tronos* (thrones). They teach shamans how to master fear and develop the courage required for confronting evil sorcery. Just below is a woman's face with Shipibo geometric patterns. She represents the

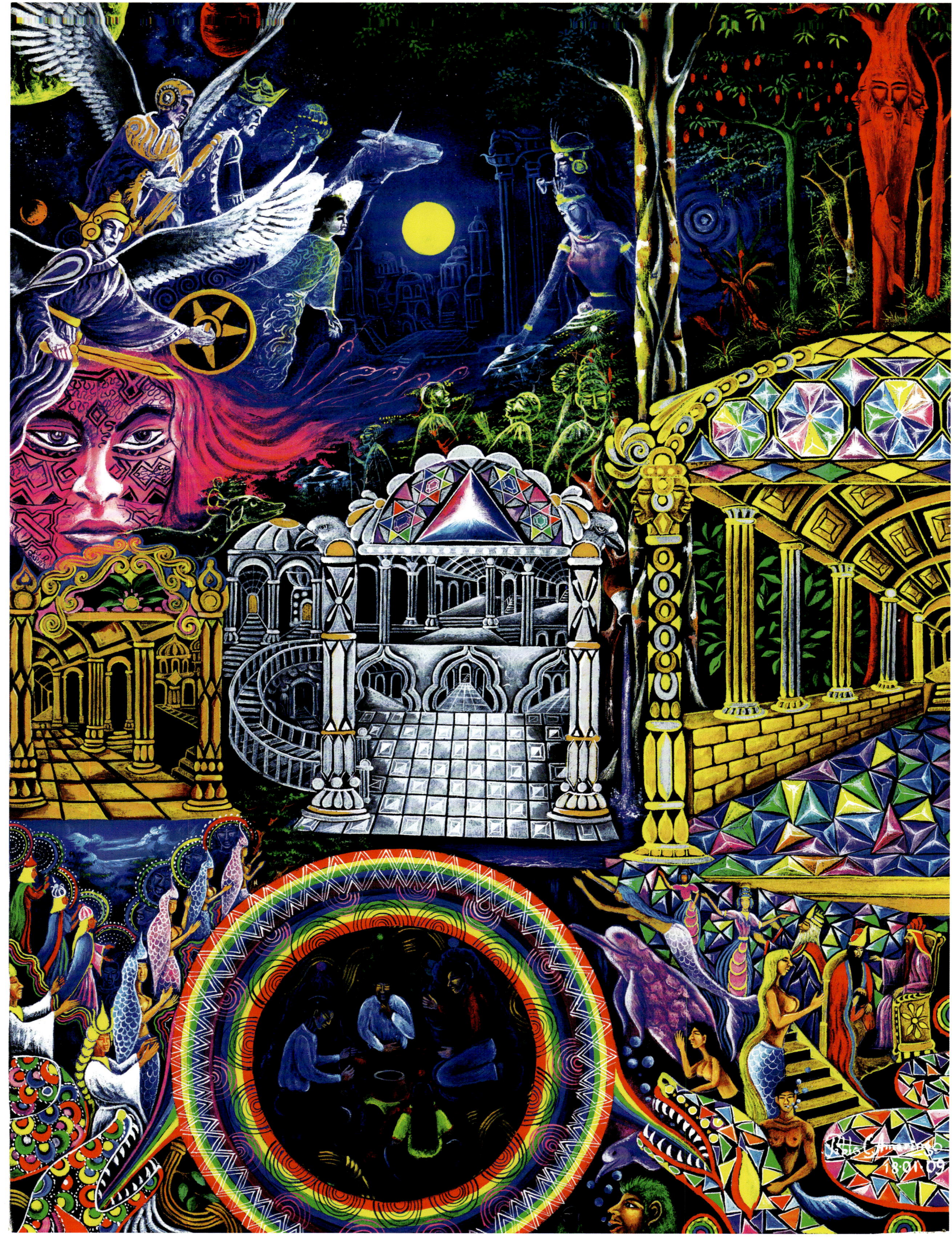

PUÑUSCA MUSCUNA
Revelación Profunda
2009, Oil on Canvas
60 x 80 cm.

nurturing love of Mother Earth, and the love of a mother for her children. It is necessary that men learn this too, for as long as the feminine power is present, all life will be cherished. Men who do not have this quality can become destructive and cause great damage in the world.

The white palace in the center is where shamans learn to heal. Ayahuasca reveals her most profound secrets when the visionary mareación (see glossary) is at its strongest. Here it shows that human beings need to create equilibrium between their good and bad sides. It is obviously wrong to be bad, but human beings are as yet imperfect, and if we are excessive about being virtuous, this is not good either. Our actions should simply be right and reasonable.

The palace on the left is where hechiceria, brujeria, black magic, and black spiritualism is learned. The golden palace on the right is the sanctuary of dignity and peace where you learn to show justice in your actions and attitudes, and to illuminate your heart with compassion, truth, and humility. Here you learn to express in thoughts, feelings, and words that "I am" and "I exist." If a person thinks or says, "I am nothing and I have nothing," he is extinguishing his spiritual strength and will be doomed to failure. It is important to have inspired thoughts and to speak enriching words about oneself and others, rather than complain about a person's negative aspects, as we all embody both positive and negative qualities.

Below the golden sanctuary is the *sachamama,* the Mother of the forest. Its skin is encrusted with precious stones and jewels, and alongside it you see the great masters and teachers of philosophy and occult wisdom.

The steps lead to the subaquatic realm where sirenas, sirenos, pucabufeos (see glossary), and the yacuruna reside. The bejewelled discs are gateways to secret tunnels under water, which connect to the rivers and cochas (lakes). They lead to hidden cities and palaces to which sumirunas and murayas (see glossary) must journey for gaining mastery of the subaquatic domains.

The yakumamas, the Mothers of the waters, are projecting powerful rainbow colored arkanas (see glossary) to protect the shamans in their ayahuasca ceremony from sorcery. To the left there are the huarmi murayas, who are like mermaids, wearing the scaled armor of celestial fish who teach the shamans the art of alchemical healing. Behind them are Oriental masters wearing turbans, who bestow wisdom to those learning from ayahuasca. As the shamans in the ceremony rise to higher states of consciousness, they understand that all of creation is in constant flux and motion toward balance and equilibrium.

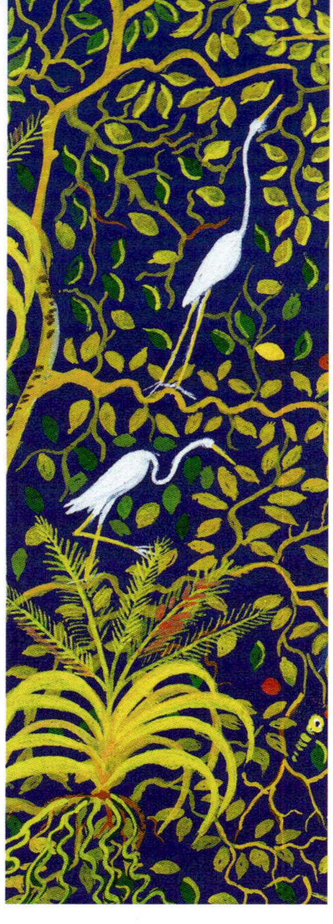

YANA YACUMAMA

BOA NEGRA

Yacumama is the black anaconda, an intrepid boa that attacks anything that threatens it. It is madre of the enchanted cocha brava seen here, and makes people afraid to hunt or fish in the area. For this reason, all kinds of animals thrive in a cocha brava. The oil of the yana yacumama is highly valued as it is so fine that if held in the hand, it will drip right through and around your hand. It opens padlocks so efficiently that even burglars use it for housebreaking. If you rub its oil on your body when there is a full moon you will be a very good shot. Otherwise it will cure rheumatism and withered limbs, but the oil should be heated first in a water bath.

The yana yacumama occasionally comes out of the water to sunbathe, and smaller individuals can pass through tunnels at the bottom of the cocha and explore rivers and other lakes. The *camungo,* which is bigger than a turkey, warns the yana yacumama when people approach, so she can use her ability to make the water level rise rapidly, flooding the area. This boa can shoot spittle with astonishing accuracy, bringing down birds and animals from the trees.

The anaconda can appear in your vision. If it has a yellow patch on its nose, it can teach you, but the one here is all black and can teach only brujeria.

You should beware when fishing in shallow waters around the renaco tree. Smaller anacondas can come and coil themselves around your legs, and in no time they can immobilize you. The young boa soon thinks you are dead and goes off to call its mother to eat you. When she comes expectantly you have already taken refuge and climbed up the renaco tree. When this happens she will angrily eat her own young for proving so inept.

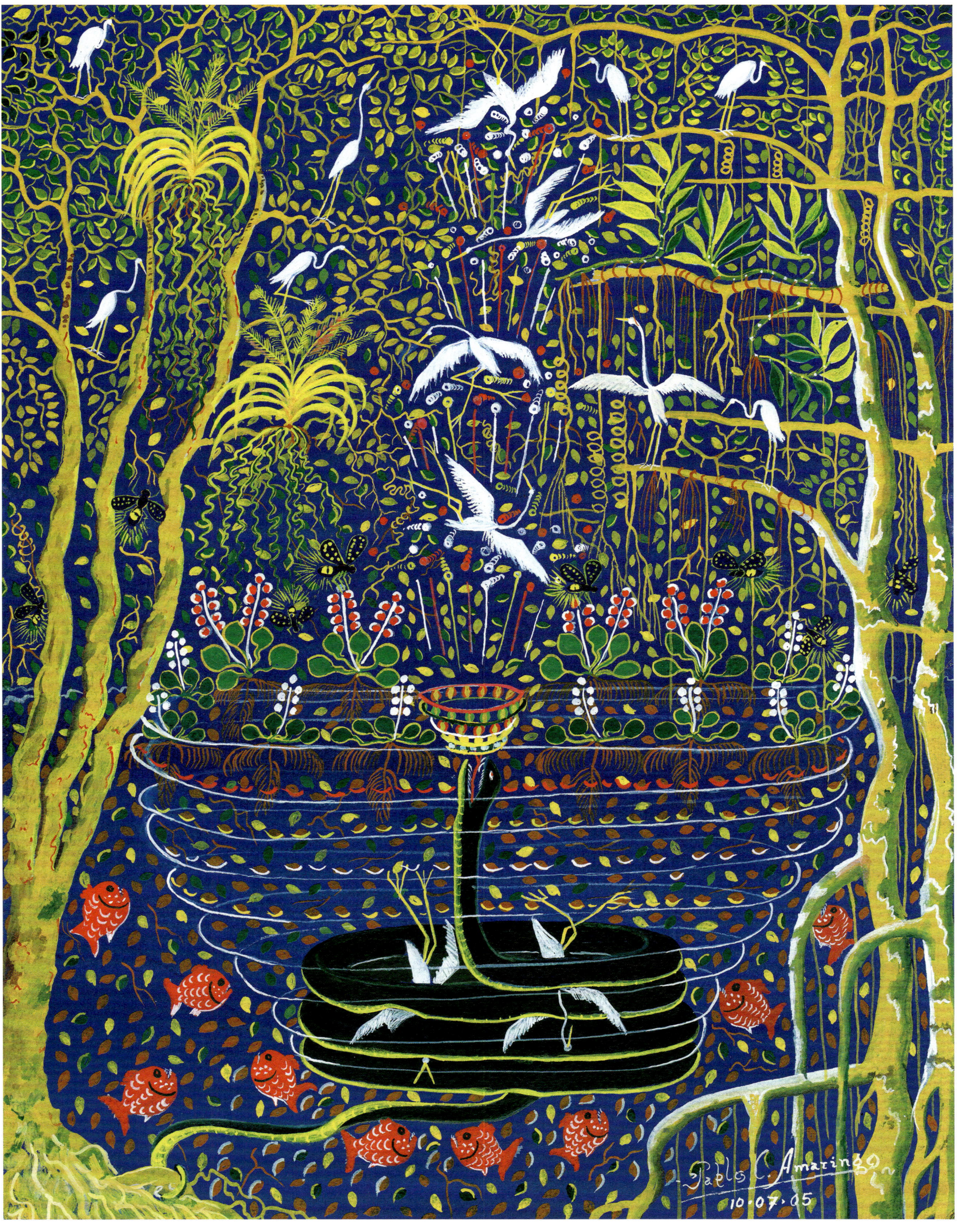

YANA YACUMAMA
Boa Negra
2005, Gouache on Arches Paper
30 x 40 cm.

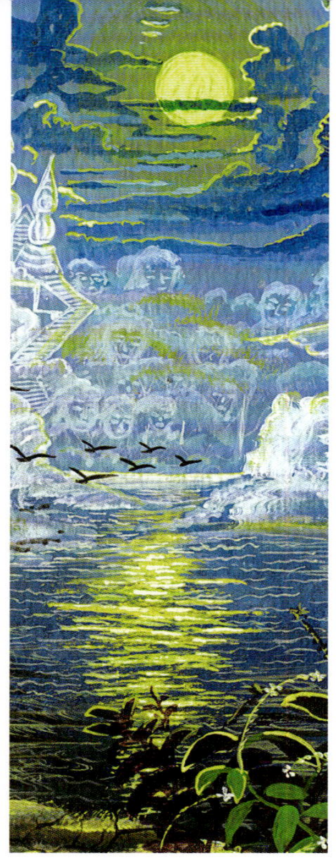

AMAZÓNICA ROMANTICA

In the lower left of this painting* are the large leaves of the cocona plant (*Solanum sessiliflorum*). Cocona fruit is greatly appreciated in the Amazon for making delicious juices and a sauce essential for eating fish: *ají de cocona*. Just behind is a Shipibo *mahuete* from which the ayahuasca liana grows. The feet of the mahuete represent the bond that ayahuasca has with Mother Earth. Above, with its heart-shaped leaves and white flowers, is the *boa sacha* tree (*Gouania lupuloides* sp.). Next on the right is *lagarto muena* (*Endlicheria* sp.), the bark of which is used against snakebites.

To the lower right is the *mucura* plant (*Petivera alliacea*), which grows widely in the Amazon and is used in baños florales to cleanse and heal saladera. Its medicinal properties help to cure asthma and bronchitis, and reduce fat and cholesterol. To the right is the chacruna plant, whose leaves are used to make ayahuasca.

Above is the *ayahuma* (*Couroupita guianensis*) tree with its large fruit. *Ayahuma* in Quechua means "spirit head," or "head of a dead person." It is an important tree for dieting, and the thick bark and seeds are used by curanderos to protect against brujeria.

At the top is the *catahua* tree (*Hura crepitans*), which is one of the strongest palos. To gain mastery of this tree requires an extensive dieta. Its resin, when cooked with tobacco, gives powerful dreams.

---

*This charming picture was one of Pablo's final works, and it heralded an intended return to his earlier genre of painting the plants and landscapes of his beloved Amazonian rain forest. The painting depicts a couple hand in hand, experiencing the mystic enchantment of the selva illuminated by the full moon.

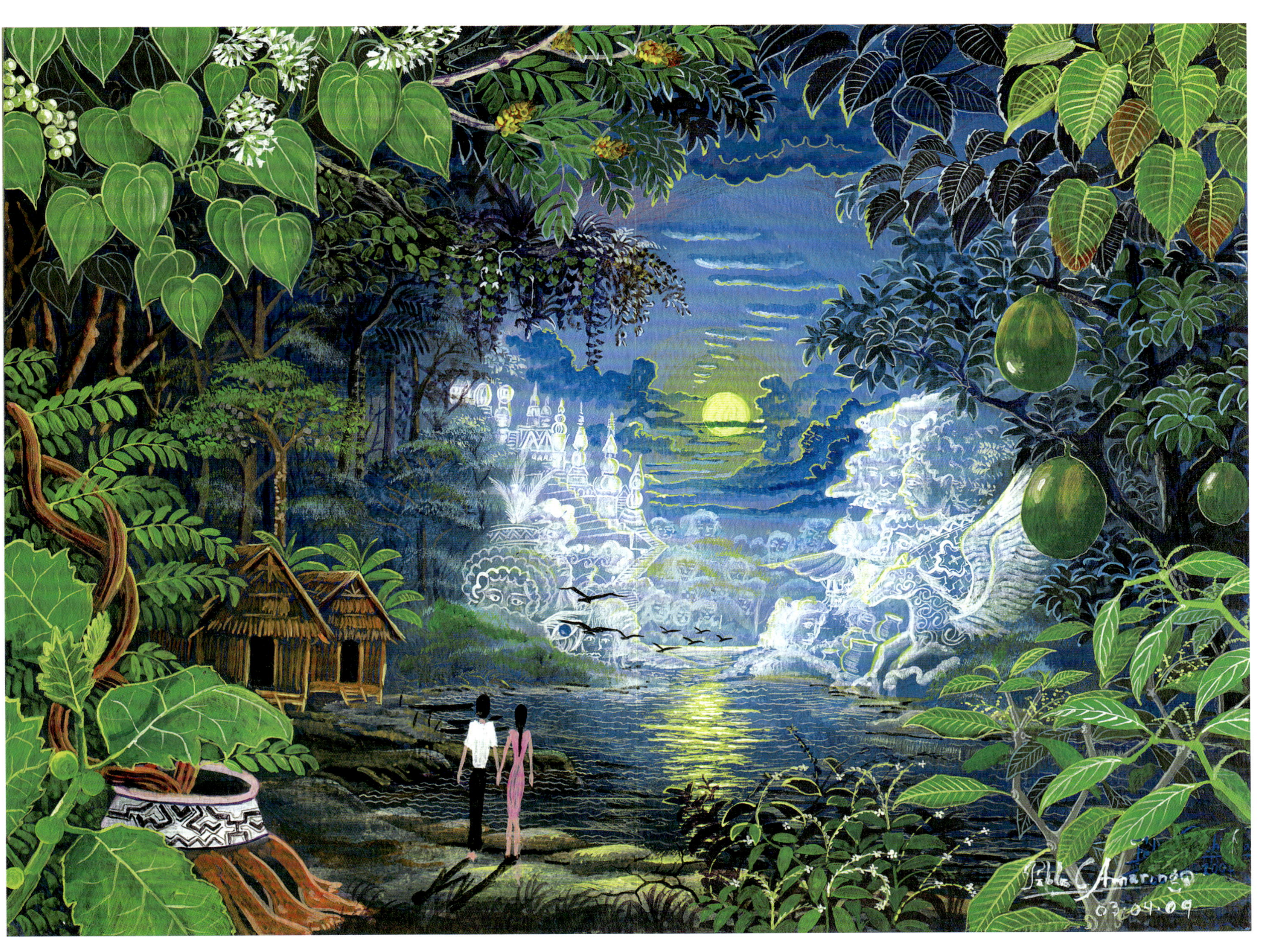

AMAZÓNICA ROMANTICA
2009, Gouache on Arches Paper
20 x 30 cm.

GLOSSARY

Authors' note: This was never intended to be an exhaustive glossary of terminology about the rich and magical *mundo Amazonico.* To do that justice would require a lengthy book of its own. Rather, it is our intent to provide some background detail to Pablo's paintings without disrupting the flow of the narratives. There is no single cohesive system of terminology or classification in the Amazon, due to linguistic differences among tribal groups such as the Shipibo, Ashaninka, Andean Quechua, and mestizo cultural influences. There are also local plant species definitions that do not conform to Western botanical classification.

Agua florida: A commercially available cologne used all over Peru by curanderos for healing and cleansing.

Aguajal: An inundated area where aguaje palms grow. Pablo regards the aguajales as a temple of nature, a beautiful sacred grove where the spirits like to gather.

Aguaje: *The Mauritia flexuosa,* or moriche, is an important palm tree in the Peruvian Amazon. Its fruit is very popular, particularly with women, as it contains high levels of phytoestrogens. The tree can grow to heights of more than thirty-five meters. When old, the aguajes fall and rot, and after a time people look for suris: large, fat white worms considered a great delicacy in the selva.

Aguardiente: In Peru, it is an alcoholic drink distilled by artisans from sugar cane. It is used for preparing medicines as well as for recreational use.

Ahuara: Red monkeys that are allies to the curandero. They are courageous and agile and have the ability to capture virotes sent by a sorcerer.

Alquimia palistica: Palero alchemy, the science of palos (trees). Paleros, specialists that work and diet with the roots, bark, and branches of trees, obtain knowledge through their dreams. Only a select few learn to be paleros. For a muraya or sumiruna, however, it is essential they undergo this apprenticeship. The dieta is stricter and longer than for an ayahuasquero, and for three to six years the apprentice is not allowed to see anyone other than his own maestro and have no contact with women. The Shipibo banco Benjamin Ochavano advises that the most important palo is the ayahuma tree (*Couroupita guianensis*), followed by the pucalupuna and the chullachaqui caspi (*Remijia peruviana*). "This is one of a number of plants that is consumed together with tobacco and is so strong that you only need to take it two times. It requires a diet of six months. You drink it in the morning and then lie down; you are in an altered state for a whole day afterward."

Angash sirenas: Blue sirenas are the mermaids who guard over aquatic plants and teach the curanderos their medicinal properties. The ícaro that the shamans sing when they work with them is called the *sirenita caya* (the mermaid princess).

Arkana: A field of spiritual protection against sorcery. The arkanas are drawn to the person(s) often at the start of an ayahuasca ceremony by the shaman singing the appropriate protective ícaros. A maestro can also give an arkana via his soplo of mapacho smoke. In his paintings Pablo often depicts arkanas as rainbow-colored ribbons.

A'tun a'tun: Quechua, meaning "great" or "vast."

A'tun mauca runa: "The great ancient ones." They are the guardians of space, time, and the stars and galaxies.

Ayahuasca: Ayahuasca is a sacred medicine of the indigenous people living in the Upper Amazon area of South America. *Ayahuasca* is a name derived from two Quechua words: *aya* means "spirit, ancestor, deceased person," and *huasca* means "vine" or "rope." Hence it is known as "vine of the dead" or "vine of the soul." It is important to note that the term ayahuasca refers to both the vine itself (*Banisteriopsis caapi*), and the psychoactive brew made from combining the vine with at least one other ingredient, typically the leaves of the chacruna plant (*Psychotria viridis*). The vine is an inhibitor that contains harmala alkaloids, and the leaf contains vision-inducing alkaloids (DMT).

Ayahuasca types: Pablo describes the following types of ayahuasca:

- Ayahuasca *cielo* (sky) can give visions of angels, arcontes, divine aralim, and celestial palaces. A maestro vegetalista is able to draw in the sublime powers of these divine beings.
- Ayahuasca *cascabel* (rattle) is a rare variety with very powerful effects. It gives visions in red and is used by shamans to heal and cleanse a person suffering from malign sorcery.
- Ayahuasca *trueno* (thunder) allows you to hear the voices of sylphs, napeas, and dryads. The thunder refers to the deep sound that originates in the stomach, not in the chest. This

ayahuasca helps you to hear the words of the celestial masters who speak through thunder. Vegetalistas who learn from trueno ayahuasca specialize in the sonorous, resonant sound of thunder and its power to command respect.

- Ayahuasca *lucero* (illuminated) gives beautiful visions of celestial palaces and brilliant colors. It also allows you to see within yourself, into your body.
- *Yana* ayahuasca (black ayahuasca) is a challenging liana and is usually reserved for knowledgeable vegetalistas, as the drinkers feel they are facing their death. The mareación is bleak and dark and brings up subconscious fears.

Ayahuma: *Couroupita guianensis,* a tree with large fruit. *Ayahuma* in Quechua means "head of a dead person," or "spirit head." It is an important tree for a palero to diet, and the thick bark and seeds are used by curanderos to protect against brujeria.

Banco: Although it is a generic term, it typically denotes a shaman of great power who has mastery over the land. There are different specializations within this; for example, a banco puma can transform into a jaguar.

Banco puma: The banco puma is a master shaman with the ability to transform into a jaguar to go hunting or hide from an enemy. The banco puma is a powerful healer with great knowledge of medicinal plants. He can also travel to other galaxies and dimensions. Pablo informed the authors that a banco puma could sometimes be so savage as to eat his own wife.

Banco sumi: A maestro who has discovered so much wisdom that he has reached the highest degree that a human can achieve and has become akin to an angel.

Baños florales: Floral baths form part of the traditional practice of vegetalistas and curanderos. Floral baths are taken for a variety of reasons, including attracting good fortune and ceremonial cleansing (*limpia*) or to clear saladera (a persistent run of bad luck). Floral baths are used in Peru today before demanding events, such as taking an exam or going to a job interview. The color, perfume, and shape of the plants and flowers used are important factors in this practice.

Barco fantasma: The supernatural steamboat, or phantom ship, is a manifestation of the yacumama and the huairamama. Also called *acero punta* (steel point) or *manchay buque* (splendid ship). In the Piro and Quechua languages it is known as the *acoron,* and in the Cocama language, *purahua*. This mythical image of a steamboat goes back to the rubber boom era, when they appeared at night and made a tremendous impact on the indigenous peoples.

Blue morpho: This iridescent blue butterfly (*Morpho menelaus*) has special significance for Pablo, and represents our higher purpose and destiny. A shaman with a true calling as a healer and teacher wears the butterfly like a tie for all to see the knowledge he possesses.

Brujeria: The Spanish word for "witchcraft." A brujo can invoke malign forces to harm another person by preparing concoctions for his clients to introduce secretly into the victim's food, drink, or bath water. In addition, through rituals performed with photos, articles of clothing, or personal possessions of the victim, the brujo can inflict bad health or misfortune (saladera) on the victim. Pablo does not regard brujeria as having the same degree of malevolence as hechicería, which can cause death.

Bufeos: These are Amazon river dolphins. Pablo's paintings usually depict the pink dolphin or bufeo colorado; there is also the gray dolphin. The Amazon is rich in legends of the bufeo colorado, in which these creatures transform themselves into handsome young men and seduce innocent young girls who become pregnant by them. The story may end with the girl having a miscarriage of a dolphinlike fetus; alternatively she is forced to agree to give the child back to the waters at a later time. Amazon River dolphins have evolved differently from maritime dolphins. They have lost the use of their eyes and navigate through highly developed sonar.

Bufeosirenas: Dolphin sirenas who can remove their tails as though they were trousers, whereupon they turn into sylphs and fly off into space to visit other worlds and star systems.

Caballococha: This is a town located on the Amazon River in the province of Loreto. Its name is a hybrid of Spanish (horse) and Quechua (lake) and means "horse lake." During the high water season, typically December to April, the forest around the town is inundated.

Cashimbo: Portuguese for "pipe." In the Peruvian Amazon the Portuguese word has long been accepted by shamans and some indigenous people, probably due to the Brazilian influence during the rubber boom.

Caspi: Quechua word used to refer to a tree. It means a "pole," "rod," "stick," or "wood."

Catahua: Catahua (*Hura crepitans*) is one of the strongest palos and its mastery requires a long and demanding diet. When boiled with tobacco, the resin provokes powerful dreams.

Chacra: Quechua word to describe small-scale arable land, typically a small farm or a field.

Chacruna: Chacruna (*Psychotria viridis*) leaves are boiled with the ayahuasca vine to produce the ayahuasca brew.

Chanca: Contemporaries of the Inca who had extensive knowledge about curing with plants. Pablo said that is why their descendants, the Ashaninka, have a deep understanding of the spiritual properties of plants.

Cherubim: The origin of the term "cherub" (plural, "cherubim") derives from the ancient Sumerian mythology, later incorporated into the Babylonian and Assyrian mythologies. Cherubim were depicted as composite creatures with components of four animals: the head of a bull, the wings of an eagle, the feet of a lion, and the tail of a serpent.

Chicua: *Piaya cayana,* or "squirrel cuckoo," is a guardian of ayahuasca and forewarns shamans of imminent danger. The brains of the chicua are eaten to promote intelligence and prescience.

Chukcabufeos: Bufeos with feathers or hair (chuka); they are like angels but come from the subaquatic world, not from the celestial. They are the spiritual guardians of bufeos.

Chullachaqui: A legendary being of the Amazon and protector of the animals of the rain forest. The name is a combination of the Quechua words *chulla,* which means "unequal," and *chaqui,* which means "foot," because it has one human foot and one larger, nonhuman or beastlike foot. Also known as a *curpira*.

Cocama: An indigenous tribe of the upper Amazon. Their culture was devastated during the Amazon rubber boom in the late nineteenth century, when many were enslaved to work as rubber tappers.

Cocha brava: A wild and mystical lake guarded by the anguilamama, the mother of the cocha brava, where people dare not venture to hunt or fish.

Colpas: Clay salt licks. Birds obtain minerals from these licks, and they often swallow small stones or grit that are mixed into the clay. The grit is essential for their digestion and helps break down seeds, since they don't have teeth.

Contour rivalry: A technique used to create different visual interpretations of an image. Pablo uses this technique in *Caspi Maman* and *Llullon Llaqui Supai.*

Copal: *Protium grandifolium,* the solidified natural resin of the tree, has a long history of use as ceremonial incense. Pablo reports that copal smoke is used to cure ear infections, as it is like a fumigant that kills bacteria.

Cushma: A traditional, loose-fitting woven cotton tunic. A Shipibo cushma is usually white cotton decorated with Shipibo geometric patterns. An Ashaninka cushma is typically dark brown or black.

Cutipa: A form of daño caused by not following certain rules of the dieta correctly, such as contact with a woman who is menstruating or inappropriate contact with the opposite sex during a diet.

Daño: Harm or illness frequently caused by sorcery.

Dieta: A discipline required of Amazonian shamans, healers, and apprentices who wish to learn directly from the plant spirits. It implies much more than mere dietary restrictions of avoiding salt, sugar, meat, and alcohol. It means refraining from libidinous thoughts, sexual activity, and contact with women who are menstruating, or anybody engaged in sexual activity. It is an extensive period of complete isolation for weeks or even months, and often the apprentice must fend for himself in the wilderness. The dieta is a complex and challenging practice. In an interview with the authors (2002), Shipibo shaman Guillermo Arevalo related that, "The period indicated by all the plants is a year, if you want a deep knowledge; three months is basic knowledge; and six months is intermediate. After a year there is no more to learn from that plant." Guillermo also commented regarding the overall perspective of the diet, "One year of dieting for a shaman is winning an extra year of your life. You are lengthening your life, because it might have been wasted. This is important for a shaman, to recuperate or gain more life and not grow old. The age can increase but life is always there. The plants always give more energy and life to those who diet." This practice goes beyond discovering a plant's medicinal properties. In a dieta, the spirit of the shaman and the plant meet in a magical world.

Encantos: Magical stones used by shamans for healing. Encantos possess hidden powers that can be combined with ícaros to heal. However, they must be kept hidden, as the spirits can harm people seeing them and cause vomiting, diarrhea, and headaches. Pablo cautions that one should be careful when encountering encantos in an ayahuasca vision, because their esoteric powers cannot be received by a person who has not first dieted and purged with ayahuasca. Some encantos are so powerful that if they are seen by a person who has not dieted properly, they can cause daño.

Espiritones: The espiritones are vibrations of quantum electromagnetic waves that permeate the fabric of multidimensional reality. Pablo describes them as the "cells" that form the spirits.

Genio: Guardian spirit of an animal or plant.

Gramalote: *Brachiaria mutica.* This plant is also used by curanderos to heal sorcery and saladera. There are different types of gramalote; puca gramalote is used primarily for healing. The shamans make a poultice by mixing it with camphor (*Alcanfor caspi,* or cinnamomum camphora) resin and Thimolina. The poultice is placed on the body, where it draws out the sorcery.

Guacamayo runa: Macaw people have the head of a guacamayo and the body of a man. The guacamayo runa teach the shaman how to interpret the characteristics of the atmosphere to predict when it is going to rain. They also have the ability to create rainfall.

Guanábana: *Annona muricata.* The fruit is taken for parasites, fevers, to increase mother's milk after childbirth, and for diarrhea. The bark, leaves, and roots are used as a sedative and antispasmodic. *Graviola,* as it is known in Brazil, has a long history of use in herbal medicine, as well as indigenous use. In the Peruvian Andes, a leaf tea is used for catarrh. In the Peruvian Amazon the bark, roots, and leaves are used for diabetes.

Hamadryades: Nymphs that enter a tree and live there. The resins of trees such as the tahuari (*Tabebuia serratifolia*), remocaspi (*Aspidosperma excelsum*), tinta caspi (*Haematoxylum campechianum*), and copal (*protium grandifolium*) are the blood of the hamadryades. Hence their resins and barks are powerful medicines.

Hechicería: Spanish word meaning "sorcery."

Hechiceros: Sorcerers that can inflict serious harm and even death. Hechiceros can kill their victims, either for their own vengeance or on behalf of their clients The early missionaries maligned shamans by calling them hechiceros.

Huairamama: Mother of the air, a giant serpent that has dominion of the earth's atmosphere. She moves like a whirlwind and creates the rainstorms that fertilize the land.

Huanarpo macho: *Jatropha macrantha* is in widespread use in Peru as an aphrodisiac, a natural libido enhancer, and a sexual stimulant for men. The powdered bark is typically used and is known as "Peruvian viagra." It is interesting that the tree is a classic example of the "doctrine of signatures," as the branch stems are shaped like male genitals.

Huanuco: Capital city of the department of Huanuco in the Peruvian highlands.

Huayco: Landslides or mudslides are frequent in the Andes during the rainy season and are commonly referred to as *huaycos,* a word derived from the Quechua word *wayqu,* meaning "river."

Huayruro: *Ormosia amazónica.* These brightly colored seeds are widely used in Amazonian crafts and jewelry; they protect travelers and attract good fortune. The huayruro macho (male) seeds are black and red, and the huayruro hembra (female) seeds are all red. Wearing them gives protection against the mal de ojo (evil eye).

Huito: *Genipa Americana,* a medicinal fruit. Also known as jaguar (in Spanish it is pronounced with an "h.")

Hyperchemical: *Hiper quimico.* A term that Pablo uses to describe the transmutation of physical matter. A grand master, such as a sumiruna or banco sumi, can develop hyperchemical abilities to transform himself into another creature, such as a machaco runa or an animal.

Ícaro: The word *ícaro* comes from the Quechua word *icarai,* meaning "to blow." Ícaros are magical chants that are sung or whistled by shamans during Ayahuasca ceremonies. There are several kinds of ícaros. At the beginning of a ceremony their purpose is to provoke the mareación, or visionary trance state, and to render the mind more susceptible for visions to penetrate. The shaman on his plant diet learns the ícaros directly from the plant spirits. Ícaros have great power and influence on the visionary experience of people drinking ayahuasca in a ceremony. Pablo also regarded the ícaro as the sound of the universe—the planets, stars, comets, and supernovas. Everything is created by music, by vibration, by sound. Ícaros are the music of creation.

Ila: Magical trees that fly into space. The trees function like a flying boat that carries the maestros. When they fly they make a thundering noise that many find unbearable.

Intisirena: This sirena of the sun is the guardian of the four cardinal points of the underwater realm.

Ishanga blanca: Ishanga blanca (*Laportea aestuans*), white stinging nettle. This plant has many medicinal uses and is used for healing rheumatism, burns, and wounds. The sap is used for its antibacterial and anti-inflammatory properties.

Ishanga moe: *Ishanga moe* (*Urea baccifera*), another type of stinging nettle with the same medicinal uses of its leaves.

Kunan versucum: The spiritual personification of music. As Pablo often said, "These spiritual vibrations resonate within us. As we are made from the pure energy of spirit, we are also made of music, the vibrations of the spirit."

Lengua de perro: (*Cynoglossum officinale*), also known as *cinoglosa,* is used medicinally as an astringent and antiseptic. Mestizo shaman Javier Arevalo informed the authors that it is used in *pusanga* (attraction medicine). It is called *lengua de perro* (dog's tongue) because it resembles a dog's tongue and will cause a person to be loyal and faithful to you, as a dog would be.

Machaco runa: A being with the head of a human and the body of a serpent. Only great masters, such as a sumiruna or banco sumi, have the hyperchemical ability to transform into a machaco runa.

Machaco sirenas: Sirenas with serpentine bodies. See *rikra machaco sirenas.*

Macua runa: Wise elder, who is called Yachay Sapa. He is a grand master of divine inspiration, and his name means "incomparable in knowledge."

Maestro curandero: Master healer.

Mahuete: Shipibo word for a large, ceremonial ceramic vessel used for preparing chicha and masato at fiesta time. It is usually decorated with the unique Shipibo geometric patterns.

Mal aire: An illness produced by the spirit of a dead person, also called *mal aire de difunto. Mal aire del monte* is produced by air from the jungle and *mal aire del agua,* evil air from the water. It is also referred to by Pablo as "an illness caused by bad or cold air," and "negative energies in the vicinity that cause sickness." In the old days, malaria was believed to be spread by vapors from water.

Maligno: A harmful spirit.

Manchari: A state of trauma and shock common in children and usually caused by some kind of accident or contact with malignos or tunchis.

Manes: The spirits of deceased people that have received the appropriate funeral rites and blessings. They return to earth to help the curanderos and to protect the plants and animals.

Mapacho: *Nicotiana rustica.* Locally grown tobacco is one of the most important plants used by shamans in the Amazon. It is used for protection during ayahuasca ceremonies, intensifying the mareación, and for giving soplos for healing. It is usually smoked in large cigarettes as *puros* (rolled in leaves similar to cigars) or in cashimbo. It is matured for long periods and macerated in aguardiente (alcohol). It can be "dieted" and taken internally, or added to the ayahuasca brew to encourage purging, and it can be used for dressing wounds.

Its use is described by Shipibo shaman Enrique Lopez in an interview (2007) with the authors: "Tobacco is very necessary for a shaman's work. Smoke protects against enemies and badness crossing your path. Before you light a mapacho you ícaro it, then you blow the smoke onto your body before the session begins. You can also cure a child of susto [fright] by blowing smoke over it."

Mapirui: Snake excrement found on the beaches in the selva (rain forest). Pablo said that sitting near the mapirui is dangerous and can cause fevers and urinary infections.

Mareación: The visionary and trance effects of ayahuasca, which may vary greatly and depend on many factors. It may be necessary to purge and purify before the ecstatic and beautiful visions can be experienced.

Mariri: This is the subtle and mysterious "magical phlegm" of the shaman. It is used in extraction of pathogenic agents or as a form of defense against sorcery. It is physically transferred from the maestro, who regurgitates this substance and passes it from his mouth to the mouth of his apprentice, and in doing so transfers his knowledge. Mariri is also obtained from plants such as the punga tree, and animals such as the shuyo fish, all of which produce a phlegmlike substance. The mariri of a sorcerer holds virotes that enable him to cast deadly spells. His mariri can contain needles, sharp objects, and the poison of snakes, wasps, and other insects. Curanderos must learn the ícaros of the many kinds of mariris so that they can neutralize and extract the pathogenic agents from a sorcerer.

Marupa: *Hechicería marupa* is a practice described by Pablo in which venomous insects, snakes, scorpions, or sharp-toothed fish, such as piranhas, are used to inflict harm. These marupas are retained and mastered in the mariri of the hechicero, who projects them magically to cause serious or fatal harm to his victims.

Marupa machaco: Marupa snake. Curanderos learn its ícaro to enable them to extract virotes and marupa sorcery from victims of hechicería.

Matico: *Piper* sp. Shamans use matico leaves to craft their shacapas, which are shaken like rattles to accompany their ícaros and assist concentration. Matico can also be used to heal machete wounds and similar injuries. The leaves are crushed and boiled in water, then the lukewarm liquid is poured over the wound.

Mishquipanga: *Renealmia alpinia,* which is Quechua for "sweet or tasty leaf." The fragrant leaves of this plant are used in floral baths to attract good fortune, love, and success.

Mucura: *Petivera alliacea.* This plant grows widely in the Amazon and is used in baños florales to cleanse, bestow positive energy, and heal saladera.

Muraya: A Shipibo term denoting one of the grades of a vegetalista. Pablo states that a muraya is an accomplished maestro with dominion over the subaquatic realm, and is able to live under water.

Neutrinos: Luminous electromagnetic cosmic particles that Pablo depicts as chromatic spirals or geometric forms. The neutrinos manifest and transmute into physical matter when their ícaro is sung.

Nina chukcha: Quechua, meaning "fire hair." They are beings with flames instead of hair—malignos (evil spirits). They are used by sorcerers to do severe harm to their victims, and unless the person is healed very quickly he will be consumed by a fever and die.

Oceanic flow: Pablo's description of how oceans flow is in line with current scientific understanding of the oceanic cycles. This includes his description of evaporative cooling and the increase in saline density in the north that generates ocean circulation. This is called "meridional overturning circulation" and describes the north-to-south characteristics of the ocean circulation.

Onaya: Shipibo term for vegetalista; means "one who knows," from the Shipibo word *ónana* (knowledge).

Pablo's spirit hierarchy: Pablo described for us the spiritual hierarchy he uses. Note: This is just for information; these terms are from ancient Greek and the Bible.

Serafine (Seraphim)
Cherubine (Cherubim)
Principados (Principalities)
Los Tronos (Thrones)
Archangeles (Archangels)
Angeles (Angels)
Arcontes (Archons)
Silfides (Sylphs)
Driades (Dryads)
Napeas (Nymphs)
Camenas (Water nymphs)
Hadas (Fairies)

Paiche (*Arapaima gigas*) is a large Amazonian freshwater fish and a living fossil.

Palos: The roots, bark, and resin of trees (typically, the larger hardwood varieties), which are prepared and taken in the context of a dieta. Vegetalistas who specialize in these are known as *paleros.*

Pambamuri: A stingray that has grown to a huge size after many years. These stingrays are also known as *rayamamas.*

Papastrueno: *Dioscorea* sp. Pablo said that this plant is difficult to find and requires a very demanding diet that must be followed in secret. A maestro shaman with good resolve will utilize the energy of a lightning storm to bring rain to their chacras so that they are abundant and luxuriant. However, if the shaman is a sorcerer, with the same energy he can kill a person or animal in an instant, wherever they may be.

Pashaca: *Microlobium acaciifolium.* Its large, brown, disk-shaped seeds are ubiquitous in Amazonian crafts and necklaces.

Patiquina: *Dieffenbachia* sp. The leaves are widely used in Peru in baños florales for counteracting brujeria and attracting positive energy. There are four varieties of patiquina: verde, blanco, negro, and pintado (green, white, black, and speckled).

Penca: *Agave* sp. is very similar to the penca common in the Sierra. It has its own ícaro and prayer and should be treated with great respect, as though it were a being. When planted on the wall around a farm or house it gives protection from thieves.

Perfumero: A specialist in the use of floral aromas and natural perfumes. Mestizo maestro Artidoro Aro Cardenas related his work with floral aromas in an interview (2003): "A smell has the power to attract. I can also make smells to attract business, people who buy. You just rub it on your face and it brings people into your business; if you are selling, people come to buy. I also make perfumes for love and others for flourishing. These are the forces of nature—what I do is give it direction with my breath so it has effect. I use my experience of the plants that I have dieted. I have a relationship with the plants and with the patient; I can't make these things on a commercial scale." Floral aromas have biological properties of attraction. Plants have evolved these attributes over millions of years to attract insects and birds to drink their nectar for their fertilization.

Piñon blanco: *Jatropha curca.* The large seeds are rich with oil and are used in many products, such as soap and candles. The oil is also extracted for use as biodiesel fuel.

Piñon colorado: *Jatropha gossypifolia* is used in floral baths for undoing sorcery and daño. Pablo states that in order to use this plant effectively, one must use leaves that have five tips, like a human hand. The seeds contain oil and have emetic properties. Artidoro Aro Cardenas, a mestizo shaman interviewed by the authors, advised that the seeds cooked in water are used as a purgative for parasites in the stomach and intestines. Two seeds are crushed for a child, six for an adult. The crushed leaves are good for cleaning the anus when it is itchy (hemorrhoids). It is also a teacher plant to be "dieted." If the rules are not respected it can work against you and make you worse, which is called *cutipa.* Mestizo shaman Javier Arevalo related that it is good for skin problems and wounds. For example, it is used after cuts have been deliberately made to make blood brothers using *chonta* (a type of tree) splinters. Not only does it heal effectively, but the scars recover the color of normal skin. All the shamans of the Rio Napo do this to speed up their apprenticeships by transmitting the wisdom from an older generation. The scars are made to take the form of an armadillo (protection). With this magical protection you can fall from high branches of trees or suffer burns and recover quickly.

Piñon negro: *Jatropha gossypifolia.* The botanical classification is the same as piñon colorado, but shamans work with different criteria for classification and regard it as a different plant with its own characteristics. Stephan V. Beyer has commented about some of the difficulties of reconciling plant names in his book, *Singing to the Plants: A Guide to Mestizo Shamanism in the Upper Amazon* (University of New Mexico Press, 2009).

Piri piri: *Cyperus articulates* is a grasslike reed that grows on the banks of rivers. Its rhizomes are used medicinally for digestive and nervous ailments. Teresa Rango, a Shipibo, informed the authors that when a girl is very young, it is customary for her mother to squeeze a few drops of piri piri seed sap into her eyes in order to give her visions of the designs she will paint throughout her life.

Pucabufeo: *Inia geoffrensis,* the pink river dolphin, is said to be able to shape-shift into human form in order to have sex with humans.

Pucalupuna: *Cavanillesia umbellata,* or *Cavanillesia hylogeiton. Puka* or *puca* is the word for "red" in Quechua. It is the most formidable tree from which a palero can learn and gain mastery. It requires a demanding dieta in isolation over a period of many months. The power of this tree is used by both curanderos and sorcerers.

Puca sirenas: Pink mermaids. In former times they seduced men with their enchanted songs and took them to live in their underwater palaces. Many years ago you could see them on the banks of the River Ucayali.

Pulsario: Pulsations or throbbing aches. Pablo said they can be cured by ícaros alone without the need for medicine. Only water that has been treated with sopladas and ícaros is required. In certain cases this condition can indicate the presence of a virote.

Puma: In Peru it refers to the jaguar, or otorongo, not the North American puma.

Punga tree: *Bombax munguba.* A fatty, phlegmlike resin is secreted from its soft wood. The maestro teaches his apprentices the ícaro of this tree so they can extract a maleficent intrusion, such as a virote or marupa. The magical phlegm, mariri, is used to absorb it and render it harmless.

Pusanga: Pusanguería is popularized as the "love medicine" of the Amazon. However, this should be more accurately referred to as "attraction medicine," as it is not only for attracting a sexual encounter or a partner. The latter is a vexing concern for Westerners, who see it as manipulation of another person. However, in the Amazonian culture this does not present an ethical problem because, in the words of mestizo shaman Javier Arevalo, "Everyone is doing it." A pusangero is a shaman who specializes in making pusangas, and there are subspecializations within this; for example, *amarres* (ties) using mapacho, and also the work of a perfumero (see above). One of the clearly unwholesome aspects is that animals are killed for their body parts; the sexual organs of dolphins and *coati mundi,* tongues of hummingbirds, and brains of birds and bats are used in pusangas. To give a broader perspective of the pusanga effect, Peruvian shaman and mystic Alonso del Rio in an interview (1993) with Peter said, "The shaman can work with animal magnetism, and of course all bodies emanate some kind of magnetism, but some shamans have the ability to make one person's magnetism be directed such that it will affect or magnetize another person. This principle is used for many purposes, not just the infamous pusanga for attraction between couples, but also for hunting and fishing. You are charging the person so that he will attract, whether it is fish, game, or a partner."

Putu putu: Water hyacinth (*Eichornia crassipes*). The flowers of this aquatic plant are mixed with chapo (a sweet drink made from bananas) and taken in the context of a diet. It can help women's period pains. The ícaro of the putu putu can heal a person suffering mental disturbance. Putu putu is also known as *wamaruiro.* The mother of this plant is the yacumama. When she navigates along the waters, the dense floating mass of putu putu opens for her and then closes again when she has passed through, thus impeding access to the cocha from the river. A valuable characteristic of this plant is that the fibrous root system absorbs and cleanses contamination that is discharged into the rivers. Pablo said that this plant provides important nutrients for the bufeos, calling it "marine maca," and that is why the leaves are smoked by shamans to gain mastery over the bufeo colorado and to heal daño caused by bufeos.

Quechua: This was the language spread widely in the Andes by the Inca, and subsequently introduced into the Peruvian Amazon. The word *ayahuasca,* for example, is Quechua; *aya* meaning "spirit" or "ancestor," and *huasca* meaning "vine." Many of the titles and names of spirits and mythological beings in Pablo's paintings are from Quechua.

Remocaspi: *Aspidosperma excelsum* is a large canopy tree of the Amazonian rain forest. The name *remocaspi* is a hybrid Spanish-Quechua word meaning "paddle wood." The wood is widely used in the Amazon for canoe paddles, being relatively light but very strong and water resistant. The bark is used medicinally as a male potency enhancer, antiseptic, and for fevers and wounds.

Renaco: A type of fig tree (*Ficus* sp.) that has an intricate, extensive trunk and root system. As seen in many of Pablo's paintings, the renaco tree offers shelter to many types of animals and beings. Pablo refers to this tree as the Temple of the Waters. The renaco is a sanctuary for animals, insects, and birds in the cosmology of the Amazonian selva.

Rikramachaco sirena: Sirenas with serpentine bodies and wings. They have the ability to fly like a bird.

Runamula: A hybrid human-mule creature, in Amazonian mythology. It is the spirit of a woman who has been unfaithful or had relations with a clergyman, and for punishment has been transformed into a runamula.

Sachamama: The mother of the forest. In the complex mythological world of the Amazon, the sachamama is a giant supernatural anaconda that, due to its immense size, can no longer move through the rain forest. When this happens it merges with the earth and becomes a part of the terrain. Trees, plants, and flowers grow around and on it so it becomes invisible and indistinguishable from the forest. It can leave its mouth wide open and unsuspecting hunters will walk straight in, never to be seen again. The sachamama is regarded as the spirit or primal life force of the forest.

Sacha yana versucum sisa: The ícaro of the forest black flower is sung to call the medicinal powers of the plants and flowers of the Amazonian rain forest. *Versucum* means "canto."

Saladera: A term used to describe a persistent run of misfortune, often considered to be caused by brujeria, envy, or malicious thoughts of others (*envida*).

Sarara: A heron, *anhinga anhinga.* Pablo describes different types of mystical sararas: the quilla (moon) sarara, puca (red) sarara, and yana (black) sarara. These birds are used by both curanderos and brujos.

Shacapa: A tied bundle of leaves used for healing by mestizo shamans, both as a fan to sweep away negative energy and as a rattle for increasing the intensity of the mareación during an ayahuasca ceremony.

Shaman: The term "shaman," or in Peru *chamán,* originates from the Turkic Asiatic word *šamán.* The term "shaman" is a recent Western import into the Amazon in the past thirty years. In the Amazonian tradition there are many specializations and categories. The traditional generic term would be *vegetalista,* which denotes they have received their power from the plant kingdom. There are many subspecializations of the vegetalista, for example:

- Palero—Specialist in the bark and roots of trees
- Perfumero—Specialist in the perfumes of plants and flowers
- Ayahuasquero—Specialist in ayahuasca
- Chontero—Specialist in chonta (darts)

Benjamin Ochavano, an elder Shipibo banco (currently in his late eighties), related to the authors in an interview (2002), "My father was known as a *muraya* or *banco*, or in Spanish, a *curandero*. A banco could specialize in being a good chontero or a shitanero who does harm to people."

Shebónal: Seasonally inundated areas where *shebón* (*Attalea* sp.) palms grow. These tall palms have dense hanging fronds like thick ropes, which are called *maromas*.

Shipibo: Indigenous tribal group. Their communities are located in the Ucayali region of Peru. They are renowned for their unique geometric-patterned textiles and ceramics.

Shungo: A hardwood post used in the construction of houses and tambos in the Amazon

Shungu: The Quechua word for "heart," also a metaphor for the biological foundation of life.

Sinchi yachai: Great teachers with braided colored hair. They are masters of the cleansing and protective power of mapacho smoke.

Sirenas: Mermaids who inhabit rivers in the Amazon rain forest, and whose legends are familiar to people in the West. The Amazonian sirenas adopt the form of beautiful women with hypnotic eyes who sing enchanting tunes to seduce young men. Eventually they are dragged under water and drown. Sirenas live at the bottom of lakes and rivers, especially where there are whirlpools. Sometimes they teach their ícaros to shamans who use them for love magic.

Sireno machaco: The snake merman has great knowledge and is a powerful ally for a muraya or sumiruna who claims mastery of the underwater realm. These maestros chant their ícaros to draw upon the powers of the subaquatic domain.

Sirenos: Mermen or tritons. Sirenos are rarely seen, because unlike sirenas, they remain in the subaquatic realm.

Soplada: From the Spanish for "to blow," *soplo* or *soplada* usually refers to the practice of blowing mapacho (*Nicotiana rustica*) smoke onto a person. The smoke is directed onto specific parts of the patient. The soplada is an important part of healing and is typically used for cleansing and as a conduit for the shaman's concentration and energy.

Suisui: *Thraupis bonariens.* This bird is also called a *bodosque.* Pablo said that the suisui has extraordinary hearing ability and can sense the heartbeat of the land and of people. It can distinguish people who mean well from those who harbor malevolent intentions and is a good guardian for the shaman.

Sumiruna: One of the highest levels of mastery that a human can attain. A sumiruna has dominion over land, air, and water.

Supay lancha: Phantom ship, supernatural steamboat; a manifestation of the yacumama and the huairamama. Also called acero punta (steel point), the manchay buque (splendid ship), or barco fantasma (phantom ship).

Supay or supai: A Quechua word meaning "spirit" or "supernatural," but can also be used to mean "devil" or "demon."

Tahuari: *Tabebuia serratifolia.* A large canopy tree, also widely known as *pao d'arco.* There are many well-documented studies on its wide range of medicinal properties.

Tamanco: A town in the district of Emilio San Martin, Province of Requena, Department of Loreto. Pablo was born here in January 1938 at his family farm, Puerto Libertad.

Tambo: In the Amazon this Quechua term refers to a simple, sometimes temporary dwelling.

Tamshi: *Heteropsis jenmanii.* The long aerial roots are split into fibers and used to make baskets, woven belts, necklaces, and bags. Children are encouraged to chew tamshi fibers to keep their teeth healthy and prevent decay.

Thimolina: A commercial antiseptic of thyme oil, eucalyptus, menthol, and pine oil dissolved in alcohol. It is used by curanderos in the Amazon.

Tibemama: An important supernatural bird ally to the shaman. Pablo depicts the tibemama as an osprey or sparrow hawk. There is also a yana tibe (black tibe). These birds possess acute vision that can penetrate to the depths of rivers and cochas.

Tinaja: Medium-size ceramic vessel of the Shipibo, usually decorated with their characteristic geometric patterns.

Tingunas: Electromagnetic emanations that can transform into corporeal matter, such as plants, clouds, or birds. In Amazonian terminology it means "lights of transformation." In Pablo's paintings tingunas are depicted as brightly colored geometric patterns. In Pablo's words, "The first particles of matter were formed by tingunas; this is something that people do not yet understand."

Tinta caspi: *Haematoxylum campechianum.* The Latin name means "blood-wood tree." The bark and leaves are used medicinally for their antibacterial, anti-inflammatory, and antiseptic properties. The resin is used as a natural dye.

Toé: *Brugmansia suaveolens,* also known as *tomapende* and *floripondio.* An important psychotropic plant in the Amazon, sometimes combined with ayahuasca to intensify visions. Pablo said that with toé you can learn what a person is thinking, and it can enable you to see spirit beings as they are in their natural form. Shamans use toé to help them delve into profound mysteries.

Troncomoro: The troncomoro is worn by indigenous Amazonian people around the waist or neck as adornment. It is made of the nuts and seeds of the pashaca (*Microlobium acaciifolium*) and sacha (*Virola calophylla*) trees, each having a different property.

Belts and bracelets made from *ampi huasca* (*Chondredendron tomentosum*, curare) offer protection from ingested poison and reduce the effect of the venom of a snakebite. *Carahuasca* (*Guatteria modesta*) is woven with ayahuasca vine to make bracelets that keep the heart strong.

Tunchis: The wandering ghosts of deceased people. Pablo depicts them as white-shrouded beings in his paintings. They are regarded as malignos and frighten those who encounter them. An encounter with a tunchi is regarded as a cause of the illness referred to as *mal aire* (bad air).

Varayoc runa: The judge who awards a credential to a shaman who has successfully learned the healing sciences.

Virote: A dart, often regarded as a maleficent intrusion that can cause serious illness or even death to its victim. The term originally came from the Spanish word for "crossbow bolt," and later it was used to refer to the darts used in native blowpipes. Chonta is another form of virote. Chonteros can project benign chontas for healing purposes. A virote is not simply a projectile, it has a spirit that needs to be nourished and mastered by the shaman. Shipibo banco Benjamin Ochavano related to the authors this story of his teacher Jose Sánchez (his uncle): "He was a chontero, a kind of shaman who works with virotes or chontas—so called because real darts and arrows for hunting are made from the black splintery bamboo called *chonta.* A chontero can send darts with positive effects like knowledge and power, too, and he knows how to suck and remove poisoned darts that have caused illness or evil spells." Some palms have spikes on their trunks that work like arkanas to protect vegetalistas from hechiceros. The *pijuayo* palm (*Bactris gasipaes*) is one of the most formidable, with clusters of long sharp spines on its trunk, like virotes. A maestro will learn the ícaro of this tree as a defense against hechiceros.

Yacumama: Mother of the waters, the great anaconda. She can transform into a supay lancha.

Yacupucarunas: Quechua "red water people." They are aquatic, red-skinned, blond-haired sirenas and sirenos.

Yacuruna: In the mythological world of the Amazon, the yacuruna (water people) are the primordial hairy ancestors of humans. They inhabit the subaquatic realm of rivers. Their hammock is a boa, their canoe a charapa (turtle) or alligator. They kidnap people to be their consorts.

Yacu warmi: These sirenas, literally "women of the waters," defend a maestro from harm when he is traveling in subaquatic realms.

Yaku sarara: A combination of a bird and a river ray, it can fly and dive deep into the water. It protects the shaman from his enemies.

Yana: Means "black" in Quechua.

Yura: Means "white" in Quechua.

Yura cukchas mallcas: Sublime healers who perform wondrous cures. In Quechua, "the old white-haired wise ones."

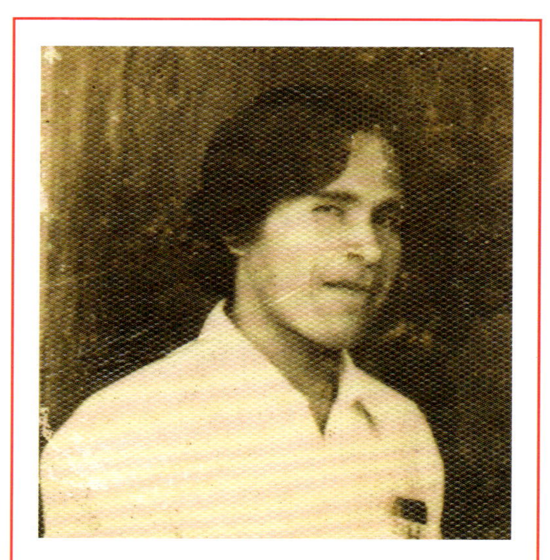